its the would-be

C. E. Montagu,
lyn Waugh, James
, Henry D. Thorec
v others. Ec

Challenge

AN ANTHOLOGY OF THE
LITERATURE OF MOUNTAINEERING

Challenge

AN ANTHOLOGY

OF THE LITERATURE OF

Mountaineering

EDITED BY

WILLIAM ROBERT IRWIN

NEW YORK 1950

COLUMBIA UNIVERSITY PRESS

FOR

W. A. I.

PREFACE

FROM THE WEALTH of the literature of mountaineering written originally in English I have selected for this anthology what I believe to be the best and the most widely representative. The range is from vigorous narrative of adventure, as in "The Conquest of Minya Konka" and "Into Spain and Back Again," to reflective essays concerned with the psychology and morality of extraordinary experience wilfully sought, as in "The Regrets of a Mountaineer." Prose fiction is represented by "Action" and "How I Stalked Wilder Game than Deer," humorous commentary in "A Tricky Bit" and "Mountains and the Public." Other selections reveal still other combinations of form and spirit. Throughout I have endeavored to illustrate the variety of non-technical prose produced by men and women who, with two exceptions, must be granted the authority which comes from personal experience as climbers.

The reader who is already well informed concerning the sport will note the absence of purely technical writing and of the poetry of mountaineering. The omission of the former from a book not intended primarily for specialists requires, I believe, no explanation. There is only a small body of poetry which derives from mountaineering itself. Although some of it, such as the work of Michael Roberts and Geoffrey Winthrop Young, is eminently worth reading, the poetry of mountaineering as a whole tends to be intramural, to rely on an already established community of experience and knowledge. Hence it is in its way also specialized. Nothing is reprinted here of the writing which has emanated from the long and thus far unsuccessful campaign to climb Mount Everest. For this the reader is referred to *Kingdom of Adventure: Everest* (1947), edited by James Ramsey Ullman, which provides an articulated narrative, largely from primary sources, of attempts through the expedition of 1938.

I am happy to express my gratitude for assistance and suggestions to Mr. Ken C. Baumann of Cornell University; to Miss Matilda

Berg, Messrs. William Bridgwater and Henry H. Wiggins, of the Columbia University Press; to Miss Helen I. Buck, librarian of the American Alpine Club; to Professors Fritz Coester, Ralph Ellsworth, Victor Harris, M. F. Heiser, and Charles T. Miller, of the State University of Iowa; to Mr. Charles Francis Meade, Meifod, Montgomeryshire; to Professor David A. Robertson, of Barnard College, and Mrs. Beridge Robertson; to Mr. Geoffrey Winthrop Young and Mrs. Eleanor Winthrop Young, Cambo, Northumberland; and to the librarians of Cornell University and the State University of Iowa. I am mindful finally of debts that lie too deep for overt acknowledgment.

W. R. IRWIN

Department of English
State University of Iowa

CONTENTS

INTRODUCTION

"WHY DO men climb mountains?" is a provocative question, to which answers are plentiful and various. One man seeks no further than the tonic of exercise amid superb scenery; another spins out a full allegory of human aspiration. All the answers are valuable, but any one soon reveals its own limitations. The literature of mountaineering is rich in professions of faith, in which the central affirmation is illuminated by the values—physical, emotional, and imaginative—which the devoted find in abundance. A brief survey of these values and of the history of mountaineering will provide a means for understanding and sharing the joy which quick-spirited men and women have discovered in their chosen world of rock, snow, ice, and challenging summits.

The first fact about the history of mountaineering is that for centuries it had no history. The ancients were awed by high places, made them the scenes of astonishing and important events, peopled them with superhuman beings. One need only recall the connotations of such names as Ararat, Sinai, Olympus, and Parnassus. But the ancients were not given to climbing, except when forced by military necessity. Overland traders of the Mediterranean world and later those of the northerly countries of Europe, like the men who penetrated the western mountains of America, sought passes and circumventing routes. Quite rightly, they saw no profit in climbing, except briefly to secure marketable commodities. Even without this reason, centuries of men would have been deterred by fear alone, not so much of dangerous terrain as of the terrible creatures, inimical to man and quick to punish any invasion of privacy, which inhabit the mountain wastes. In the first essay of *The Playground of Europe* Sir Leslie Stephen describes the population of the Alps as conceived in Swiss folklore—dragons, giants, monstrous *Lämmergeier*, even Pontius Pilate and his wife in baleful residence on a mountain near Lucerne. And this kind of fear is not beyond recall in the twentieth century. Anyone who wishes can induce it simply by getting caught above timber line in a storm; he will scarcely escape the intimidating persuasion that every bolt and blast is aimed at his destruction.

This early attitude can be inferred also from the connotations of the word "mountaineer," which meant originally, not a person who climbs for pleasure, but one indigenous to mountain areas. Such could easily be thought outlaws or at least rough and uncivilized folk. Quotations from the period before 1700 cited in the *New English Dictionary* uniformly suggest barbarism; the best the mountaineers are accorded is excellence as soldiers, presumably because of their durability and cruelty. Reflecting this connotation, Dante represents mountain dwellers as rude and clownish, tending to malignancy; Gonzalo in *The Tempest* remembers from his boyhood stories of "mountaineers dew-lapp'd like bulls"; and in Milton's *Comus* the mountaineer is classified with savages and bandits, hags, ghosts, goblins, and faeries, as a creature which does not dare assault true chastity, despite his native propensity to evil.

Long before mountaineering became an established sport this venerable dread began to yield to isolated bold and curious men who invaded the fastnesses and returned unharmed. Several of these forerunners deserve special mention. Apparently to satisfy a longstanding desire, Petrarch ascended Mont Ventoux near Avignon in April, 1336. The significance of this exploit has sometimes been overstated. It did not inaugurate the Italian Renaissance or make Petrarch the first modern man. Its importance here lies rather in Petrarch's motive, a combination of curiosity and sober pleasure-seeking. In 1492, Antoine de Ville, an officer of Charles VIII of France, led a party to the top of Mont Aiguille in Dauphiné and had a mass said there. About the same time Leonardo da Vinci, chiefly interested in phenomena of climate and color, reached an elevation of 8,000 feet on the southern slope of the Monte Rosa chain. Konrad von Gesner of Zurich, a naturalist sometimes called "the German Pliny," made a number of minor ascents during the mid-part of the sixteenth century and left written testimony to the joys and benefits of climbing. Gesner also publicly doubted the legend concerning Pontius Pilate.

More significant than individual anticipations, however, was a slowly developing change in the generally held concept of physical nature. Even while ancient superstitions were being handed on, the structure of a new attitude toward nature was taking shape. To state the matter with deceptive simplicity, the old concept of nature as animated yielded to the view that nature operates according to physical laws which can be known by man. "Animated nature" is almost necessarily fearsome. Its parts move by mysterious and erratic principles, which often manifest themselves in disaster; it is hospitable to an endless variety of beings which seem inimical to man and are obviously more powerful. Greek mythology provides abundant evidence of this. But such was the progress of the enlightened speculation often associated with the name and influence of Sir Isaac Newton that by the early years of the eighteenth century physical nature could be regarded as a grand mechanism, divinely instituted but accessible to the unaided human understanding.

Both as a consequence and a concomitant there occurred a change in taste, whereby objects of nature and art once thought disgusting became estimable. This too was a slow and far-reaching development. It included growing preferences for natural rather than highly formal gardens, for "ancient" English and Scandinavian poetry, for the appurtenances and expressions of chivalry, for Gothic architecture, and for parts of physical nature somewhat wilder than Windsor Forest. This development was greatly assisted by the Scottish-born James Thomson, who liberally represented mountain scenery, particularly in its grim and forbidding aspects, in "Winter," which is generally the most sombre of the four parts of his long poem *The Seasons*. Despite the circumlocution and recurrent moralizing for which he is often blamed, Thomson's descriptions of nature reveal a perception which was frequently acute. His attention to mountains has a further significance in itself. Generations of poets before him had rendered to admiration the more smiling aspects of nature; Thomson was the first considerable English poet of mountains.

It was established, then, that there is an æsthetic value in the sensation which Joseph Addison, in describing the Alps near Geneva, had characterized as "an agreeable kind of horror." This "horror" was elaborately examined by Edmund Burke in his

Philosophical Enquiry into the Origins of Our Ideas of the Sublime and Beautiful (1757). The sublime, he believed, has its psychological origin in the delightful terror, accompanied by astonishment, which we feel in the presence of obscurity, power, privation, magnitude, infinity, and the like, when these are manifested on a grand scale but without apparent danger to the beholder. In a section entitled "Vastness" he writes, "An hundred yards of even ground will never work such an effect as a tower an hundred yards high, or a rock or mountain of that altitude. . . . A perpendicular has more force in forming the sublime, than an inclined plane; and the effects of a rugged and broken surface seem stronger than where it is smooth and polished." As if to illustrate, Thomas Gray in several letters written in 1739 emphasizes the feelings of awe inspired by the torrents and precipices of the Alps. He was particularly impressed with the road leading to the Grande Chartreuse, which opened "one of the most solemn, the most romantic, and the most astonishing scenes I ever beheld." Understandably enough, when the "horrors were accompanied with too much danger to give one time to reflect on . . . beauties," he reverted to the traditional complaints against mountains, but even Gray's incomplete enlightenment is significant of a major change.

Thus two movements in the history of ideas—the one divesting nature of terrors, the other revalidating much the same terrors, but only as stimulants to the imagination—combined to promote a favorable view of mountains and to forecast the prominence of mountain poetry during the Romantic Revival. Those who contributed to forming the new attitude were not themselves climbers, but these were not long absent from the scene. During the second half of the eighteenth century, while Jean Jacques Rousseau's rapturous descriptions of low-level Alpine scenery were yet fresh, Mont Blanc became the object of a group of Swiss aspirants. The principals were Horace Bénédict de Saussure, a university professor from Geneva; Marc Bourrit, an artist and musician; Dr. M. G. Paccard, a Chamonix physician; and Jacques Balmat, a young crystal-hunter. For the development of alpinism and its literature the most influential person was de Saussure. For more than twenty-five years after 1760 he conducted geological explorations in the

Alps and particularly on Mont Blanc, which he finally ascended in 1787. He recorded his peregrinations in a series of books, entitled *Voyages dans les Alpes*, which are valuable equally for detailed scientific information and for lyrical description. In his recent book, *The Swiss without Halos*, J. Christopher Herold states, "De Saussure was not merely the founder of a new sport. Unwittingly he had from the first found words for the mystical passion that binds the mountain climber and the mountain and for its ambivalent feelings of hatred and love."

For half a century the combination represented in de Saussure did not conspicuously recur. Various other persons prepared further for the sport and its literature. The English and German Romantic poets discovered the Alps and propounded the myth of the freedom-loving Swiss. But for all its glory, theirs was a poetry of mountains and political tendency, not of mountaineering. The poets themselves looked up from the valleys. Intermittently from about 1800 to 1843 the English painter J. M. W. Turner visited Switzerland and made many studies and sketches, some of which were developed into finished pieces which gained considerable repute. Natural philosophers continued to frequent the Alps. Perhaps the most noteworthy were Jean Louis Rodolphe Agassiz, Pierre Jean Edouard Desor, and James David Forbes. All were interested primarily in geological phenomena, particularly in glaciers. Desor and Forbes together ascended the Jungfrau in 1841. Since then the association of mountaineering and scientific study has never been completely broken. Theodolites, aneroid barometers, various kinds of thermometers, and such gear have been hauled up countless peaks; medical investigators have taken extensive note of the effects of altitude on bodily functioning. *The Alpine Journal* has retained its original subtitle, "a record of mountain adventure and scientific observation." The Everest expeditions of the 1920's and 1930's included scientists and were sponsored not only by the Alpine Club but by the Royal Geographical Society. During the recent war the journals of several climbers' clubs were filled with articles about the contribution of mountain craft to military science.

No one can say precisely when the number of young English gentlemen, chiefly from Oxford and Cambridge, taking holiday walking tours in Switzerland, Bavaria, and northern Italy, became sufficient to mark the inception of climbing as an organized sport. Probably it was during the decade of the 1850's, when the fourth volume of Ruskin's *Modern Painters*, entitled *Of Mountain Beauty*, was published and Alfred Wills ascended the formidable Wetterhorn. The Alpine Club was founded in 1858. The great men of the heroic age of mountaineering—Wills, Leslie Stephen, John Ball, F. F. Tuckett, A. W. Moore, to name a few—were beginning their pioneer exploits. Important first ascents were made every season; basic principles of mountain craft were established. In a remarkably short time the new sport acquired an impressive number of devotees and began to emerge into public prominence. This early conspicuousness may be attributed in part to the social rank of most of the early climbers, in part to their quickly achieved reputation as seekers of death, the result of a few spectacular accidents. Equally important, however, was the publicity which they themselves gave the sport, for the early climbers were with few exceptions highly literate and articulate. Thus the growth of a literature of mountaineering was contemporaneous with the growth of the sport, and many of its great books—Wills's *Wanderings in the High Alps* (1854) and the first two series of *Peaks, Passes, and Glaciers* (1859, 1862), for example—come from its earliest period. Fortunately, the sport and the literature have maintained their vigor and their concurrency.

Such a rapid efflorescence demands explanation. The most obvious fact is that, from the first, climbing has attracted persons of high intellectual and artistic capacity. Sir Leslie Stephen was a philosopher and a man of letters, Sir Alfred Wills a jurist, Sir Martin Conway an historian of art, George Leigh Mallory a university lecturer in history—the roll of scholars, clergymen, physicians, lawyers, diplomats might be long extended. It is in accordance with this tradition that Michael Ransom, the protagonist of *The Ascent of F6*, by W. H. Auden and Christopher Isherwood, is presented as a scientist, a translator of Confucius, a student of Goya, a player of the viola da gamba, a compelling leader, and an adventurer—a kind of Alpine Lawrence of Arabia.

At first, of course, participation in the sport required a competence of money and time, which was in the possession chiefly of university and professional people and of the hereditarily wealthy. Mountaineering developed within a clearly defined and somewhat restrictive social and economic framework and is just recently becoming open to many.

It is not enough, however, to point out that the makers of the literature of mountaineering have been fortunate in their incomes, educations, and prose styles. One must still ask why the sport has attracted such men, what values they have discovered in it. Certain values, though of great importance, need only be mentioned here. The magnificence of mountain scenery and the pleasure of a kind of exertion which is both exhilarating and exhausting are sufficient values for many, and these are major themes in the literature of mountaineering. But expressions of simple joy do not need the services of a commentator.

It is sometimes said that devotion to climbing can scarcely be made intelligible to those not of the cult. I doubt this. It can, I believe, be demonstrated that the emotional and imaginative benefits which climbers derive from their sport closely resemble those to be found in a variety of demanding experiences.

Mountaineering is arduous. By an act of will the climber surrenders comfort and subjects himself to mortification from hunger, exertion, tedium, and frustration. He is slave to terrain and weather and heir to frostbite, snowblindness, contusions and abrasions. Danger is his silent companion. In brief, the inescapable conditions of mountaineering are such as contribute to an experience which more than superficially resembles the ascetical way. It is worth recalling here that "ascetic" derives from ἀσκεῖν, one basic meaning of which is "to exercise physically." This may seem high-flown; certainly as a group mountaineers do not avow devotion to the science of the saints. But the fact remains that, like the ascetics, they seek conditions which require continuous self-discipline and sacrifice of lower values to achieve higher. What do they get in return? First, an intensified observation of physical nature from the very small to the very large. The climber must be as careful to note minutiae as Mark Twain's ideal river pilot, and for the same reason. The slope of a shelf of rock, the precise degree of hardness of ice, the meaning of a small midday cloud or of a shift in the wind must be determined accurately and often very quickly. At the other end of the scale the pleasure and profit of "observation with extensive view" are his in abundance. Only the flier and the climber can fully understand the organization of the gross components of nature and the reality which a good map represents. Microcosm and macrocosm are simultaneously within the range of his sharpened perceptions, as well as all forms from those of Euclidean regularity to the fantastically misshapen. He is at once in and out of this world.

Further, the climber has a remarkable opportunity to gain self-knowledge. He must learn the limits of courage, ingenuity, and strength, both his own and of the qualities themselves. There is nothing like a resistant mountain for proving that no one virtue —intellectual or moral—can safely be developed to the disadvantage of others. The climber can also learn what he is in relation to physical nature: that his capacity for overcoming its onslaughts is astonishing, but that his own power, measured against nature's, is as nothing. Few men are less likely than the thoughtful mountaineer to fall into the error of believing that man can conquer nature; few are less likely to be paralyzed by the perception of nature's might. Thus the climber discovers in his sporting experience what is constantly being discovered throughout a wide variety of other kinds of experience, the paradox of man's strength and weakness, alternating, coexisting, interpenetrating. He has good reason to recall Pope's summation of man, "the glory, jest, and riddle of the world."

Previously I discounted the notion that mountaineers are consciously ascetical. Yet the analogy between climbing and religious aspiration cannot be ignored. Many of the makers of the literature of mountaineering show a tendency toward animistic myth-making. Sir Leslie Stephen remarks that, were he to fabricate a new paganism, he could think of no more proper objects of worship than the snowy giants of the Bernese Oberland. The imaginative climber seems always to be aware that on the mountain he is in the Presence. He venerates and fears, loves and loathes, feels powerful attraction and repulsion, but always he aspires. Further, mountaineers often take a peculiar interest in the local superstitions which people the lofty fortresses with mighty beings. Thoreau on Mount Katahdin felt a hostile presence. Himalayan climbers do not usually dismiss as simply benighted the natives who steadfastly believe that the mountain prosaically called Everest is really Chomolungma, Goddess Mother of the Snows. There have, of course, been many climbers either ignorant of or indifferent to these nameless pressures. As athletic machines they were not harmed by their immunity, but they missed the emotional value of temporary superstition, which is one way of apprehending the sublime.

The climber, then, has a means for organizing and expressing an aspiration which is characteristically human. The resistance provided by the mountain and by the retrograde part of his own spirit is necessary also, for aspiration cannot be realized except against opposition. Because he has a clearly definable object, lacking in much human activity, the climber enjoys the psychological benefits of simplification and direction. In *Brave New World* Aldous Huxley describes a dreary sport sanctioned in the inverted Utopia which he projects. Known by the arresting name Centrifugal Bumblepuppy, its main feature is a fundamental complexity and, consequently, the use of elaborate equipment. To the layman the equipment of mountaineering—ice axes, pitons, crampons, and the varied impedimenta of a Himalayan expedition—may suggest the same essential complexity. But the great majority of mountaineers combat real mechanization of the sport and hold to the original belief that the primary object is ascent and the primary means human effort. Thus the sport has retained its essential simplicity and its pleasure.

Plainly, the discovery in action of a source of unified sensibility is in great part what gives mountaineering its emotional force and validity. This is difficult to convey by analysis. But it appears vividly in an essay entitled "The Mountaineer as Artist," by George Leigh Mallory, one of the great climbers, whose achievement and disappearance on Mount Everest have become part of the heroic legend of mountaineering. Exploring the analogy of musical experience and climbing he wrote:

Mountain scenes appear to recur, not only in the same quality with tunes from a great work, say, Mozart or Beethoven, but from the same differentiating cause. It is not mere intensity of feeling that determines the places of tunes in my subconscious self, but chiefly some other principle. When the chords of melody are split, and unsatisfied suggestions of complete harmony are tossed among the instruments; when the firm rhythm is lost in remote pools and eddies, the mind roams perplexed; it experiences remorse and associates it with no cause; grief, and it names no sad event; desires crying aloud and unfulfilled, and yet it will not formulate the object of them; but when the great tide of music rises with a resolved purpose, floating the strewn wreckage and bearing it up together in its embracing stream, like a supreme spirit in the glorious act of creation, then the vague distresses and cravings are satisfied, a divine completeness of harmony possesses all the senses and the mind as though the universe and the individual were in exact accord, pursuing a common aim with the efficiency of mechanical perfection. Similarly, some parts of a climbing day give us the feeling of things unfulfilled; we doubt and tremble; we go forward not as men determined to reach a fixed goal; our plans do not convince us and miscarry; discomforts are not willingly accepted as a proper necessity; spirit and body seem to betray each other: but a time comes when all this is changed and we experience a harmony and a satisfaction. The individual is in a sense submerged, yet not so as to be less conscious; rather his consciousness is specially alert, and he comes to a finer realisation of himself than ever before. It is these moments of supremely harmonious experience that remain always with us and part of us. Other times and other scenes besides may be summoned back to gleam across the path, elusive revenants; but those that are born of the supreme accord are more substantial; they are the real immortals.[1]

The reward which Mallory suggests is rich and wonderful. Fortunately, it can be shared, at least in part, by anyone who will read the literature of mountaineering in a spirit of emotional participation. Such a reader will discover information highly interesting in itself and the zestful recounting of adventure. He will discover also a remedy for dejection and a testament of human worth in record upon record of joyful experience, in which men achieved, perhaps but briefly, a harmony of the active and the contemplative which most of us are toiling all our lives to find.

[1] *The Climbers' Club Journal*, I, N.S. 3 (1914), 28–40. Reprinted by permission of The Climbers' Club.

Challenge

SIR LESLIE STEPHEN

1832–1904

A SERIOUS STUDENT of nineteenth century English culture is obliged to give attention to the life and works of Sir Leslie Stephen. He was widely known and respected in the literary society of his time; he contributed notably to the periodicals—*Pall Mall Gazette, Cornhill, Fraser's, Fortnightly*—which raised journalism to perhaps the highest level it has ever reached. He performed permanently valuable services to literary and philosophical scholarship in his *History of English Thought in the Eighteenth Century;* in his lives of Hobbes, Swift, Pope, Johnson, and George Eliot—all written for the English Men of Letters series; and in the *Dictionary of National Biography*, of which he was editor from 1882 to 1891 and to which he contributed almost four hundred articles. Once acquainted with his work, few would choose not to read his shorter essays in biography, criticism, and ethics.

To his Alpine Club contemporaries Stephen's accomplishments and somewhat astringent personality, "in its quaint glooms, keen lights, and rugged trim," were almost heroic. He was eminent among those who first made the Alps the playground of Europe. After a few vacation walking tours on the Continent, he began earnest mountaineering on Monte Rosa, and through several seasons climbed the Bietschhorn, Dom, Rimpfischorn, Allalinhorn, Blumlisalphorn, Schreckhorn, Monte della Disgrazia, the Weisshorn, Lyskamm, Zinal Rothhorn, and Jungfrau. Several of these were first ascents. He was also fond of climbing high passes. Even after he professedly abandoned the giants, in 1867, and wrote "The Regrets of a Mountaineer," his feats were those of an athlete. He joined the recently organized Alpine Club in 1858, in 1865 became president for three years, and edited *The Alpine Journal* from 1868 to 1872. In his later years he became a kind of elder statesman among mountaineers and at the time of his death was described by Lord Bryce as the "recognized head of the Alpine confraternity in England."

Stephen's biographer suggests that it was in writing of his mountain experiences that he discovered a talent for expression and went far toward forming the clear and economical style which served him well throughout his life. Certainly his earliest works were entirely Alpine essays, and few of the early volumes of *The Alpine Journal* lack a high-spirited paper by the Rev. Leslie Stephen, M.A. Most of these and some later pieces he collected in the volume entitled *The Playground of Europe* (1871); they range from crisp and entertaining narrative to essays of sustained reflectiveness and unobtrusive lyricism, tones entirely consonant with the recurrent grave wit. According to his daughter, Virginia Woolf, the elderly Stephen thought "Sunset on Mont Blanc" the best thing he ever wrote.

Stephen's influence on the formation of the sport and on the nascent literature of mountaineering was strongly directive. He had no use for a "mere athletic machine"; he scorned false heroics in narrative and in action. With a converse consistency he labored steadily against the widespread opinion among the uninformed that the new sport was actually a new lunacy. Stephen's Alpine writings furnish a reliable index of a man who achieved a remarkable integration of the muscular and the spiritual.

The following selection is reprinted from Sir Leslie Stephen, *The Playground of Europe*, edited by H. E. G. Tyndale, Oxford, Basil Blackwell, Ltd., 1936, by permission of Longmans, Green & Co., Ltd.

Sunset on Mont Blanc

I PROFESS MYSELF to be a loyal adherent of the ancient Monarch of Mountains,[1] and, as such, I hold as a primary article of faith the doctrine that no Alpine summit is, as a whole, comparable in sublimity and beauty to Mont Blanc. With all his faults and weaknesses, and in spite of a crowd of upstart rivals, he still deserves to reign in solitary supremacy. Such an opinion seems to some mountaineers as great an anachronism as the creed of a French Legitimist. The coarse flattery of guidebooks has done much to surround him with vulgarising associations; even the homage of poets and painters has deprived his charms of their early freshness, and climbers have ceased to regard his conquest as a glorious, or, indeed, as anything but a most commonplace exploit. And yet Mont Blanc has merits which no unintelligent worship can obscure, and which bind with growing fas-

---

[1] Mont Blanc is the monarch of mountains;
    They crowned him long ago
   On a throne of rocks, in a robe of clouds,
    With a diadem of snow.

(Byron, *Manfred*, I, i, 60–63.)

cination the unprejudiced lover of scenery. Tried by a low, but not meaningless standard, the old monarch can still extort respect. He can show a longer list of killed and wounded than any other mountain in the Alps, or almost than all other mountains put together. In his milder moods, he may be approached with tolerable safety even by the inexperienced; but in angry moments, when he puts on his robe of clouds and mutters with his voice of thunder, no mountain is so terrible. Even the light snow-wreaths that eddy gracefully across his brow in fine weather sometimes testify to an icy storm that pierces the flesh and freezes the very marrow of the bones. But we should hardly estimate the majesty of men or mountains by the length of their butcher's bill.

Mont Blanc has other and less questionable claims on our respect. He is the most solitary of all mountains, rising, Saul-like, a head and shoulders above the crowd of attendant peaks, and yet within that single mass there is greater prodigality of the sublimest scenery than in the whole mountain districts of inferior elevation. The sternest and most massive of cliffs, the wildest spires of distorted rock, bounding torrents of shattered ice, snowfields polished and even as a seashell, are combined into a whole of infinite variety and yet of artistic unity. One might wander for days, were such wandering made possible by other conditions, amongst his crowning snows, and every day would present new combinations of unsuspected grandeur.

Why, indeed, some critics will ask, should we love a ruler of such questionable attributes? Scientifically speaking, the so-called monarch is but so many tons of bleak granite determining a certain quantity of aqueous precipitation. And if for literary purposes it be permissible to personify a monstrous rock, the worship of such a Moloch has in it something unnatural. In the mouth of the poet who first invested him with royal honours, the language was at least in keeping. Byron's misanthropy, real or affected, might identify love of nature with hatred of mankind: and a savage, shapeless, and lifeless idol was a fitting centre for his enthusiasm. But we have ceased to believe in the Childe Harolds and the Manfreds. Become a hermit—denounce your species, and shrink from their contact, and you may consistently love the peaks where human life exists on sufferance, and whose message to the valleys is conveyed in wasting torrents or crushing avalanches. Men of saner mind who repudiate this anti-social creed should love the fertile valleys and grass-clad ranges better than these symbols of the sternest desolation. All the enthusiasm for the wilder scenery, when it is not simple affectation, is the product of a temporary phase of sentiment, of which the justification has now ceased to exist. To all of which the zealot may perhaps reply most judiciously, Be it as you please. Prefer, if you see fit, a Leicestershire meadow or even a Lincolnshire fen to the cliff and glacier, and exalt the view from the Crystal Palace above the widest of Alpine panoramas.

Natural scenery, like a great work of art, scorns to be tied down to any cut-and-dried moral. To each spectator it suggests a different train of thought and emotion, varying as widely as the idiosyncrasy of the mind affected. If Mont Blanc produces in you nothing but a sense of hopeless savagery, well and good; confess it honestly to yourself and to the world, and do not help to swell the chorus of insincere ecstasy. But neither should you quarrel with those in whom the same sight produces emotions of a very different kind. That man is the happiest and wisest who can draw delight from the most varied objects: from the quiet bandbox scenery of cultivated England, or from the boundless prairies of the West; from the Thames or the Amazon, Malvern or Mont Blanc, the Virginia Water or the Atlantic Ocean. If the reaction which made men escape with sudden ecstasy from trim gardens to rough mountain sides was somewhat excessive, yet there was in it a core of sound feeling. Does not science teach us more and more emphatically that nothing which is natural can be alien to us who are part of nature?

Where does Mont Blanc end, and where do I begin? That is the question which no metaphysician has hitherto succeeded in answering. But at least the connection is close and intimate. He is a part of the great machinery in which my physical frame is inextricably involved, and not the less interesting because a part which I am unable to subdue to my purposes. The whole universe, from the stars and the planets to the mountains and the insects which creep about their roots, is but a network of forces eternally acting and reacting upon each other. The mind of man is a musical instrument upon which all external objects are beating out infinitely complex harmonies and discords. Too often, indeed, it becomes a mere barrel-organ, mechanically repeating the tunes which have once been impressed upon it. But in proportion as it is more vigorous or delicate, it should retain its sensibility to all the impulses which may be conveyed to it from the most distant sources. And certainly a healthy organisation should not be deaf to those more solemn and melancholy voices which speak through the wildest aspects of nature.

"Our sweetest songs," as Shelley says in his best mood, "are those which tell of saddest thought." [2] No poetry or art is of the highest order in which there is not blended some strain of melancholy, even to sternness. Shakespeare would not be Shakespeare if it were not for that profound sense of the transitory in all human affairs which appears in the finest sonnets and in his deepest dramatic utterances. When he tells us of the unsubstantial fabric of the great globe itself, or the glorious morning which "flatters the mountain tops with sovereign eye," only to be hidden by the "basest clouds," or, anticipating modern geologists, observes

> The hungry ocean gain
> Advantage on the kingdom of the shore,

he is merely putting into words the thoughts obscurely present to the mind of every watcher of the eternal mountains which have outlasted so many generations, and are yet, like all other things, hastening to decay. The mountains represent the indomitable force of nature to which we are forced to adapt ourselves; they speak to man of his littleness and his ephemeral existence; they rouse us from the placid content in which we may be lapped when contemplating the fat fields which we have conquered and the rivers which we have forced to run according to our notions of convenience. And, therefore, they should suggest not sheer misanthropy, as they did to Byron, or an outburst of revolutionary passion, as they did to his teacher Rousseau, but that sense of awe-struck humility which befits such petty creatures as ourselves.

It is true, indeed, that Mont Blanc sometimes is too savage for poetry. He can speak in downright tragic earnestness; and anyone

2 "To a Skylark," l. 90.

who has been caught in a storm on some of his higher icefields, who has trembled at the deadly swoop of the gale, or at the ominous sound which heralds an avalanche, or at the remorseless settling down of the blinding snow, will agree that at times he passes the limits of the terrible which comes fairly within the range of art. There are times, however, at which one may expect to find precisely the right blending of the sweet and the stern. And in particular, there are those exquisite moments when the sunset is breathing over his calm snowfields its "ardours of rest and love." Watched from beneath, the Alpine glow, as everybody knows, is of exquisite beauty; but unfortunately the spectacle has become a little too popular. The very sunset seems to smell of Baedeker's Guide. The flesh is weak and the most sympathetic of human beings is apt to feel a slight sense of revulsion when the French guests at a *table d'hôte* are exclaiming in chorus, "*Magnifique, superbe!*" and the Germans chiming in with "*Wunderschön!*" and the British tourist patting the old mountain on the back, and the American protesting that he has shinier sunsets at home. Not being of a specially sympathetic nature, I had frequently wondered how that glorious spectacle would look from the solitary top of the monarch himself. This summer I was fortunate enough, owing to the judicious arrangements of one of his most famous courtiers—my old friend and comrade M. Gabriel Loppé—to be able to give an answer founded on personal experience. The result was to me so interesting that I shall venture—rash as the attempt may be—to give some account of a phenomenon of extraordinary beauty which has hitherto been witnessed by not more than some half-dozen human beings.

It was in the early morning of August 6, 1873, that I left Chamonix for the purpose. The sun rose on one of those fresh dewy dawns unknown except in the mountains, when the buoyant air seems as it were to penetrate every pore in one's body. I could almost say with Sir Galahad

> This mortal armour that I wear,
> This weight and size, this heart and eyes,
> Are touch'd and turn'd to finest air.[3]

---

[3] Tennyson, "Sir Galahad," ll. 70–72.

The heavy, sodden framework of flesh and blood which I languidly dragged along London streets has undergone a strange transformation, and it is with scarcely a conscious effort that I breast the monstrous hill which towers above me. The pinewoods give out their aromatic scent, and the little glades are deep in ferns, wild-flowers, and strawberries. Even here, the latent terrors of the mountains are kept in mind by the huge boulders which, at some distant day, have crashed like cannon-balls through the forest. But the great mountain is not now indulging in one of his ponderous games at bowls, and the soft carpeting of tender vegetation suggests rather luxurious indolence, and, maybe, recalls lazy picnics rather than any more strenuous memories.

Before long, however, we emerged from the forest, and soon the bells of a jolly little company of goats bade us farewell on the limits of the civilised world, as we stepped upon the still frozen glacier and found ourselves fairly in the presence. We were alone with the mighty dome, dazzling our eyes in the brilliant sunshine, and guarded by its sleeping avalanches. Luckily there was no temptation to commit the abomination of walking "against time" or racing any rival caravan of climbers. The whole day was before us, for it would have been undesirable to reach the chilly summit too early; and we could afford the unusual luxury of lounging up Mont Blanc. We took, I hope, full advantage of our opportunities. We could peer into the blue depths of crevasses, so beautiful that one might long for such a grave, were it not for the awkward prospect of having one's bones put under a glass case by the next generation of scientific travellers. We could record in our memories the strange forms of the shattered séracs, those grotesque ice-masses which seem to suggest that the monarch himself has a certain clumsy sense of humour.

We lingered longest on the summit of the Dôme du Goûter, itself a most majestic mountain were it not overawed by its gigantic neighbour. There, on the few ledges of rock which are left exposed in summer, the thunder has left its scars. The lightning's strokes have covered numbers of stones with little glass-like heads, showing that this must be one of its favourite haunts. But on this glorious summer day the lightnings were at rest; and we could peacefully count over the vast wilderness of peaks which already stretched far and wide beneath our feet. The lower mountain ranges appeared to be drawn up in parallel ranks like the sea waves heaved in calm weather by a monotonous ground-swell. Each ridge was blended into a uniform hue by the intervening atmosphere, sharply defined along the summit line, and yet only distinguished from its predecessor and successor by a delicate gradation of tone.

Such a view produces the powerful but shadowy impression which one expects from an opium dream. The vast perspective drags itself out to an horizon so distant as to blend imperceptibly with the lower sky. It has a vague suggestion of rhythmical motion, strangely combined with eternal calm. Drop a pebble into a perfectly still sheet of water; imagine that each ripple is supplanted by a lofty mountain range, of which all detail is lost in purple haze, and that the furthest undulations melt into the mysterious infinite. One gazes with a sense of soothing melancholy as one listens to plaintive modulations of some air of "linked sweetness long drawn out." Far away among the hills we could see long reaches of the peaceful Lake of Geneva, just gleaming through the varying purple; but at our backs the icy crest of the great mountain still rose proudly above us, to remind us that our task was not yet finished. Fortunately for us, scarcely a cloud was to be seen under the enormous concave of the dark blue heavens; a few light streamers of cirrus were moving gently over our heads in those remote abysses from which they never condescend even to the loftiest of Alpine summits. Faint and evanescent as they might be, they possibly had an ominous meaning for the future, but the present was our own; the little puffs of wind that whispered round some lofty ledges were keen enough in quality to remind us of possible frost-bites, but they had scarcely force enough to extinguish a lucifer match.

Carefully calculating our time, we advanced along the "dromedary's hump" and stepped upon the culminating ridge of the mountain about an hour before sunset. We had time to collect ourselves, to awake our powers of observation, and to prepare for the grand spectacle, for which preparations were already being made. There had been rehearsals enough in all conscience to secure a perfect performance. For millions of ages the lamps had been lighted and the transparencies had been shown with no human eye to observe or hand to applaud. Twice, I believe only twice, before, an audience had taken its place in this lofty gallery; but on one of those occasions, at least, the observers had been too unwell to do justice to the spectacle. The other party, of which the chief member was a French man of science, Dr. Martens, had been obliged to retreat hastily before the lights were extinguished; but their fragmentary account had excited our curiosity, and we had the pleasure of verifying the most striking phenomenon which they described.

And now we waited eagerly for the performance to commence; the cold was sufficient to freeze the wine in our bottles, but in still air the cold is but little felt, and by walking briskly up and down and adopting the gymnastic exercise in which the London cabman delights in cold weather, we were able to keep up a sufficient degree of circulation. I say "we," but I am libelling the most enthusiastic member of the party. Loppé sat resolutely on the snow, at the risk, as we might have thought, of following the example of Lot's wife. Superior, as it appeared, to all the frailties which beset the human frame suddenly plunged into a temperature I know not how many degrees below freezing-point, he worked with ever increasing fury in a desperate attempt to fix upon canvas some of the magic beauties of the scene. Glancing from earth to heaven and from north to south, sketching with breathless rapidity the appearance of the eastern ranges, then wheeling round like a weathercock to make hasty notes of the western clouds, breaking out at times into uncontrollable exclamations of delight, or reproving his thoughtless companions when their opaque bodies eclipsed a whole quarter of the heavens, he enjoyed, I should fancy, an hour of as keen delight as not often occurs to an enthusiastic lover of the sublime in nature. We laughed, envied, and admired, and he escaped frost-bites.

I wish that I could substitute his canvas—though, to say the truth, I fear it would exhibit a slight confusion of the points of the compass—for my words; but, as that is impossible, I must endeavour briefly to indicate the most impressive features of the scenery. My readers must kindly set their imaginations to work in aid of feeble language; for even the most eloquent language is but a poor substitute for a painter's brush, and a painter's brush lags far behind these grandest aspects of nature. The easiest way of obtaining the impression is to follow in my steps; for, in watching a sunset from Mont Blanc one feels that one is passing one of those rare moments of life at which all the surrounding scenery is instantaneously and indelibly photographed on the mental retina by a process which no second-hand operation can even dimly transfer to others. To explain its nature requires a word or two of preface.

The ordinary view from Mont Blanc is not specially picturesque—and for a sufficient reason. The architect has concentrated his whole energies in producing a single impression. Everything has been so arranged as to intensify the sense of vast height and an illimitable horizon. In a good old guidebook I have read, on the authority (I think) of Pliny, that the highest mountain in the world is 300,000 feet above the sea; and one is apt to fancy, on ascending Mont Blanc, that the guess is not so far out. The effect is perfectly unique in the Alps; but it is produced at a certain sacrifice. All dangerous rivals have been removed to such a distance as to become apparently insignificant. No grand mass can be admitted into the foreground; for the sense of vast size is gradually forced upon you by the infinite multiplicity of detail.

Mont Blanc must be like an Asiatic despot, alone and supreme, with all inferior peaks reverently couched at his feet. If a man, previously as ignorant of geography as a boy who has just left a public school, could be transported for a moment to the summit, his impression would be that the Alps resembled a village of a hundred hovels grouped round a stupendous cathedral. Fully to appreciate this effect requires a certain familiarity with Alpine scenery, for otherwise the effect produced is a dwarfing of the inferior mountains into pettiness instead of an exaltation of Mont Blanc into almost portentous magnificence. Grouped around you at unequal distances lie innumerable white patches, looking like the tented encampments of scattered army corps. Hold up a glove at arm's length, and it will cover the whole of such a group. On the boundless plain beneath (I say "plain," for the greatest mountain system of Europe appears to have subsided into a rather uneven plain), it is a mere spot, a trifling dent upon the huge shield on whose central boss you are placed. But you know, though at first you can hardly realise the knowledge, that that insignificant discoloration represents a whole mountain district. One spot, for example, represents the clustered peaks of the Bernese Oberland; a block, as big as a pebble, is the soaring Jungfrau, the terrible mother of avalanches; a barely distinguishable wrinkle is the reverse of those snowy wastes of the Blumlisalp, which seem to be suspended above the terrace of Berne, thirty miles away; and that little whitish stream represents the greatest icestream of the Alps, the huge Aletsch Glacier, whose monstrous proportions have been impressed upon you by hours of laborious plodding. One patch contains the main sources from which the Rhine descends to the German ocean, two or three more overlook the Italian plains and encircle the basin of the Po; from a more distant group flows the Danube, and from your feet the snows melt to supply the Rhone. You feel that you are in some sense looking down upon Europe from Rotterdam to Venice and from Varna to Marseilles. The vividness of the impression depends entirely upon the degree to which you can realise the immense size of all these immeasurable details.

Now, in the morning, the usual time for an ascent, the details are necessarily vague, because the noblest part of the view lies between the sun and the spectator. But in the evening light each ridge, and peak, and glacier stands out with startling distinctness, and each, therefore, is laden with its weight of old association. There, for example, was the grim Matterhorn: its angular dimensions were of infinitesimal minuteness; it would puzzle a mathematician to say how small a space its image would occupy on his retina; but, within that small space, its form was defined with exquisite accuracy; and we could recognise the precise configuration of the wild labyrinth of rocky ridges up which the earlier adventurers forced their way from the Italian side. And thus we not only knew, but felt that at our feet was lying a vast slice of the map of Europe. The effect was to exaggerate the apparent height, till the view had about it something portentous and unnatural: it seemed to be such a view as could be granted not even to mountaineers of earthly mould, but rather to some genie from the *Arabian Nights*, flying high above a world tinted with the magical colouring of old romance.

Thus distinctly drawn, though upon so minute a scale, every

rock and slope preserved its true value, and the impression of stupendous height became almost oppressive as it was forced upon the imagination that a whole world of mountains, each of them a mighty mass in itself, lay couched far beneath our feet, reaching across the whole diameter of the vast panorama. And now, whilst occupied in drinking in that strange sensation, and allowing our minds to recover their equilibrium from the first staggering shock of astonishment, began the strange spectacle of which we were the sole witnesses. One long, delicate cloud, suspended in mid-air just below the sun, was gradually adorning itself with prismatic colouring. Round the limitless horizon ran a faint fog-bank, unfortunately not quite thick enough to produce that depth of colouring which sometimes makes an Alpine sunset inexpressibly gorgeous.

The weather—it was the only complain we had to make—erred on the side of fineness. But the colouring was brilliant enough to prevent any thoughts of serious disappointment. The long series of western ranges melted into a uniform hue as the sun declined in their rear. Amidst their folds the Lake of Geneva became suddenly lighted up in a faint yellow gleam. To the east a blue gauze seemed to cover valley by valley as they sank into night and the intervening ridges rose with increasing distinctness, or rather it seemed that some fluid of exquisite delicacy of colour and substance was flooding all the lower country beneath the great mountains. Peak by peak the high snowfields caught the rosy glow and shone like signal-fires across the dim breadths of delicate twilight. Like Xerxes, we looked over the countless host sinking into rest, but with the rather different reflection, that a hundred years hence they would probably be doing much the same things, whilst we should have long ceased to take any interest in the performance.

And suddenly began a more startling phenomenon. A vast cone, with its apex pointing away from us, seemed to be suddenly cut out from the world beneath; night was within its borders and the twilight still all round; the blue mists were quenched where it fell, and for the instant we could scarcely tell what was the origin of this strange appearance. Some unexpected change seemed to have taken place in the programme; as though a great fold in the curtain had suddenly given way, and dropped on to part of the scenery. Of course a moment's reflection explained the meaning of this uncanny intruder; it was the giant shadow of Mont Blanc, testifying to his supremacy over all meaner eminences. It is difficult to say how sharply marked was the outline, and how startling was the contrast between this pyramid of darkness and the faintly-lighted spaces beyond its influence; a huge inky blot seemed to have suddenly fallen upon the landscape. As we gazed we could see it move. It swallowed up ridge by ridge, and its sharp point crept steadily from one landmark to another down the broad Valley of Aosta. We were standing, in fact, on the point of the gnomon of a gigantic sundial, the face of which was formed by thousands of square miles of mountain and valley. So clear was the outline that, if figures had been scrawled upon glaciers and ridges, we could have told the time to a second; indeed, we were half-inclined to look for our own shadows at a distance so great that the whole villages would be represented by a scarcely distinguishable speck of colouring.

The huge shadow, looking ever more strange and magical, struck the distant Becca di Nona, and then climbed into the dark region where the broader shadow of the world was rising into the eastern sky. By some singular effect of perspective, rays of darkness seemed to be converging from above our heads to a point immediately above the apex of the shadowy cone. For a time it seemed that there was a kind of anti-sun in the east, pouring out not light, but deep shadow as it rose. The apex soon reached the horizon, and then to our surprise began climbing the distant sky. Would it never stop, and was Mont Blanc capable of overshadowing not only the earth but the sky? For a minute or two I fancied, in a bewildered way, that this unearthly object would fairly rise from the ground and climb upwards to the zenith. But rapidly the lights went out upon the great army of mountains; the snow all round took the livid hue which immediately succeeds an Alpine sunset, and almost at a blow the shadow of Mont Blanc was swallowed up in the general shade of night.

The display had ceased suddenly at its culminating point, and it was highly expedient for the spectators to retire. We had no time to lose if we would get off the summit before the grip of the frost should harden the snows into an ice-crust; and in a minute we were running and sliding downwards at our best pace towards the familiar Corridor. Yet as we went the sombre magnificence of the scenery seemed for a time to increase. We were between the day and the night. The western heavens were of the most brilliant blue with spaces of transparent green, whilst a few scattered cloudlets glowed as if with internal fire. To the east the night rushed up furiously, and it was difficult to imagine that the dark purple sky was really cloudless and not blackened by the rising of some portentous storm. That it was, in fact, cloudless, appeared from the unbroken disc of the full moon, which, if I may venture to say so, had a kind of silly expression, as though it were a bad imitation of the sun, totally unable to keep the darkness in order.

> With how sad steps, Oh moon, thou climb'st the sky,
> How silently and with how wan a face! [4]

as Sidney exclaims. And truly, set in that strange gloom the moon looked wan and miserable enough; the lingering sunlight showed by contrast that she was but a feeble source of illumination; and, but for her half-comic look of helplessness, we might have sympathised with the astronomers who tell us that she is nothing but a vast perambulating tombstone, proclaiming to all mankind in the words of the familiar epitaph, "As I am now, you soon shall be!" To speak after the fashion of early mythologies, one might fancy that some supernatural cuttlefish was shedding his ink through the heavens to distract her, and that the poor moon had but a bad chance of escaping his clutches.

Hurrying downwards with occasional glances at the sky, we had soon reached the Grand Plateau, whence our further retreat was secure, and from that wildest of mountain fastnesses we saw the last striking spectacle of the evening. In some sense it was perhaps the most impressive of all. As all Alpine travellers know, the Grand Plateau is a level space of evil omen, embraced by a vast semicircle of icy slopes. The avalanches, which occasionally descend across it, and which have caused more than one catastrophe, give it a bad reputation; and at night the icy jaws of the great mountain seem to be enclosing you in a fatal embrace. At

[4] Sidney, *Astrophel and Stella*, xxxi.

this moment there was something half grotesque in its sternness. Light and shade were contrasted in a manner so bold as to be almost bizarre. One half of the cirque was of a pallid white against the night, which was rushing up still blacker and thicker, except that a few daring stars shone out like fiery sparks against a pitchy canopy; the other half, reflecting the black night, was relieved against the last gleams of daylight; in front a vivid band of blood-red light burnt along the horizon, beneath which seemed to lie an abyss of mysterious darkness. It was the last struggle between night and day, and the night seemed to assume a more ghastly ferocity as the day sank, pale and cold, before its antagonist. The Grand Plateau, indeed, is a fit scene for such contrasts; for there in mid-day you may feel the reflection of the blinding snows like the blast of a furnace, where a few hours before you were realising the keenest pangs of frost-bite. The cold and the night were now the conquerors, and the angry sunset-glow seemed to grudge the victory. The light rapidly faded, and the darkness, no longer seen in the strange contrast, subsided to its ordinary tones. The magic was gone; and it was in a commonplace though lovely summer night that we reached our resting-place at the Grands Mulets.

We felt that we had learnt some new secrets as to the beauty of mountain scenery, but the secrets were of that kind which not even the initiated can reveal. A great poet might interpret the sentiment of the mountains into song; but no poet could pack into any definite proposition or series of propositions the strange thoughts that rise in different spectators of such a scene. All that I at last can say is that some indefinable mixture of exhilaration and melancholy pervades one's mind; one feels like a kind of cheerful Tithonus "at the quiet limit of the world," looking down from a magic elevation upon the "dim fields about the homes

Of happy men that have the power to die." [5]

One is still of the earth, earthy; for freezing toes and snow-parched noses are lively reminders that one has not become an immortal. Even on the top of Mont Blanc one may be a very long way from heaven. And yet the mere physical elevation of a league above the

[5] Tennyson, "Tithonus," ll. 69–70.

sea-level seems to raise one by moments into a sphere above the petty interests of everyday life. Why that should be so, and by what strange threads of association the reds and blues of a gorgeous sunset, the fantastic shapes of clouds and shadows at that dizzy height, and the dramatic changes that sweep over the boundless region beneath your feet, should stir you like mysterious music, or, indeed, why music itself should have such power, I leave to philosophers to explain. This only I know, that even the memory of that summer evening on the top of Mont Blanc has power to plunge me into strange reveries not to be analysed by any capacity, and still less capable of expression by the help of a few black marks on white paper. . . .

CHARLES EDWARD MONTAGUE

1867–1928

C. E. MONTAGUE was another for whom mountaineering was an integral part of an active life. Except for the four years of the First World War, he served from 1890 to 1925 as reviewer, dramatic critic, and leader writer for the *Manchester Guardian*. Early in the war he enlisted as a private. Invalided home, he soon returned to France as an officer in intelligence. His first assignment was to conduct distinguished visitors on tours of the battle front; later he became a press censor. During a busy life of journalism, much of it polemical, he found time to write numerous essays and short stories and four novels. The citation read on the occasion of his receiving an honorary degree from Manchester University praises his "immense natural gusto and zest for living hard, and his passion for intenser ways of life, like mountaineering or the theatre or rock-climbing."

Montague spent many vacations, long and short, tramping and climbing. He was intimately familiar with the Alps near Chamonix, with the uplands of England, particularly the Pennine Chain and the Cumbrian Mountains. Although he achieved no records and made no important first ascents, he was elected to the Alpine Club in 1906 and was a member of its controlling committee in 1926 and 1927.

Many of his writings urge the spiritual regeneration possible through violent physical activity and danger. These, he believed, resolve the divided loyalties and inconclusive efforts of common living; the climber who concentrates every power of mind and body on straining up the pitch which lies immediately before him is approaching the intense unity of aspiration and faculty which characterizes the artist and the saint. Safely on the summit, though fatigued and sore, he appreciates profoundly the joy of life, partly because he has risked death. He is a better man for having been cleansed by his toil. If, however, he should slip and be killed, there is no occasion for grief. To Montague a violent death, encountered suddenly during joyous exertion, is a positive blessing, far to be preferred to the wasting of illness. This is the doctrine of an extremist, which Montague would happily have confessed himself to be.

It is not surprising that Montague found war, despite the horror which he did not minimize, the ultimate in adventure, "the great sport to which all the delicious sports of the field lead up, and for which they serve as practice games." In all his activities he was a happy warrior, somewhat misplaced in time, and a knightly spirit invests his writings.

The following selection is reprinted from *Action and Other Stories,* by C. E. Montague. Copyright 1929 by Doubleday and Company, Inc.

Action

I

WHEN CHRISTOPHER BELL was just fifty-two he woke up one September morning to feel a slight numbness all down his right side. Some of the numbness was in his right arm; a good deal of it in his right thigh, along its outside, rather less in his right foot; and just a little in his head—all over the hinterland of his right ear.

It seemed a big percentage of a man to "go to sleep" at one time. He lay still for a minute, to let it pass off. But it didn't. So he began to speculate. When he got up, would he be able to stand? And to walk straight? Would his head go on working all right, with that bit of it stiff? Just how hard a punch would it turn out to be, that some god or devil had given him in the night?

He tried. Yes, he could stand, walk, dress and shave. No portion of him was absolutely on strike. But the numbness went on. And somehow he couldn't feel sure that some part of the right flank of his body or brain would not give way, without notice, and give him a cropper. You never know how deliciously sure you have been of yourself, of every scrap of yourself, all the days of your health, till some small gadget inside you is put out of action. Bell made this deep reflection while going downstairs to his solitary breakfast. He kept one hand on the banisters.

II

Christopher Bell was the reigning sovereign of a respectable dynasty of "merchant princes" in Manchester. For several generations his clan had embraced the higher civilisation so far as English Public schools and universities lead to such embraces. He had read with understanding and relish, and he had travelled with open eyes. He could value the great things in the arts and in science—indeed, in the whole ampler life of the race. And always, till now, his blood had pretty well bubbled with health. He had rowed, run, swum and ridden well. To his body, at forty years old, the War had brought a second boyhood of happy absorption in efforts merely physical.

Half-way through the war, the wife he had loved in every tissue of body and soul had died of something brought on by too passionate overwork for the cause. The news came to Bell in a hospital where he had just begun to grow a new skin on a face and hands well flayed and charred by chemical warfare. He could not see at the time, so a nurse read the telegram out. His face was buried deep in a canary-coloured mask of wadding stained with picric acid, so the nurse could not see how he took it—only knew that he thanked her very civilly through the little blow-hole left for his mouth. I fancy Bell was hanging on hard to the thought that he still had two children, a boy and a girl, both in their teens. Soldiers, even educated ones, are apt to grow sentimental, especially when wounded. Bell, the war widower, lay, week by week, behind his fancy-dress mask, staying his mind on an ingenuous vision of an improved world, to come after the war. He saw it as a young man and a young woman standing in summer twilight, under the stars, with their eyes all a-shine at the loveliness of the life which it had taken so much pain and shame to make possible for them.

Many soldiers hugged these quaint fancies, in their bad times. They helped, for the moment. It was afterwards that they had to be paid for. In the foul enervatory air that filled England and Europe just after the war Bell's boy and girl drifted feebly into failure. Both were married lovelessly now, each to another small waste product of that waste-producing time. Somewhere out of Bell's sight these forfeited objects of his pride and joy were shuffling punily through life. He gathered that they were rather ashamed of him as an old slow-coach provincial.

Bell was not given to wallowing in self-pity. Still, as you see, he had had his losses, like another.

III

Your merchant prince, in these days, is prone to lose heart, get himself up as an owner of land and beeves, and melt weakly into the common herd of squires who know not, poor fellows, what it is to go on 'Change. Bell was different. He had pride. He stuck, as his father had done, to his post among the garrison of the smutty city that had done well by them. He lived where he could hear the Town Hall clock strike twelve when the traffic was quiet at night, and a North wind blowing. He liked the sound, he was so oddly civic a person.

To this old-fashioned hobby Bell added some cheap habits less rare in rich men. He stood on guard against his wealth, lest it should cut him off from the sight and sound of ordinary and unprincely men, for whom his regard had been re-doubled by four years of living with them in the war. Because of this fad he nearly always went in to the city by tram. This morning he walked the three hundred yards from his house to the tram's stopping-place with deliberate caution. He could not be sure of that sleepy right leg. He was still distrusting it temperately when he had taken his seat and was tendering his fare to town.

The conductor rejected the tender, at sight. "We doan't taäke bootons," he said with civil composure.

Bell examined the bright disc that he had offered as a sixpence.

Behold! a silvery trouser-button. Last night it had come off and he had slipped it into a pocket. He put his finger-tips ruefully up to his eyes. "I'm sorry," he said to the man, as he gave the right coin.

"It's aal reet, Sir," the conductor said quietly. Once he saw that no pulling of legs had been intended, his tact and sympathy were perfect.

He passed on to collect other fares. But a new care remained in Bell's mind. Sight, too? Was that going? Sight, touch, the whole sensory business, losing precision, entering on the long slope to decay—the silver cord going loose and the golden bowl cracking? When a man who has known how to read feels the first clap of the hand of Time on his shoulder, he has plenty of ready prompters to ruefulness; so many excellent poets have found handsome words for the mists and mellow poignancy of man's autumn, the lapse from old vigour and vision into mere drug-takers' dreams while we are led down the avenue lined with overblown roses, to lie in the dust at its end.

Bell kept his head. But his memory was beginning to bulge with lovely quotations not conducive to high spirits—"Bare ruined choirs where late the sweet birds sang," and all that lot.

IV

The morning's office work did him good, while it lasted. He had more than most men of the gift of forgetting himself in the excitement of getting a job to come right—any old job, the dictating of letters, anything. And just now the affairs of his firm were of quite stirring interest. Like many others it had been making large losses for several years. Bell's game was to keep these losses as low as he could without stopping the work and wages of a moorland villageful of people who spun and wove cotton for Bell to sell for less than it cost to make it. This unacquisitive practice brought Bell into great infamy. Most of his fellow-employers wanted to close all the factories down, or half close them down, and leave the work-people to live on their fat. So Bell was an arrant traitor to them. Still, he was an employer: and so, to ardent Socialist eyes, he was a sucker of blood, *ex officio*. This lively crossfire of censures braced Bell. If it had to be woe unto you when all men spoke well of you, it might be safer when everyone slated you hard. Anyhow it livened you up, like a good stinging wind that has blown across snow. While he schemed to find some not quite ruinous sale for the stuff that piled itself up at the mills, Bell could forget the thing that had clawed him in its clutch during the night.

But the clouds return after the rain: luncheon-time set his mind free to worry, the way your sore tongue returns and returns to the amusement of hurting itself on the sharp point of a tooth lately broken. He lunched at the club; and twice in the one hour it took him his mind accused younger members of paying him the pestilential kind of un-arguing deference which is really the civil refusal of youth to keep its communications open with age. Could they have noticed the way he walked down the stairs—a canny way, like a horse's when it is afraid on a slippery slope? One younger man opened the door of the billiard-room for him. Damn these good manners that ain't good at all.

Going home at twilight, in the tram, Bell thought over all this so absorbedly that he kept his legs crossed the whole way. So, when he stood up, to get off, his right leg had gone clean asleep. It was only asleep in the common and blameless way. Still, he couldn't know that, at first. For all he could tell, a second stroke might have fallen, and this time a real knockout. Of course he kept his fears dark; still, he stepped off the car with such unconcealable care that the conductor slipped a friendly hand under his arm and led him slowly to the safety of the footpath, like a blind man or a drunk.

When Bell had walked a few yards by himself the extra numbness was gone. But the other numbness remained. And so did the feel of that patiently guarding hand under his arm. Of course he had not needed it. Still, perhaps he would, presently, "Mene, mene," etc.— every wall seemed to be covered with sinister shreds of writing. An object for everybody's protection, a call on everyone's forbearance— that was the kind of pest that he might become. Soon, too, perhaps. This kind of plague crept on and on. It never turned back. Five years might bring an invalid-chair and a male nurse to put him to bed and to see that he was carted securely about from place to place, to sprawl in the sun—Mentone, the Canaries, Egypt, all the places to which the *passés* butterflies of our commonwealth were brought to lie out and doze in the warmth when too much eating and idling had brought them back all the way to the status of larvae. Disgusting!

V

Bell gazed steadily into this smiling future, while eating his dinner alone. From the table he went straight, like a man who knew what he needed, to that shelf in his study on which there were all his pet Alpine books. No other sport had ever so wholly ravished his soul as mountaineering. On the high snows it seemed as if magical fires were lit in your blood; the flame of life burned amazingly; something was added unto a man as divine as whatever it is that makes its way into the vapid juice of a fruit and turns it to wine. Nowhere else in the world was the taste of success so wholly and indefeasibly sweet as it was on the tip of some spire of granite and ice that had all but turned you back in despair by the Daphnean rigour of its resistance. There, uplifted on the swell of the round earth, you could see how men had come to dream Gardens of Eden and Ages of Gold.

He took from the shelf a great climber's narratives of his greatest adventures. Two of these, in especial, could always entrance Bell as soon as he had read a few lines: their vividness gave him an almost physical sense of what they described. Each was a case of cutting steps up a long and extremely steep slope of ice. And in each case the slope had, at one point, ceased even to slope. For just a few feet of its height it had become as vertical as the wall of a house: each man of the party had had to hold himself in to the perpendicular wall by sheer strength and good hand-hold, against gravitation.

In each case the party had come safely through. But with how big a margin of safety, as engineers say? Bell wondered. A pretty big one, he fancied. Few good climbers slipped in really difficult places; all their faculties were bent up too intently for that, with danger about; they were above their own everyday form. But what if such a party were to try paring and paring away at that pretty wide margin? Something like an experiment, that! To what untold heights of achievement might not the party attain before all the margin was gone! And of course the party might be a party of one.

Bell had once had a holiday dream of climbing a crag that grew steeper and steeper till it was vertical first, and then overhung, more and more, but still he climbed on and on and because the crag beetled out over a warm summer sea, so that, when he lost hold in the end, he would only fall from one pleasure into another, out of a mountaineer's paradise into a swimmer's. Cut out the old fear of death in that way, or some other, and—why, you could do anything.

As he sat back with the open book on his knees, a light wind stirred the trees in the garden. It may have been this that called up another old notion of his. This one had visited him in a wood close to Arras, in 1916. During some dark windless weeks of that autumn the unfallen leaves had been fading inertly from green to a dull rusty red, and so down to a dead russet brown; the whole burning heart of the year was collapsing into shabby ashes. Then a night of frost came and then a gale on a day of broken sunshine thrown wildly about between clouds. As the gale stripped the trees it had seemed almost to blow them aflame; sparks of brave yellow flew in the air; the dun beech-leaves took light and fell lustrously. Somehow the sight had filled Bell at the time, with a wish that, when he had to go, he might do it like that—all a-stir and a-glow, by one of the "violent" deaths, as most of the easy ones seemed to be called. Anything but to lie on a bed in a hushed room with the lights low and life's jolly noises shut out, and people whispering among the shadows. One wrench for the undecayed body, and then unbreakable sleep—what end could equal it?

Now, almost suddenly, these several notions ran into one, as raindrops do on a newly wet window. Here was the moment to put into practice that old and sound choice of his between the long decrepitude of the flesh and the one clean cut and summary pang that save you it all. Suicide? Oh! no. But just to carry on, right to the end, the piquant experiment of paring and paring away that limiting and restraining margin of safety which mountaineers, even the boldest, keep in reserve. Had not all things conspired to free him from too much love of remaining alive—bereavement and baulked hope and now this first lick from heaven, soon to blast the whole of him by degrees? Why, fate had brought him the fulfilment of his old dream. No precipice in the world would now have an abhorred death waiting at its foot—merely a warm quiet sea of painless forgetfulness.

Only—he must be quick, before the accursed thing that was setting to work on him could pith so much of the vigour out of his body that he could not make his own way to a place—already he had a good place in his mind—where he might try the thing out.

VI

At the end of September a savoursome blend of jollity and melancholy pervades the little Val d'Anniviers. The summer hotels at Zinal, at the head of the valley, are closing. Down the bridle-path, through forests of fir, the hotel staffs stream along joyously, laden with the year's vintage of tips, to their snug winter homes in the

Rhone Valley below. Reconverted, after four months of restraint and disguise, into young, natural Swiss men and women, they caper like Alpine cows let out in the spring. Shouting, chaffing and singing, they seem to flout with their merriment Nature's yearly menace to marmots and men. And Nature answers them back. Almost hour by hour the new snow creeps down the forested slopes of the valley and grizzles more of its firs; the morning dew lies late, and even at noon the weakening sun hangs lazily low above the main chain of the Alps. You feel, all about you, a big closing-in, the rustle of a heavy curtain falling upon a good time that is played out at last.

As Bell walked the six miles up from Vissoye to Zinal, he breasted that jovial current of waiters and chamber-maids thawed and re-humanised. Jove! They were good to see and to hear, with their jokes and catches and bold, friendly, unobsequious looks at any man and brother they met. But everything was good in this place. Even the smell of Vissoye and its pigs, as he passed, had been the smell of the best holiday of his boyhood. How he had liked life— every bit of it, coloured or plain, the high lights and the low! Even the jars had been part of the makings of the incomparable adventure. He wondered whether the mere feel of things—common things, all sorts of things—could ever have given anyone else such raptures of secret contentment as they had given to him.

He had made sure of a room at Zinal. He dined by the light of one lamp in a corner of the hotel's dining-room, now empty and shadowy. An elderly woman waited upon him; everyone else in the house had gone down the valley; she had been left for a week or two more, to cook, wait, make a bed and draw out a bill for anyone mad enough to turn up so belatedly. Bell had known her for thirty years— ever since her marriage to an old guide of his, recently killed on the Meije. She told him how their son Pierre was now a guide too, rather to her alarm. She seemed amazingly glad to see Bell, as if he were a bit of some good old world that had been slipping away. And he . . . ? she asked. Was he making a *grande course*, as always? Surely not, at this time of year?

He fenced with her apt, friendly questions. He felt like a liar. Indeed, he was one, pretty well; for he fully meant to deceive. He would go for a walk by himself, he said, after breakfast tomorrow—perhaps to the Arpitetta Alp only, perhaps rather further.

She looked at him sadly, with peasant directness. "All alone now!" she said simply. "And once it was you and Madame—and Gaspard and me. Ah! the good times." She had all humanity's fate in her face, like an old woman drawn by Rembrandt—hopes and happy love and then the dust of the day, dimming the roses, and then great loneliness and unconsolable tears. Would Monsieur have coffee? she asked.

Bell could face her no longer. It was too treacherous. No, he said, he would want nothing more. Let her go to bed early, like all the good marmots. So would he too, when he had smoked a little end of tobacco.

When she was gone, he sat by a fire of logs she had lit for him in the small smoking-room. To his surprise he found he had nothing to do. There could be no saying good-bye, no specious last letter to write, no will to be made, no manifesto of any sort to be left. People do not do such things before unforeseen accidents—for the wood must look raw at the break. A real good tip for the widow of Gaspard would have to be left in an obvious place: that was all.

It went beyond having nothing to do. There was nothing to think. He had no fear of *post mortem* torture to busy his brain, for the God of his faith was no fiend. He was equally void of covetous hopes of a sensational "good time" when the breath should be out of his body. So far he might have expected his mind to be free. The strange thing was to find how much of one's usual matter for thought is taken away if, in twenty hours or so, one will have nothing whatever to fix up or to see to, no house or business to run, no social beat to patrol, no arts or letters to care for, nor "public duties" to mind. It was a release. But it was a queer one—a kind of vacuous and disquieting freedom, such as a man might attain who was suddenly let off the pressure of gravitation, so that he needn't keep his feet down to the earth any more—in fact couldn't press on it hard if he tried, and so couldn't get any purchase for putting forth his strength upon anything at all. Bell's released mind did its best to think firmly of what he was going to do the next day. But no firmness came: the levers

of thought could not find any fulcrum; they worked at a loss feebly
and fumblingly.

He brought over the lamp to review the Inn's tiny library—two
shelves freakishly peopled with the printed leavings of guests, let-
tered, half-lettered, unlettered, conventional, independent and odd.
There was the common aphrodisiac novel of commerce; there was
The Vicar of Wakefield, all golden sunshine and wit; there were
Nat Gould and the wise, humane book of the great William James
on the incessant endeavour of men to find or to imagine some larger
life on which to rest the frail and soon-tired figure of their own.
Yes, that was it: something to lean against: something sure not to
give when you put your whole weight on it, in any state of yourself:
that was where peace and strength were to be had; nowhere else. So
he fancied, at least: he could not be sure: he was still in that vacuum
where his thoughts had no pivot to work on: the wheels did not
bite on the road; the cogs would not engage; he thought and he felt,
but gropingly, not with the sure and eager drive of a mind and heart
that have found themselves by forgetting themselves.

VII

The place that Bell had picked for his purpose was on the West
side of the Schallijoch. The Schallijoch, as you may know, is a dip
in the ridge that joins the Weisshorn to the Schallihorn. Even the
lowest point of the dip is more than 12,000 feet high. The last part
of the rise to the ridge from the West is up one of the steepest
slopes of ice that are climbed. That is if you mount it where it is
least steep. At some other points it is steeper than any slope that is
climbed, or thought to be climbable. The surface of this wall of ice
undulates like a sheet of hammered copper—here a concave patch
and there a convex one. Though the wall, at its steepest, leans back
from the straight, as a whole, it has parts—the upper halves of these
hollows and lower of these bulges—at which it is vertical for some
feet at a time; and at two or three parts it even overhangs slightly.
These last, avoided by climbers happily wedded to life, were what
Bell had in mind. He would start up the wall at the steepest part he
could find; as he went on, he would make, at each stage, for the point

where there seemed to be most an overhang. He would do the thing honestly—try all that was in him to bring the climb off, reach the ridge and prove that, in this small matter, man could do more than he knew. With careful timing he would be up, if up at all, about dusk. In that unlikely event he would carry the test a step further and try to come down his ice ladder by feel, in the dark, instead of descending the gentle snow slopes on the Eastern side of the pass.

He worked out a time-table. Three hours' walk up to the Arpitetta Alp from Zinal. Three more up from the Alp to the foot of the final ice-wall. Half an hour for eating; another half hour for sundries and lateage. Four for the ultimate work on the wall. Eleven hours in all. To-morrow's evening dusk would be over by seven. He would push off at eight in the morning.

VIII

Probably you would have thought him rather a pleasant sight as he quitted Zinal—the outward figure of a hale, fit mountaineer; just a little stricken with years, but vigorous; brindled but not at all bald; leanly and brownly good-looking, turning out by himself, with his axe under his arm and a little luncheon in his pocket, for a walk among the feet of sporting old friends like the Weisshorn and Rothhorn. How can you tell by the looks of a man that he would not feel the point of a pin if you ran it into his thigh, or that this exemption from pain is causing any disturbance of his spirits?

Nobody was to be seen at the emerald Alp of Arpitetta. Like the almost deserted Zinal, like yesterday's valley path streaming with walkers carrying bundles, the empty hovels on the Alp recalled the sight of a whole countryside in flight before the army of an invader. The ashes left from the cheesemaker's fire were wet with drippings from the roof; the rough wooden crane used for swinging the cauldron over the flames flapped in a draught from the door. Outside, the intoxicant beauty of gentian and orchis was over for the year; the rich grass had spread back over the trodden mud of the milking-place; but snow was lying a few hundred feet higher up. The invader was near.

Bell's legs were liking the work. The numb one was numb, but it did not give out; it would not let him down. By one o'clock he had

reached the tail end—some would call it the snout—of the big
Weisshorn Glacier, eaten his rations and set a first foot on the
rough convex swell of honey-combed ice with water flushing out
its millions of cells; for the sun was on it. He pawed the stuff tenderly
with his axe. Perdition catch his soul but he did love it—strong
as iron, carvable as cheese: what genius could have conceived so
delicious a union of opposites if, by some disaster, no glaciers had
been made?

By three o'clock he was through the freak shapes of the ice-fall,
across the snowfield above it and close to the wall that he sought.
Yes, its great width and height had the wavy surface that he remembered. It showed like a vast relief map of some low rolling
downland, modelled in ice and then set up to stand on its edge. Off
to his right, as he looked up, the general angle was easiest. That was
the regular way—very steep but quite practicable. That was of no
use for his purpose. Far away to his left the slope looked ferocious
enough. But down it an almost continuous fall of stones of all sizes,
broken away from the sun-warmed rocks of the Weisshorn, came
sliding and hissing, or bounding and smashing explosively. That was
no use either. That way would be suicide, not experiment.

He soon saw what he wanted—almost directly above him. There,
nearly all the way up to the ridge, the ice was steep and bare and
blue, and the face of it waves more at this place than anywhere
else. Several broad bosses of rocks must have overlain the smooth
surface. Over these the close-fitting ice swelled like a stocking upon
a bent knee. Up to the centre of each of these bosses it bulged out
overhangingly; just above each centre it would recede at a more
merciful angle; but nowhere in the whole thousand feet of ascent
would a man have a foothold to stand on, unless he made it.

Bell conscientiously tightened each boot-lace and puttee-string.
Then he set off for the point where he had descried the best overhangs. It was half-way, as he judged, to the top of the wall. If he
should conquer that one, then he would look for another, more
bulgy.

He cut his steps with almost fanatical care. He had a disagreeable
sense of doing something furtive: he couldn't help asking himself,
against his own will, "What if somebody saw?" Damn somebody,

another part of him said. Still, he cut every step as if he defied the
whole solar system to say that it was not the work of a good crafts-
man bent upon keeping alive. So he rose slowly. It took a good two
hours' work to mount a third of the way to the ridge. But then
he was close to what mattered more—the great bulge that he was
making for.

The bulge stood out like a gigantic blister upon the face of the
ice. It must have been forty feet in diameter and it jutted so much
that a stone dropped from its outermost point would only have
touched the slope again some fifty feet lower. So the climax had
come. To reach that outermost point he would have to climb for
about twenty feet as you climb up the under side of a ladder that
leans against a wall. And he would have to make the ladder, rung
by rung, as he climbed it—fashion each rung out of the ice with his
axe, held in one hand, while with the other hand and both feet he
clung to three of the rungs made already, and held up the body
against the drag of its weight. Every rung would have to be made
like a letter-box in a door, big enough for the toe of a boot to go in,
but so shaped that, when a hand entered, the fingers could bend
down inside and grip as you grip the top of a fence. The grand,
the crucial question was how long one hand and one arm could
hold the body in to the projecting ice-wall. For what part of the
two hours or so that the other labouring hand might require to cut
that fantastical staircase? Of course, if his axe should slip out of
his hand, or if one step should break, that would end the affair.
But away with the thought of any such bungling.

The moment the overhang started Bell discovered the theory of
gravitation to be exceedingly true. The work was amazingly hard.
When he had carved five letter-boxes, and used them, an hour had
gone. He carved five more and observed that daylight was failing.
Behind his back an unsensational sunset was going on at its ease.
His left hand was chilled almost dead with all the ice it had gripped;
his right wrist was swollen and sore with the intensity of the axe-
work; his right knee had begun to shake as uncontrollably as chattering teeth; he heard his breath as if it were somebody else's:
it made a dry rustling noise, like a bird struggling silently in the
hand.

The centre of the boss was now, he reckoned, some eight feet above his head. Beyond it he could see nothing as yet, but a tranquil sky with a rose-coloured flush dying out of it. Five letter-boxes more, he thought, might take him up to the nipple of this frozen breast and bring the receding slope of its upper half into his sight. It was just at this point that it struck him as a clear, sober matter of fact that he could not get up those eight feet. His strength was running out fast: one more good letter-box was all that he could conceive himself able to make. He made it, hacking away with slow, painful strokes, his axe-handle slippery with his sweat. He reached up his left hand to grab the new hold and dragged a foot up to its new place below. Then, just to go down fighting, he went through the movements of starting to chip out yet another step. Second by second the effort held out; his strokes were the taps of a child; his wrist felt like breaking; yet somehow he finished the hole and forced his left hand to rise up to it: then he even hauled up in its turn a right foot of infinite weight: the poor quivering knee had to straighten out next, and did it, after a long, doubtful struggle. But that was the end, he felt, of all possible effort.

By this time all his senses had the morbid exultation that will some-times come of fierce physical effort. His mind was at leisure, after a fashion. He was fully aware of the sunset; he did not miss the charm of its sabbatical calm; the majesty and mystery of mountains were still there, all right. A verse he had liked as a boy came into his head, as beautiful things that have built themselves into your mind are apt to do at a crisis—as people who once went to church will cry out "Oh! God!" when a smash comes.

> And here indeed might death be fair
> If death be dying into air
> And souls evanished mix with the
> Illumined sky, eternal sea.

But no pretty dying for him, if death could be still headed off. He started desperately to try again, sweating and straining. No good: the feeble strokes of his axe scarcely scratched the bare ice; his left hand was frost-bitten now, past feeling anything. Only five feet to relative safety, but five more than any spur worn by his will could drive the spent body. "I'm done," he said, and ceased to struggle upwards.

IX

Some innate impulse to take the thing well and not let human dignity down at a pinch kept him resolved to hold on, hand and foot, to the last moment possible.

While he clung so, the sun left him. A high Alpine sunset is sudden, like tropical ones. A cold, sharp-edged shadow raced up from the valley, chasing the sunlight before it. Pursuer and fugitive scudded up over the tops of the firs and across the bright green of the Alp Bell had passed, and then up the ice-fall and on up the wall till the shadow came down like a great frigid hand on the sweaty back of his neck. Next moment the last warmth and light fleeted up out of sight, over the bulge. As his gaze followed, his cheeks felt the sting of a few falling granules of ice; little chips of it, rather; even a few rather big ones. A trickle of ice scraps seemed to be sliding down the upper half of the bulge, to dive into space on reaching its centre—most of them clear of his back.

Queer! Was an ice avalanche coming? No need to suppose it, though. Glaciers, crushed and huddled things, always heaving and cracking, played curious tricks and ground out all sorts of freak rubbish. Oh! let the ice do what it liked, all his business with it was done; all that he could now attend to was a kind of dream noise, big, muted and almost asleep, that the torrent was making, enormously far off, down in the blackening trench of the valley—that and a kind of emotional dream of himself, the dying man doing his best to take leave as was meet—a figure at which he could look, as it were, from outside, and dreamily feel it to be rather touching.

Into this semi-dream there managed to enter, also, a sound more abrupt—a little noise like the low startled cry that some women give when they see a horse fall or a big window is smashed. The cry worked itself into his dream, but also it roused him. "Getting light-headed," he thought. But he wasn't. Almost as quick as that thought, a new sound, a light hissing rub, rushed down to his ears and an ice-axe slid over the bulge overhead and out into the air: it whizzed past the back of his head.

To anyone versed in high mountains an ice-axe loose and falling
in any such place is a portent of horror, like a child's pony galloping
riderless home or a boat adrift, bottom uppermost in a Thames lasher.
It means that somebody may have just lost the power to move, without help, at a place where a man unable to move will soon be unable
to live. Suddenly Bell's mind took eyes to itself; it saw a party of
some sort above him, trying to cut its way down the ice wall, straight
towards the deadly bulge that now beetled over himself. At this
hour! And by such a route! They must be mad; so he thought—
forgetting himself. And now one of them was disabled—perhaps had
disabled the whole of his party—tethered it to the ice-wall. The
idea was frightful to Bell.

Another sound came. From somewhere not far overhead there
broke, like an explosion, the singular cry that Swiss peasants and
some mountaineers employ as a long-distance hail. No other noise
of purely human production will carry so far. Harsh, wild and
long, it starts, as the noise of a rocket does, at its maximum loudness,
and then wails itself out in a dying fall that has an effect of collapse
into despair. Though commonly uttered on quite cheerful occasions, it might be the passionate scream of some wretched animal
terrified by the solitude of a desolate place and trying to empty into
one impetuous lamentation all its burden of loneliness and desire.

Bell held his breath as the sinking shriek thinned away into
silence. Then he counted off the seconds half-aloud, by guess work,
as bomb-throwers learnt how to do in the war. The count ran to
seven-eight-nine—and, just as Bell was muttering "Ten," the great
yell smashed into the silence again. Yes: he had expected that. Someone above was in the last extremity of danger—was trying the last
shift of all, the most all-but-hopeless of all—was sending out the
Alpine signal of distress into this stone and snow desert where
autumn and night had joined to make it utterly certain that no
answer could come. It was like praying to God, for dear life, that
a well of fresh water might open itself in the dry middle of the
Sahara.

X

Up to that point of time, as you have seen, Bell had been the kind of dual creature that most of us are for nearly the whole of our days. Part of him had toiled, sweated and ached and another part of him had been sorry for that one. But, from the moment the second yell came, this twofold arrangement was somehow abolished. All craving or need for any part of himself to be troubled about any other was over; now there was nothing at all to work out any more, no next move to be consciously planned, nor hesitant will to be coaxed or hustled, nor any plaguey choice to be made. All of the man was one unit at last, and it lived intently and intensely, moved by some force which it had no more desire to question than flames have to ask "Why burn upward?"

The next mystery was that out of the mind so suddenly lightened there seemed, as it were, to overflow lightness into Bell's body of lead. Strangely empowered, his left foot was rising already to thrust itself into the next letter-box; almost gaily his right arm, freed from its preoccupation with pain, was beginning to hack a new hand-hold above. How long it took him to make he could not have told, then or after. For time, too, was abolished; long trains of executive, practical thought could run on to their end instantaneously; courses, whole courses, of study of relevant things—of the state of the ice, minute changes of gradient, the swift re-gelation following sundown—were carried out without any sense of duration. One of the revelatory trances had come, in which even a plain man sees for once that an eternity need not be long and that in a single moment he may have everlasting life.

A minor, but still a piquant, discovery was that he had never really known till now what it was to cut a good sizable strip off that old margin of safety which he had imagined himself to have all but used up. His new letter-boxes were marvels of sketchy adequacy; they were high art in the skimpiness of the means that they took to their end; triumphs of confident "cheek" to Nature, they bluffed that august power quite wittily. Almost before the vocalist overhead had completed the long S.O.S. of the mountains—it takes three minutes in all—Bell had his chest up to the dead centre of the bulge and saw what he had come for.

Some thirty feet higher up, a woman in mountain kit, with no axe and no hold for hand or foot, was dangling at a long rope's end. Her body revolved a little as it hung against the steep ice, but she was making no voluntary movement. The rope constricting her chest was held with one straining hand by a man perched eighty feet higher up. He was clearly unable to move, hand or foot, without being dragged off his stance by the weight of the woman. He stood on one foot—his right: it seemed to be firmly placed, on a tiny step; and a little above his hand, he had the pick of his axe driven well into the ice. To the steel bracket thus formed by the axe-head the man was holding on stoutly with his right hand.

The sorry sight explained itself. The woman must have been cutting steps down the slope; she must have slipped from a step, and dropped her axe with the shock. The man had checked her fall well, but both were hung up as immovably as a couple of stoats nailed to a gamekeeper's door. And now the rope must be slowly killing the woman. Just as Bell's head topped the bulge she called out in a strangled voice to the man, "Can you cut the rope, Teddy? I'm done, anyhow. Think of the kiddies. You *must*." The man held on.

Bell gave tongue as loud as the dry brown fur lining his mouth would allow. "Well held, Sir," he roared. "It's all right, I'm coming."

Not once in a long and respectable Alpine career had Bell thought he would ever entrust his person to ledges quite so narrow as those on which he made the rest of his way up to that pendant woman. And yet he had never, in any hard place, felt such absolute freedom from any uneasiness. As he romped up, he sang out, at intervals "There in three minutes," "Just two minutes more," "Only one minute more," "Half a shake—I'm just there." Then he arrived. He cut a big step close to where the woman's feet hung, planted his own firmly on it, and then stooping and straightening up again, took the weight of her, sitting, on his right shoulder. Lest she be fainting he put up his right hand behind her, to hold her in place.

She was no fainter, though she was white, yellow, greenish—all the bad colours that beauty itself may have to put on in bad times. "She's a good 'un," Bell thought, as she sat quiet, panting.

"*You're* a great sportsman," she gasped, when she had breath enough.

Feeling all the weight off the rope of a sudden, the man above shouted down thickly, "Sure you have got her, Sir?"

"Right as rain," she called up from her perch.

Bell added, "Leave the rope slack, and dig in. We'll come up when you're comfy."

The man gave a tuneless yodel of joy and was plying his axe the same instant; chips and wedges of ice came pelting down from the great step that he must be cutting, from which to make the whole caravan fast. In five minutes he ceased hacking, braced himself, drew in the slack of the rope and announced that now he could hold up a cow for a day.

Bell let the woman cannily down till her feet found a trim ledge that he had managed to scratch out while holding her up. But some four or five feet of smooth ledgeless ice intervened between this and the lowest step the woman had cut, coming down, before she slipped off. Some new ones had to be made. "Care to cut 'em?" Bell asked. "Or shall I?"

She ruefully opened the hands in which no axe was now held. "I dropped it," she said, "like a mug. I feel sick with shame."

"Have mine," he said holding it out.

Her open boy face shone with joyous relief, as if at a gift of free absolution from sin. Even now their lives hung on this axe that he was entrusting to her, the convicted axe-dropper. She took it. "You are a very generous person," she said. "Now I'll unrope, and go up by myself, and you shall tie on."

He shook his head firmly. "You mustn't unrope."

Her eyes broke out in a quick sparkle of anger. "You've *got* to rope up," she said, flushing. "I know that I've done a dud thing and can't preach. But what about you? Climbing alone! coming up out of nowhere, almost at night. Up a worse slope than this beast! Think it bears looking into? Eh? Well, do you mean to rope up, or shall both of us climb in this way that you seem to think right?"

Bell fairly funked the scrutiny of this young woman's spirited simplicity. When once simplicity sets out to inquire, what else is so penetrating? "Well, you tie on in the middle," he said, "and I at the end."

"That's fair," she agreed. A few feet of spare rope were let down by her husband. In two or three minutes, at most, the man who would have shuffled off the mortal coil was securely girt with the most delectable of its loops, the cheerfullest symbol of human determination not to withdraw from the banquet of life—only to salt a dish now and then with a few little hazards.

XI

The last daylight was gone when the three stood safe on the level roof of the ridge, scrunching its gritty granular snow somewhat shyly, though partly kept in countenance by the dark, which is itself a shy, friendly thing. Bell, now a mere dual creature again, had been wondering, all the way up the last flight of ice stairs, how he should give these married lovers a chance to re-assert their lately threatened right to possession of each other's lips. Best, he thought, just to turn his back on them when he got up, and try to look busy, coiling the rope.

But they also seemed to have some sort of plan. The man was waiting above the last step, to shake Bell by the hand—really to shake him—and mumbling something which Bell did not desire to make out more clearly. The cup of his consternation was filled when the lady raised his disengaged hand to her lips, a gesture for which he had not been prepared by her vivacity lower down.

Then, with one silent consent, they all stampeded away from the key of emotion. "You travel light, Sir," said Bell, just to say something trivial. The other two seemed to carry not so much as a prune or a biscuit between them.

"Well——" said the man, and then Bell imagined the man must be having a quiet laugh in the dark.

"Oh! I know I can't talk," Bell admitted. "The fact is I didn't expect to be coming right over the Pass."

"Same here," said the man. "We just walked up from Randa— meant to go only as far as the hut for the Weisshorn, eat our sandwiches there and go back to dinner. Then—it *was* rather mad, but the snow was so toppingly good—we thought we might just risk the Schallijoch before dark, sleep at Zinal and come back to-morrow."

"Gosh! it was rash!" exclaimed Bell, off his guard. He felt sure the next instant, the man was quite seeing the humour of such a rebuke from such a sinner. Hastily trying to cover the slip, Bell made another. He asked, "How on earth did you miss the way down?"

The man didn't exactly say, "How did *you* miss the way up?" but he did say, "Yes, it was stupid, but—well you know how it isn't so easy to see a way down from above as it is from below?"

"Hadn't we better push off?" said Bell rather hurriedly. "We'll be getting friz, up here." But it was not the cold that he minded. It was the heat. It felt as if he couldn't move his tongue without burning his fingers.

The three truants had luck. Just such a full moon as they needed, not having a lantern, was on the point of rising from behind the snowy mass of the Mischabel, beyond the forest glen of the Visp. The mounting light could no longer contain itself. Its bright animation was pulsing up the dark violet of the sky in tremulous waves. It would be easy, by such a light as was coming, to follow the downward track left by the couple, on their way up, almost to the door of the old Weisshorn hut, a refuge squat, squalid, flea-haunted and cramped, but divinely rich in raw materials for manufacturing heat, against a long night of hard frost.

At any time it is rather exciting to walk in the dark, and in silence, with anyone whom you like but don't yet know very well. What is he thinking about? You? And, if so, in what way? Barring you? Liking you? Wanting to throw down the conventional fence and talk frankly? An hour or two of this blindfold contact between mind and mind may so work on them both that when their eyes meet under a lamp at the end of the walk it may feel as if they had had a long and intimate conversation, leaving each of them just slightly anxious to know that the other has taken nothing amiss. Even thus, with friendly and deprecatory looks, did Bell and the strangers regard each other by candle-light two hours later, among the strong shadows and smells of the hut.

In ten minutes more the man's wife, who had walked like a true

Joan of Arc, was exercising the blessed privilege of healthy and tired young people of thirty or so. While she slept like a prosperous babe, her man and Bell smoked as they lay in the hay at the big sleeping-shelf's other end. Smoking helps to keep talk good. A man can puff at his pipe between each thing he really wants to say and the next. No gap-filling rubble is required.

Bell ascertained first that the man's name was Gollen and that he was a doctor—the Harley Street species of doctor. Bell gave in return his own name and description. Then they enjoyed one of those unembarrassing pauses. Then Bell said, somewhat brusquely, "There's one thing we have to get straight."

"Go it," said Gollen.

"You seem to imagine you're under some sort of obligation to me."

"Well, you see, we're alive. And, before you appeared, our number was up."

"So was mine."

"Oh! everyone's is, in a sense. 'All condemned to death,' doesn't somebody say, 'with an indefinite reprieve.' But ours wasn't indefinite. We were booked to go West in five minutes."

"I was to do it in one. In less. I should have dropped off my holds in ten seconds if you people hadn't blown in."

"Hullo?"

"Sure thing. I was done. I had never known until then how far doneness could go. That's how it felt, anyhow. Then your wife's axe came along. That by itself held me on for a jiffy or two. And then you hollered—gad! you *can* holler—and everything changed. There was something new in me, or round me, at work on me somehow. Every bit of soreness and worry and funk was taken right off me—nothing was left in the world but one energy—just an enveloping, mastering sort of a push. It went up like a flame and it took me along—it made everything easy and light. And it wasn't only a thing in the mind. Old brother body himself was roped into the movement: some of the waft of this impulse seemed to get itself into my muscles. D' you follow these ravings?"

"Rather. Physicians aren't the fools that they were. We don't go on missing out what the mind—or the soul, if you like—has to say to all the dynamic affairs of the body."

Bell puffed his pipe for a while. Then he said "See? That's how you two preserved me. So if thanking is what we're about, thanky kindly."

Gollen, too, smoked in silence for the next minute or two, before asking "The ice overhung where you were when I first caterwauled?"

"Can't tell you the angle. Hadn't got a clinometer thing. Of course it wasn't a motoring road."

Gollen laughed. Bell liked Gollen's face when he laughed, so far as it could be seen among the tangle of wry shadows thrown about the hut by a small flame that still leapt in the stove. Gollen's face made Bell think of a trade term—"good ordinary." He had blunt goodish features, strong and goodtempered. A straight, friendly man, you would say, and easily amused; a good man to be in a hole with. Bell enjoyed such men. They made the world go round. As he was thinking so, Gollen suddenly asked, "I say—why did you do it?"

As Bell did not answer at once, Gollen added, "Of course, it's cheek—asking. Tell me to go to Hell, if you like, and I'll warmly approve. Only, well—I'm a doctor."

Bell cut the thing short. He answered at once what Gollen might go on to ask in another few minutes. "Yes—the spring's running dry. The salt losing its savour, you know—the wine going flat. And worse coming."

Again Gollen did the bold thing. "Any particular evil?" he said.

Bell liked the man. And when two men would both have been dead a few hours ago if either had failed at a pinch, they may soon get on terms. Bell avowed the whole business—his symptoms, his surmises and disgusts and his specious experiment.

Gollen listened as wise doctors do. "Did that numbness cramp you today?" he asked at the end.

"No. But it was there all the day—except just the time—ten minutes or so, I suppose—when——" Bell hesitated for a moment.

"When you were in action?" said Gollen.

"Action?"

"Oh! I don't mean just doing violent things out of doors—pressing triggers or lassoing cows. I mean getting every Jack fibre

there is in your nature alive and utterly turned on to something
outside you—absorbed in it, lost in it—every bit of your consciousness taken up into some ecstasy of endeavour that's passion and
peace."

Bell nodded, and Gollen went on. "I guess the great artists—all
sorts of 'em—know how to bring the fit on, or it comes when they're
at the top of their form—they seem to get further and further above
'emselves—hold the note out in a way that we can't—bring every
tissue they have in their being to bear on the effort to get a wee
touch to come right. Saints too, I suppose—the pukka ones, like
Francis, the man at Assisi: they have the knack too: they can get
more alive: they've found how to exist at a sort of top pressure.
I fancy all of us get just a glimpse of the thing now and then—
of what living might be, you know—at a great turn in a game, or
when we're in love, or if some beautiful thing in a book bowls us
over. Only, we can't hold the note, or we can't do it yet: the pitch
is too high for our reach; so we flop back into flatness. But we shall
get there. I do believe that. What we've done since we started as
jelly-fish is to get more and more of ourselves into action, and we
shall go on until we are as much more in action—real true action—
than now, as we are now than when we were jelly-fish. Why, in a
few thousand years we may all be able to live half our time as you
lived today for ten minutes."

"Something in that," Bell assented.

Gollen apologised meekly. "Sorry to verge upon 'uplift.' Still,
one can't always bother about the convention that talk has got to be
pessimist piffle."

Bell nodded. Reigning conventions had few less dutiful followers
than he.

They smoked again for a while. Presently Gollen said, "How goes
the weather?" He rose and opened the door of the hut very quietly.
Bell followed him out to the hut's tiny terrace.

Nothing at all was wrong with that night. Beyond the queenly
white shape of Mont Rose [1] the moon rode gloriously high, burnished
and flashing with frost, above sleeping Lombardy. Gowned in new
snow and bejewelled with sparkles of light, the Weisshorn, the

---

[1] Commonly known as Monte Rosa.

greatest great lady in Nature, looked as lovely to Bell as when the first sight of that pale supreme grace had taken his breath away in his youth. At the height where they stood the frost had silenced every trickle of water, leaving all space to be filled with subtler challenges to the ear. The air almost crackled with crispness: it was alive with the massed animation of millions of infinitesimal crystallisations. The Schalliberg Glacier, a little away to their right, had its own living whisper, the sum of the innumerable tiny creaks and fractures of its jostling molecules of ice. Up here, where the quiet of night was suffused with this audible stir of the forces fashioning the earth, it felt as if some murmurous joint voice of all existence were abroad and life itself were trying to make its high urgency felt.

"Pretty good!" Gollen said presently.

"Yes, it's all right," answered Bell.

Gollen waited a minute or two. Then he asked, "Is it all right—enough?"

"Oh! yes," said Bell. "I'm sticking on."

THE MATTERHORN ACCIDENT

JULY 14, 1865

THE EARLY HISTORY of mountaineering as a sport was made chiefly by Englishmen who climbed in the Alps from 1854 to 1880. Although a few peaks—the Jungfrau, the Finsteraarhorn, and several eminences in the Monte Rosa group, for example—had been ascended earlier, most of the major heights were conquered during this period by men whose names have become legendary, despite the greater skill and more spectacular feats of their successors. F. F. Tuckett, A. W. Moore, John Ball, Alfred Wills, John Tyndall, T. W. Hinchliff, Leslie Stephen, Edward Whymper are figures from an heroic age.

Among early climbers and guides the precipitous, storm-riven Matterhorn —less commonly known as Mont Cervin and Il Cervino—had a fearsome reputation. Many thought an ascent impossible. But Edward Whymper, a young wood-engraver and water-color artist, sent to the Alps to make sketches for the second series of *Peaks, Passes, and Glaciers,* fixed his ambition on climbing it. Between 1861 and 1865 he made seven defeated attempts from the Italian side. One of the following selections tells of his final victory and the disaster which quickly succeeded, in which four of the party of seven were killed. This was the first major accident of mountaineering, and an intense controversy ensued. In letters and leading articles printed in newspapers throughout Great Britain and western Europe, Whymper himself, the expedition, and the whole sport were vigorously attacked and defended. The sporting public has never completely forgotten this accident. Whymper's own *Scrambles amongst the Alps in the Years 1860–'69* (1871) confirmed the memory as it went through a series of editions and became a classic of the literature of mountaineering. In August, 1947, *Life* recapitulated the whole affair, with illustrations and diagrams, for its millions of readers.

Four of the many immediately contemporary documents are given here. One presents an account of the essential facts, never since effectually challenged. The other three state standard arguments in a disagreement which has never been and probably never will be resolved, despite the efforts of apologists and the persistent fact that most mountaineers, like most hunters and yachtsmen, grow old and die of the customary natural causes.

No doubt the Matterhorn accident has received attention disproportionate to its significance. But the shattering suddenness with which catastrophe followed success, the helplessness of the victims, the setting—a wasteland of ice and rock, the sickening distance of the fall, the always lurking, easily stimulated fear of implacable Nature combine to make the event, even in Whymper's dispassionate narrative, work powerfully on the imagination. There is a quality of myth about the elements of the story. One is reminded of the terrible vengeance of the gods on imprudent man, as in the story of the fall of Phaëton. Like the names and exploits of the early climbers, the Matterhorn accident has become part of the living legend of mountaineering.

The following selections are reprinted from *The Times* (London), August 2, 1865; July 27, 1865; August 14, 1865; and from Anthony Trollope, *Travelling Sketches*, London, Chapman and Hall, Ltd., 1866. The titles of these selections have been supplied.

Edward Whymper's Account

SIR,—After the direct appeals which I have received from the President of the Alpine Club and from yourself to write an account of the accident on the Matterhorn, I feel it is impossible to remain silent any longer, and I therefore forward to you for publication a plain statement of the accident itself, and of the events that preceded and followed it.

On Wednesday morning, the 12th of July, Lord Francis Douglas and myself crossed the Col Théodule to seek guides at Zermatt. After quitting the snow of the northern side we rounded the foot of the glacier, crossed the Furgge Glacier, and left my tent, ropes, and other matters in the little chapel at the Lac Noir. We then descended to Zermatt, engaged Peter Taugwalder, and gave him permission to choose another guide. In the course of the evening the Rev. Charles Hudson came into our hotel with a young friend, Mr. Hadow, and they, in answer to some inquiries, announced their intention of starting to attack the Matterhorn on the following morning. Lord Francis Douglas agreed with me it was undesirable that two independent parties should be on the mountain at the same time, with the same object. Mr. Hudson was therefore invited to join us, and he accepted our proposal. Before admitting Mr. Hadow

I took the precaution to inquire what he had done in the Alps, and, as well as I remember Mr. Hudson's reply was, "Mr. Hadow has done Mont Blanc in less time than most men." He then mentioned several other excursions that were unknown to me, and added, in answer to a further question, "I consider he is a sufficiently good man to go with us." This was an excellent certificate, given as it was by a first-rate mountaineer, and Mr. Hadow was admitted without any further question. . . .

We left Zermatt at 5:35 on Thursday morning. . . . No rope was taken from Zermatt, because there was already more than enough in the chapel at the Lac Noir. It has been repeatedly asked, "Why was not the wire rope taken which Mr. Hudson brought to Zermatt?" I do not know; it was not mentioned by Mr. Hudson, and at that time I had not even seen it. My rope alone was used during the expedition, and there was—first, about 200 ft. of Alpine Club rope; second, about 150 ft. of a kind I believe to be stronger than the first; third, more than 200 ft. of a lighter and weaker rope than the first, of a kind used by myself until the Club rope was produced.

It was our intention on leaving Zermatt to attack the mountain seriously . . . , and we were provided with everything that long experience has shown to be necessary for the most difficult mountains. On the first day . . . we mounted accordingly very leisurely, left the Lac Noir at 8:20, and passed along the ridge connecting the Hörnli with the actual peak, at the foot of which we arrived at 11:20, having frequently halted on the way. . . . Before 12 o'clock we had found a good position for the tent, at a height of 11,000 ft. . . .

We were astir long before daybreak on the morning of the 14th, and started directly it was possible to move. . . . At 6:20 we had attained a height of 12,800 ft., and halted for half an hour, then continued the ascent without a break until 9:55, when we stopped for fifty minutes, at a height probably of about 14,000 ft. Thus far we had ascended by the north-eastern face of the mountain, and had not met with a single difficulty. For the greater part of the way there was, indeed, no occasion for the rope; and sometimes Hudson led, sometimes myself. We had now arrived at the foot of that part which from Zermatt seems perpendicular or overhanging, and we could no longer continue on the same side. By common consent, therefore, we ascended for some distance by the arête—that is by the ridge descending towards Zermatt—and then turned over to the right, or to the north-western face. Before doing so we made a change in the order of ascent; Croz now went first, I followed, Hudson came third. Hadow and old Taugwalder were last.[1] The change was made because the work became difficult for a time, and required caution. In some places there was but little to hold, and it was therefore desirable those should be in front who were least likely to slip. The general slope of the mountain at this part was less than forty degrees, and snow had consequently accumulated and filled up the irregularities of the rock face, leaving only occasional fragments projecting here and there. These were at times coated with a thin glaze of ice, from the snow above having melted and frozen again during the night. Still it was a place over which any fair mountaineer might pass in safety. We found, however, that Mr. Hadow was not accustomed to this kind of work, and required continual assistance; but no one suggested that he should stop, and he was taken to the top. It is only fair to say that the difficulty experienced by Mr. Hadow at this part arose, not from fatigue or lack of courage, but simply and entirely from want of experience. Mr. Hudson, who followed me, passed over this part, and, as far as I know, ascended the entire mountain without having the slightest assistance rendered to him on any occasion. Sometimes, after I had taken a hand from Croz or received a pull, I turned to give the same to Hudson; but he invariably declined, saying it was not necessary. This solitary difficult part was not of great extent, certainly not more than 300 ft. high, and after it was passed the angles became less and less as we approached the summit; at least the slope was so moderate that Croz and myself detached ourselves from the others and ran on to the top. We arrived at 1:40 P.M., and the others about 10 min. after us.

I have been requested to describe particularly the state of the party on the summit. No one showed any signs of fatigue, neither did I

---

[1] Whymper here neglects to mention Lord Francis Douglas and Peter Taugwalder, the younger.

hear anything to lead me to suppose that anyone was at all tired. I remember Croz laughed at me when I asked him the question. Indeed, less than ten hours had elapsed since our starting, and during that time we had halted for nearly two. The only remark which I heard suggestive of danger was made by Croz, but it was quite casual, and probably meant nothing. He said, after I had remarked that we had come up very slowly, "Yes; I would rather go down with you and another guide alone than with those who are going." As to ourselves, we were arranging what we should do that night on our return to Zermatt.

We remained on the summit for one hour, and during the time Hudson and I consulted, as we had done all the day, as to the best and safest arrangement of the party. We agreed that it would be best for Croz to go first, as he was the most powerful, and Hadow second; Hudson, who was equal to a guide in sureness of foot, wished to be third; Lord F. Douglas was placed next, and old Taugwalder, the strongest of the remainder, behind him. I suggested to Hudson that we should attach a rope to the rocks on our arrival at the difficult bit, and hold it as we descended, as an additional protection. He approved the idea, but it was not definitely settled that it should be done. The party was being arranged in the above order while I was making a sketch of the summit, and they were waiting for me to be tied in my place, when someone remembered that we had not left our names in a bottle; they requested me to write them, and moved off while it was being done. A few minutes afterwards I tied myself to young Taugwalder and followed, catching them just as they were commencing the descent of the difficult part described above. The greatest care was being taken. Only one man was moving at a time; when he was firmly planted the next advanced, and so on. The average distance between each was probably 20 ft. They had not, however, attached the additional rope to rocks, and nothing was said about it. The suggestion was made entirely on account of Mr. Hadow, and I am not sure it even occurred to me again.

I was, as I have explained, detached from the others, and following them; but after about a quarter of an hour Lord F. Douglas asked me to tie on to old Taugwalder, as he feared, he said, that if there was a slip Taugwalder would not be able to hold him. This was done hardly ten minutes before the accident, and undoubtedly saved Taugwalder's life.

As far as I know, at the moment of the accident, no one was actually moving. I cannot speak with certainty, neither can the Taugwalders, because the two leading men were partially hidden from our sight by an intervening mass of rock. Poor Croz had laid aside his axe, and in order to give Mr. Hadow greater security was absolutely taking hold of his legs and putting his feet, one by one, into their proper positions. From the movements of their shoulders it is my belief that Croz, having done as I have said, was in the act of turning around to go down a step or two himself; at this moment Mr. Hadow slipped, fell on him, and knocked him over. I heard one startled exclamation from Croz, then saw him and Mr. Hadow flying downwards; in another moment Hudson was dragged from his steps, and Lord F. Douglas immediately after him. All this was the work of a moment; but immediately we heard Croz's exclamation Taugwalder and myself planted ourselves as firmly as the rocks would permit; *the rope was tight between us, and the shock came on us both as on one man.* We held; but the rope broke midway between Taugwalder and Lord F. Douglas. For two or three seconds we saw our unfortunate companions sliding downwards on their backs, and spreading out their hands endeavouring to save themselves; they then disappeared one by one, and fell from precipice to precipice on to the Matterhorn Glacier below, a distance of nearly 4,000 feet in height. From the moment the rope broke it was impossible to help them. . . .

Immediately we had descended to a safe place I asked for the rope that had broken, and to my surprise—indeed, to my horror—found that it was the weakest of the three ropes. As the first five men had been tied while I was sketching, I had not noticed the rope they employed, and now I could only conclude that they had seen fit to use this in preference to the others. It has been said that the rope broke in consequence of its fraying over a rock: this is not the case; it broke in mid-air, and the end does not show any trace of previous injury. . . . There is no occasion to say more of the descent. I looked frequently but in vain, for traces of my unfortunate companions, and we were in consequence surprised by the night when still at a height of about 13,000 feet. We arrived at Zermatt at 10:30 on Saturday morning.

Immediately on my arrival I sent to the President of the Commune, and requested him to send as many men as possible to ascend heights whence the spot could be commanded where I knew the four must have fallen. A number went and returned after six hours, reporting they had seen them, but that they could not reach them that day. They proposed starting on Sunday evening, so as to reach the bodies at daybreak on Monday; but, unwilling to lose the slightest chance, the Rev. J. M'Cormick and myself resolved to start on Sunday morning. . . . We started with [several guides] at 2 A.M. on Sunday, and followed the route we had taken on Thursday morning until we had passed the Hörnli, when we went down to the right of the ridge and mounted through the séracs of the Matterhorn Glacier. By 8:30 we had got on to the plateau at the top, and within sight of the corner in which we knew my companions must be. As we saw one weather-beaten man after another raise the telescope, turn deadly pale, and pass it on without a word to the next, we knew that all hope was gone. We approached; they had fallen below as they had fallen above—Croz a little in advance, Hadow near him, and Hudson some distance behind; but of Lord F. Douglas we could see nothing. To my astonishment, I saw that all of the three had been tied with the Club, or with the second and equally strong, rope, and consequently there was only one link—that between Taugwalder and Lord F. Douglas—in which the weaker rope had been used. . . .

This, Sir, is the end of this sad story. A single slip, or a single false step, has been the sole cause of this frightful calamity, and has brought about misery never to be forgotten. I have only one observation to offer upon it. If the rope had not broken you would not have received this letter, for we could not possibly have held the four men, falling as they did, all at the same time, and with a severe jerk. But, at the same time, it is my belief that no accident would have happened had the rope between those who fell been as tight, or nearly as tight, as it was between Taugwalder and myself. The rope, when used properly, is a great safeguard; but whether on rocks, or whether on snow or glacier, if two men approach each other so that the rope falls in a loop, the whole party is involved in danger, for should one slip or fall, he may acquire, before he is stopped, a momentum that may drag down one man after another and bring destruction on all; but if the rope is tight this is all but impossible.

I am, Sir, your obedient servant,

EDWARD WHYMPER

The Iniquities of Mountaineering

THERE ARE OCCASIONS on which a journal must brave certain un-
popularity and ridicule, even in quarters where it may most wish to
stand well. We desire the sympathies of the young, the courageous,
and the enterprising, and we can feel their taunts. But we have our
Matterhorn as well as they—not without a cause. Why is the best
blood of England to waste itself in scaling hitherto inaccessible peaks,
in staining the eternal snow, and reaching the unfathomable abyss
never to return? We believe it was the heir presumptive to one of
our noblest titles, but, far more than that, one of the best young
fellows in the world, who fell, with three [*sic*] others and a guide,
down a precipice of 4,000 feet. . . . The two English gentlemen
who shared his fate . . . were all just the men that England is
proud of, and that would be the salt of any age, even more corrupt,
more self-indulgent, than our own. They were scholars and gentlemen. They were men who had distinguished themselves at school
and at college, and in the path of honourable employment. They
were admired and loved. . . . So many of our readers have "done"
Zermatt that it is almost needless to describe the well-known scene.
As you stand in that deep valley and look to the southern sky, you
see across it, and almost overhead, a vast shelf of rock and snow—a
very pathway in the heavens, along which the Olympian deities
might be imagined to drive their cars. Upon this shelf stands a mass,
in shape between an obelisk and a pyramid, for all the world like
an immense ornament of alabaster and frosted silver upon a gigantic
marble mantelpiece. . . . But this charming ornament, this Pelion
upon Ossa, is itself loftier than Snowdon. To the humble beholders
in the valley below it looks about as accessible as the dome of St.
Paul's. If compelled to make the choice, we might reasonably prefer
to scale with fingers and toes the front of a well-built London house,
with good stone window-sills, cornices, and water-courses. If anybody wants to know what 200 feet sheer is, let him go to the top of
the Monument.[1] This is 4,000 feet, and looks very sheer. As the suc-

[1] Erected in 1677 in commemoration of the great fire of 1666.

cessful ascent is utterly incomprehensible, of course we do not wonder at the disastrous descent. Indeed, throughout these many hours
of continual and painful effort there must have been few places
where the climbers could rest their limbs and close their eyes with the
momentary feeling of safety. Well, this is magnificent. But is it life?
Is it duty? Is it common sense? Is it allowable? Is it not wrong?

There are certainly limits to audacity. We may go even further,
and dispute that a wanton exposure to peril is the best school of
courage. It is not the best and coolest rider who takes the most headlong leaps. English common sense leaves to young Irish gentlemen
the steeplechases in which a certain average loss of men and horses
is found necessary to keep up interest. . . . There is a point of danger which, if gratuitous, becomes ridiculous, if not disgusting. Five
hundred years ago the young Romans of noble or Papal families
thought to revive the glories of the Amphitheatre with bull-fighting.
"Every champion," says GIBBON, "successively encountered a wild
bull; and the victory may be ascribed to the quadrupeds, since no
more than eleven were left on the field." One cannot contemplate
this without a smile at the utter folly of staking the life of a COLONNA
against that of a wild bull; but a time may come when the historian
will tell us irreverently how English noblemen, scholars, and divines,
passed in endless succession to the loftiest peaks of the Alps, accepting the equal alternative of an idle boast and a horrible death. Surely,
courage, to be respectable, ought to be reasonable, and ought also
to have some regard to the end? What is the use of scaling precipitous rocks, and being for half an hour at the top of the terrestrial
globe? There is use in the feats of sailors, of steeple-climbers, vane-
cleaners, chimney sweepers, lovers, and other adventurous professions. A man may be content to die in such a cause, for it is his life's
battle. But in the few short moments a member of the Alpine Club
has to survey his life when he finds himself slipping, he has but a
sorry account to give of himself. What is he doing there, and what
right has he to throw away the gift of life and ten thousand golden
opportunities in an emulation which he shares only with skylarks,
apes, cats, and squirrels? Life requires a great deal of courage, moral
as well as physical, whatever the meaning of the distinction. Every
gentleman with a sphere of duties and a station in society requires

courage and presence of mind, otherwise he is sure to be scorned and to become an object of civil contempt. A man cannot hold his own in a parish vestry, or in the committee of a coal fund, without knowing what he is about, and standing to his colours, and defending his rights. . . . But this courage is not acquired in a series of desperate adventures. The Age of Chivalry is over. A man does not now learn temperance by a toilsome journey through a desert. By these processes a man only makes himself the slave to a necessity, and reduces himself to the helpless and pitiable condition of being obliged to do something disagreeable, whether he likes it or not. His whole existence centres for the time in that one act or that one suffering, and he can no longer be called a responsible being.

All this we shall be told, is utilitarian, matter of fact, calculating, coldblooded, and so forth. But there is no harm in considering the end and counting the cost. The wisdom of all ages points to the very great advantage which valour itself gains by the connexion. Discretion compels a man to contemplate and realize his danger, and to face it, instead of rushing at it with a wild, unthinking impulse, and perhaps closed eyes. In these days there is a great waste of energy, that often ends in bringing the impulsive and adventurous into disagreeable collision with their mother earth or a stone wall. When a man of middle age turns to look about him, he sees the path of life behind him strewn with as many sufferers as the half-burnt moths that cover our carpets these summer nights. These are the martyrs of passion. They are the men whose first notion of life was a grand adventure, in which they rush at some object or other of which they were enamoured, and win it with a blow. That is the theory of human life which is shadowed in the Alpine expeditions. But, of course, our young men will go to Switzerland, and they will ascend mountains, and they will feel a very natural and irresistible desire to do what everybody has done before, and, still more, what nobody has done. This is the great prize which caps and leads on the lesser attempts. It was the blue riband of the Alps that poor Lord FRANCIS DOUGLAS was trying for the other day. If it must be so, at all events the Alpine Club, that has proclaimed this crusade, must manage the thing rather better, or it will soon be voted a nuisance.

If the work is to be done, it must be done well. They must advise youngsters to practice, and make sure of their strength and their endurance. . . . They must devise implements of a practical character, unless they are above such weaknesses. They must instil a habit of caution, and calculation as to rests, and such particulars. Above all things, their ropes must not break. If a people chose to despise the aid of improved weapons and defences as unworthy of a true military genius, it would soon find itself under the heel of its more scientific and mechanical neighbour. We do not see why the Matterhorn must be conquered with sinew alone. With every aid that can be applied it will still be a work of great labour and peril; and we entertain no doubt that the man who submits to be assisted, and incurs no more danger than is necessary, will be a more useful member of society than the other who thought only of the glory of a desperate enterprise. We trust we have not said a word to increase the grief of surviving friends. Our argument shows the value we set on the lives that have been lost. These were no common men, and we could not afford to lose them. They fell into a fashionable rivalry, as was but natural to their time of life and to a forward age. They will not have died in vain if this warning is taken as it is meant.

Defence of Alpinism

S<small>IR</small>,—The terribly simple and intelligible story of the Matterhorn disaster is now known to us all. Mr. Whymper's clear and manly narrative, told with a candour and honesty which give him an additional claim on the sympathy of every feeling heart, strips the calamity of all mystery or doubt. One lesson it inculcates with awful distinctness you have already pointed out. Young and inexperienced climbers should neither go nor be taken on expeditions of this kind. Another warning, hardly less distinctly uttered and hardly less important, but valuable chiefly to those who engage in similar undertakings, is against the slackened rope—the best friend of the climber converted only too easily into his most insidious and dangerous foe.

But I do not propose to enlarge on these topics. I have been urging prudence and caution, as the members of the Alpine Club well know, till I fancy some of my younger friends have almost begun to think that I was losing nerve and enterprise; and both at the Club and in private I have not ceased to express my conviction that the insulted majesty of nature would repudiate by some terrible example the notion that her grandest and most solemn fastnesses might be safely won by every novice in the mysteries of mountain craft. If the sad lessons she has read us, in the untimely deaths of men whom to know was to admire and to love, do not find their way home to those to whom they are addressed, it is certain that no words of mine can be of any avail. . . . But it is, perhaps, not an unfitting moment to refer to another danger, less obvious and more insidious, but of which I think quite as seriously as of the actual risk of instant loss of life or limb which threatens many of our mountaineers, especially the younger ones, and that is the danger of over-exertion.

To those who have a taste for such pursuits the delights of Alpine adventure are unspeakably fascinating. For my own part, in the whole range of life I know no mere enjoyment to come near them, however incapable some persons to whom they are unknown may be of appreciating or understanding them. The season for such enterprises is so short, the air is so marvellously exhilarating, the pleasure is so pure, so enduring, and so intense, the spirit of emulation among Alpine explorers is so keen, that for the time all sense of fatigue is banished, and men who have passed ten months of the twelve in sedentary pursuits, living the life of our large towns, seem to have become all at once superior to all the common wants of nature—to undergo the most severe and protracted physical exertion with less and worse food and far less rest than would have sufficed them in their ordinary life at home. They return hardened in muscle and bronzed in aspect, and sometimes none the worse for it; but I am very sure that this kind of excess cannot, any more than excesses of a grosser and less excusable order, be practised with impunity, and sooner or later it will tell upon the constitutions of all but either those who are so strong as to be exceptions to the general rule, and therefore no fit example for others, or those whose circumstances and occupations permit them on returning home to take an excess of rest to counterbalance the previous excess of labour—a process, however, not always to be relied upon. Of course, it is the younger men who stand most in need of a caution on this head. This species of excess is more natural to them than to their seniors. They are better able to do without food and rest at the time, and they suffer more from it afterwards.

I believe such warnings to be nearly useless. There is the large balance at the banker's; it is so easily drawn upon, and all goes so smoothly and pleasantly at the time that it seems incredible that anything should really be amiss, or that the time can come when, instead of the orders being cheerfully honoured, the overdraught will be demanded back with interest and with relentless rigour. I did not pay much heed to such considerations when I was younger, and I have not too much expectation of being listened to myself; but, if, by the kindness and confidence of my Alpine friends, I have been placed in a position of some influence among them, the least I can do is so far to justify their choice as to show that the rashness and folly which some persons who have little taste for mountain pleasures themselves are so fond of attributing to the members of the Alpine Club are not the qualities for which they have elected their principal officer. The Alpine Club has to answer for giving a new direction to as well as some extension of that intense love for beautiful scenery which, I venture to think, is a good characteristic of our day. It has to answer for opening a new field—and, I venture to think, a glorious field—for the expenditure of that physical energy which active men, when they get their leisure, will work off in some way or other—in shooting, fishing, hunting, boating, or cricketing, if not in climbing. It has to answer for bringing together men of common tastes in these matters, and enabling them to compare their different experiences and to profit by one another's successes, difficulties, and failures: and by so doing it has, I believe, saved many a life and prevented many an accident, not only to its own members, but to those who benefit indirectly by a slow but certain improvement which is taking place in the race of guides, and which has already reached beyond the higher class of men who are brought more directly within the influence of the Alpine Club. But I say unhesitatingly that the Club has not only not given its sanction and encouragement to rash and ill-considered enterprises, but has done what it could to ascertain and make known the conditions under which a kind of enjoyment, blameless and elevating when pursued with due regard to safety and duty, may be properly and prudently indulged in, and to place within the reach of those who may be willing to profit by its labours information, appliances, and facilities without which the element of dangers, from which no manly sport is wholly free, would have been infinitely greater and more calamitous.

I am, Sir, your most obedient servant,

ALFRED WILLS
President of the Alpine Club

A Further Defence

IT WOULD HAVE BEEN easier and much pleasanter to write of the Alpine Club man, and to describe his peculiarities and his glories, if that terrible accident had not happened on the Matterhorn. It is ill jesting while the sad notes of some tragic song are still sounding in our ears. But the Alpine Club man has of late made himself so prominent among English tourists,—has become, with his ropes, his blankets, and his ladders, so well-acknowledged and much-considered an institution, that it would be an omission were he not to be included in our sketches. And, moreover, it may not be amiss to say yet a word or two as to the dangers of Alpine Club pursuits, —a word or two to be added to all those words that have been said in these and other columns on the same subject.

It may well, I think, be made a question whether we are not becoming too chary of human life; whether we do not allow ourselves to be shocked beyond proper measure by the accidental death of a fellow mortal. There are two points of view from which we look at these sudden strokes of fate, which are so distinctly separated in our minds as to turn each calamity into two calamities; and the one calamity or the other will be regarded as the more terrible according to the religious tendencies of the suffering survivor. There is the religious point of view, which teaches us to consider it to be a terrible thing that a man should be called upon to give up his soul without an hour for special preparation; and there is the human point of view, which fills us with an ineffable regret that one well loved should be taken from those who loved him, apparently without a cause. . . . As regards the religious consideration, we know of course that we are constantly praying, with more or less of earnestness, that the evil of sudden death may not come upon us, as we pray also that battles may not come. But yet, if occasion require it, if the honour of the country seems to demand it, we do not hesitate about battles. We may say, at least, that we never hesitate on account of the death that must ensue, though we do hesitate with extreme caution on the score of the money that must be spent.

And we consider,—if the cause has been good,—that the blood spilt on battle-fields has been well spilt, and that the lives gallantly rendered there have been well rendered. But the carnage there has all been the carnage of sudden death. It may be,—and yet it may hardly be,—that the soldier, knowing the chances of his profession, shall keep himself prepared for the death-dealing blow; but if the soldier on the eve of battle can do so, then why not he who is about to climb among the mountain snows? But, in truth, the subject is one which does not admit of too curious an inquiry. As we pray to be removed from sudden death, so do we pray that we may always be prepared for it. We are going ever with our lives in our hands, knowing that death is common to all of us; and knowing also,—for all of us who ever think do know it,—that to him who dies death must be horrible or blessed, not in accordance with an hour or two of final preparation, but as may be the state of the dying man's parting soul as the final result of the life which he has led. It suits us in some of our religious moods to insist much on the special dangers of sudden death, but they are dangers which come home in reality to very few of us. . . . In war, in commerce, not unfrequently in science, we disregard utterly the perils of sudden death; and if, as regards religion, these perils do not press on us in war and commerce, or in science, neither should they do so in reference to other pursuits. Is there any man with a faith so peculiar as to believe that salvation will be refused to him who perishes among the mountains of Europe because his employment is regarded as an amusement; but that it will be given to the African traveller because his work is to be accounted as a work of necessity? For myself, I do not think that there is a man who so believes.

And as to the human point of view,—that wearing regret which almost melts the heart into a stream of woe when the calamity comes home to oneself,—the argument is nearly the same. The poor mother whose dear gallant boy has fallen in battle . . . cannot reconcile herself to the need of war, nor unless she be a Spartan, can she teach herself to think that that dear blood has been well shed for the honour of her country. And, should he have fallen from some snowy peak, her judgment of the event will be simply the same. It will be personal regret, not judgment. It is equally impossible that she should console herself in either event by calculating that the balance of advantage to the community of which she is a member is on that side to which courage and the spirit of adventure belong.

In our personal regrets we must all think of our individual cases; but in discussing such a question as belonging to England at large, we can only regard the balance of advantage. And if we find that that spirit of enterprise which cannot have its full swing, or attain its required momentum without the fatality which will attend danger, leads to happy results,—that it makes our men active, courageous, ready in resource, prone to friendship, keen after gratifications which are in themselves good and noble; that it leads to pursuits which are in themselves lovely, and to modes of life which are worthy of admiration, then let us pay the necessary cost of such happy results without repining. That we should, all of us, have a tear of sorrow for those gallant fellows who perished on the Matterhorn is very good;—

> For Lycidas is dead, dead ere his prime,
> Young Lycidas, and hath not left his peer;
> Who would not sing for Lycidas?

But shall it be said among us that no boat is again to be put off from our shores because that one "fatal and perfidious bark" was "built in the eclipse."

There is a fate infinitely worse than sudden death,—the fate of him who is ever fearing it. "Mors omnibus est communis." We all know it, and it is the excitement coming from that knowledge which makes life pleasant to us. When we hear of a man who is calm and collected under every danger, we know that we hear of a happy man. In hunting, in shooting, in yachting, in all adventures, in all travelling,—I had almost said in love-making itself,—the cream of the charm lies in the danger. But danger will not be danger long if none of the natural results of danger come; and the cream of such amusements would, under such safe circumstances, soon become poor and vapid as skim-milk. I would say that it is to be hoped that that accident on the Matterhorn may not repress the adventurous spirit of a single English mountain-climber, did I not feel so sure that there will be no such repression as to leave no room for hoping. . . .

GERTRUDE MARGARET LOWTHIAN BELL

1868–1926

MOUNTAINEERING was only an incidental activity in Gertrude Bell's busy life of travel and diplomacy. Having learned mountain-craft in Scotland, she spent parts of the seasons of 1901, 1902, and 1904 in the Alps, during which she explored the Engelhörner group, near Meiringen, in the Bernese Oberland, and underwent the famous ordeal on the then unclimbed northeast face of the Finsteraarhorn. Her conduct evoked the unqualified praise of her guide, Ulrich Führer, and of J. P. Farrar of the Alpine Club, and she enjoyed immediate reputation as a climber. But she did not devote herself to the sport. The scene of her major activities was rather the deserts of Arabia. Here she traveled extensively, usually alone, and trained herself to a high degree of competence in Near Eastern languages, archaeology, and politics. During the first World War she joined the British Army's Arab Intelligence Bureau in Cairo. Then, after a brief mission in India, she became Oriental Secretary to the Mesopotamian Expeditionary Force; one of her close collaborators during the war and at the Paris Peace Conference was T. E. Lawrence. Afterwards she continued as adviser to Sir Percy Coxe and the Arab ministers in the delicate diplomacy which preceded the establishment in 1921 of the independent state of Iraq under King Feisal. During this period her knowledge of desert ways and her personal friendship with the sheiks were invaluable. Her last undertaking was the promotion of a national museum in Baghdad, one wing of which was, after her death, named in her honor.

The boldness and energy which Gertrude Bell displayed on the Finsteraarhorn were characteristic of her conduct during a varied life of action and negotiation. Though more adroit, she reminds one in many ways of another illustrious Englishwoman, Florence Nightingale.

The following selection is reprinted from *The Letters of Gertrude Bell,* edited by Lady Bell, D.B.E., Two Volumes, London, Ernest Benn, Ltd., 1927, by permission of Ernest Benn, Ltd. The title of the selection has been supplied.

Ordeal on the Finsteraarhorn

Meiringen, Sunday, August 3, 1902.

TO H[UGH] B[ELL]

F OR ONCE I must begin by acknowledging that Domnul's [1] gloomy forebodings came very near to being realised, and I am now feeling some satisfaction in the thought that my bones are not lying scattered on the Alpine mountains cold. Don't be alarmed, however, they are all quite safe and sound in the Grimsel and if it were not for a little touch of frostbite in the feet I should be merrily on my way to fresh adventures. . . . The matter we had in hand was the ascent on the face of the Finsteraarhorn: it is a well-known problem and the opinions of the learned are divided as to its solution. . . . We have looked at it for 2 years and decided for it and other authorities agree with us in what I still think is a right opinion. The mountain on the side facing the Schreckhorn comes down in a series of arches radiating from the extremely pointed top to the Finsteraar glacier. . . . The arête, the one which has always been discussed, rises from the glacier in a great series of gendarmes and towers, set at such an angle on the steep face of the mountain that you wonder how they can stand at all and indeed they can scarcely be said to stand, for the great points of them are continually overbalancing and tumbling down into the couloirs between the arêtes and they are all capped with loosely poised stones, jutting out and hanging over and ready to fall at any moment. But as long as you keep pretty near to the top of the arête you are safe from them because they fall into the couloirs on either side, the difficulty is to get on to the arête because you have to cross a couloir down which the stones fall, not to speak of avalanches; the game was beginning even when we crossed it an hour after dawn. We left the hut at 1.35 A.M.

Thursday. Crossed the séracs just at dawn and by 6 found ourselves comfortably established on the arête, beyond the reach of

[1] Gertrude Bell's nickname for Sir Valentine Chirol (1852–1929), traveller, diplomat, author. He was Director of the Foreign Department of *The Times* (London) from 1899 to 1912.

[torn fragment, partially legible:] at us (fortunately with the rock. We breakfasted ... It was difficult because ...ow and then we had to ...nney—one in particular ...sequently had the very ... face of a tower or cut ...gendarmes and it was ...tcherous. I found ...p'd into the crack ...mpoundations of thir... ...and knocked ... ...pany with it o... ...led up by the

rock w... About 2 feet square or rock tum... a little way down the hill till I managed to p... a tiny ledge. I got back on to my feet without being pull... rope, which was as well for a little later I happened to pass the rope through my hands and found that it had been cut half through about a yard from my waist when the rock had fallen on it. This was rather a nuisance as it shortened a rope we often wanted long to allow of our going up difficult chimneys in turn. So on and on we went up the arête and the towers multiplied like rabbits above and grew steeper and steeper and about 2 o'clock I looked round and saw great black clouds rolling up from the west. But by this time looking up we also saw the topmost tower of the arête far above us still, and the summit of the mountain further still and though we could not yet see what the top of the arête was like we were cheered and pushed on steadily for another hour while the weather signs got worse and worse. At 3 just as the first snow flakes began to fall, we got into full view of the last two gendarmes—and the first one was quite impossible. The ridge had been growing narrow, its sides steeper as we mounted, so that we had been obliged for some time to stick quite to the backbone of it; then it threw itself up into a great tower leaning over to the right and made of slabs set like slates on the top with a steep drop of some 20 feet below them on to the col. We were then 1000 feet below the summit I should guess, perhaps rather less, anyway we could see our way up, not easy but possible, above this tower and once on the top we could get down the other side in any weather. It had to be tried: we sat down to eat a few mouthfuls the snow fall-

...ck and let Ulrich ...ng of the tower. He ...up. The ledge was very ...otten. Anything was better ...the tower: there was a very ...e foot of the rock on that side for ...would be well. Again we let ourselves ...the foot of the tower, again to find that ...ssible. A month later in the year I believe this ...er a warm August there would be no ice in it, ...very steep the rocks so far as one could see under ...ed climbable. But even with the alternative before us of the descent down the terrible arête, we decided to turn back; already the snow was blowing down the couloir in a small avalanche, small but blinding, and the wind rushed down upon us carrying the mists with it. If it had been fine weather we should have tried down the arête a little and then a traverse so as to get at the upper rocks by another road. I am not sure that it could be done but we should have tried anything—but by the time we had been going down for half-an-hour we could see nothing of the mountain side to the right or to the left except an occasional glimpse as one cloud rolled off and another rolled over. The snow fell fast and covered the rocks with incredible speed. Difficult as they had been to go up, you may imagine what they were like going down when we could no longer so much as see them. There was one corner in particular where we had to get around the face of a tower.

We came round the corner, down a very steep chimney, got on to a sloping out rock ledge with an inch of new snow on it; there was a crack in which you could stand and with one hand hold in the rock face, from whence you had to drop down about 8 feet on to steep snow. We fixed the extra rope and tumbled down one after the other on to the snow; it was really more or less safe because one had the fixed rope to hold on to, but it felt awful: I shall remember every inch of that rock face for the rest of my life. It was now near 6. Our one idea was to get down to the chimney—the mid-day chimney which was so very difficult—so as to do it while there was still only a little snow on it. We toiled on till 8, by which time a furious thunderstorm was raging. We were standing by a great upright on the top of a tower when suddenly it gave a crack and a blue flame sat on it for a second. . . . My ice axe jumped in my hand and I thought the steel felt hot through my woollen glove—was that possible? I didn't take my glove off to see! Before we knew where we were the rock flashed again—it was a great sticking out stone and I expect it attracted the lightning, but we didn't stop to consider this theory but tumbled down a chimney as hard as ever we could, one on top of the other, buried our ice axe heads in some shale at the bottom of it and hurriedly retreated from them. It's not nice to carry a private lightning conductor in your hand in the thick of a thunderstorm. It was clear we could go no further that night, the question was to find the best lodging while there was still light enough to see. We hit upon a tiny crack sheltered from the wind, even the snow did not fall into it. There was just room for me to sit in the extreme back of it on a very pointed bit of rock; by doubling up I could even get my head into it. Ulrich sat on my feet to keep them warm and Heinrich just below him. They each of them put their feet into a knapsack which is the golden rule of bivouac. The other golden rule is to take no brandy because you feel the reaction more after. I knew this and insisted on it. It was really not so bad; we shivered all night but our hands and feet were warm and climbers are like Pobbles in the matter of toes.[2] I went to sleep quite often and was wakened up every hour or so by the intolerable discomfort of my position, which I then changed by an inch or two into another which was bearable for an hour more. At first the thunderstorm made things rather exciting. The slaps followed the flashes so close that there seemed no interval between them. We tied ourselves firmly on to the rock above lest as Ulrich philosophically said one of us should be struck and fall out. The rocks were all crackling round us and fizzing like damp wood which is just beginning to burn—have you ever heard that? It's a curious exciting sound rather exhilarating—and as there was no further precaution possible I enjoyed the extraordinary magnificence of the storm with

[2] Edward Lear, "The Pobble Who Has No Toes," in *Laughable Lyrics* (1877).

a free mind: it was worth seeing. Gradually the night cleared and became beautifully starry. Between 2 and 3 the moon rose, a tiny crescent, and we spoke of the joy it would be when the sun rose full on to us and stopped our shivering. But the sun never rose at all—at least for all practical purposes. The day came wrapped in a blinding mist and heralded by a cutting, snow-laden wind—this day was Friday; we never saw the sun in it. It must have snowed a good deal during the thunderstorm for when we stepped out of our crack in the first grey light about 4 (too stiff to bear it a moment longer) everything was deep in it. I can scarcely describe to you what that day was like. We were from 4 A.M. to 8 P.M. on the arête; during that time we ate for a minute or two 3 times and my fare I know was 5 ginger bread biscuits, 2 sticks of chocolate, a slice of bread, a scrap of cheese and a handful of raisins. We had nothing to drink but about two tablespoonfuls of brandy in the bottom of my flask and a mouthful of wine in the guides' wine skin, but it was too cold to feel thirsty. There was scarcely a yard that we could come down without the extra rope; you can imagine the labour of finding a rock at every 50 feet round which to sling it, then of pulling it down behind us and slinging it again. We had our bit of good luck—it never caught all day. But both the ropes were thoroughly iced and terribly difficult to manage, and the weather was appalling. It snowed all day sometimes softly as decent snow should fall, sometimes driven by a furious bitter wind which enveloped us not only in the falling snow, but lifted all the light powdery snow from the rocks and sent it whirling down the precipices and into the couloirs and on to us indifferently. It was rather interesting to see the way a mountain behaves in a snowstorm and how avalanches are born and all the wonderful and terrible things that happen in high places. The couloirs were all running with snow rivers—we had to cross one and a nasty uncomfortable process it was. As soon as you cut a step it was filled up before you could put your foot into it. But I think that when things are as bad as ever they can be you cease to mind them much. You set your teeth and battle with the fates; we meant to get down whatever happened and it was such an exciting business that we had no time to think of the discomfort. I know I never thought of the danger except once and then quite calmly. I'll tell you about that presently. The first thing we had to tackle was the chimney. We had to fix our rope in it twice, the second time round a very unsafe nail. I stood in this place holding Heinrich, there was an overhang. He climbed a bit of the way and then fell on to soft snow and spun down the couloir till my rope brought him up with a jerk. Then he got up on a bit of rock on the left about half as high as the overhang. Ulrich came down to me and I repeated Heinrich's process exactly, the iced extra rope slipping through my hands like butter. Then came Ulrich. He was held by Heinrich and me standing a good deal to the left but only half as high up as he. He climbed down to the place we had both fallen from, asking our advice at every step, then he called out "Heinrich, Heinrich, ich bin verloren," and tumbled off just as we had done and we held him up in the couloir, more dead than alive with anxiety. We gave him some of our precious brandy on a piece of sugar and he soon recovered and went on as boldly as before. We thought the worst was over but there was a more dangerous place to come. It was a place that had been pretty difficult to go up, a steep but short slope of iced rock by which we had turned the base of a tower. The slope was now covered with about 4 inches of avalanche snow and the rocks were quite hidden. It was on the edge of a big couloir down which raced a snow river. We managed badly somehow; at any rate Ulrich and I found ourselves on a place where there was not room for us both to stand, at the end of the extra rope. He was very insecure and could not hold me, Heinrich was below on the edge of the couloir, also very insecure. And here I had to refix the extra rope on the rock a little below me so that it was practically no good to me. But it was the only possible plan. The rock was too difficult for me, the stretches too big, I couldn't reach them: I handed my axe down to Heinrich and told him I could do nothing but fall, but he couldn't or at any rate, didn't secure himself and in a second we were both tumbling head over heels down the couloir, which was, you understand, as steep as snow could lie. How Ulrich held us I don't know. He said himself he would not have believed it possible but hearing me say I was going to fall he had stuck the pointed end of the ice axe into a crack above and on this alone we all three held. I got on to my feet in the snow directly I came to the end of my leash of rope and held Heinrich and caught his ice axe and mine and we slowly cut ourselves back up the couloir to the foot of the rock. But it was a near thing and I felt rather ashamed of my part in it. This was the time when I thought it on the cards we should not get down alive. Rather a comforting example, however, of how little can hold a party up. About 2 in the afternoon we all began to feel tired. I had a pain through my shoulder and down my back which was due, I think, to nothing but the exertion of rock climbing and the nervous fatigue of shivering— for we never stopped shivering all day, it was impossible to control one's tired muscles in that bitter cold. And so we went on for 6 hours more of which only the last hour was easy and at 8 found ourselves at the top of the Finsteraar glacier and in the dark, with a good guess and good luck, happened on the right place in the Bergschrund and let ourselves down over it. It was now quite dark, the snow had turned into pouring rain, and we sank 6 inches into the soft glacier with every step. Moreover we were wet through: we had to cross several big crevasses and get down the sérac before we could reach the Unteraar glacier and safety. For this we had felt no anxiety having relied upon our lantern but not a single match would light. We had every kind with us in metal match boxes but the boxes were wet and we had not a dry rag of any kind to rub them with. We tried to make a tent out of my skirt and to light a match under it, but our fingers were dripping wet and numb with cold—one could scarcely feel anything smaller than an ice axe—and the match heads dropped off limply into the snow without so much as a spark. Then we tried to go on and after a few steps Heinrich fell into a soft place almost up to his neck and Ulrich and I had to pull him out with the greatest difficulty and the mists swept up over the glacier and hid everything; that was the only moment of despair. We had so looked forward to dry blankets in the Pavillon Dollfuss and here we were with another night out before us. And a much worse one than the first, for we were on the shelterless glacier and in driving drenching rain. We laid our three axes together and sat on them side by side. Ulrich and I put our feet into a sack but Heinrich refused to use the other and gave it to me to lie on. My shoulders ached and ached. I insisted on our all eating something even the smallest scrap, and then I put a wet pocket-handkerchief over my face to keep the rain from beating on it and went to sleep. It sounds incredible but I think we all slept more or less and woke up to the horrible discomfort and went to sleep again. I consoled myself by thinking of Maurice [3] in S. Africa and how he had slept out in the pouring rain and been none the worse. We couldn't see the time but long before we expected it a sort of grey light came over the snow and when at last I could read my watch, behold it was 4. We gathered ourselves up; at first we could scarcely stand but after a few steps we began to walk quite creditably. About 6 we got to where we could unrope—having been 48 hours on the rope—and we reached here at 10 on Saturday.

They had all been in a great state of anxiety about us, seeing the weather, and had telegraphed to Meiringen, to Grindelwald, to know whether we had turned up. So I got into a warm bath and then discovered to my great surprise that my feet were ice cold and without any sensation. But having eaten a great many boiled eggs and drunk jugs of hot milk I went to bed and woke about dinner time to find my toes swollen and stiff. Frau Lieseguay then appeared and said that a S. American doctor had passed through in the afternoon and had seen Ulrich and Heinrich and had bound up their hands and feet in cotton wool and told them to keep very warm; so she bound up my feet too—my hands are nearly all right but I think my feet are worse than theirs. Still they seem better now and I don't expect I shall be toeless. They are not nearly as bad as my hands were in the Dauphiné, but the worst of it is that with swollen toes bound up in cotton wool one can't walk at all and I shall just have to wait till they get better. I slept for about 24 hours only waking up to eat, and it's now 4 in the afternoon and I'm just going to get up and have tea with Mr. Campbell, who has, I hear, been an angel of kindness to my guides. They seem to be none the worse except that Ulrich had a touch of rheumatism this morning, and as for me, I am perfectly absolutely well except for my toes—not so much as a cold in the head. Isn't it remarkable! . . . Isn't that an awful drefful adventure! It makes me laugh to think of it, but seriously now that I am comfortably indoors, I do rather wonder that we ever got down the Finsteraarhorn and that we were not frozen at the bottom of it. What do you think?

[3] Gertrude Bell's younger brother.

GEOFFREY WINTHROP YOUNG

BORN 1876

As a boy G. Winthrop Young had the good fortune to spend holiday seasons among the British hills and to find in his school library a copy of Edward Whymper's *Scrambles amongst the Alps in the Years 1860–'69*, a book which has excited the imagination of many potential mountaineers. Thus began a lifelong devotion to active climbing, to writing, and to educating young climbers.

Before the First World War Mr. G. Winthrop Young spent several seasons in the Alps, where he performed mountaineering feats of great daring, endurance, and imagination. One of these is recounted in the present selection. In 1914 he turned his energy to relief work in Europe. He commanded the Friends' Unit of the British Red Cross at the battle fronts in Belgium, France, and Italy. He was cited in despatches and decorated by the Italian, British, French, and Belgian governments for humanitarian services.

A severe wound received in action resulted in the high amputation of one leg, but failed to end his active climbing. Increasingly, however, he devoted himself to writing and to introducing mountaineering, with its adventure and discipline, into the British educational system. He was President of the Alpine Club from 1941 to 1944, and founder and first president of the British Mountaineering Council, which represents thirty climbers' organizations. His most important work of instruction and guidance is *Mountain Craft,* first published in 1920 and now in the seventh edition (1949). He is the author of three volumes of mountain poetry—*Wind and Hill* (1909), *Freedom* (1914), and *April and Rain* (1923), all available in a collected edition (1936). *On High Hills* (1927), in which "A Memory of the Mischabel" originally appeared, is an experiment in mountain autobiography which is already one of the great books of the literature of sport. It recreates scene, adventure, and emotional response in their original intensity and should communicate even to the inexperienced an understanding of the passion which makes men climb.

The following selection is reprinted from Geoffrey Winthrop Young, *On High Hills*, London, Methuen & Co., Ltd., 1927, by permission of Methuen & Co., Ltd.

A Memory of the Mischabel

Let him who seeks the monarchs of our quest
challenge their wakened might,
his diadem
wrested from summits crowned with summer light.
Not his to tempt their rest
when winter rigours and cold snows encumber:—
the sleeping ones have but to stir in slumber,
and he shall sleep with them.

"TIME AND FAIR WEATHER are apt to prove fatal to most alpine esti-
mates." But the years have passed, and the south face of the Täschhorn [1] stares at me across the interval, a height and depth of sensation unreduced by a longer perspective and unobscured even by the
ranges of emotion traversed during the excitement and the depressions of the war.

But the war years have produced one slight, perhaps temporary
change. In difficult or dangerous undertakings men of action have
always had to take "nerves"—their own or their company's—very
thoroughly into consideration; but it was thought indelicate to allude
to them publicly, in forecast or reminiscence. It is now conceded
that they may form a necessary part of the nature of a man, not in-
consistent with manliness or even with heroism. The story, therefore, of the Täschhorn climb can now be told with less likelihood of
seeming to do an injustice to the gallantry and endurance of our
company of the day. For one reason especially I am glad of the new
licence. Franz Lochmatter's mountaineering feat was the greatest I
have witnessed, and after a number of years I can still say the greatest I can imagine. It is right that it should be recorded; for I do not
suppose that in its mastery of natural difficulty, in its resistance to
the effects of cold and fatigue and to the infections of depression and
fear, it has often been equalled on any field of adventure or conflict.

After this exordium—the story will probably read very flat. Our
own feeling is the light by which we see a scene. We know, after-

[1] The Täschhorn is one of five connected peaks which make up the Mischabel.

wards, what our own feeling was, and we can rekindle it for ourselves. But we cannot reproduce the feeling in words simultaneously with the description of the incidents which produced it, and which were seen by us only as reflected in its light.

I have confessed to a period when it seemed that the early romance of alpine climbing could best be recaptured by inventing novel routes up the great peaks; and have mentioned that this occasionally brought me across the path of that comet of the Alps, V. J. E. Ryan, and Josef and Franz Lochmatter. Into their tail—if they had one—little Josef Knubel and I were willingly swept, in somewhat irregular conjunction. So long as there was no danger, in the mountain sense, we all climbed unroped. In a danger-zone we grouped as a trio and a duet working independently. But where, as sometimes happened, there was no safe holding for any member of the party of three or the party of two, we joined up our ropes. There are few mountain passages which do not allow of good holds for at least one member of a party of five spaced out along four hundred feet of rope. Since upon this plan it was usually possible for several of us to be moving simultaneously, we gained the extra security which a span of five men can give, and climbed almost as quickly as a rope of three.

We had decided from the top of the Weisshorn opposite that the Täschhorn from the south could be climbed. I based my opinion on what I used flippantly to call prima facie evidence: every south "face" must have a route up it, and all the better if we were the "first." Ryan had sounder advices: he had looked down the wall itself from above. There are two couloirs up the face, which, as they approach the pyramidal summit, fork out to left and right on to the western and south-eastern ridges. The final diamond of precipice which they thus enclose we thought, as we examined it from Zermatt, might prove the ace of trumps against us. But we could possibly cut out, by the couloirs, on to either ridge; and as it lay with us to lead off, we were safe in opening the game with a high heart.

We idled up to the luxury of a night at the Täschalp. A first grey dawn of mist, mizzling and "lowand," whose drench freezing at higher levels was responsible for much of our later trouble upon the

peak, we spent in a false start up the wet grass slopes, and in a cheerful return down them again, to a day of chess and wild-raspberry
jam. Our second start was in an earlier darkness; and we came up
among the snow levels, to meet a colder, clearer grey light glimmering ominously from ice-frore and snow-fleck on the high peaks. We
sprinted up the north bay of the Weingarten glacier, to its snow
rim under the south face.

To this, our first near view of the cliffs, their foreshortening, and
the cunning lie of the strata, gave a most deceitful impression of
their brevity and retrogression, and of their darkling innocence of
snow. One prophet murmured of the top at half-past nine; another
conceded until mid-day. But the great central chimney up the face,
although clear of any traces of stone-fall, we had at once to reject
from among our alternative lines. It was festooned and freakishly
upholstered with ice, and a frash of new snow on its corbels gave me
a qualm of doubt as to all that might be lying hidden on the less
visible belts of the face.

A steep but plausible buttress on the west of the chimney was our
unanimous choice. It mounted genially out of the glacier, and gave
us all we could wish of erect furrow and rib, with wrinkle holds of
the Welsh cliff pattern. Higher up we began to find that the ledges
sloped wrong, and that each rock tilt, as it became visible, held a
white plastering of snow. I have a recollection of an ill-looking
crooked funnel, upright and bitten into the nose of the buttress, with
its snowy lining dark-dappled and smirched by the up-wriggling of
my predecessors, where I first suggested to little J., who was climbing
below me, that convention suggested our roping together. And, later,
there follow several flash-light records of Franz' brown face—he was
climbing last of the trio ahead—looking down at me pensively: his
fashion of expressing a more vocal guide's "How goes it?" or "What
about a rope to help here?"

Higher again, I was not disinclined to use a spare rope, fixed and
considerately left behind for me in a glaciated and knobbly perpendicular groove; and not far above this we all collected for breakfast
on a relenting, snow-laden rock bracket, which projected over the
emptiness of the great chimney on the east of our buttress. It was
half-past seven; and this halt—a chilly standing and a swallowing of

food from frozen mittens—proved to be our last "rest" or convenient platform of assembly during the whole ascent. Above us the buttress merged into the face. Against the sky overhead, the snow fringe, upon the crest of the west ridge, caught the sunlight and looked very near. Between the two, the rock terraces, slanting upward across the face to the east, leaned back promisingly. We were only gradually to discover that each lift of the smooth friable rock was surmounted by no gratifying shelf, but by a rounded glacis, steep and slippery and holdless, vexed with snow, and sliding up against the sheer rise of the following step.

But already at intervals, as we climbed on again, there came to me from above and below atmospheric hints of that depression in the guides' humour which often warns us, through the instinct of the best of the hill-men, that there is grave work in prospect even before their eyes have discovered it. Ryan was, however, as always, bent upon the immediate "forward"; and his imperious staccato sentences, as little modified as his own fearlessness by any hush of breathless circumstance, had their usual effect upon his high-mettled team.

The buttress slid us stealthily up, and out on to the cliffs. The cliff-terraces drew us insidiously up and on. I soon forgot any atmospheric warnings in the exhilaration of clinging up smooth facet after smooth facet of rock, and of crawling and hand-pressing up the disappointing shelves, sloped like desk-lids, which joined steep to steep. I was not concerned with "stances," such as would allow me to stop and anchor our rope. Where I could go, little J. could more than follow safely; and surely the next shelf must be as level as it looked from below? Meanwhile, I was only intent to keep our duet up to the tremendous pace set by the trio ahead.

There is nothing lulls a leader's judgment more fatally to sleep than another party, or even a man "off the rope," climbing ahead of him. The task of settling *whether* or not to proceed is taken from him. He has only to think *how* to pass where another has already gone. If little J. and I had been climbing by our cautious selves we should, I think, have begun to doubt much sooner whether we would find it wholesome to descend all that we were grappling up so confidently. As it was, although a separate, we were no longer a responsible unit; and the strength of a climbing party is its collective, self-contained discretion. My own attention was bobbing ahead, concerned chiefly with the growing interval between myself and the speedy rhythm of the trio above me. They also were probably in much the same case. The presence of a cheerful amateur, similarly out of touch with the unison and "feeling" of their rope and rattling tin-cannily if always more distantly at their heels, may have had a good deal to say to Josef Lochmatter's pushing on, until well beyond the time when his better judgment would have perceived the risk of what we were doing and all that it threatened in the event of our retreat. It may well be so. But then again what was there, upward, downward, or across in the mountain world, which Josef, Franz, and Ryan might not justifiably have attempted, and confidently have faced as a return?

I began to notice that the trio, dotted up the diagonal markings on the grey face above, were pausing from time to time, as if to wait for us. This spurred me on the more. About the same time that recording angel, sensation, signalled to me that I was wrestling up the steepening walls and their lean-to roofs more awkwardly and slowly. Experience teaches us early to distinguish between the causes that may produce this feeling; and I was able to assign it now to the fact that the class of difficulty was getting beyond me, and not to a fluctuation in my own "standard of the day."

The precipices beetled their brows always more harshly over us. They restricted us more and more to lines of treacherous diagonal traverse, upward to the right and along the trend of the strata towards the central chimney. Traversing up these orbic, slithery bands without a vestige of good hold was no work for a rope of two. Little J., even if he went ahead, could be of no more protection to me than I was to him. But, imperceptibly still, the promise of a better stance above the next wall, and again above the next wall, each ending in disappointment, led us up and on. It was an optical illusion familiar in design. The gentler lateral inclination of the rock bands continued to lead the eye astray. They prevented it from appreciating the actual, and exceptional, steepness of the precipice, to which we were now all too deeply committed.

Ryan called back to me, to suggest that I should rope on behind Franz, in our usual fashion for danger-zones. I believe this to have been his generous reply to a suggestion made to him about this time that the trio ought to try and push ahead, while little J. and I should be advised to make our own way down. I recall the incident merely to indicate how doubtful already seemed the prospect of a successful issue, and how far the peculiar method which we followed, of separate ropes—so successful on other occasions, but so dangerous on this owing to the insidious character of the climbing—had already succeeded in hustling our mountaineering discretion.

Reassured by the pleasant moral of Franz' rope, the more agreeable for its rarity, I found the immediate business of not falling off the planes of traverse less preoccupying. It is an illustration of the psychic value of the rope, that we were no sooner united by it physically than I began to be more sensible of the nervous depression which had been gathering in the lead; although, spatially, we were in no closer touch than before. I felt it to the extent at least of realizing that the element of cheerfulness, the oxygen of a confident climbing atmosphere, needed replenishing.

The day was still bright and young, and the men obviously in fine climbing form. It was, therefore, no effort to telephone hearty remarks up and down the rope, or to emerge at Franz' feet after each struggle with a breathless but honest grin. But still the cliffs leaned out at us; still the unchancy upward and sideways traversing was forced upon us. A little cloud of anxiety crept upon the edge of my mind. My eye glanced unwillingly up or down: it was beginning to dodge, instinctively, the questions that the sight suggested. Our hands and feet grew gradually numb with the uninterrupted clinging to rounded, cold and slippery ledges.

At last—and how vividly the scene starts to mind—I stood on such a shelf, looking up at Franz' head and shoulders as he poised over a sheer wall above me, his prehensile feet balancing him erect upon a gutter-slope whose gracelessness I was yet to discover. The wall up to him bothered me a little, and as I got one arm over the coping and felt only the comfortless incline of the narrow band, I called out in joking patois, "Watch out, Franz, for my rope!" He looked down at me and out beyond me thoughtfully, almost abstractedly, without the customary flash of big brown eyes and big white teeth: "You must do what you can; *here* we can no longer help one another!" And then he turned away, dropping my rope symbolically from his hand and watching his brother, whose struggles, invisible to me, were audible far up round a black, repulsive corner.

From such a man the words had the effect of an icy douche. The detachment of mind which a leader may never lose whatever his occupation with his own struggles returned upon the instant. I looked down over my arm: to see the deadly continuity of descending precipice with its narrow snowy eavelets leaning out one above another, and still one above another, dizzily; and seeming to shrug even the glance of my eye off into space. And I realized in a flash what a return down them must mean. I looked up; to discover that worse lay before us, if we failed to force a way up the chimney into which we were traversing for an escape. For hours already, deceived by our spacing from each other up a seeming ladder of terraces that were no terraces, we must have been climbing in reality at our several risks: each of us unprotected by the man above: the slip of any one imperilling the rest. For how many more hours would this, or could we, continue?

A slight, pricking snow began to drift across us. From the exposed height of our great pyramidal wall, surging above other ranges, we looked out across a frozen and unheeding stillness of white peak and glacier, disappearing under darker clouds to the south. We seemed very much removed from the earth, and very much alone. As I turned back to the rock I could see nothing but antagonism in the ice-wrinkled face of the crags upon which we were venturing; and I had the feeling—it was too formless at the time to take a definite shape I must now give to it—as if somewhere low beyond the horizon behind me a great grey bird was just lifting on its wings into heavy flight. As the hours wore on, this shadow at our backs seemed to be approaching soundlessly and covering more and more of the sky. Gradually it was enclosing us within its spread of cold wings, and isolating us from all the world of life and movement in our contest with the frigid wall of grey precipice.

Precariously we crawled up to and along, and up to and along the sloping ribbons, silky with chill snow, and leading interruptedly upward towards the projecting corner which shut us off from the big couloir. On the decrepit mantelpiece by which we turned the corner itself, we could use a rock "hitch" for the rope, one of the only three we found on all this upper face! We edged round into the couloir, a forbidding chasm; and found ourselves on a slim, shattered ledge, that continued inwards at a high level across the sheer wall of rock forming our side of the rift.

We were more or less together now; and no one could any longer pretend that some one above saw a gleam of hope denied to himself. Forty feet below, the slabby back of the chasm slanted steeply outward, and down into space. Past us, the same backing of slabs mounted precipitously, to splay out in an amphitheatre of over-leaning walls far above. And every hopeless curve of slab was glassy with ice and glitter-film. The couloir, as an upward escape, needed no second glance. Josef was already clinging down our wall into the chasm below. His object was plain. The same belt or flaw by which we had entered the rift appeared again, at a lower level, upon the wall opposite to us, and disappeared round the profile of the further containing buttress. What could be seen of its re-start was no more than a sloping shelf, that wound steeply upwards and out of sight round the all but vertical corner. But Josef had evidently made up his mind that our only chance, now the couloir had failed, was to resume our perilous ribbon-traverses along the bands; in the hope—if they continued far enough—of finding the second, smaller chimney, the branch which forked out on to the south-east ridge, accessible; and if accessible, less icy-hearted. It appeared to me, and probably to him, a very faint and rather fearsome chance. Even the slabs below us, which gave difficult access to the crazy re-start of the traverse, looked villainous enough.

Was there no alternative? Far above us on our right, and above the vanishing top of the hopeless couloir, I could see the snow crest of the west ridge slanting down the sky, as it descended steeply from the peak. That part of the crest looked very remote; and there was no way to it. But in a direct line above our ledge, since the west ridge descended very rapidly, our wall must surely be meeting the crest at no such very great height above us? Stuck like stamp-paper as we were on to the wall, it was impossible for us to see more than a short initial overhang, then twenty feet of rock almost sheer but bristly as a clothes-brush, and above that a silvery fringe of snow which *must* mean some set-back in the angle of the cliff. It seemed to me certainly worth trying, and far shorter, if it would go! Franz waved it aside without comment. Little J. gave it longer consideration; but he was away along the ledge, and could not count. Josef was already more than occupied with the slabs below us, and, therefore, not to be distracted. But I still think it might have proved the less desperate alternative.

Josef moved tentatively about on the smooth shoot of the slabs, steadied by Ryan with the rope from our ledge. He never looked like crossing them; and I think that the nearer view of the re-start of the traverse was weakening his resolution. The dark chilly depths of the chasm gave muffled answer to his agitated comments. Franz, beside me on the ledge, watched him, hissing a gay little French song between his teeth, the only sign of excitement I have ever known him show. Then—"It won't go!" came in a hollow shout from below; and—"But it *must* go!" echoed from Franz, who at once leaped into action. I untied my rope to him. He was down and out on to the slabs in a breath, still singing to himself. He caterpillared his way across the ice-bosses above Josef. Josef, and other great guides, on slabs moved with the free poise of an athlete and the foot-cling of a chamois. Franz, in such case, had the habit and something of the appearance of a spider or crustacean. His curled head disappeared altogether. His body and square shoulders split and elongated into four steely tentacles, radiating from a small central core or hub of intelligence, which transmitted the messages between his tiny hands and boots as they clung attached and writhing at phenomenal angles and distances.

At the far side of the slabs he crawled onto and up the sloping shelf of the disappearing traverse, only keeping himself on it, so far as could be seen, by thrusting one foot firmly out against the aether. Presently Ryan followed, out of sight; and then Josef. Even with little J. playing my rope from high up on the wall behind me, I found the crossing of the iced slabs of the couloir upon a descending diagonal nasty enough. More specially towards the farther side, when the rope, sagging across from above, began to pull me back with a heavy draw. But the start of the traverse looked unspeakable. A downward and outward leaning shelf, with nothing below and an overhanging wall above, it screwed steeply upward out of sight round the buttress. From far up along it came Josef's voice, thinly crying caution. How was I to keep on the shelf—and, much more wriggle up it?

Little J. joined me on the ice-nicks in the slabs; and after many attempts the end of Josef's rope, slung from above and weighted with a stone, was lassoed back and round to a point on the slabs from which we could recover it. I tied on, and started. Once up on the shelf, I found that there was nothing to keep me on it against the urgency of that slant into space. A hailing match between little J. and Josef only produced the information that while he was "good" to hold—but not to pull—along the diagonal upward line of the shelf, he would be helpless against any direct downward strain, such as must result if I fell off the shelf. There was nothing for it but to thrust myself desperately upward, relying only upon the friction of my outer knee on the hem of the sloping ribbon to resist an outward drag to which the weight of the world seemed to be added. Of service, also, were two or three painful finger-tip pinches on the down-sloping prickles of the wall above my head.

When I reached Josef, I found him sprawled over rugosities on the buttress. His "hitch"—the second of our dauntless three—was no more than a prong of rock sticking downward like a tusk from the overhang above him, and of course useless against a pull from any but the one, sideways, direction. Little J., who had by now begun his assorted collection of all our sacks and axes, followed up magnificently.

I have no clear recollection of the series of traverses up and across the face that followed. After a short easier interval, they became, if anything, more steeply inclined and more outwardsloping than before. The snow on them grew slimier and colder, the day darker, the sprinkling pepper of snowfall denser and keener. Hands and feet grew lifeless and lost their touch; and there was never a single sound holding-ledge for any one of the party. We began that monotonous beat of any unoccupied toe or hand against the rock which alone kept the blood in circulation during the long cold hours of halt and fight and creep, and creep and fight and halt. On the next day my own toes and finger-tips were bruised blue—though I had felt no pain at the time; and a few fingers still retain the lowered vitality that follows on frost-bite. But during the climb no lesser trouble could get its head above the dark tide of oppression which filled all the spaces of consciousness. The fight went on doggedly, with that determination to take no long views but to make just the next hold good and the one more step secure, which enables a human atom to achieve such heights of effort and to disregard such lengths of suffering.

The next clear memory is of finding ourselves inside the second, smaller, chimney, a precipitous narrow cleft up the face, of worn, skull-smooth rock. It was all dirty white and bone-blue in the gloomy afternoon light, with blurred ice-nubbles bulking through the adhesive snow. But at least there was the singular rest for eye and nerves which the feeling of enclosing walls gives us after long hours on an exposed cliff. We even found a nominal stance or two, in ice-pockets on chockstones, where we could *almost* hold on without help from the hands. Franz, who was back again above me resting from the lead, could spare me a few partial hoists with the rope. I began to feel my muscles slackening with the relief, and I became conscious of the cold. I had time to notice that I was climbing less precisely, a symptom of relaxed tension: time, too, to admit ungrudgingly that nothing in the universe but Franz' rope could have got me up to and over some of the expulsive ice bulges in the chimney. Ignorant in my remote position of what the front men saw awaiting us above, I even thawed into a congratulatory remark or so; but I drew no response.

And then, it all ended! The chimney simply petered out: not under the south-east ridge, as we might have hoped, but in the very hard heart of the diamond precipice some six hundred feet below the final and still invisible summit. The vague exit from the chimney faded out against the base of a blank cliff. One of its side walls led on for a little, and up to the left. There it too vanished, under the lower rim of a big snowy slab, sloping up and slightly conical, like a dish-cover. I have reason to remember that slab. It formed the repellent floor of a lofty, triangular recess. On its left side, and in front, there was space and ourselves. On its right, and at the back, a smooth leap of colossal cliff towered up for a hundred feet of crystallized shadow, and then arched out above our heads in a curve like the dark underside of a cathedral dome. A more appalling-looking finish to our grim battle of ascent could hardly have been dreamed in a "falling" nightmare; and we had not even standing room to appreciate it worthily! As I looked up and then down, I had an overpowering sense of the great grey wings behind us, shadowing suddenly close across the whole breadth of precipice, and folding us off finally from the world.

But our long apprenticeship to discouragement stood us in good stead. Muscles braced anew obstinately; determination quickened resentfully. The recess on whose lip we hung had been formed by the sliding of a great wedge of rock off the inclined, dish-cover slab, once its bed. But on our right the cliff continued the original line. My impression of this, therefore, was as of a high building viewed from under one corner. Its sheer front wall stretched away to the right, flush with the sill of our slab. The end wall of the building formed the right side of our recess, and overhung the slab. The rectangular house-corner, where the two walls joined, rose immediately above us, vertical and iced, but a little chipped by the rending out of the wedge. Again, the front wall of this projecting house did not rise to the same height as the cliff that backed our recess. Forty feet up—my measures are merely impressions—the wall slanted steeply back in a roof, receding out of sight. Presumably another huge wedge had here slid from its bed, on a higher plane. Above and beyond this roof the precipices rose again into sight, in the same line and of the same height as the cliffs which backed our recess. Only, the cliff vertically above us was crowned by the great dome or overhang. There must be, therefore, invisible above, some rough junction or flaw where the line of cliffs above the receding house-roof linked on to the forward jut of our dome. Four vital questions suggested themselves: Could the house-corner be climbed? Was the roof, if attainable, too steep to crawl up? Might there be a flawed connexion where the precipice upon which the roof abutted joined on to the side of the dome? If there was such a flaw, would this yield us a passage out on to the face of the convex dome *above* its circle of largest dimension, on its retreating upper curve, or *below* it, under its hopeless arch? These details are tiresome, perhaps unintelligible. But they may help other climbers to a better understanding of Franz' remarkable feat.

Right up in the angle of the recess there was a rotund blister of rock modelled in low relief on the face of the slab; and round this a man, hunched on small nicks in the steep surface, could just belay the rope. Josef and Franz were crouching at this blister up in the recess. The rest of us were dispersed over freezing cling-holds along the lower rim of the slab. And the debate proceeded, broken by gusts of snow. The man to lead had clearly to run out a hundred to a hundred and fifty feet of rope. He could be given no protection. His most doubtful link would come some eighty feet up, above the roof. If he found a flaw there, and it served him favourably, he would be out on the convex of the dome fully a hundred feet above us, and outside us in a direct line above our heads. If, at this point, he could not proceed—well, it was equally unlikely that he could return.

Franz showed no hesitation. The hampered preparations for the attempt went on hurriedly. We had all to unrope as best we could, so as to arrange for the two hundred feet of possible run-out, and we hooked on to our holds with difficulty, while the snow-frozen rope kinked and banged venomously about us. In the end little J. and I had to remain off the rope, to leave enough free. Then—

> as a flame
> Stirred by the air, under a cavern gaunt—

Franz started up the corner, climbing with extraordinary nerve but advancing almost imperceptibly. It was much like swarming up the angle of a tower, rough-cast with ice. Ryan and little J. crept up near the blister; but as there was no more room I remained hanging on to the fractured sill of the slab. In this position I was farther out; and I could just see Franz' two feet scratting desperately for hold to propel him up the tilt of the roof above the corner. The rest of him was now out of sight. The minutes crawled like hours, and the rope hanging down to us over the gable-end hardly seemed to stir upwards. The snow gusts distracted us cruelly. A precipice in sunshine seems at least interested in our microscopic efforts. Its tranquillity even helps our movement by giving to it a conspicuous importance. But when the stable and the unstable forces of nature join in one of their ferocious, inconclusive conflicts, the little human struggle is carelessly swallowed up in uproar, and tosses unregarded and morally deflated, like a wet straw on a volcanic wave.

Suddenly I heard that unmistakable scrape and grit of sliding boot-nails and clothes. Above my head, over the edge of the roof to the right, I saw Franz' legs shoot out into space. Time stopped. A shiver, like expectancy, trembled across the feeling of unseen grey wings behind me, from end to end of the cliff. I realized impassively that the swirl of the rope must sweep me from my holds before it tightened on the doubtful belay of the blister. But fate was playing out the game in regions curiously remote. My mind watched the moves, itself absorbed into the same remote, dispassionate atmosphere. It seemed unwilling to disturb the issue by formulating a thought, or even a fear. The fact of the body seemed negligible; it had not part in the observant aloofness into which all consciousness had withdrawn. Something of the same feeling of separation between the body and the watching mind is the experience of men actually falling or drowning, when action is at an end and there is not even pain to reunite bodily and mental sensation. But during the crises of this day the condition lasted, with me certainly, for spaces that could only be measured by hours.

Franz' boots again disappeared above the edge. No one in the recess had known of the slip, out of their sight and lost in the gusts. He had stopped himself miraculously on the rim by crushing his hands on to ice-dimples in the slab. The hanging rope began again to travel up along the slanting gable-end of the roof. There was a long interval, and now and then the sound of a scratting boot or the scrabble of loose surface. Then the rope began, jerkily, to work out and across far above our heads. Franz had found a flaw in the joint of the cliffs above the roof, and he was creeping out on to the projection of the dome. The lengthening rope now hung down well *outside* the men in the recess, and it might have hung outside me on the lower rim, had they not held in its end. Its weight upon Franz, as it swayed down through the snow, must have added to his immense difficulties. He was well out of sight, clinging somewhere above on the upper curve of the overhang.

An indistinct exchange of shouts began, half swallowed by echo, wind, and snow. Franz, it appeared, was still quite uncertain if he could get up any further. For the time he could hold on well enough to help one man with the rope; but he had not two hands free to pull. I could hear his little spurt of laughter at the question—"Could he return?" He suggested that Josef should join him, and the rest wait until they two might return with a rescue-party. Wait, there!— for at best fifteen hours, hanging on to the icy holds, in a snow wind! Well, then, what if we four tried to get down, and he would go on alone—if he could? "Get down? Ho, la, la!"—Josef was at his resourceful wits' end. I suggested, pacifyingly, that Ryan might join and reinforce Franz, and that we remaining three could attempt the descent together. This provoked the crisis, which had been long threatening. Josef's competence and control were second to none in the Alps; but the responsibility, the physical strain, and this last disappointment had overstrained the cord. It snapped; and in somewhat disconcerting fashion.

Harsh experience can teach us that when these accidiae occur, as they may to the most courageous of men if tested unfairly, the only remedy is to soothe or to startle. The first was impracticable in our situation. I spoke sharply in reproach, but without raising my voice. The experiment succeeded surprisingly. Self-control returned upon the instant, and for the rest of the day Josef climbed and safeguarded us with all his own superb skill and chivalrous consideration.

He was right in so far that, at that hour of the day and upon those treacherous cliffs, now doubly dangerous under accumulating snow, all the odds were against any of us who turned back getting down alive. Franz in any case could not get back to us, and he might not be able to advance. We were committed, therefore, to the attempt to join him, however gloomy its outlook. As many as possible must be got up to him—and the rest must be left to chance.

Josef started his attempts on the corner. This left room for me to move up to Ryan on the slab. He asked me, I remember, what I thought were the chances of our escape. I remember, too, considering it seriously, and I can hear myself answering—"About one in five." As we talked fragmentarily, and listened to the distant scraping of Josef's feet up the roof, I recalled—with a grim appreciation of this new, first-hand example—having often remarked in the stories of shipwreck or other catastrophe how inevitably and usefully the "educated" man plays up to the occasion. For the audience of his own mind as much as for anybody else he sustains almost unconsciously the part which his training imposes upon him as alone consistent with his self-respect.

The end of the long rope hooted down past us. It hung outside the recess, dangling in air; and I could only recover it by climbing down again over the rim of the slab and reaching out for it one-handed with my axe. I passed it up; and then I stayed there, hanging on, because I could no longer trust hands or feet to get me up the slope again. Ryan began the corner; but if I have described the position at all intelligibly, it will be seen that while the corner rose vertically on our right, the long rope hung down on a parallel line from the dome directly above our heads. So it came that the higher we climbed up the corner the more horizontal became the slanting pull of the rope, and the more it tended to drag us sideways off the corner and back under the overhang. Very coolly, Ryan shouted a warning before he started of the insufficient power left in frozen hands. Some twenty feet up, the rope tore him from his inadequate, snowy holds. He swung across above our heads and hung suspended in mid-air. The rope was fixed round his chest. In a minute it began to suffocate him. He shouted once or twice to the men above to hurry. Then a fainter call, "I'm done," and he dangled to all appearance unconscious on the rope. Franz and Josef could only lift him half-inch by half-inch. For all this hour—probably it was longer—they were clamped one above the other on to the steep face of the dome, their feet on shallow but sound nicks, one hand clinging on, and only the other free to pull in. Any inch the one lifted, the other held. The rough curve of the rock, over which the higher portion of the rope descended diminished by friction the effectiveness of each tug. The more one considers their situation, the more superhuman do the co-operation and power the two men displayed during this time, at the end of all those hours of effort, appear. Little J. and I had only the deadly anxiety of watching helplessly, staring upward into the dizzy snow and shadow: and that was

enough. J. had followed silently and unselfishly the whole day; and
even now he said nothing: crouching in unquestioning endurance
beside the freezing blister on the slab.

Ryan was up at last, somehow to the overhang; and being dragged
up the rough curve above. A few small splinters were loosened,
and fell, piping, past me and on to me. I remember calculating apa-
thetically whether it was a greater risk to try and climb up again
into the recess, unroped and without any feel in fingers and toes, or
to stay where I was, hanging on to the sill, and chance being knocked
off by a stone. It is significant of the condition of body and mind that
I decided to stay where I was, where at least stiffened muscles and
joints still availed to hold me mechanically fixed on to my group
of rounded nicks.

Ryan was now out of sight and with the others. When the con-
striction of the rope was removed he must have recovered amazingly
toughly, and at once; for down once more, after a short but anxious
pause, whistled the snow-stiffened rope, so narrowly missing me
that little J. cried out in alarm. I could not for a time hook it in
with the axe; and while I stretched, frigidly and nervously, Josef
hailed me from seemingly infinite height, his shouts travelling out
on the snow eddies. They could not *possibly* pull up my greater
weight. Unless I felt sure I could stick on to the corner and manage
to climb round to them by Franz' route, it was useless my trying!
At last I had fished in the rope, with a thrill of relief, and I set mental
teeth. With those two tied on to the rope above, and myself tied
on—in the way I meant to tie myself on—to the rope below, there
were going to be no more single options. We were all in it together;
and if I had still some faith in myself I had yet more in that margin
of desperation strength which extends the possible indefinitely for
such men as I knew to be linked on to me above. And if I were once
up, well, there would be no question after that about little J. coming
up too!

I gave hands and feet a last blue-beating against the rock to re-
store some feeling to them. Then I knotted the rope round my
chest, made the loose end into a triple-bowline "chair" round the
thighs, and began scratching rather futilely up the icy rectangular
corner. For the first twenty-five feet—or was it much less?—I could

just force upward. Then the rope began to drag me off inexorably. I clutched furiously up a few feet more; and then I felt I must let go, the drag was too strong for frozen fingers. As I had already resolved, at the last second I kicked off from the rock with all my strength. This sent me flying out on the rope and across under the overhang, as if attached to a crazy pendulum. I could see J., crouching in the recess far below, instinctively protecting his head. The impetus jumped the upper part of the rope off its cling to the rock face of the dome above, and enabled the men to snatch in a foot or two. The return-swing brought me back, as I had half hoped, against the corner, a little higher up. I gripped it with fingers and teeth, and scrambled up another few feet. But the draw was now irresistible. I kicked off again; gained a foot or so, and spun back.

I was now up the corner proper, and I should have been by rights scrambling up the roof on the far side of my gable-edge. But the rope, if nothing else, prevented any chance of my forcing myself over it and farther to the right. Another cling and scratch up the gable-end, and I was not far below the level of the dome overhanging above and to my left. For the last time I fell off. This time the free length of the rope, below its hold upon the curve of the dome, was too short to allow of any return swing. So I shot out passively, to hang, revolving slowly, under the dome, with the feeling that my part was at an end. When I spun round inward, I looked up at the reddish, scarred wall freckled with snow, and at the tense rope, looking thin as a grey cobweb and disappearing frailly over the forespring of rock that arched greedily over my head. When I spun outward, I looked down—no matter how many thousand feet—to the dim, shifting lines of the glacier at the foot of the peak, hazy through the snowfall; and I could see, well inside my feet, upon the dark face of the precipice the little blanched triangle of the recess and the duller white dot of J.'s face as he crouched by the blister. It flashed across me, absurdly, that he ought to be more anxious about the effect of my gymnastics upon the fragile thread of alpine rope, his one link with hope, than about me!

I was quite comfortable in the chair; but the spinning had to be stopped. I reached out the axe at full stretch, and succeeded in touching the cliff, back under the overhang. This stopped me, face inward. I heard inarticulate shouting above, and guessed its meaning, although I was now too close under the dome to catch the words:— "They could not lift my dead weight!" I bethought me, and stretched out the axe again; got its point against a wrinkle of the wall, and pushed out. This started me swinging straight out and in below the dome. After two pokes I swung in near enough to be able to give a violent, short-armed thrust against the cliff. It carried me out far enough to jump quite a number of feet of rope clear of its cling down the rope above. The guides took advantage of the easing to haul in, and I pendulum'd back a good foot higher. The cliff facing me was now beginning to spring out in the Gothic arch of the overhang; so it could be reached more easily. I repeated the shove-out more desperately. Again they hauled in on the released rope. This time I came back close under the arch; and choosing a spot as I swung in, I lifted both feet, struck them at the wall, and gave a convulsive upward and outward spring. The rope shortened up; and as I banged back the cornice of the arch loomed very near above my head. But the free length of rope below it was now too short to let me again reach to the back of the arch with leg or axe. I hung, trying in vain to touch the lowest moulding of the cornice above with my hands. I heard gasps and grunts above quite distinctly now. The rope strained and creaked, gritting over the edge of the rock above me. I felt the tremor of the sinews heaving on it. But for all that, I did not move up. I reached up with the axe in both hands, just hooked the pick into a lucky chink of the under-moulding, and pulled, with a frantic wriggle of the whole body. It was a feeble lift, but enough for the sons of Anak above to convert into a valuable gain. The axe slipped down on to my shoulder, held there by its sling. I reached up and back with both arms, got hold of a finger-grip, and gained another inch. Infinitesimal inches they seemed, each a supreme effort, until my nose and chin scratched up against a fillet of the cornice. Then the arms gave out completely, so much at the end of their strength that they dropped lifeless. But the teeth of the upper jaw held on a broken spillikin and, with the stronger succour of the rope, supported me for the seconds while the blood was running back into my arms.

Wrestle by wrestle it went on. Every reserve of force seemed exhausted, but the impulse was now supplied by a flicker of hope. Until, at last, I felt my knee catch over a moulding on the edge, and I could sink forward for an instant's rest, with rucked clothes clinging over the rough, steep, upward but *backward* curving of the dome. It is impossible to suggest the relief of that feeling, the proof that the only solid surface which still kept me in touch with existence had ceased to thrust itself out for ever as a barrier overhead, and was actually giving back below me in semi-support.

But there was no time, or inclination, to indulge panting humanity with a rest or a realization. I crept up a few feet, on to small, brittle, but sufficient crinkles. The dark figures of the three men above were visible now, clinging crab-like and exhausted on to similar nicks, indistinct in the snow dusk, but still human company. I had to stay where I was, and untie my rope, knotting up a coil at the end of the heavy length so that I could swing it inward to little J. back and out of sight beneath me in the recess. The second cast was true: I felt him handle it, and then I let it go for those in the more direct line above to hold. Presently I saw it writhing away from me across the few visible feet of stooping crag, as J. below moved away to start the icy corner. He had, I think, two sacks beside his own and at least three extra axes slung on to him; but he grappled up the corner masterfully and forced his way out on to the roof. Hopeless of lifting him as they had lifted us, the men above had learned, from pure fatigue, to leave him more free upon the rope. But he was naturally a very long time; and there was all too much leisure in which to realize how irrevocably our descent was now cut off, and how improbably our ascent could be continued.

The first flare of blinding relief died down. The obscure future settled round again like a fog. The precipice receding into murky uncertainty above looked more than ever dark with discouragement for a vitality ebbing on the tide of reaction. The shadowy, humping figures above were silent; there was none of that heartening talk that greets us over a difficult edge, giving us assurance that the worst is past. With no longer even the rope about me as a reminder of companionship, the sense that others were near me and in like case passed out of mind. My thoughts wandered drowsily, and all

life in the limbs seemed suspended, as we feel it to be sometimes
in the moments just preceding sleep.

The snow began to fall in large, soft flakes; not the tingling darts
that assail us with the crisp hostility of intruders upon our alien
earth, but flakes like wings, instinct with life, surrounding and wel-
coming a visitor to their own region of air with vague but insistent
friendliness. A few of them settled inquisitively, to gleam and fade
for a second like fallen starlight, on the short arc of brown crag
racing into shadow between my feet. The rest drifted lightly and
recklessly down past my heels, to disappear over the rim of void:
suggesting how easy and restful might be my own descent could
tired muscles but be persuaded to relax their tenacious hold upon
the few remaining feet of inhospitable rock. Far below and to the
right, a brow of bending and frosted precipice frowned into sight;
and against and round its more familiar obstruction, lit by a pale
glare diffused through the low clouds, the white flakes twirled and
circled intimately, already forgetful of their more timid flight past
the stranger above. When they sank from it, it was into an immensity
of grey haze, featureless but for the black ribbons of moraine which
floated high and distinct above their unseen glaciers, as reeds seem
to sway and float high over the reflecting depths of a transparent
stream. Into these immeasurable grey depths everything seemed to be
descending, unresistingly and as of choice,—the long lines of ice-
fast crag, the shifting eddies of snow, the rays of darkness under the
storm-clouds, even the eye and the tired mind. Some rebellious
instinct of hand and foot alone appeared to defy a universal law.

The ceaseless movement of the snow spread to the rock. We must
all have felt, when we look up at overhanging cliffs, how they lean
out, rushingly, above us, and yet never visibly stir; as if their furious
motion were not in space but through some other dimension. The
same sensation came as I clung on to the rough short bend of rock
islanded in the sky. The dome swayed out and out perpetually
under me, and yet did not move for sight or touch. Not common
"giddiness"; my eyes held the crags as firmly in place as my feet and
hands were holding me. Then the movement became general; an
impetuous hurtling across the sky, which yet left heights and depths

in their fixed relation to one another. And imagination conjectured that this must be the spin of the earth, perceptible upon one of its pre-eminent spires.

Back with a slight shock, came the realization of the loneliness, of the long waiting, and of the still probable end to it. What do we think of at these times? While action is still possible for us, we think, deliberately, of that alone. But when action is suspended? We do not think for long about our fears. We cannot continue to feel frightened of a certainty, or even of a probability. Any keen fear must be constantly fed by new danger, and the drug be kept effervescing by fresh uncertainty, for its fumes to maintain their strength. Fear for ourselves, unstirred and undiluted, soon tastes flat: we cease to feel afraid of being frightened. And when that point is past, our mere instinct to avoid a very common experience cannot hold more than a part of our interest.

Nor do we think much about death itself, or what may come after. That which follows after cannot happen to us as we are; and therefore, to a condition of mind too pre-occupied about the tremendous present to have leisure for speculation about other or abstract states, it seems immaterial. As for the matter of our dying— we have already accepted the event. The ending of our personality, in all its aspects and in all its consequences for others, has been envisaged; and, with that, it also has become no longer of the first importance.

Thought, in fact, seemed to me to be released just as much from human cares and compassions as from any supernatural concern. It pursued a deeper, or at least a different path, into a region of impressions, stern, unemotional, and strangely impersonal. The flaring up of the essential personality under a sudden threat of extinction . . . was not perceptible: the realization of the threat, under the gradual closing of the grey wings, had been too cumulative and too slow. The sense of myself as an individual seemed indeed to have been gradually lost, or all but lost. In its place I had the feeling of belonging to, or of being myself, some infinite experience, at the moment passing through a cloud. I am illustrating and not attempting to explain the feeling, when I say that it was as if my consciousness, when the door was almost closed upon an existence for me personally, had become again all but absorbed into the continuous and transmitted principle of life within me. It was a sphere of sensation—or of absence of sensation—which I could only describe in meaningless words, illimitable, unhuman, all-comprehending, all-disregarding and their like. During my experience of it, it was more dark with the knowledge of its ages of recurring interruption by individual death, than alight with the assurance of its perpetual reappearance in new lives. For this prevalence of shadow at the time my own situation may have been responsible; because my life-tenancy of the transmitted principle was still holding good, and the extinction which threatened this personal tenure could not, therefore, but continue to colour any thought of mine however far withdrawn.

Certainly, my personal interest in living, although reduced, was not at an end. The purpose, for instance, to battle out the remainder of the climb if only for the time remaining to me needed no reinforcement. But it had become subordinate: whether I remained alive or not had become a minor, if still a surviving, interest.

When we began to climb again, I noticed that the value of being alive as myself grew greater, with the greater opportunity which action gives us for individual assertion. At the same time the feeling of belonging to an impersonal, timeless existence diminished; but it remained uppermost in thought. When, later, and without warning or gradual preparation, the probability if not the certainty of our safety suddenly broke in upon me, the first result was a comic reversal in the precedence of these interests in thought. I laughed to myself to feel how the importance of my being alive immediately and truculently reasserted itself; how the sense of personality expanded, until it exceeded even its own normally large dimensions. And, a little later still, I had to laugh again, to think that I of all people should ever have been brought to the point of laughing at myself for being in love with life!

That last laugh was perhaps the best. It was one of the predicates of a friendlier understanding of life in all its presentments, of a lesson in detachment—or humour—learned, which came back with me from that shadowy exploration. Men who survived the weeks of dedication to "services of special danger" in the war could give better account. But no one who had lived through even the few hours we

spent upon the southern precipice, under the grey wings, could have
emerged from them—and felt in himself no change.

The appearance of little J. as he clambered, a clattering brown
goblin of sack-humps and axe-points, over a boss on the shadowy
dome beside me brought me back to the world of human company,
and struggle. The day was darkening steadily—or is my memory of
darkness only the shadow of our circumstance? for it was not yet
four o'clock: but the snow stopped, having done its worst where it
could most impede us. We roped up patiently, and began again our
age-long crawl and halt up icy slabs as little kindly as before; and
every fifty feet above us loomed still the threat of a total interruption. If it came now—it must just come! We had none of us, I think,
any apprehension left: or, for that matter, any comprehension of
much more than hanging on and forcing up. In my own case—and a
truthful record of sensation limits me to thinking only of myself—
the capacity to feel or to remark was exhausted. Franz must have
been more nervously alert, for he ground out a devious upward line
through the upheaving of giant slabs without a halt or a false attempt.
I can recall nothing but obscurity, steepness, and an endless driving
of the muscles to their task. Still no message of hope reached us from
above; and yet we must have left another four hundred feet of rib
and crack, snow-ice and equivocal holds below us. Even fancy
dared not whisper to itself of the summit: the next five feet, and still
the next five feet were the end of all effort and expectation.

And then, something was happening! There came a mutter of
talk from the dusk above. Surely two shadows were actually moving
at one time? I was at the foot of a long icy shelf, slanting up
to the right. It was overhung by cliff on the left, as usual. It was
falling away into space on my right, as usual; and it had the usual
absence of any holds to keep me on it. I began the eternal knee-
friction crawl. The rope tightened on my waist. "Shall I pull?"—
called Josef's voice, sounding strange after the hours of silence, and
subdued to an undertone as if he feared that the peak might still hear
and wake up to contrive some new devilment. "Why not?—if you
really can!"—I echoed, full of surprise and hope; and I skimmered
up the trough, to find Josef yoked to a royal rock hitch, the third and
best of the day! And, surely, we were standing on the crest of a great

ridge, materialized as if by magic out of the continuous darkness of cliff and sky? And the big, sullen shadow just above must be the summit! It was indeed the mounting edge of the south-east ridge upon which we had arrived; and sixty feet above us it curled over against the top of the final pyramid. Josef unroped from me, while I brought up little J.; and as we started to finish the ascent together in our old-time partnership, I saw the silhouettes of the other three pass in succession over the pointed skyline of the peak.

We found them, relaxed in spent attitudes on the summit-slabs, swallowing sardines and snow, our first food since half-past seven in the morning. It was now close upon six o'clock. Franz came across to meet me, and we shook hands. "You will never do anything harder than that, Franz!" "No," he said reflectively, "man could not do much more."

The end of the story follows the usual route down hill as easily as we did; and it must hurry down those ten thousand feet as quickly. Little J. and I raced ahead down the evening snow-slopes with the advantage of being only two. Darkness caught us as we reached the moraine at the end of the Kien glacier. We scattered to search for the then new Kien hut, to shelter in for the night. J. found the track to it, but Franz had dashed on ahead and down, and the rest of us were already far enough below to make it unwise to recall us uphill again. We struggled and tumbled down through the precipitous woods, vainly seeking for the subtle evasions of the old Randa path. The candle-lamps proved, as always, consolatory but ineffective. I believe I found the track first, by falling headlong down a bank of pine-roots and alighting on the abrupt surprise of a horizontal surface. On lower alps at night, this is the surest indication that we have hit the path.

Into Randa we trudged at half an hour before midnight, for a genuine meal. And then, leaving the guides to sleep, and to forget all but the greatness of their exploit, Ryan and I started again and drove and walked the long historic miles up to Zermatt. At a quarter past three we began our last dinner and our first breakfast, rounding off a circle of sensation which had lasted twenty-six hours in time, and left some impressions as deeply graven as those of the five later years of war.

Since then Josef, great guide and good comrade, has left us. The incomparable Franz and my own unique little J., I rejoice to think, still head the glorious band of Skt. Niklaus guides. But of the Täschhorn by the south face there has not yet been a re-ascent— or a revised version.

WILLIAM CECIL SLINGSBY

1849–1929

ACCORDING TO HIS OWN RECOLLECTION it was in 1872 that W. C. Slingsby first viewed from a distance the group of unexplored mountains known as the Horungtinder in the Jotunheim (giants' home) region of Norway and resolved to make the first ascent of Skagastölstind, "the grandest European mountain north of the Alps." Thus began a career during which Slingsby, often accompanied by the Norwegian climber Emanuel Mohn, traversed the whole mountain system of Norway and opened the northern playground to sportsmen. Between 1874 and 1912 Slingsby is credited with twenty-four first ascents and new routes; his other expeditions, chiefly for reconnaissance, were far more numerous.

Feeling an "hereditary affinity" for Norway, he not only climbed its mountains but acquired a comprehensive knowledge of all aspects of Norwegian popular life—contemporary, historical, and legendary—and became a self-appointed publicist of that nation's excellences. For thirty-five years he was vice-president of the Norwegian Club of London. He is reputed to have introduced skis, indigenous to Scandinavia, among sportsmen in the Alps. His book *Norway: the Northern Playground* is a work of description and celebration. The Norwegians responded to this active friendship by making Slingsby something of a national hero. Several prominent physical features of the Horungtinder bear his name. He was an honorary member of the major Norwegian mountaineers' club. His daughter, now Mrs. Eleanor Winthrop Young records that on Slingsby's last visit to Norway, made in 1921 to dedicate at Bergen a memorial to the Norwegian fishermen who died in the First World War, "his welcome had the dignity of a royal progress."

Slingsby's exploits in the Alps, from 1878 to 1913, though not pioneering, are also famous. Often in the company of A. F. Mummery, Norman Collie, and Geoffrey Hastings, he specialized in guideless first ascents, then an innovation. In Great Britain he was one of the first to engage in rock-climbing, a sport which did not become popular until some years after Englishmen began frequenting the Alps. His last climbs, undertaken when he was more than seventy, were on severe cliffs in the mountains of the Lake District.

The following selection is reprinted from W. Cecil Slingsby, *Norway: the Northern Playground*, edited by Mrs. Eleanor Winthrop Young, Oxford, Basil Blackwell, Ltd., 1941, by permission of Mrs. Eleanor Winthrop Young.

The Conquest of Skagastölstind

W<small>HEN I UNROLLED MYSELF</small> from my Scotch plaid, and crept from under the sheepskin coverlet at three o'clock, on the morning—ever memorable to me—of Friday, July 21st, 1876, I did not feel that early rising was exceptionally virtuous. How could I do so, when I heard the musical voices of the bright-eyed Live and Oliva calling their cattle to come and give their rich store of morning milk? No, I felt that though Mohn had won his laurels,[1] mine depended on the day before us, and I longed to be up and doing, and to get the most I could out of Knut on this his last day with us, as we had every reason to believe that the ascent of Skagastölstind would prove to be very severe. Vormelid is only about 1600 feet above the fjord at Aardal, and as Skagastölstind is 7874 feet, there was a considerable ascent to be made, in addition to the crossing of a high spur, before the actual base of the mountain could be reached.

Early rising, when mountaineering, is not of such prime importance, in the almost nightless days of July in Norway, as it is in the Alps in the same month; still, when we waved an adieu to our hostesses, we could not help feeling that seven o'clock was at least two hours later than it ought to have been. . . .

Though the barometer had risen during the night, the weather was unpromising, and all the neighbouring heights were enshrouded with dense clouds. Knut said, "You cannot climb anything today," to which I replied, "Possibly not; but we must go and do our best, and for anything we know, the whole of the higher Horungtinder may even now be quite clear above the clouds. . . ."

As Knut was evidently tired, owing to hard work and a succession of bad nights, I engaged to carry both my own rope and one of his, as well as most of the food. A steep, zigzagging cattle path led us easily alongside a fine cataract, the Maradalsfos, into the Maradal, a short valley so far as vegetation is concerned, which is headed by the Maradalsbrae. This is the finest glacier in the range of Horung-

---

[1] Emanuel Mohn, Slingsby, and the guide Knut Lykken made the first ascent of the Gjertvastind.

tinder, and several grand mountains rise out of its cold ice, one being the Gjertvastind, on whose snowy crest we had been the previous day.

At the top of the fos, which is 1295 feet in height, just above the birch-tree limit, and where the dwarf willows begin to grow, we called a halt, nominally to admire the view, but in reality because our limbs and lungs demanded it. Truly it was a fair picture to look upon, the peaceful saeter, with cattle and goats browsing around it in greenest of pastures; the foaming river Utla below, here a tempestuous rapid, there a deep pool; then, beyond the river, crag piled upon crag, terrace upon terrace, where until some rude avalanche shall suddenly come and sweep them away, grow the sombre pines and graceful silvery birches, which blend in most harmonious colours with the purest emerald of the mosses, and the rocks of greyish blue and brown. Other crags, as black as darkest winter's night, formed a strong contrast to the snows, the gauze-like cloud veils, and the milk-white cataracts. Of sunshine there was little, and up the valley, where we were to go, clouds reigned supreme, and left much for our lively imaginations to picture.

A short rest sufficed, and Mohn led us up the valley. . . . A short distance from the glacier we turned to the left, to cross the buttress of Rolandsnaasi, then we descended 314 feet into a valley, which was there and then dubbed the Skoddedal—cloud-valley—where we could not see twenty yards in front of us. The ground was new to us all, and the maps were faulty, so we erected many diminutive cairns to guide us on our return. The weather was decidedly unpromising, we could see nothing, and nearly ran our heads against the base of that grim obelisk, the eastern Maradalstind.

Mohn and I had often noticed that, after being enveloped in thick mist for nearly a whole day, the higher Horungtinder frequently shone out with double beauty late in the afternoon or evening, and we told Knut that such would be the case today, though I fear we thought otherwise.

On nearing the top of a second ridge, 3276 feet above Vormelid, we found that the higher we got, the lighter were the clouds, so I ran forward to the highest point, and saw a most glorious sight.

Across the cloud-filled Midt Maradal were the serrated ridges of the Midt Maradals and the Dyrhougs-tinder, which form a colossal and nearly perpendicular wall between 2000 and 3000 feet in height. The contrast which the top of this black wall showed to the white clouds below was wonderful. I shouted to Mohn and Knut to hurry up, and when they arrived they shared my delight.

Soon after their arrival we saw the trough of Midt Maradal, 1500 feet below us. . . . Clouds again swept up the valley and for a few minutes blotted out the whole of the view. Then a grand and inaccessible-looking peak, a continuation of our ridge, appeared.

"Is that Skagastölstind?" we all exclaimed. We could only see the top, and the clouds lent it such additional grandeur that we had no proper conception of its height, nor of its relative position. It disappeared from our view as quickly as it had come, and all was gloom again once more.

After a minute or two, a truly noble aiguille appeared, a never-to-be-forgotten sight. Further doubt was impossible. This was Skagastölstind, and the former peak, Mohn rightly said, was only one of the Maradalstinder. Another peak then appeared between the two, and for a while each seemed to be floating in clouds. The marvellous panoramic changes caused by the drifting of the cloud curtains are far beyond my descriptive powers. Suffice it to say that we gazed in wonder and bewilderment until the guardian clouds were dissipated, and in a few moments all was clear.

Our excitement and anxiety were intense, as may be easily imagined. No thought of fatigue now. No memory of the meagre fare, the hard beds, and the short snatches of fitful sleep, with which we had perforce been contented during the last ten days. No. Our task lay unfettered before us, and without a word being spoken we began scrambling at noonday down the rugged crags into Midt Maradal.

A walk of a mile or so over horrible débris brought us at one o'clock to the flattened snout of Midt Maradalsbrae, at the actual base of our mountain, and 4396 feet from the top. Here we lunched in the glowing sunshine, and carefully reconnoitred the proposed route. The guiding was all left to me, as Skagastölstind was considered to be my special mountain, though of course I consulted the others.

The grandeur of Midt Maradal is in great measure due to the fact that the lowest pass across the range of the Horungtinder happens to be close to the highest mountain, and entirely cuts it off from its near western neighbours, and this mountain is only connected with the peaks on the eastern side of the pass by a narrow ridge 518 feet below the summit. Hence, too, Skagastölstind possesses a delightful isolation. It rises majestically some 3000 feet above the head of the pass, and out of two fine glaciers, the Midt Maradalsbrae and the Skagastölsbrae on the north side. There is also a much steeper and wilder glacier descending like a cataract of ice from the heights of the eastern range. This glacier skirts the south-eastern walls of Skagastölstind, and Norse mountaineers with the generosity of their race have honored me by associating it with my name. At the time of which I write, this glacier ended abruptly at the top of a line of crags 60 or 70 feet in height, over which their terminal séracs fell, and formed the nucleus of a minute secondary glacier below. The stream which drained the glacier made a waterfall into the snow, and added variety to the wild scene. . . .

I proposed that we should cross the fan of the lower glacier, that we should climb up a little gully between two bosses of rock, which would lead us on to the right bank of our wished-for icy highway, and so gain the glacier itself. In fact, it was our only chance thus late in the day, though a few years later the route entirely by rocks, now almost universally followed, was discovered from the Midt Maradalskar—also called Bandet, the band—on the south-west.

On looking upwards, we saw a narrow belt of dark rocks at the head of the glacier which separates it from a steep snow-slope above. Here we apprehended difficulty, and Knut said, "De kan ikke komme frem der, sneen er alt for brat." (You cannot get forward there, the snow is much too steep.) I replied that it was the only way where there was even a ghost of a chance, and that we must try it. Mohn loyally supported me, as he and I, having both seen the mountain from the north, thought that there was no possibility of climbing it on that side, whilst Knut, who had never been near it before, was inclined to think "our best as bad." The snow-slope leads up at a very steep angle to a gap or skar, rather more than 500 feet from the top, and though from the base we could not see whether it continued farther up the mountain, as it was hidden by a projecting crag, we rather expected a chimney or a friendly ridge to lead from the skar to the summit. The south-eastern face rises almost perpendicularly out of the glacier, so nothing could be done there.

We had no difficulty in crossing the fan of the lower glacier, and soon got up the gully, and on to a spur which separates the two glaciers. Here great caution was required, as the rocks were smooth and steep. We presently reached a snow-patch which we had to cross—where we saw before us footsteps! Crusoe's surprise at finding footprints in the sand could not have much exceeded ours. Horrid thought! "Have we been forestalled?" "Is some unknown party of mountaineers now on the top?" "Surely not; we must have heard if other climbers were in this wild region." A close inspection revealed the fact that they were the fresh tracks of a bear. What Bruin could have been doing up there, out of the way of all vegetation, we could not divine, but there were his traces, quite recent too. Perhaps he too was on a tour of exploration, or possibly we had frightened him the previous day, when we threw stones down the overhanging precipice of the Gjertvastind. He had proceeded in the direction we were taking, and when we reached the glacier a few minutes later, we found his tracks again, and followed them to our advantage, through an intricate maze of crevasses, until they turned off towards the lower crags of Centraltind. . . .

We had some interesting step-cutting through some séracs where a jutting crag contracted the glacier. After this, we turned a little to the left quite under Skagastölstind, which towered proudly 3000 feet above us. Hardly any débris seemed to have fallen from this awful precipice on to the glacier; a good sign for us, which suggested firm rocks above, whilst on the other hand an avalanche thundered down to the far side of the glacier from the ridge above it, and echo answered echo again and again.

Near the top of the glacier, there about 500 yards wide, a large crevasse stretched nearly across. Where we first reached it about the middle of the glacier, it looked like a ravenous, open-jawed monster, awfully deep and ready to swallow a whole Alpine Club. As there were no snow-bridges here, we followed it to the western side where the friction of the rocks had broken down the snowy wall and had partially choked up the crevasse. Here we made sure of crossing. In the best place, however, there was a wall of névé, 12 feet high, above the snow in the crevasse. My companions anchored themselves safely and paid out my rope while I climbed down into the hollow. Twice I cut my way up the wall, but though I cut a dozen large steps, I could not get over on the top, as the snow, at that late hour of the day, was too soft for my ice-axe to hold in, and twice I came down again to the soft snow in my fruitless endeavours. The second time, my feet passed through and revealed uncanny depths and a blue haze which was not reassuring. If the snow had been strong enough to hold a second man safely, we could have got up the wall, as I could have stood on his shoulders and have hacked away a sloping staircase to the platform above. I tried once more, and though I failed, I all but succeeded. For some time, Knut had been calling out "Til höire" (To the right). . . . We retraced our steps and, to our great joy, found a substantial bridge close to the eastern side.

The glacier became steeper, but we soon reached the black belt of rock, where from below we expected to find considerable difficulty or possibly defeat. Fortunately the bergschrund at the head of the glacier and at the foot of the rocks was choked up with a snow avalanche, which gave us a ready-made road on to the rocks.

Though we were still 1114 feet below the summit, Mohn said he felt tired and needed rest. Both of my companions on principle wore boots which were quite innocent of nails or spikes, and in consequence they had found the steep portion of the glacier to be very trying, and they both acknowledged that their theories were wrong, and that Alpine nails were excellent and prevented many a fall.

As it was nearly 5 P.M., and the great tug of war was yet to come on, I said that we could not afford time for a rest, so I untied myself and soon reached the steep snow-slope at the top of the belt of rock. This snow-slope was nearly 600 feet high. As it was partially frozen it required very great care, and an ice-axe was a *sine qua non*. I rather feared the descent of this part, as being in the shade the snow crust was then hardening, the angle was severe, and a fall was not to be thought of. Where the rocks were feasible I preferred them, and left the snow until the rocks were too steep to climb.

An hour after leaving my friends I reached the top of the skar, and then took a look around. On the north or opposite side to that which I had ascended, instead of a friendly glacier or couloir close at hand, there was a grim precipice, and at its base was a glacier, the Skagastölsbrae, the sister to the Midt Maradalsbrae, which projected its icy foot into a mountain tarn, on the placid surface of which many quaint little icebergs were floating. Above the tarn and glacier rose the black precipices of the northern Dyrhougstinder, a grand wall.

Looking towards the true Skagastölstind, 518 feet above the skar, I felt that I was beaten after all, and my dream at an end, as it is difficult to imagine any mountain presenting a more impracticable appearance than is shown at first sight by this peak from the skar. The skar consists of a narrow and flat ridge, perhaps 100 yards in length, of which one end abuts against a huge oblong tower of gabbro, the great peak itself. On the right is the precipice above the tarn, and on the left the base of the tower springs from the glacier which we had ascended nearly perpendicularly and almost entirely without ledges. There seemed to be no proper arête to connect the peak with the skar, and merely a narrow face, mostly consisting of smoothly polished and almost vertical slabs of rock. The first 150 or 200 feet seemed to be the worst, and I thought that if those could be surmounted, the top might be won, but really I did not then think there was the slightest possibility of doing it. Of course there was no snow couloir, as the rocks were much too steep to allow snow to accumulate there in any quantity.

Behind me, and rising some 300 feet at a comparatively gentle angle from the other end of the ridge, was another peak now called Vesle, or the little Skagastölstind. As this seemed to be relatively easy to ascend, and thinking that it was better than none, I set off to climb it before my companions arrived. When I had gone a short way I looked down and saw the others rounding a rock just below the skar, so I hurried down and joined them.

"What do you think of it, Mohn?"

"Well, I suppose that we can now say it is perfectly impossible."

"We have not yet proved it to be so; we must not give it up without a try. Will you come?"

"No."

"Knut, will you?"

"No, I shall not risk my life there."

"I will at least try, though I do not think I can manage it."

Fortunately I was perfectly fresh, and of course had an excellent stimulant in the uncertainty of my enterprise and the delights of entering still further into the unknown; and besides this, it is rarely safe to say that a mountain wall which you have never studied in profile, but have face to face with you, is unclimbable.

I recommended the others to climb the lesser peak—then unascended. Mohn said philosophically, "Aut Caesar, aut nihil." Then I left them and passed under a snow cornice which overhung the northern precipice like a wave arrested when about to break on a shingly beach, and I soon reached the rock wall. Now! farewell to snow, that great aider of mountain ascents, and!—500 feet of cold rock! I found a small buttress projecting from the face of the rock a little to the south of the skar. It formed a corner. Up there I must go or nowhere else: of choice there was none; but still, when viewed closely it looked more hopeful than at the first glance. I soon found that the rocks were firm; the ledges, though so tiny, were secure. The strata of the rock inclined the right way, downward from the out-face towards the centre of the mountain. Better than all, I was quite cool and in perfect training. Still, no trifling must be indulged in here.

After being hidden from my friends by the snow cornice, I came into view again, and every movement was eagerly watched by my well-wishers. Soon I got into difficulties in the corner, and, but for a ledge not so broad as my hand, from which I had to knock away the ice, I should thus early have been defeated, because without the aid of this foothold the mountain, on this side, at least, would be inaccessible. My friends saw me at this place, and vainly tried to call me back, but with the help of my well-tried ice-axe I surmounted the difficulty. I avoid going into details about this and other places, though I made minute notes the following day because if I were to attempt to describe them I should undoubtedly be accused either of exaggeration or perhaps of foolhardiness by readers unaccustomed to alpine work, when at the same time I might be guilty of neither. Suffice it to say that what under the most favourable conditions must be a tough piece of work, was made more so by the films of ice with which every little ledge was veneered. Three times I was all but beaten, but this was my especial and much-longed-for mountain, and I scraped away the ice and bit by bit I got higher and higher. In sight of the others I reached what from the skar we had judged to be the top. I raised a cheer, which was renewed below, when I found that there was a ridge—a knife-edged affair—perhaps sixty yards long, and that the highest point was evidently at the farther end. There are three peaklets, and a notch in the ridge which again almost stopped me. For the first time I had to trust to an overhanging and rather a loose rocky ledge. I tried it well, then hauled myself up to terra firma, and in a few strides, a little over half an hour after leaving my friends, I gained the unsullied crown of the peerless Skagastölstind, a rock table four feet by three, elevated five or six feet above the southern end of the ridge.

As to the view, which was perfectly free from clouds, it would be futile for me to attempt to describe it at length, except to say that on every hand, some of the wildest crags, aiguilles, and glaciers in "Gamle Norge" [Old Norway] looked their very wildest. On one hand, our luncheon place 4307 feet below, seemed to be only a stone's-throw off. On another, below an almost vertical precipice 3000 feet in height, was a portion of the glacier which we had ascended. On another, some 4000 feet down lay the mountain tarn with its icy flotilla, and above it the glacier and terrible cliffs I have before alluded to. Forests and green pastures here and there relieved the scene of most of its harsher characteristics, and in the distance the many beautiful domes and subtle curves of purest snow which together form the great Justedalsbrae showed for a distance of 45 miles from the Kamphammer pass to the snowy heights of Fjaeland, a most lovely and harmonious horizon, a beauty which insensibly grows upon one year after year, and which is seldom appreciated when first seen.

The exquisite colouring for which Norway is so deservedly famous appeared in all its richness and variety; but in such a place, alone, out of sight of every living creature, one of the greatest desires of my heart granted to me, it will be easily understood, when I say that a feeling of silent worship and reverence was more suitable than the jotting down of memoranda in a note-book. The scene was too overwhelming for notes. I longed to have my trusted friend Mohn by my side, and his absence was a bitter disappointment to me. Had he been with me his enthusiasm would have been boundless. . . .

Such was the first ascent of what is usually called the finest mountain in Norway. The illusion of its inaccessibility had been at last dispelled, most probably too at the first determined attack upon its grisly towers, and a solid fact took the place of an ancient fable.

Though the ascent has become a favourite amongst experienced mountaineers, it will never become what in the Alps is termed "a fashionable mountain" for tourists such as those whom one meets at Zermatt, and who are pulled and shoved up fine mountains by indifferent guides. The last bit is too bad for that. I for one would never have attempted alone rocks such as those upon any other mountain, but it was the particular one upon which I had centred my energies, and those 518 feet which I climbed in solitude, I always look back upon with a feeling of veneration. They formed an event in my life which can never be forgotten; and although I have climbed very many of the higher Norse mountains, yet the ascent of none has left such a vivid impression in my mind as this. We had set off in the misty morning with feelings of hope perhaps, certainly not of expectancy. The first portion had been all in clouds, and we were oppressed by doubts; the second was in brilliant sunshine. Success had been granted to me at all events and, better still, a safe return to us all.

DOROTHY E. PILLEY

(Mrs. I. A. Richards)

IN THE PREFACE to *Climbing Days* Mrs. Richards says, "I began to write this book in China, being homesick for European hills. It was a substitute for climbs in Britain and the Alps." The experiences which in this mood she describes with a happy combination of tenderness and verve covered two decades, three continents, and multitudinous pleasures. Like many another excellent climber, she received her early sporting education in the high regions of Great Britain. In southwestern Europe she left little unvisited, having climbed throughout the various Alpine ranges, in the Pyrenees, and in the mountains of Corsica. In the years 1925 to 1927 she tried the opportunities offered by the Canadian Rockies and the Selkirks, by the mountains of Glacier National Park and the Cascade Range, and by the Himalayas near Kanchenjunga.

On many of her trips she was accompanied by her husband, I. A. Richards, also an accomplished mountaineer, although better known as literary critic, semanticist, and deviser of Basic English. Another frequent and favorite companion was the guide Joseph Georges. Indeed, throughout *Climbing Days* persons are easily as important as places and adventures. Mrs. Richards is acutely aware of the heightened rapport existing among mountaineers in their proper habitat and sensitively records the social as well as the athletic pleasures of the sport. Likewise she is aware of the imaginative stimulation which transforms a bodily recreation into significant experience with no loss of simple delight. *Climbing Days* is a specialized autobiography which becomes a testimony.

The following selection is reprinted from Dorothy E. Pilley (Mrs. I. A. Richards), *Climbing Days*, New York, Harcourt, Brace and Company, Inc., 1936, by permission of the author.

Into Spain and Back Again

CORSICA had been so successful that in 1923 we decided to go abroad again for Easter. So off we went, Dorothy Thompson, John Hall Paxton, a new American recruit, and ourselves, to the Pyrenees. On the map the great barrier between France and Spain offers an easy and alluring field to explore. We made scores of plans. In imagination we penetrated all the valleys, ascended all the peaks in that wild romantic country—about which we knew no more than the map and Belloc's books [1] could tell us. In such amiable planning space contracts; time expands like a concertina; handholds are plentiful everywhere; snow bears your weight; difficulties vanish and the weather is always perfect. Soon, alas, our schemes came up against the immutable laws of real mountaineering in late winter conditions. And of that host of dream expeditions a few minor summits and a crossing of the frontier into Spain were alone to materialize. . . .[2]

We made enquiries about guides. Presently there entered François Bernard Salles. How our hearts sank! With crude, unseeing eyes we looked at him. Tall and bowed with a stoop which brought his head far forward of his knees, his shoulders, drawn together, gave him a narrow broken-down appearance. Indefinitely old, worn-out he looked. His hands, gnarled and corded with great veins, drooped low as he sat, fidgeting with his ancient beret. But a grim, peasant strength was in his haggard face, in the great hooked nose, the narrow, high, bony forehead fringed with ragged, short grey hairs, and in the hollow toothless jaws and indrawn burnt-out mouth stained at the corners with tobacco juice.

We looked at one another wildly but sympathetically. His responses to our questions were mainly made up of grunts and *patois* exclamations. Yes, we could get over to Spain if the weather were good. Yes, he could use ski; but why need we worry about them,

---

[1] See Hilaire Belloc, *The Pyrenees* (1909).
[2] In the omitted pages Mrs. Richards recounts the party's leisurely progress to Gavarnie, a frontier village in southern France, Département des Hautes-Pyrénées.

we could get on better without them! If we started at 6 A.M., not later, we could be in Torla by the evening. No need to take provisions with us. Something to eat on the Col, yes; but we could get all we wanted certainly on the other side. He rose and we shook hands, wondering at his gaunt aspect, his strange bony frame poised in a curious way as if he were about to spring. He went and we did not know what to make of him. We might hope for the best but it did not look very promising. At least we could get over and have a look at Spain.

In the morning he surprised us. Between grunts and expectorations we gathered that he could lend one of us (who had been improvident) an axe—he had a spare one. Had we a rope? . . . As we followed him out of the village in the early light over crisp snows, we could see that here was a guide of the old school—one who, instead of displaying his own agility, concentrates rather on setting a steady, rhythmic pace. Salles walked with a masterly gait; it had a strange swing, almost a stumble, in it, which ate up the slopes but never seemed to be fast, was easy to keep up with yet would have been hard to outstrip. Up to the sun we mounted.

The Col de Boucharou (or Port de Gavarnie) is a long trough in its upper regions, flanked by fine peaks, the Gabiétous and Taillon on the left, beyond them, on the French side, the Cirque de Gavarnie, the Pyramide and Mont Perdu—great limestone precipices banded with shelves of glacier. There is an easy, frequented mule-track here in summer, but now all the hollow valleys and all the slopes, except the sheer rock walls, were deeply clad in snow. We mounted smoothly. The perfect day wore on, but not faster than our journey. Up the long floor of the trough in well-judged tracks with a few steeper zigzags at its head, we followed; exhilaration, hope and a sense of well-being steadily growing greater.

On the top the old man was pleased, unmistakably. In the brilliant sunlight he looked even older, sixty-five we thought, as he grunted with satisfaction. We made out he was telling us that it was an extraordinarily beautiful day and that we had come very fast, much faster than usual, and that the snow was good. The snow indeed was perfect, firm to walk on and crisp, so that granules of ice chased each other over the Port with a scurrying sound. Above us the gloss on the ice of the Gabiétous was almost too bright to contemplate in the sunny, limpid air.

Beyond was Spain, the country we had longed to see. It stretched in a deep valley at right angles to the one we had ascended, though we had no sight yet of the ground below the snow-line. Opposite, limestone ranges sharp but tremulous in the brightness of the early sunshine stretched away, more and more yellow, into the distance.

Soon, wishing to escape the wind, we set out again at a little run bearing along and around the hollow curves of the flank of the Gabiétous. Suddenly brown leafage poked up over the edge of the snow-drifts, and we were in a bare, tawny, grassless region where box bushes grew in tangled masses and a narrow stony path, cut by water channels from the melting snows, led steeply down to a wasted, trench-like valley far below. Through this, like a twisted ribbon, wound a river bordered on either side by burnt-out levels. Nowhere was there any sign of life. Nothing below the snows but the reddish earth, red rocks and dark patches of the box bushes. Heat struck up from the ground; a full, almost pungent scent rose from it—aromatic, southern, a smell of Spain.

We ate, and drank from the streams and from the wine gourd— that rank drink tasting of goat and tar grows upon one with experience. Then we went down and round the corner. Boucharou appeared. We had heard much about this "village." Here, so Salles said, we were to find all we could want; wine, bread, sausage and cheese. Now we saw it—a barn-like hovel with an unfinished stone building beside it. Picturesque certainly but hardly encouraging to our hopes of pastoral banquets.

Between us and it a narrow humped-backed bridge spanned the river. We went down, to be struck at once, when we reached the level, by a hot blast which seemed to rush out of the ground. Much conversation now ensued between Salles and a number of men; a confused, prolonged grunting from him, violent gestures from them. An old, very dirty patriarch appeared, dressed exactly like a pirate, a red handkerchief about his brow, and white, strangely clean expansions of linen hanging out at his knees and flapping about his calves.

We were glad to go inside into the cool darkness and were led upstairs to the main dwelling-room. This was a large space surrounding a central, blackened, circular chimney-shaft through which, thirty feet above, the sunlight could be seen slanting diagonally downwards and shining through the little streamers of soot which clung to its wide stone cowl and supporting pillars. A small fire was burning, its wisp of smoke spiralling up through the sunrays. Three days later we were to see all this under very other circumstances. A suppressed disappointment fell on the party on account of the non-appearance of the promised baskets of fresh fruits and cold delicacies. True, we were given anisette, said by some to be a cooling and refreshing drink, and we bought a piece of garlic sausage which looked so terrible that we all silently and independently resolved to leave it to Salles—who devoured it with avidity.

Down the valley the heat increased out of all measure. We could understand now why the landscape looked so bare, yet it was only April. Only the dark box bushes throve; they surrounded us as we went on, following the winding, deep-worn, narrow path towards the forests. We passed a chapel set high on a knoll and almost hidden by surrounding fir trees, and in time came into the shadow of a cliff beside the river, now foaming through a series of rapids. Here hours passed. When at last it seemed as though it must be cooler we went on, stumbling along a stony way which wandered round shoulder after shoulder of the hills, sometimes with great drops and overhangs below—gorges where the river disappeared in roaring plunges, and always with greater and greater precipices rearing themselves above us.

At last a final shoulder threw us out to where, commanding the opposite side of the ravine, we could look over it and into the main valley soaked with a rich, stain-like sunshine. Black, small and remote, upon a slight rise in its midst, stood Torla, a huddled patchwork of roofs above low walls, rising in the centre to a square, dark tower. Green meadows lay about it; beyond, to a vague horizon, an unbounded corridor stretched between declining hills. At our feet a bridge—the Pont des Navarrais—stretched across the gulf. Up to our left another higher-level valley ran back at right angles, walled (few other valleys have so strict a right to the word as the Val d'Arazas) on both sides by mind-shaking ramparts of smooth, sheer limestone, banded in ochre and russet; streaked, where streams dissipated themselves into air upon them, with black and purple. Every shelf and all their crests were overlaid with snow. . . .

Our programme was to go up to Ordesa in the Val d'Arazas and round the Mont Perdu to the cabane behind it. Failing that, a return to Gavarnie by the Brèche de Roland would have satisfied us. But the next day was filled with a queer lassitude. We wandered, listlessly, up into the Val d'Arazas—the primroses and violets by the wayside were unusually beguiling. What odd things one remembers. Our American friend surprised us by saying that there were no primroses in America! At the opening of the valley a whole forest was lying flat—cast down by the wind-pressure of an avalanche which had not reached them. Higher up a deep clear pool attracted us irresistibly. The icy shock of our dip was followed by a dreadful lazy faintness. Bathes in the heat on the way *up* anything are a temptation to be resisted. So we lay about on the grass while Salles spent half an hour hiding the rucksacks from the chance discovery of any Spanish "brigand" (i.e. peasant) who might pass. He found it necessary to cut down a whole grove and replant them over the bulgy sacks before he was fully satisfied! Then we lit a giant bonfire and toasted ourselves round it in the woodlands before turning back to Ordesa. This is two small whitewashed cottages standing on a grassy knoll under some of the most appalling cliffs in the world. We went to bed, dragging ourselves away reluctantly from one of those wood fires which by themselves make a Pyrenean journey worth while.

We awoke in the morning with a sense of bewilderment that turned to dismay. The ceilings of our rooms shone with a "strange, unheavenly glare." Leaping up, we saw snow all about the little house—snow not in any sprinkling but in beds and layers. All day long it rose higher and higher. The wind moaned and roared, and two-thousand-foot-high cataracts of snow-dust fell from time to time from the almost invisible cliffs opposite. By evening the problem of returning to France had become serious. But we had hardly any alternative. For two of our party time was up. The only other route, by the Canfranc tunnel, meant two days lost and trouble and delay for lack of passports. After much discussion we resolved to attempt the recrossing of the Col de Boucharou, though we knew it would be no easy matter.

At dawn we set out through a blanched, obliterated world. Nothing to be seen through the veil of falling particles. The new snow filled in the gaps between the lower bushes and covered them leaf by leaf with little soft light heaps which clung to one another. To step through them or between them was much the same. Here and there a clump of trees had kept the ground clearer, and the dark pine-needles, showing through, might be an indication of a path. We went on steadily, almost swiftly, winding without halts downwards across the broken hillside. A stumble broke the silence from time to time: broke rather the steady, low roar of river and wind which seemed to come up heavily to the ears and blurred. With his coat collar turned up, Salles appeared more bent forwards than ever. He seemed all the time as though screwing himself through some narrow place, head down, shoulders drawn, legs bowed and knees bent, feet together.

After a while we turned more steeply down—there was less snow here—and came out at the bridge from which we had first seen Torla. There was little to be seen now as we took the upward way to Boucharou—except coloured rocks rising into a yellow opaqueness out of which snow-flakes steadily silted downwards, the darkness of the roaring gulfs below and the laden, uneasy forest trees. As we rose again we began to take notice of the wind. At times the boughs above us would thrash together, swinging and swaying with a hoarse angry sound and brushing thick clouds of accumulated snow from their needles to fall in blinding showers. Above the nearer noises we could hear—high, sustained, almost note-like in quality—the prolonged rushing of the gale against the upper ridges. The same thoughts were in all our minds.

Above the gorges, where the forest gives way to open, bush country, the wind seemed less menacing. From time to time wild white clouds of snow-dust would sweep by, twisting and writhing upon themselves and sucking up all loose snow from the ground to pile it up in the sheltered sides of bushes so that the path became almost free. With the cessation of the forest noises our hopes rose.

We were warm, making quick progress, and Boucharou was at hand to retreat to, if need be, from the upper reaches. It was true that, even at the clearest moment, only a beginning of vague slopes rising into impenetrable obscurity showed; but the snowfall seemed to be diminishing, or were the flakes merely passing by more thickly at a higher level overhead? We did not know, but cheered by the now near loom of the houses we pushed on rapidly, enjoying that peculiar pleasure which people who have been out enduring a storm feel at the thought of encountering fireside folk.

Inside, a truly Pyrenean fire was blazing. Half a dozen four-inch saplings were laid together across the wide dogs in the middle of the room and piled high with lighter pieces and bits of charcoal. As it burnt, the numerous population, crouching on low stools, pushed the wood forward, sending swarms of sparks upwards to the wide aperture above, through which fell to meet them a ceaseless stream of snowflakes, dwindling and vanishing before they reached the flames. An occasional hiss would indicate the survival of a giant. Through the aperture the wind entered, catching the smoke streams and whirling them in spiral about the chimney. However, few of these gusts got into the room, which was astonishingly free from smoke. Here amid three generations of mountain dwellers we sat to dry ourselves, to eat a little and to listen to the storm outside. The prospects of crossing, we presumed, were the topic of conversation. Not a phrase was intelligible. Even gestures—we were watching Salles closely now—meant little. They consisted of shrugs for the most part, accompanied by grunts of violent though entirely vague emphasis.

Suddenly Salles turned, and without any diminution of his grunts made a statement in his patois: *"Moi, ughah, ça m'est égal! Périr là haut, ça m'est égal. Moi, je suis vieux ughah! J'ai vécu, mais vous, ughah, vous êtes jeunes, deux jeunes demoiselles périr là haut dans la neige! C'est dommage!"*

The choice appeared grave.

We did not know what to decide. From time to time it seemed that the wind might be dropping, but soon its flurrying would begin again. In the end we agreed to start, taking with us a Spaniard, who might be supposed to know his own side of the pass, sloping up as it did from his very doorstep, and thus should have been an added strength to our party.

He began by calling to his aid a singularly light-headed and incompetent dog who gambolled about in the most carefree fashion in and out of the track—pushing past us in the awkward trough which we were ploughing through deep snow-drifts. The next moment he would get lost and have to be called in by his master, most of whose small energy was dissipated in strident shoutings and whistles. Encumbered by a flapping overcoat, he took turns with Salles at breaking the track, already no easy business. As we mounted it became more and more arduous. Sometimes for a few yards we would find a streak of hard surface which the wind had swept clear of power-snow, crusted, glistening and slippery. But in a few steps we would be in the waves again, plunging thigh-deep through an element which offered no resistance except when we tried to extricate ourselves or to advance. In the brief trances of the blast we could see dimly a circle twenty yards across of streaky white surface ending in mist. Then the wind would begin again, the circle would close in, and we would be drowned in a whirling tide of hard, stinging particles. Eyes closed, half choking, we could only just stagger on against it.

After a time the slope steepened and we came to a halt. The Spaniard had already complained a good deal of cold. We had in fact to lend him our gloves. Now it appeared, through Salles' disgusted gruntings, that the Spaniard was afraid; he wished to return home to safety. Salles was doubtful himself and was scrutinizing his party for signs of fatigue. *"Ça va? Hein? Faut essayer encore? Que pensez vous?"* The dog had long ago given up the expedition and returned, reasonably, to the fireside. How often during the hours that followed we were to envy him! After a moment we sent the Spaniard after his dog, rather relieved to be rid of him.

We were now, we reckoned, about half-way to the pass. Though the old man showed no signs of flagging, it was time to relieve him of some of the toil, and from now on we all took turns at going ahead. The drifts became deeper. It was often no longer possible to walk. The only way to make even a yard of progress up the slope was in a peculiar spread-eagled, frog-like position. Sometimes we crawled on all-fours for a hundred yards together, trying desperately to keep on the surface of the yielding welter by spreading our weight upon shins and elbows. Every few moments the blast which roared endlessly overhead would drop upon us, and the slope would dissolve into a race of white writhing smoke that seemed to eat one's skin. All sense of where we were and even of what we were doing vanished at these moments. A lull would come and we toiled on.

Every fifty yards, at most, a new leader was required. Following exhaustedly behind in the track, we waited for our turn to come again; changing slowly from a feeling that another step as leader was impossible to the sense that after all there was not much difference between going first and following! But we realized that Salles' spells ahead were longer than we could any of us achieve. Buried to the hips or flopping like a huge frog on the billowy surface that old man seemed to belong to a race of giants. His strides were immense and unfaltering. His hunched shoulders seemed to bore into the storm. We gradually grew to feel a puzzled wonder at his stamina. He had seemed to us, on account of his age, a liability. Now we felt instead a thankful reliance in his strength.

At last the drifted snow thinned; we could walk again, and with a final zigzag we came to the pass itself and a glimpse of downward stretching snow-slopes in place of the blank unending whiteness into which we had been pushing. It was time: one at least of the party, less experienced than the others, had been feeling that despair which precedes breakdown, and a collapse here would have been a desperate business. How transformed from the gentle walk of two days before.

We plunged down in a completely changed mood, thinking that now our troubles were nearly over. One thinks indeed that downhill over easy slopes one can always contrive to travel somehow. It took perhaps half an hour to disillusion us! On the French slope the drift was even deeper and seemed even stickier. The downhill going drove our feet in still further, and our spells at leading became shorter and more exhausting. It is a strange experience to lie in the snow unable to take another step, to know that prostration must come again and again before there is relief.

Half-way down, on a little hummock, stands a Pyrenean cabane. It had brightened our imaginations for hours with a promise of shelter and rest. But it bore no resemblance to any of the cabanes of the Alps. Not high enough to stand up in, built of loose stones and roofed with insecure slabs and more used by sheep than by men even in autumn, it offers little protection and no comfort. Yet we reached it at last almost with a sense of home-coming. Aften ten minutes' rest a chill struck which drove us out shaking from head to foot. We had to go on or collapse.

The wind at this lower level had moderated. Up above in the dim, white, cloud-hidden heights it was still howling. We held fast to the thought that it must be packing the new snow above fairly tight, for we had now to cross the mouths of many gullies to emerge out of the funnel of the valley on to the more open slopes above Gavarnie. It was a place evidently much exposed to avalanches. Following in the track, we had ample time to gaze up into the vagueness above and imagine the drifts piled up on tilted ledges which hung above us ready to fall. Across the gullies we moved singly. By so doing we ran less risk of disturbing the equilibrium of the slope, and there would be some left to dig out the engulfed should anything happen. The danger under the circumstances was not too great, and it was carefully weighed. If the weather had been clearing up it might have been prohibitive. The place has a bad name, and the tales of lost Spaniards which we heard that evening in the village made us feel lucky.

Beyond, on the wider, gentler slopes which hang over Gavarnie, we thought once more we had reached the end of our toiling. Again we were tricked. But now it was more exhaustion than the depths of the drifts which held us up. We were tired as no ordinary mountain expedition in fair weather can tire climbers of some experience. We found ourselves back in a state familiar to those wandering for the first time in mountains. There below loomed the valley, blackness working unevenly through the mist. Now and then, as the wind cleared it away, we could even see the village church and separate houses, and after a while, lights glimmering here and there in windows. We toiled on and they seemed to come no nearer. A kind of impatience and fretfulness which belongs only to one's very first expeditions assailed us. Our legs seemed to have become the wrong kind of things for walking downhill. Even Salles, fighting through the snow to the last with an energy worth all the rest of us put to-gether, seemed to feel the same weakness. We limped and lumbered down, stumbling and slipping. When the snow ceased at last and we came to grass and scree, we went no better; we had almost reached the limit of our resources.

As we joined the valley path two men came out unexpectedly, looking like two ravens in long black cloaks that trailed the ground. They stood and watched us with curiosity. One of them was Salles' grandson, that year's champion ski-runner of the Pyrenees. He greeted his grandfather in a peculiar fashion. [Charles Stuart] Cal-verley was once asked by the Dean of his College how he regarded the Decalogue. Not knowing precisely what it was, he replied, "With feelings of reverence mingled with awe." It seemed to be with similar feelings that François Bernard Salles was regarded by his grandson. But it was no uncertainty that inspired these feelings. Later on, rested and refreshed, and sitting in a glow of congratula-tions by the fireside, we had it impressed upon us that no other man in the valley would have dreamed of crossing the Port in such weather. He had done it before when younger, but no other guide had cared to risk the expedition. We enquired his age and were told that he was seventy-two.

Already in his own valley he is a legendary figure round whom tales of exploits worthy of Samson or Milo of Crotona have gathered. We had seen enough ourselves to credit them without difficulty. Mr. Haskett-Smith tells the story of how a stove which no one else could lift was carried by him up the Vignemale to one of Count Russell's grottoes. All the other porters had gone off with lighter loads. Salles looked at the stove a moment, then went off to collect a load of wood with which to fill it! "What's the use of a stove without wood?" he had demanded. And there were other tales. How a mule which collapsed under too heavy a load on a cliff path had been caught as it fell and hoisted back into safety by him alone. How it was he, when no one else could, who had taken the great bronze Virgin up to the Touquerou. Today's performance, they said, was just like him!

Sitting by the great log fire listening to the hiss of the still falling snow in the wide chimney we thought of what would have happened if he had not been so remarkable. The chill of the cabane, though now a distant memory, had lost none of its vividness. With an ordinary man we should still have been there if lucky; or, if unlucky, in the snow on the Spanish side. The thought was sobering. That night we went to bed with a profound feeling of respect towards the grand old man who had preserved us from that necessity. An epic figure from a vanished age.

JAMES BRYCE

(VISCOUNT BRYCE OF DECHMONT)

1838–1922

YEARS BEFORE HE DIED James Bryce had become an international institution. His honors were as many and diverse as his accomplishments. Throughout the world and particularly in America and the United Kingdom his name signified triumphs as historian, student of political institutions, teacher, and diplomat. He was one of the most successful of British ambassadors to the United States, for, not content with the knowledge which had enabled him to write *The American Commonwealth*, he visited every state, participated in every variety of public function, and won the affection of the nation.

The energy, intelligence, and good fortune by which he achieved renown enabled him also to be an eager and observant traveler. And wherever he traveled, if possible, he climbed—among the hills of Great Britain, in the Alps, the Dolomites, the Pyrenees, the Carpathians, in the Caucasus. Even remote mountains, such as Hekla in Iceland and Mauna Loa in Hawaii, claimed his attention. He neither sought new and dangerous ascents nor scorned the easy. His taste was catholic, for climbing was to him not the tyrannizing end of all travel but an activity enjoyable in itself and proper for an inquisitive man. It served the enlightened curiosity which Sir Frederick Pollock believed his primary motivation in all his affairs. Nonetheless, his achievements in mountaineering commanded the respect of the Alpine Club. He was elected to membership in 1879, and served as president from 1899 to 1901, having been proposed by his friend and climbing companion Sir Leslie Stephen. Proud of the honor, Bryce was a very active leader and spoke often to the club in addresses which, in the opinion of Pollock, "were perhaps the most alive of his writings." The quality of his love of mountains is revealed most clearly in the valedictory delivered on his retirement from the presidency: "No future generation will find any pleasure more pure or more intense than that which we . . . have drawn from the days and nights we have spent among the mountains, with the silence of the snow-fields around us and the waterfalls faintly calling from the valleys beneath, in the solemn presence of Nature." Lord Bryce's monument is fittingly permanent, the triple-peaked mountain in British Columbia which bears his name.

The following selection is reprinted from James Bryce, *Transcaucasia and*

Ararat, Fourth Edition, London, Macmillan and Co., Ltd., 1896, by permission of the executors of the late Lady Bryce.

The Ascent of Ararat

A T 8 A.M. on the morning of the 11th of September [1876] we set out from Aralykh to ascend the mountain.[1] We had arranged to start at sunrise, knowing how terrible the heat would be for the first part of the road, but to get a large party under way is always troublesome, and certainly not least so in these countries, where there is no sense of the value of time, and no conception of the conditions of a successful mountain expedition. Indeed, what with the collecting of the soldiers, the packing of provisions, the hundred little things that occur to one's mind at the last moment—a compass, snow spectacles, warm gloves, and, above all, the indispensable lemons—more than three hours would have been consumed had we been in any hands but those of our genial and energetic host. The last thing was to write a few lines home, wondering what the next lines would have to report, and then we filed out of the cantonment amid adieux and good wishes given in strange tongues. We were nine in all, six soldiers of the Cossack detachment, the gentleman who had undertaken to interpret, and our two selves.[2] The soldier in command was a Kurd named Jaafar, a man of great mental as well as bodily force, in whom the colonel [3] reposed full confidence, and whose singularly keen and expressive glance made us wish that we could have held some direct communication with him. Remembering that on the same day of the year, five years before, I had started to climb the Schreckhorn, and three years before the Maladetta, it amused me to think how unlike this cavalcade of ours was to the parties of loud-voiced Englishmen and stalwart guides that issue from an

[1] Great Ararat (16,916 feet) is on the boundary line between Iran and Turkey.
[2] Bryce's companion was Aeneas Mackay (1839–1911), an old college friend.
[3] Colonel Shipshef, commander of the Russian garrison at Aralykh.

Alpine inn before daylight to "do" some stimulating peak or pass. We were all mounted, though certainly on no fiery chargers, and might rather have been taken for a reconnoitring or marauding party, sent to plunder some village across the Persian border, which lay six miles off. The Cossacks were of course fully armed and equipped, while my friend and I, in addition to pistols stuck in the belt, brandished heavy ice-axes, the management of which, together with that of the bridle and a big white umbrella, required some dexterity. An umbrella and a horse do seem rather incompatible, not only with one another, but with a mountain ascent; but we would willingly have looked even more ridiculous for the sake of some protection against the fiery shower of beams that descended from the cloudless sky, and was reflected from the whitish wastes over which we took our way.

We were traversing, in a southerly direction, the outermost and extremely gentle slope of Ararat, a region of fine sand or hard yellowish clay, covered with dwarf, prickly, almost leafless bushes, but no grass, and with no creatures save butterflies and lizards of every hue scuttling about. Each mile was like the last; the want of landmarks on the almost level expanse prevented us from noticing our progress; and the air was so clear that, when we had marched for three hours, the mass of the mountain seemed no nearer than it had done from Aralykh. Looking up the smooth and featureless slope, we had, of course, grossly underestimated the distance which separated us from the base of the cone. Such heat we had never felt before. Probably it was only the thrice blessed umbrellas that saved us from a sunstroke, since we had no better head protection than light felt wide-awakes, whereas the Cossacks cover their solid skulls with thick caps of sheepskin. Yet it was not an enervating heat: the air had that fresh stimulating quality which is said to make travelling in the Arabian desert so healthy; and the sight of the glittering peak above, which was now, like an Eastern beauty, beginning to draw over its face the noonday veil of cloud, seemed to shoot a thrill of coolness through our burning veins.

After a time the ground became rougher as we came to a region where winter torrents had cut deep gullies in the volcanic soil; the slope, too, grew steeper, and the air was fresher as we mounted, while a stray cloud or two, detached from the mountain, deigned us a passing shadow as it sailed across the blue. About noon we were fairly on the side of Ararat himself, and felt that every step was a gain. Here there projects from the body of the mountain . . . a huge rounded, dome-shaped spur or buttress, 7091 feet in height, and evidently formed by eruptions from one or more volcanic vents rising through it. . . . Its name is Takjaltu, not to be confounded with another Takjaltu much farther to the north-west, in the upper Araxes valley. We made for the point where this mass joins Great Ararat, following a path which mounts between them, and crosses a succession of rocky ridges that descend steeply from the east side of the latter.

Pursuing our way along the hillside, we had to dip into more than one rocky ravine, but nowhere was there a stream at the bottom: everything dry as a chalk down in Sussex. This path brought us out on a little grassy plain, hemmed in by two of these ridges, and on the third or eastern side by the heights of Takjaltu, where to our surprise several tiny fields appeared, and one or two men and women at work in them, with a cluster of huts, built of stones and earth, standing near. Jaafar rode across to the men to inquire if any Kurds could be got to take our baggage up the mountain, on the backs of oxen, while we halted in the hope of a drink from the well that was said to be somewhere near. At last a man came, carrying a rude bowl, but as it was filled with liquid mud instead of water, we preferred thirst. The men were Kurds, and this was one of their few autumn or spring settlements on the mountain. As it lies 6000 feet or more above the sea, they do not stay in it through the winter: at this season they were beginning to descend hither from the higher pastures. Remounting, we continued to coast round the mountain towards the south, scaling several more of the black rocky ridges that descend its flank, the path being in some places so steep and rugged that we were obliged to dismount and lead the horses. Among these rocks there grew rose-bushes enough to have inspired all the poets of Persia. They were pretty even in berry, but imagine what the scene must be in July, when the whole mountain-side is gay with these delicate pink blossoms, whereof I saw only one left now in September, and the sweet scent fills the keen mountain air. On rounding the last ridge, the conical peak of Little Ararat came in view, its base about two miles distant, across an open slope, and just beneath us, nestling under the ridge, was a Kurdish encampment. . . . To slake our thirst, they brought us bowls of sourish milk mixed with water, a frequent drink in these countries, and we found it refreshing, if less palatable than the fresh milk of a Swiss *chalet*.

Five minutes' more riding up the grassy slope brought us to the spot for which we had so often, and latterly, time drawing on, so anxiously, inquired, the well of Sardarbulakh. As the only high permanent camping-ground on the mountain, and the place which will be chosen for an alpine hotel, if such a thing ever comes into existence on Ararat, Sardarbulakh is entitled to a few words of description. It stands nearly in the middle of a wide semicircular valley, or rather a sloping plain, between the two Ararats. Towards Great Ararat, which bears about west, the ground rises, at first gently, then steeply, in a series of rocky ridges of nearly equal height, separated by long, narrow hollows, and mostly running nearly west-north-west and east-south-east. About five miles, as the crow flies, from this plain these ridges merge in the great cone, whose summit may be some six or seven miles from Sardarbulakh in a straight line through the air, though more than twice that distance to walk.

On the opposite or south-south-east side of this small plain, Little Ararat springs up 5000 feet, in an almost perfect truncated pyramid, with steep, smooth sides, grassy, except where they are seamed by deep cuts, running from top to bottom, into the sand and gravel with which those smooth sides are covered. Its base may be two, its top about four, miles distant in a straight line drawn along the earth. If Great Ararat is the most majestic, Little Ararat may claim to be the most elegant of mountains; the eye is never tired of its beautiful lines. The two peaks are connected by a rough-topped ridge which forms the back of the sloping plain I have described, and also marks the frontier between the Russian and Turkish empires. . . .

The height above the sea of this sloping plain varies from 8818 feet . . . to 7000 feet; and Sardarbulakh in the middle is 7514 feet. Its lumpy volcanic hillocks—I have called it a plain, but it is far from being level—are covered with good grass; and about a mile

off, near the foot of Little Ararat, appears the only bit of wood on
the whole mountain—a grove of low birches, whose dimensions
the wasteful Kurds are rapidly reducing. Near the birch trees is a
sort of subterranean village, huts formed by hollowing out the
ground and laying a few boughs, covered with turf, across the top,
through which comes such light as can penetrate. These huts are
often uninhabited: I fancy it is mostly when cold weather comes
on that the Kurds take to them. There is a tale told that they were
once an Armenian village, inhabited by people whom the Sardar
had transported hither, but who forsook the place when his power
ended. Sardar, or Sirdar, a name with which Anglo-Indians are
familiar, means general or governor, and was the title of the Persian
governor of Erivan. Sardar-bulakh is therefore translated as the
Sardar's well. It is, of course, the presence of drinkable water that
has made the Kurds and Cossacks fix themselves here, for (as has been
said already) there is no other constant spring nearer than the
valley of Arguri, four hours' journey. Probably some Persian vice-
roy may have stationed a garrison here in the old days when they
carried on constant wars with the Turk. A pleasanter frontier post
to be sent to out of the hot valley of the Aras could not be imagined;
exquisitely keen fresh air, noble prospects over the plains and mountains to the east, and a superb peak on either hand. It is just the place
which those who love the Riffel or the Aeggischhorn would enjoy.
However, we thought little more of these charms than probably
the Persian officers did long ago, when they grumbled at being
banished from the luxuries of the city, for it was two o'clock, and
we were still many hours from the base of the cone. Every one who
had spoken to us about the ascent had wound up with the same advice: "Whatever chance of success you have . . . depends on your
sleeping very high up, close to the snows, and starting before dawn to
try the main peak." Knowing that we were out of training, and that,
as we should have to find our own way up, plenty of time would be
needed, we recognised the force of this advice, and were most anxious
to get to the foot of the cone, a point 11,000 feet high, by nightfall.
To push straight on was impossible, for horses could go no farther,
and the Cossacks absolutely refused to carry even the few things we
needed for a bivouac; it was therefore necessary to procure Kurds for

the purpose, and that was a slow business. Minutes and half-hours slipped away while they were being found and brought to Jaafar, who had been charged by the colonel with the arrangements for our expedition. When they came, the bargaining began, and that seemed interminable. We knew nothing of what was going on, for even with Jaafar, who spoke Russian, we could not communicate directly, and were, of course, one remove further from the Kurds, whose tongue the companion who was interpreting did not understand.

It is always vexatious to be checked by difficulties and delays of merely human origin in a mountain expedition; and here we were in full sight of our goal, the glorious snows seeming to beckon us on, while the minutes which might make all the difference to success were being wasted in wranglings we could not abridge or even understand. Once or twice we struck in to urge that, at all hazards and whatever the cost a start should be made; but to little purpose, for the Kurds, like true children of nature, found difficulties in every course proposed, and were, as far as I could make out, not so much pleased by the prospect of earning what to them was a fortune as anxious to improve the occasion by squeezing out more. Perhaps the idea of working at all was distasteful to them: one generally finds in wild and simple people a greater disposition to prefer their inclination to their interests, and in particular more disinclination to earn money by doing anything they are not accustomed to, than in civilised man. Jaafar's plan had been to send our baggage on the backs of Kurdish oxen as far up as a place which they call the Hermitage, where, however, there is no anchorite's cell, but only a grassy hollow among the rocks with sometimes a little water, and let us either sleep there, 2000 feet higher than Sardarbulakh, or else, leaving the animals there, get on as much farther as we could before nightfall.

But these discussions had now brought us to half past four o'clock. At least half an hour more would be consumed in packing and preparations for departure. There would then remain little more than an hour's daylight to reach a higher camping ground, where, of course, we should have much less chance to sleep than here below in the tent which the Cossacks had vacated for us. Yielding, therefore, most unwillingly to circumstances, and believing that we were practically abandoning our chances for the morrow, I suggested that we should remain and sleep at Sardarbulakh, and make a start upwards as soon as the moon rose, shortly after midnight. This idea, like anything which delayed a move, was accepted. Jaafar engaged four Kurds to go with us and carry what baggage we had, some wrappings to sleep in, and a little food—it would have been a load for one Swiss porter and a half—and told off no less than seven Cossacks to act as a guard, not merely a guard of honour, it seemed, but an actual guard to defend us against these four ferocious Kurds, who looked to me wild indeed, but by no means terrible. However, so it was settled. Whether, having really no say in the matter, we ventured to suggest that seven Cossacks were not needed, I hardly remember, but believe we were told that the Cossacks refused to go at all unless they were allowed to go in that number. The terrors of the mountain and the Kurds would have been too great for a smaller detachment. . . .

When our plans for the ascent had been settled there was just time for a stroll up the slope towards the pass leading to Bayazid. I scrutinised the south-east face of the great cone, which looked in the marvellously clear air much nearer than it turned out to be, and sketched out mentally a line of attack for the morrow. Clouds still clinging to the summit made it difficult to say whether there might not be impracticable precipices in the upper part. There was, of course, no light to be had from either Kurds or Cossacks: the former never go higher than the limits of pasture, and the latter have no motive to go nearly so high. One could therefore only rely on the general structure of the ridges, which seemed to promise a route either up the edges of the snow-beds or along the rocky crests that rose between them. Returning at sunset to the tent, we found some Cossacks sent out to meet us by the watchful Jaafar, who feared we might be picked off by stray marauders, and looked rather reproachfully at us for having gone forth alone. It was very odd: I suppose now that there really may have been a risk, but the habit of security was so strong that, in gazing round on those silent slopes, we could no more expect robbers than we could have done on the Wengern Alp.

Supper was prepared, the Cossacks cooking theirs and ours in a big pot over a fire kindled on the hillside, which lit up their figures and the still more picturesque figures of the Kurds, who crouched round it just like the brigands in an opera scene. The Russian has a turn for cooking; the Cossack, though his taste may be less refined, rivals to Zouave in the power of getting on in a bivouac. After the meal, which consisted of boiled mutton and milk, both procured from the Kurds, we had some of the unfailing tea, and lay down for a little sleep. Four years before we had shared a tent under the snow-storms of Iceland, an experience which somewhat diminished the romantic pleasure young travellers find in life under canvas. Here, to be sure, we were twenty-five degrees nearer the equator; but then we were 7500 feet above the sea, with a breeze shaking the tent walls and forcing us to cover down their bottom, piling up stones and hay outside, and to turn every shred of clothing into account. One feels little inclined for sleep on these occasions; we stayed long outside watching the Cossacks and the stars, by whose light it was just possible to make out the lines of Little Ararat in front. The silence of the mountain was astonishing. No calling of torrents to one another, such as one hears in the Alps, no rippling of rills or rustling of boughs, not even the noise of a falling stone, only the whistling of the west wind, the home wind, over the pass. About nine we crept into the tent and fell asleep. Waking at midnight, which was lucky, for the rest were deep in sleep, we roused them by degrees, and packed up what we needed, while they gathered the food and the rugs as well as they could in the darkness, making four bundles, one for each Kurd. The moon had risen over the Karabagh mountains beyond Aralykh, but she was so far gone in waning that there was only sufficient light to see a yard or two around you.

About 1 A.M. we got off, thirteen in all, and made straight across the grassy hollows for the ridges which trend up towards the great cone, running parallel in a west-north-westerly direction, and enclosing between them several long narrow depressions hardly deep enough to be called valleys. The Kurds led the way, and at first we made pretty good progress. The Cossacks seemed fair walkers, though less stalwart than the Kurds; the pace generally was better than that with which the Swiss guides start. However, we were soon cruelly undeceived. In twenty-five minutes there came a steep bit, and at the top of it they flung themselves down on the grass to rest.

So did we all. Less than half a mile farther, down they dropped again, and this time we were obliged to give the signal for resuming the march. In another quarter of an hour they were down once more, and so it continued for the rest of the way. Every ten minutes' walking—it was seldom steep enough to be called actual climbing—was followed by seven or eight minutes of sitting still, smoking and chattering. How they did chatter! It was to no purpose that we continued to move on when they sat down, or that we rose to go before they had sufficiently rested. They looked at one another, so far as I could make out by the faint light and occasionally they laughed; but they would not and did not stir till such time as they pleased themselves. We were helpless. Impossible to go on alone; impossible also to explain to them why every moment was precious, for the acquaintance who had acted as interpreter had been obliged to stay behind at Sardarbulakh, and we were absolutely without means of communication with our companions. . . .

I can say very little about the ground we traversed in the darkness, except that it was quite waterless, and that I fancy we passed, in a grassy hollow at about 9000 feet above the sea, the spot which they call the Hermitage, which seems to be the site of General Chodzko's meteorological camp of July and August 1850. He told me there was a spring there, but either it is dry at this season or else we missed it. There was pasture in many places but we saw no cattle; doubtless they had already been driven down to the lower slopes. What we were able to remark and enjoy was the changing aspect of the sky. About 3 A.M. there suddenly sprang up, from behind the Median mountains, the morning star, shedding a light such as no star ever gives in these northern climes of ours, a light that almost outshone the moon. An hour later it began to pale in the first faint flush of yellowish light that spread over the eastern heaven, and first the rocky masses above us, then Little Ararat, throwing behind him a gigantic shadow, then the long lines of mountains beyond the Araxes, became revealed, while the wide Araxes plain still lay dim and shadowy below. One by one the stars died out as the yellow turned to a deeper glow that shot forth in long streamers, the rosy fingers of the dawn, from the horizon to the zenith. Cold and ghostly lay the snows on the mighty cone; till at last there came upon their topmost slope, 6000 feet above us, a sudden blush of pink. Swiftly it floated down the eastern face, and touched and kindled the rocks just above us. Then the sun flamed out, and in a moment the Araxes valley and all the hollows of the savage ridges we were crossing were flooded with overpowering light.

It was nearly six o'clock, and progress became easier now that we could see our way distinctly. The Cossacks seemed to grow lazier, halting as often as before and walking less briskly; in fact, they did not relish the exceeding roughness of the jagged lava ridges along whose tops or sides we toiled. I could willingly have lingered here myself, for in the hollows, wherever a little soil appeared, some interesting plants were growing, whose similarity to and difference from the alpine species of Western Europe alike excited one's curiosity. Time allowed me to secure only a few; I trusted to get more on the way back, but this turned out to be impossible. As we scrambled along a ridge above a long narrow winding glen filled with loose blocks, one of the Kurds suddenly swooped down, like a vulture, from the height on a spot at the bottom, and began peering and grubbing among the stones. In a minute or two he cried out, and the rest followed: he had found a spring, and by scraping in the gravel had made a tiny basin out of which we could manage to drink a little. Here was a fresh cause of delay; everybody was thirsty, and everybody must drink, not only the water which, as we afterwards saw, trickled down hither under the stones from a snow-bed 700 feet higher, but the water mixed with some whisky from a flask my friend carried, which even in this highly diluted state the Cossacks took to heartily. When at last we got them up and away again, they began to dawdle and straggle; after a while two or three sat down, and plainly gave us to see they would go no farther. By the time we had reached a little snow-bed whence the now strong sun was drawing a stream of water, and halted on the rocks beside it for breakfast, there were only two Cossacks and the four Kurds left with us, the rest having scattered themselves about somewhere lower down. We had no idea what instructions they had received, nor whether indeed they had been told anything except to bring us as far as they could, to see that the Kurds brought the baggage, and to fetch us back again, which last was essential for Jaafar's peace of mind. We concluded therefore that, if left to themselves, they would probably wait our return, and the day was running on so fast that it was clear there was no more time to be lost in trying to drag them along with us.

Accordingly I resolved to take what I wanted in the way of food, and start at my own pace. My friend, who carried more weight, and had felt the want of training on our way up, decided to come no farther, but wait about here, and look out for me towards nightfall. We noted the landmarks carefully, the little snow-bed, the head of the glen covered with reddish masses of stone and gravel, and high above it, standing out of the face of the great cone of Ararat, a bold peak, or rather projecting tooth of black rock, which our Cossacks called the Monastery, and which, I supposed from the same fancied resemblance to a building, is said to be called in Tatar Tach Kilissa, "the church rock." It is doubtless an old cone of eruption, about 13,000 feet in height, and is really the upper end of the long ridge we had been following, which may, perhaps, represent a lava flow from it, or the edge of a fissure which at this point found a vent. . . . We were now at a height of about 12,000 feet. Everything lay below us, except Little Ararat opposite, and the stupendous cone that rose from where we sat, its glittering snows and stern black crags of lava standing up perfectly clear in a sea of cloudless blue. Tempting it was, but it was also awe-inspiring, and as the summit was hidden behind the nearer slopes, I could not tell what the difficulties of the ascent might be. Still less could we have learnt them from our companions. The Kurds never come higher on the mountain than their flocks can find pasture, and on this side at least the pasture does not reach so high as where we were. Moreover, they have a superstitious reverence for the mountain, scarcely less than that of the Armenians: only, while the Armenian faithful believe it to be guarded by angels, the Kurds hold it to be the favourite haunt of devils and Jinn, who are ready to take vengeance on the disturber of their revels. . . .

At eight o'clock I buckled on my canvas gaiters, thrust some crusts of bread, a lemon, a small flask of cold tea, four hard-boiled eggs, and a few meat lozenges into my pocket, bade good-bye to my friend, and set off. Rather to our suprise, the two Cossacks and one of the Kurds came with me, whether persuaded by a pantomime of encouraging signs, or simply curious to see what would happen. The ice-axe had hugely amused the Cossacks all through. Climbing the ridge to the left, and keeping along its top for a little way, I then struck across the semi-circular head of a wide glen, in the middle of which, a little lower, lay a snow-bed, over a long steep slope of loose broken stones and sand. This slope, a sort of talus or "screes," as they say in the Lake country, was excessively fatiguing from the want of firm foothold, and when I reached the other side, I was already so tired and breathless, having been on foot since midnight, that it seemed almost useless to persevere farther. However, on the other side I got upon solid rock, where the walking was better, and was soon environed by a multitude of rills bubbling down over the stones from the snow-slopes above. The summit of Little Ararat, which had for the last two hours provokingly kept at the same apparent height above me, began to sink, and before ten o'clock I could look down upon its small flat top, studded with lumps of rock, but bearing no trace of a crater. Mounting steadily along the same ridge, I saw at a height of over 13,000 feet, lying on the loose blocks, a piece of wood about four feet long and five inches thick, evidently cut by some tool, and so far above the limit of trees that it could by no possibility be a natural fragment of one. Darting on it with a glee that astonished the Cossack and the Kurd, I held it up to them, made them look at it, and repeated several times the word "Noah." The Cossack grinned, but he was such a cheery, genial fellow that I think he would have grinned whatever I had said, and I cannot be sure that he took my meaning, and recognised the wood as a fragment of the true Ark. Whether it was really gopher wood, of which material the Ark was built, I will not undertake to say, but am willing to submit to the inspection of the curious the bit which I cut off with my ice-axe and brought away. Anyhow, it will be hard to prove that it is not gopher wood. And if there be any remains of the Ark on Ararat at all, . . . here rather than the top is the place where one might expect to find them, since in the course of ages they would get carried down by the onward movement of the snow-beds along the declivities. This wood, therefore, suits all the requirements of the case. In fact, the argument is, for the case of a relic, exceptionally strong: the Crusaders who found the Holy Lance at Antioch, the archbishop who recognised the Holy Coat at Treves, not to speak of many others, proceeded upon slighter evidence. I am, however, bound to admit that another explanation of the presence of this piece of timber on the rocks at this vast height did occur to me. But as no man is bound to discredit his own relic, and such is certainly not the practice of the Armenian Church, I will not disturb my readers' minds, or yield to the rationalising tendencies of the age by suggesting it.

Fearing that the ridge by which we were mounting would become too precipitous higher up, I turned off to the left, and crossed a long, narrow snow-slope, that descended between this ridge and another line of rocks more to the west. It was firm, and just steep enough to make steps cut in the snow comfortable, though not necessary; so the ice-axe was brought into use. The Cossack who accompanied me —there was but one now, for the other Cossack had gone away to the right some time before, and was quite lost to view—had brought my friend's alpenstock, and was developing a considerable capacity for wielding it. He followed nimbly across; but the Kurd stopped on the edge of the snow, and stood peering and hesitating, like one who shivers on the plank at a bathing-place, nor could the jeering cries of the Cossack induce him to venture on the treacherous surface. Meanwhile, we who had crossed were examining the broken cliff which rose above us. It looked not exactly dangerous, but a little troublesome, as if it might want some care to get over or through. So after a short rest, I stood up, touched my Cossack's arm, and pointed upwards. He reconnoitred the cliff with his eye, and shook his head. Then, with various gestures of hopefulness, I clapped him on the back, and made as though to pull him along. He looked at the rocks again, and pointed to them, stroked his knees, turned up and pointed to the soles of his boots, which certainly were suffering from the lava, and once more solemnly shook his head. This was conclusive; so I conveyed to him by pantomime that he had better go back to the bivouac where my friend was, rather than remain here alone, and that I hoped to meet him there in the evening, took an affectionate farewell, and turned towards the rocks. There was evidently nothing for it but to go on alone. It was half-past ten o'clock, and the height about 13,600 feet, Little Ararat now lying nearly 1000 feet below the eye.

I am no disciple of that doctrine of mountaineering without guides

which some English climbers have of late preached zealously by
example as well as precept, and which others, among them so high
an authority as my friend Mr. Leslie Stephen, have wisely set themselves to discourage. But if there is any justification for the practice,
that justification exists when guides are not to be had. Here not only
had the Cossack and the Kurd refused to come on, but they really
could not have been of use if they had. They were not guides in any
sense of the word; they were an escort. They had never been so high
in their lives before, knew nothing either of climbing in general or
of this particular mountain, were not properly equipped for the
work. In fact, their presence could have been no gain in any way,
except that, if one of us had hurt himself on the rocks, the other
two might have carried him down or taken news to the party below.
There was no ground for complaining of them, seeing that the mountain was terrible not only by its legends, but by its solitude and silence; and the idea of going to the top for the sake of getting to the
top would have been quite incomprehensible to them. What had
happened was so obviously what might have been, and indeed had
been expected, that it would have been folly for a man to come so
far unless he was now prepared to proceed alone. The weather
looked pretty steady, although clouds were gathering round the
top, and there seemed to be so little snow on this side that the usual
risks of solitary mountaineering were absent, and a single climber
would be just as well able to get along as a party. Convincing myself
by these reasonings that there was nothing rash in proceeding, I fell
to work upon the trachytic crags in front, but found them so nasty
that it soon became necessary to turn off to the left (west). There I
emerged on a very long, straight slope of volcanic stones, fragments
of trachyte, basalt, amygdaloid, and so forth, lying at so high an
angle (probably over 33 degrees) that they were often rolling down
of themselves, and always gave way under the foot and hand, so
that I slipped down nearly as much as I went up. It was nearly two
hours' incessant toil up this bit of "screes," owing partly to its nature, but chiefly to the state of fatigue and breathlessness in which I
found myself, and which was no doubt due to the thinness of the
air. Having never before experienced, even on top of Monte Rosa,
any of the discomforts ascribed to this cause, I had fancied that my

present sensations, which had begun in crossing the first slope of stones at a height of only 12,300 feet, were caused simply by want of training and of sleep. Now, however, when between every two steps one had to stop and gasp for breath, it was plain that the rarity of the air must be the real cause, though there was no headache, nausea, gushing of blood from the nose and ears, nor any other of those symptoms of mountain sickness on which the older travellers dilate. Oddly enough, it grew no worse as I mounted; in fact, was felt rather less at 17,000 feet than at 13,000. . . .

The practical question at this moment was whether with knees of lead, and gasping like a fish in a boat, I should be able to get any farther. Another element of difficulty was added by the clouds, which had now established themselves, as they usually do at this hour, a good way down from the top, and might prevent me from finding it, or at least beguile me into a wrong track, which there would not be time to retrace so as to reach the desired goal. I had not seen the summit that morning, and was obliged to guess at its whereabouts from the direction of the ridges running up the face of the cone (I say "cone" for convenience, though it is really more a dome than a cone, and is so huge that in climbing the sides you do not think of it as a cone at all). With these grounds for reflection I sat down to eat an egg and take stock of the position. The conclusion was that, whenever a "bad place" presented itself, or three o'clock arrived, it would be prudent, indeed necessary, to turn back were the top never so near. "Bad places" are more serious things when one is alone, especially in descending, not so much because you lose the help of a companion as because they are more likely to affect the nerves and oblige the climber to proceed with more deliberation. In this case, moreover, time was everything, because the place of bivouac must be reached by 6 P.M., after which there would be no light fit for walking, and a night without food or wrappings in the open air, even at 12,000 feet, might have had permanently disagreeable results. In coming to this decision, there was a sense of relief; and both lungs and legs were so exhausted that the bad place, or three o'clock, would have been almost welcome.

This repulsive stone slope abuts at its upper extremity upon a line of magnificent black cliffs, from which there were hanging several glittering icicles, 200 feet long, frozen waterfalls in fact, produced by the melting of the snow on a snow-slope behind. Before reaching this, I had grown so weary of the loose stones, up which it was difficult to advance except by a succession of spurts with the aid of hands and ice-axe, as to turn still farther to the left, and get on to another rock-rib, composed of toppling crags of lava, along whose farther or western side, the *arête* itself being too much broken, it was possible to work one's laborious way over the fallen masses. Here a grand sight, perhaps the grandest on the whole mountain, presented itself. At my foot was a deep, narrow, impassable gully, a sort of gigantic *couloir*, in whose bottom snow lay where the inclination was not too steep. Beyond it a line of rocky towers, red, grim, and terrible, ran right up towards the summit, its upper end lost in the clouds, through which, as at intervals they broke or shifted, one could descry, far, far above, a wilderness of snow. Had a Kurd ever wandered so far, he might have taken this for the palace of the Jinn.

This gully is, no doubt, one of those ancient volcanic fissures with which the mountain is seamed, and from which a great part of its lava has been discharged. The same phenomenon appears in most volcanic regions: in Iceland, for instance, tremendous eruptions have taken place from similar rifts or *gjas*, as they are called there, opening on the sides or even at the base of a mountain. This particular fissure, which runs north-west and south-east, is on the main axis of the mass, midway between the craters of Kip Ghöll on the north-west and Little Ararat on the south-east, and indicates the line along which the volcanic forces acted most powerfully. Following its course towards the base of the cone, I could see that line prolonged in a series of small cones and craters along the top of the ridge which connects Great and Little Ararat. Some of these craters, into which I looked straight down from this point, were as perfect as if their fires had but just cooled, each basin-shaped hollow surrounded by a rim of miniature black cliffs, with heaps of ashes and scoriae piled on their sides. In the bottom of one or two water had gathered in greenish tarns or pools.

Not knowing how far the ridge I was following might continue passable, I was obliged to stop frequently to survey the rocks above, and erect little piles of stones to mark the way. This not only consumed time, but so completely absorbed the attention that for hours together I scarcely noticed the marvellous landscape spread out beneath, and felt the solemn grandeur of the scenery far less than many times before on less striking mountains. Solitude at great heights, or among majestic rocks or forests, commonly stirs in us all deep veins of feeling, joyous or saddening, or of joy and sadness mingled. Here the strain on the observing senses seemed too great for fancy or emotion to have any scope. When the mind is preoccupied by the task of the moment, imagination is checked. This was a race against time, in which I could only scan the cliffs for a route, refer constantly to the watch, husband my strength by morsels of food taken at frequent intervals, and endeavour to conceive how a particular block or bit of slope which it would be necessary to recognise would look when seen the other way in descending.

Keeping mostly on the south-western side of this same rock-rib, and mounting at last to the top of it, I found myself on the edge of a precipice, which stopped farther progress in that direction. From this precipice, the summit, or at least the place where it must lie, since there was a great deal of cloud about in these higher regions, could be made out, barely 1000 feet above me. Fortunately, the clouds were really clouds, and not a generally diffused mist; so that, when I was not actually in them, it was possible to see clearly all round. Two courses were open. One, which would probably have been the better, was to bear off to the right, and get up the low cliffs at the top of the long stone slope which I had deserted, on to the upper slopes of rock, or gently inclined snow, which lead to the top. The other was to turn back a little, and descend to the left into a vast snow basin lying immediately south-east of the summit, and whose north-west acclivity formed, in fact, the side of the summit. This acclivity looked a likely place for crevasses, though I do not remember to have seen any, and was steep enough to require step cutting. Its *névé* would have been quite practicable for a party, but not equally so for a single man, who might have had some trouble in stopping himself if once he slipped and went off. Luckily there was on the east side of the basin, close under the range of precipice on a projecting point of which I was standing, though separated from it by a narrow snow-bed, a steep slope of friable rocks, quite free from snow, which ran up to a point where the clouds hid them, but where there seemed no sign of any cliff to bar the way. Forced to decide between a course which was difficult, but almost certainly practicable, and another probably easier, but possibly impracticable, I could not hesitate long in choosing the former. Retracing my steps a little from the precipice, and climbing along the border of a treacherous little ice-slope, where there was fortunately some handhold on the rocks enclosing it, I got into the great snow basin aforesaid, just where the gully or fissure I have already mentioned descends from it, and attacked the friable rocks. Their angle (38 to 43 degrees) would have made them simple enough if they had only been firm, but they were so rotten that neither hands nor feet could get firm hold, and I slipped down and scrambled up and floundered about pitiably, having no longer steel enough in the muscles for a rush. . . .

All the way up this rock-slope, which proved so fatiguing that for the fourth time I had almost given up hope, I kept my eye fixed on its upper end to see what signs there were of crags or snow-fields above. But the mist lay steadily at the point where the snow seemed to begin, and it was impossible to say what might be hidden behind that soft white curtain. As little could I conjecture the height I had reached by looking round, as one so often does on mountain ascents, upon other summits, for by this time I was thousands of feet above Little Ararat, the next highest peak visible, and could scarcely guess how many thousands. From this tremendous height it looked more like a broken obelisk than an independent summit 12,800 feet in height. Clouds covered the farther side of the great snow basin, and were seething like waves about the savage pinnacles, the towers of the Jinn palace, which guard its lower margin, and past which my upward path had lain. With mists to the left and above, and a range of black precipices cutting off all view to the right, there came a vehement sense of isolation and solitude, and I began to understand better the awe with which the mountain silence inspires the Kurdish shepherds. Overhead the sky had turned from dark blue to an intense bright green, a colour whose strangeness seemed to add to the weird terror of the scene. It wanted barely an hour to the time when I had resolved to turn back; and as I struggled up the crumbling rocks, trying now to right and now to left, where the foothold looked a little firmer, I began to doubt whether there was strength enough left to carry me an hour higher. At length the rock-slope came suddenly to an end, and I stepped out upon the almost level snow at the top of it, coming at the same time into the clouds, which naturally clung to the colder surfaces. A violent west wind was blowing, and the temperature must have been pretty low, for a big icicle at once enveloped the lower half of my face, and did not melt till I got to the bottom of the cone, four hours afterwards. Unluckily, I was very thinly clad, the stout tweed coat reserved for such occasions having been stolen on a Russian railway. The only expedient to be tried against the piercing cold was to tighten in my loose light coat by winding round the waist a Spanish *faja*, or scarf, which I had brought up to use, in case of need, as a neck wrapper. Its bright purple looked odd enough in such surroundings, but as there was nobody there to notice, appearances did not matter. In the mist, which was now thick, the eye could pierce only some thirty yards ahead; so I walked on over the snow five or six minutes, following the rise of its surface, which was gentle, and fancying there might still be a good long way to go. To mark the backward track I trailed the point of the ice-axe along behind me in the soft snow, for there was no longer any landmark: all was cloud on every side. Suddenly, to my astonishment, the ground began to fall away to the north; I stopped, a puff of wind drove off the mists on one side, the opposite side to that by which I had come, and showed the Araxes plain at an abysmal depth below. It was the top of Ararat.

Two or three minutes afterwards another blast cleared the air a little to the west, which had hitherto been perfectly thick, disclosing a small snow valley, and beyond it, a quarter of a mile off, another top, looking about the same height as the one I stood on. Remembering, what I had strangely forgotten on the way up, that there are two tops—one sees them distinctly from Erivan and Aralykh—I ran down the steep, soft sides of the snow valley, across it in the teeth of the blast, and up the easy acclivity to the other top, reaching it at 2.25 P.M. It is certainly the higher of the two, but the difference was not great to my eye, only some fifty feet or so, and I cannot understand how General Chodzko comes to speak of it as something amounting to thirty-six metres. The longitudinal depression between them is 100–150 feet deep. Both tops are gently sloping domes or broad convex hummocks of snow, on which there is not a trace of rock, nor a trace of the crosses which first Parrot and afterwards Chodzko set up,[4] just as little as of Noah's ship itself. One thought of the pictures of childhood, the Ark resting on a smooth, round grassy eminence, from which the waters are receding, while the Patriarch looks out of the window, and compared them with this snow-filled hollow, just large enough to have held the vessel comfortably, raised 15,000 feet above the surrounding country. Neither is there any sign of a crater. You might describe the whole top as a triangular un-dulating plain, rather more than half as big as the Green Park in Lon-don, descending gently on the north-west, with extensive terraces like fields of *névé*, less gently towards the north-north-east, but steeply on all other sides, and on the east breaking off, after a short snow-field, in the tremendous precipices that overhang the chasm of Arguri. There was nothing about it to suggest an extinct volcano, were it not known to be one. But in the ages that have elapsed since the time when eruptions took place from the great central chimney of the dome, a time probably far more remote than that when the minor cones that stud the flanks of the mountain were active, all sorts of changes may have taken place, and the summit we now see may be merely the bottom of an ancient crater, whose craggy rim has been altogether broken away. Looking around, it was hard to imagine that volcanic fires had ever raged on such a spot, robed as it now is in perpetual winter.

Immeasurably extensive and grand as the view was, it was also strangely indefinite. Every mountaineer knows that the highest views are seldom the finest; and here was one so high that the dis-tinctions of hill and valley in the landscape were almost lost. Ararat towers so over all his neighbours, much more than Mont Blanc or even Elbruz do over theirs, that they seem mere hillocks on a uni-form flat. The only rivals are in the Caucasus, which one can just make out all along the northern sky. Kazbek and Elbruz, the latter 280 miles away, are visible, but I could not be sure that I saw those

---

[4] Mount Ararat was first climbed in 1829, by Dr. Johann Parrot. Others who suc-cessfully ascended before Bryce include Otto von Abich (1834), General Chodzko (1850), and Douglas W. Freshfield (1868).

particular summits (though I saw white snow tops where they ought
to lie), for the sky was not very clear in that direction. More distinct
were the mountains of Daghestan, rising 150 miles off, over the nearer
ones that engirdle the Goktcha Lake, a little bit of whose shining
level appeared. Beyond the dreary red-brown mountains of the
Karabagh one strained to discover a line that might be the Caspian
or the plain of the lower Kur, but, of course, at such a distance (260
miles) it would be impossible to distinguish a sea-surface. Besides,
the Caspian is below the horizon; so one must reject, unless the aid of
refraction be called in, the stories of mariners who, sailing on it, have
been able to make out the white cone of Ararat. Nearer at hand,
only forty miles to the north, rose the huge extinct volcano of Ala
Göz, with its three sharp black rocky peaks enclosing an ancient
crater, in whose bottom were patches of snow; and, nearer still, the
dim plain of Erivan encircled the mountain to the north and east,
with the Araxes winding like a faint streak of silver through it. A
slight rise in the ground showed where Erivan itself lay, but the
bright green of the orchards and vineyards round it was lost at this
distance, though, standing in the market-place of the city, Ararat
seems to tower right over the spectator's head. Looking due west, the
extreme ranges of Taurus mingling with the Bingöl Dagh in the
neighbourhood of Erzerum were hidden by the clouds which the
wind kept driving up; but north-west the upper valley of the Araxes
could be traced as far as Ani, once the capital of the Armenian kingdom, and the great Russian fortress of Alexandropol, and the hills
where Kars, its enemy, looked forth defiance. To the south and
south-west the eye ranged over a wilderness of bare red-brown
mountains, their sides seamed by winter torrents that showed in the
distance like dark lines, not a tree nor a patch of green on their
scorched and arid slopes, scarcely even a fleck of snow on their tops,
though many rose more than 10,000 or 11,000 feet above the sea.
Prominent among them was the long stern line of hills that enclose
the upper course of the Euphrates (the Eastern Euphrates or Murad
Su), whose source could be distinguished about forty miles to the
south, beyond the hollow where Bayazid lies, the houses of which
were hidden by a low ridge. Still farther to the south, from the shores
of the Lake of Van, rose the great volcanic peak of Sipan Dagh, and

to the south-east the stupendous masses of Savalan Dagh, that look over all Azerbijan to the waves of the Caspian. Neither the Lake of Van nor the still larger Lake of Urumia was visible; for both, though high above the sea, are enclosed by lofty hills. But far beyond them, more than two hundred miles away, I could just descry the faint blue tops of the Assyrian mountains of Southern Kurdistan, the Quardu land, where Chaldee tradition places the fragments of the Ark, mountains that look down on Mosul and those huge mounds of Nineveh by which the Tigris flows. Below and around, included in this single view, seemed to lie the whole cradle of the human race, from Mesopotamia in the south to the great wall of the Caucasus that covered the northern horizon, Mount Kaf, the boundary for so many ages of the civilised world. If it was indeed here that man first set foot again on the unpeopled earth, one could imagine how the great dispersion went as the races spread themselves from these sacred heights along the courses of the great rivers down to the Black and Caspian Seas, and over the Assyrian plain to the shores of the Southern Ocean, whence they were wafted away to other continents and isles. No more imposing centre of the world could be imagined. In the valley of the Araxes beneath, the valley which Armenian legend has selected as the seat of Paradise, the valley that has been for three thousand years the high-road for armies, the scene of so much slaughter and misery, there lay two spots which seemed to mark the first and the latest points of authentic history. One, right below me, was the ruined Artaxata, built, as the tale goes, by Hannibal, and stormed by the legions of Lucullus. The other, far to the north-west, was the hollow under the hills in which lies the fortress of Kars, where our countrymen fought in 1854, and where the flames of war were so soon again to be lighted.

Yet how trivial history, and man the maker of history, seemed. This is the spot which he reveres as the supposed scene of his creation and his preservation from the destroying waters, a land where he has lived and laboured and died ever since his records begin, and during ages from which no record is left. Dynasty after dynasty has reared its palaces, faith after faith its temples, upon this plain; cities have risen and fallen and risen again in the long struggle of civilisation against the hordes of barbarism. But of all these works of

human pomp and skill not one can be discerned from this height.
The landscape is now what it was before man crept forth on the
earth; the mountains stand about the valleys as they stood when the
volcanic fires that piled them up were long ago extinguished. Nature
sits enthroned, serenely calm, upon this hoary pinnacle, and speaks
to her children only in the storm and earthquake that level their
dwellings in the dust. As says the Persian poet:—

> When you and I behind the veil are passed,
> Oh but the long long while the world shall last,
> Which of our coming and departure heeds
> As the Seven Seas should heed a pebble's cast.[5]

Yet even the mountains change and decay. Every moment some
block thunders from these crags into the glens below. Day by day
and night by night frost, snow, and rain are loosening the solid rock,
and the ceaseless action of chemical forces is dissolving it into its primal elements, setting free the gases, and delivering over the fragments to torrents that will sweep them down into the plain. A time
must come, if the world lasts long enough, when even the stately
peaks of Ararat will have crumbled away and be no more. "Of old
hast thou laid the foundations of the earth: and the heavens are the
work of thy hands. They shall perish, but thou shalt endure: they all
shall wax old as doth a garment; and as a vesture shalt thou change
them, and they shall be changed; but thou art the same and thy years
fail not." [6]

Withal I am bound to say that the view, despite the associations
it evoked, despite the impression of awe and mystery it gave, was
not beautiful or splendid, but rather stern, grim, and monotonous.
The softer colours of the landscape seemed to be lost; the mountains,
seen from above, and seldom showing well-marked peaks, were
uncouth, rough-hewn masses. One had a sense of vast sterility and
dreariness as the vision ranged over this boundless expanse of brown,
and sought, almost in vain, a point to recognise. For most of these
huge mountains are nameless on our maps; and these bare valleys are
peopled by races of whom we know little except that they live now
much as they may have lived when that first dispersion of mankind

[5] *The Rubaiyat of Omar Khayyam* (Third Edition), XLVII. Slightly altered.
[6] Psalm CII, 25–27.

took place. Then suddenly, while the eye was still unsatisfied with gazing, the curtain of mists closed round again, and I was left alone in this little plain of snow, white, silent, and desolate, with a vividly bright green sky above it and a wild west wind whistling across it, clouds girding it in, and ever and anon through the clouds glimpses of far-stretching valleys and mountains away to the world's end.

The awe that fell upon me with this sense of utter loneliness made time pass unnoticed; and I might have lingered long in a sort of dream had not the piercing cold that thrilled through every limb recalled a sense of the risks delay might involve. It was half-past two o'clock, so that only four hours of daylight remained; there might be some difficulty in retracing the morning's path, even by the help of the piles of stone set up: a night on the mountain without food or wrappings would be a more serious matter than any obstacle that had yet presented itself. Besides, as night approached, my friend below would grow anxious; the rather as he could not communicate with the Cossacks, and their stock of provisions would scarcely enable them and him to wait till the next day. It was clear, therefore, that the hope of descending the summit towards the west and north for the sake of better examining its structure, which no one seems to have properly described, must be abandoned. So I ran down the easy slope into the little valley between the two tops, climbed the snow wall of the eastern one, and followed the marks made by my ice-axe in the snow back to the spot where I had left the rocks. The mist was now so thick that it would otherwise have been impossible to hit the right direction; for though I had a compass, on a volcanic mountain like Ararat, with plenty of iron in the rocks, one could not have trusted it. I have seen the needle on the basaltic top of Ben Nevis point every way in succession. Once on the slope of friable rock the way was pretty clear, since a snow-bed lay on each hand, though the treacherous nature of the surface made caution necessary and progress slow. Towards the bottom I was tempted to try a glissade on the narrow left-hand snow-bed, but it turned out to be much too rough and too hard for the purpose; so my glissade ended in a slip and some bruises, the only little mischance which befell me during the day.

A few minutes more brought me to the upper end of the great

fissure of eruption already mentioned, along whose eastern side I
had climbed in the morning, partly on the slope, partly on the top of
the rock-rib or *arête* which encloses it on the east. Surveying the
declivity below me from the top of this rock-rib, it seemed possible
to descend by a route considerably shorter than that which I had
then followed, viz. by striking diagonally across the slopes of loose
rock towards the east-south-east, instead of due south-east down the
cone. Taking this line, which presented no great difficulty except
where the loose, angular blocks became so large that much time was
lost in climbing over and among them, I dropped down at last upon
a large snow-bed, and in crossing it had the ill-luck to break the shaft
of my ice-axe, which had been unskilfully fixed by the military
carpenter of Aralykh. It was well that the inclination was not steep
enough to make the rest of the way dangerous; by caution and the
use of the head of the ice-axe to cut steps or take hold of the ice, I
got safely across, and on to another mass of loose rocks, down which
I pursued the same south-eastward course, and thought I began to
recognise the long ridge up which we had toiled in the morning. To
the left rose the sharp peak which is called, in Tatar, Tach Kilissa,
and at the foot of it, on the top of the ridge I have just mentioned, was
the spot where my friend and the Cossacks had halted—the spot I
had now to make for. By this time the sun had got behind the south-
western ridge of the mountain, and his gigantic shadow had already
fallen across the great Araxes plain below, while the red mountains
of Media, far to the south-east, still glowed redder than ever, then
turned swiftly to a splendid purple in the dying light.

Quickening my pace as the risk of missing the encampment became greater—feeling, in fact, that it was now a race against the
onward striding night in which defeat would be serious—I caught
sight at last of two Cossacks loitering on the edge of the slope of
sand and gravel which had proved so fatiguing in the morning, and
after a while made them hear my shouts. When I reached them it was
six o'clock; and though at this height (12,200 feet) there was still
good twilight, Aralykh and the ruins of Artaxata below lay already
shrouded in gloom. Twenty-five minutes' more walking brought
us to the place where the Kurds and the other Cossacks had biv-
ouacked; and here, when it was already so dark that we could barely

recognise one another a few yards off, my friend came forward and met me. He had spent most of the day near the spot where we parted, coming down eventually to this point, which was a little lower, had seen the Kurd return, but of course could get no tidings from him of me, had slept about a good deal among shady places in the rocks, making up for the vigils of the last week, and had latterly, as the evening deepened, wandered round, keeping a sharp lookout on the slopes above. We examined the provisions, and found that nothing but a lump of bread, a mere scrap of meat, two eggs, and a thimbleful of cold tea were left. Happily neither of us had much appetite; the sun had kept hunger at bay for him, and meat lozenges had done the same for me; so our frugal evening meal was soon despatched. A little hot tea would have been welcome—four weeks under the sceptre of the Czar had made us perfect slaves to tea; but as there was neither fuel, nor water, nor a vessel to boil it in, the hope was no sooner formed than abandoned. Accordingly, about half-past seven, we lay down on the hillside, my friend valiantly on the top of the ridge, I a yard or two below him on the eastern side, the Cossacks and Kurds all round where they severally pleased, and we courted sleep. . . .

After packing our scanty stock of camping gear as well as we could in the darkness, and counting the bundles on the Kurds' backs, we set off [7] down the dark ridges and darker valleys, stumbling about over huge rocks under the feebly glimmering moon, losing often our companions, and sometimes the way itself. How we got safe down was a marvel to us at the time; but one frequently has the same cause for wonder in night walks. Perhaps the muscles and sinews, knowing what depends upon them, acquire a sort of preternatural elasticity and readiness, which enables them to adapt themselves to an emergency, and carry one safely through innumerable risks. There was no track, but the Kurds seemed to have an idea where they were going. Many were the halts which the Cossacks made, stretching themselves on the grass to laugh and talk; nor was it now worth while to hurry them. Now and then we tried to get a nap during these delays, but though scarcely able to walk for drowsiness, as soon as we lay down and shut our eyes we became bolt awake. At

[7] The descent was resumed about midnight.

length the morning star rose in unearthly brightness, and not long after we came to a sweet little grassy plain, where two or three Kurds, whose flocks were pasturing hard by, had lit a fire of withered bushes, to which our Kurds led us up in a friendly way, bidding us (as we guessed) warm ourselves. The Cossacks had nearly all gone on out of sight, and we were (as it afterwards struck us) entirely at the mercy of these wild, swarthy fellows, on whose glittering daggers and matchlocks the firelight played. However, they had no thought of mischief; perhaps, if it had occurred to them, the sense of hospitality, which is proverbially strong in the East, would have restrained them from harming those with whom they had eaten. Then between four and five o'clock another glorious dawn began; and just before sunrise we reached the tent at Sardarbulakh, much to the relief of Jaafar's mind, and flung ourselves down on the tent floor to sleep the sleep of the weary.

Roused again at eight or nine o'clock—both the watches had stopped, so we could only guess at the time of day—we ought clearly to have gone up Little Ararat, and obtained from his top a fuller notion of his great brother's structure. Provisions, however, ran short, and the Cossacks were anxious to return to Aralykh, taking back with them their comrades whom we had found in the two tents, as the post was to be withdrawn for the season. Accordingly the tents were struck, everything packed on the baggage horses, the Kurds paid for their day's and night's service on the hill. Then, before starting, the Cossacks gathered in a ring in front of the spot where the tents had stood, and began singing Russian songs. The words we, of course, could not follow—I believe they were mostly camp songs, some commemorating military exploits, some farewells to departing comrades—but the airs, usually lively, but occasionally tender and plaintive, dwelt long in our memory. One stood in the middle and led, firing off a gun at intervals, the others sometimes singing with him, sometimes merely joining in the refrain or chorus. The voices were good, and the time perfect. . . .

Before noon we bid a regretful farewell to Sardarbulakh, and rode down into the plain, this time taking a track outside of the buttress of Takjaltu, instead of behind it, and thence across the arid slopes to Aralykh, which we reached about four o'clock without further incident, though once during the way an alarm was given that there were strange people about, and Jaafar rode ahead to reconnoitre. Owing, I suppose, to the bracing quality of the keen dry air, we were much less fatigued than we had expected to be. Colonel Shipshef welcomed us with characteristic heartiness, and we spent a pleasant evening with him, lamenting more than ever that unhappy event at the tower of Babel which made our communications so limited. Next morning we mounted the tarantass once more, and drove off across the Araxes and through the dusty villages back into the furnace of Erivan.

Two days later I found myself at the Armenian monastery of Etchmiadzin, near the northern foot of Ararat, and was presented to the archimandrite who rules that illustrious house. It came out in conversation that we had been on the mountain, and the Armenian gentleman who was acting as interpreter turned to the archimandrite and said: "This Englishman says he has ascended to the top of Massis" (Ararat). The venerable man smiled sweetly. "No," he replied, "that cannot be. No one has ever been there. It is impossible."

ALBERT FREDERICK MUMMERY

1855–1895

BEING A MAN OF MEANS and leisure, A. F. Mummery devoted his time to two major interests—political economy and mountaineering. The only relic of the former is a book, *The Physiology of Industry* (1889), done in collaboration with J. A. Hobson, later a voluminous writer on economics.

As a climber Mummery quickly gained a reputation for daring, ingenuity, and verve. He spent a number of triumphal seasons in the Alps, where he specialized in new routes and the solution of problems of mountain-craft. Mummery was durable and agile, but his back had been weakened so that he could carry scarcely any load. Accordingly, he learned to travel with light supplies of food and devised various weight-sparing pieces of equipment, most useful of which was the so-called Mummery tent. Thus he contributed to the climber's mobility, an advantage which becomes necessity in remote regions such as the Andes and the Himalaya.

In the final chapter of *My Climbs in the Alps and the Caucasus* Mummery discusses the climber's personal risk. While far from glorying in danger, he quietly points out that more than a few of the most competent mountaineers have been killed. It is proper, he believes, for the live climber to acknowledge his luck and to remain aware without dismay that for his surpassing pleasure he may be suddenly required to pay an awful price. The book was published in May, 1895. In the summer of the same year a party composed of Mummery, Geoffrey Hastings, Norman Collie, C. G. Bruce, and several Gurkha porters made the first campaign against the Himalayan peak Nanga Parbat (26,620 feet) in northwestern Kashmir. With one Gurkha, Mummery reached 20,000 feet, the last 5,000 of which required two days and a night. They were forced back by the porter's illness. The group then determined to attempt the mountain from the northern side. Mummery and two Gurkhas were to cross to the north by the 20,000 foot Diama Pass, which was unexplored but apparently easy. They started on August 24, but never arrived at the agreed rendezvous and never returned to the old camp. Searchers were unable, because of heavy snow, to follow Mummery's course. Upon reaching a height commanding the pass, they observed it to be swept frequently by avalanches, which could not be seen from below. Doubtless the three were buried without warning.

Nanga Parbat was not approached for more than thirty-five years after Mummery's death. During the 1930's several expeditions were made. Two of these, in which German climbers participated, were all but annihilated in 1934 and 1937, one by storm and the other by an avalanche. The mountain is yet unclimbed.

The following selection is reprinted from A. F. Mummery, *My Climbs in the Alps and the Caucasus*, London, T. Fisher Unwin, New York, Charles Scribner and Sons, 1895.

Dych Tau

THOUGH THE FAITHFUL CLIMBER is, in his essence, a thoroughly domesticated man and rarely strays from his own home, the Alps, a spirit of unrest occasionally takes hold upon him and drives him forth to more distant regions. Seized with such a fit of wandering, the first days of July, 1888, found me camped on the right bank of the Bezingi Glacier, where, in the cool air of the snow fields, on slopes white with rhododendron and with the silent unclimbed peaks above, I could rest from the rattle and roar of trains, the noise of buffets, and the persecutions of the Custom-Houses.

My sole companion was Heinrich Zurfluh, of Meiringen. The experience of ten days' continuous travel, culminating in two and a half days on the peculiarly uncomfortable Tartar saddle—we had ridden from Patigorsk to Naltcik, and thence to Bezingi and the foot of the glacier—had sufficed to make him a confirmed pessimist. "Es gefällt mir nicht" was the burden of his song, and though this phrase may, perhaps, be regarded as summarising the conclusions of modern philosophy, it struck me that it was scarcely a fitting watchword for the mountaineer face to face with the hugest of unclimbed giants.

Our camp was of a most Spartan simplicity, for we had outwalked our baggage, and Zurfluh's knapsack, which I had fondly imagined contained sleeping-bags and soup-tins, proved to be mainly filled with a great pot of most evil-smelling boot grease—brought with much labour all the way from Meiringen—a large hammer, an excellent stock of hobnails and a sort of anvil to assist in their insertion. These various articles were doubtless of great value, but hardly useful as bedding, for, whatever may be the case with rose-leaves, a man need scarcely be a sybarite to object to crumpled hobnails as a mattress. Luckily various portions of a sheep, a large loaf of Russian bread, and a load of firewood had been piled on an active native whom we had met and appropriated before leaving the rest of the caravan.

The night proved remarkably cold, and we were glad to turn out at 4 A.M. and start on a preliminary examination of our peak. I soon discovered, however, that Zurfluh had more ambitious views, and was possessed of the wild idea of taking a mountain 17,054 feet high, as a training walk! It was, however, desirable to see what lay behind the Misses Glacier, so I limited my protests and followed the rapid advance of my leader. We kept up a long couloir which was separated from the Misses Glacier by a low ridge of rock. Reaching its head we ought to have crossed over on to the glacier, but we disliked the long snow slopes leading up to the ridge amongst which we thought, I believe erroneously, that we detected the sheen of ice. In consequence, we kept up the rocks to our left, and, about eight o'clock, reached a point where it was, perhaps, possible to traverse on to the great slope, but the whizz of the train was still in my ears, and the limpness of English life still ached in my muscles, and I failed to give my leader the moral support that was needed. He looked at the traverse and did not quite care for its appearance. He looked at the slope above and thought it very long. He gazed at the ridge leading to the summit and denounced it as interminable. A confident Herr, and he would have hurled himself at the difficulties, and his great skill, quickness, and strength would, I verily believe, have enabled us to reach the summit; but for the nonce I adopted the destructive rôle of critic. I pointed out that it was already late, that a night on the ridge would be chilly, and that the traverse and the slope beyond had every appearance of being stone-swept. My mind, however, was as flabby as my muscles, and instead of declaring for a prompt and immediate retreat, I followed Zurfluh languidly up the cliff to see whether a second and easier traverse could be found.

There proved to be no such possibility, and about 9 A.M. we abandoned the ascent. . . .

We found to our sorrow that the camp had not yet arrived, and a
second cold and comfortless night ensued. The next morning, as a
consequence, Zurfluh was too unwell to start, so with the energy of
an amateur I explored the approaches to the southern face of the
mountain. In the course of my solitary wander I scared a herd of
seventeen Tur, and subsequently reached the extreme south-western
buttress of the peak, a point almost worthy of a distinctive title, as
it is separated from the mass of the mountain by a broad col, and is
only to be reached by a long and not wholly easy ridge. Its height
is about 13,500 feet, or possibly more, and one looks over the Zanner
pass into Suanetia and across the Shkara pass to the mountains on
the further side of the Dych Su Glacier. The face of Dych Tau,[1]
however, had all my attention. The peak seen from this side has two
summits, and I found it quite impossible to decide which was the
higher, the great tower to the right and apparently behind the main
mass of the mountain looking as if it might be the culminating point.
This doubt, and the fact that much snow was still lying on the huge
rock face, determined me to cross the passes I was anxious to see
before attempting the ascent, so that by distant views the doubt as to
the true summit might be settled, and by the lapse of time and the
Caucasian sun the snow might be, in a measure, melted from the
rocks. On my return to the Misses kosh I found that fortune was
smiling on me, the camp had arrived and Zurfluh was once more
ready for work.

The next two weeks were devoted to excursions in the valleys of
Balkar, Suanetia, the Bashil Su, and Cheghem. Returning from the
latter by a grass pass to Tubeneli, we once more made our way
toward the Bezingi Glacier. Near the foot of this latter a thick and
wetting mist, combined with the offer of new milk, induced us to
halt at a cow kosh and we pitched our tent by the side of a great
boulder. During the night a goat mistook the tent for a stone and
jumped off the boulder on to the top of it, subsiding amongst its

---

[1] Dych Tau (17,085 feet) is in what is now the Karachaev Autonomous Area of the
U.S.S.R., of which Nalchik (Naltcik) is the capital.

startled inmates. Though I am quite willing to guarantee the be-
haviour of this make of tent on an exposed ledge in a gale of wind,
it must be admitted that it is wholly unequal to the attack of a
daring goat. After many efforts Zurfluh and I succeeded in extricating ourselves from the tangled *débris* and rebuilt our mansion,
though, when morning dawned, it exhibited a miserably baggy and
disreputable appearance. During breakfast our Tartar porter gave
us to understand that a palatial kosh, replete with all the luxuries
of life, was to be found on the left bank of the glacier nearly
opposite the Misses kosh. The weather looked so threatening that
Zurfluh urged me to go to this Capua of the mountains where, as he
wisely said, we could wait till sufficiently fine weather set in for our
great expedition. This seemed so excellent a proposition that we at
once packed up the camp and started. Zurfluh and the Tartar soon
began to exhibit symptoms of rivalry and gradually lapsed into a
walking match for the honour of their respective races, creeds, and
foot-gear. I had no ambition to join, and the men quickly disappeared
from sight. Injudiciously following some directions which Zurfluh
had given me, and which he averred were faithful interpretations of
the Tartar's remarks, I tried to get along the left moraine. This latter,
heaped up against the cliffs and scored by deep water-channels,
soon demonstrated Zurfluh's inefficiency as interpreter. After some
trouble, not to say danger, I succeeded in reaching the glacier, and
tramped merrily over its even surface. Before long, however, a
thick mist settled into the valley and suggested the possibility that
I might fail to find the kosh, for, unluckily, I had only the vaguest
idea of its whereabouts. Fearing to miss it, I felt my way through
some tangled crevasses to the left bank and explored a tenantless alp.
Beneath a great boulder I found a most excellent cave. Where
natural walls were lacking, it had been skilfully built in with stones,
and the whole was roomy, clean, and dry. It undoubtedly affords
the best shelter to be found anywhere above Bezingi. However,
there were no sheep on the pasture and no sign of Zurfluh, shepherd,
or porter, so I had to betake myself to the ice again, here crumpled
and torn into the wildest confusion. After some protracted struggles
and much hewing of steps I reached a second oasis. This likewise
appeared tenantless, and I was beginning to think I should have to

return to my previously discovered cave when, rounding a big rock, I heard the welcome bleating of sheep and walked almost into Zurfluh's arms. He had been much alarmed for my safety. Owing to more erroneous interpretation, he had gone considerably out of his way to take the séracs at exactly their worst and most broken point. Believing this worst passage to be the only one practicable, he not unnaturally concluded that I should come to untold grief.

Having mutually relieved our anxieties, I asked Zurfluh to take me to the much vaunted kosh. We found at first some difficulty in locating it, but the shepherd came to our help and led us to a black mark against a perpendicular cliff; this black mark defined the place where he lit his fire on the rare occasions when he had any firewood. At the present moment, he explained, he had not got any. Other pretence of habitation or shelter there was none. Even our small tent which had formed part of the Tartar's load had disappeared, and the Tartar himself had vanished into space. Zurfluh, indeed, was inclined to think a crevasse his probable resting place, but my experience of his skill made me pretty confident that he had not chosen that particular method of joining the houris in Paradise. The misty rain pervaded everywhere; the lee side of the rocks was as wet as the weather side, and we gradually lapsed into that soddened condition, which depresses the spirits even of the most cheerful. Moreover, we had depended on one or other of the active sheep we saw around us for our dinner; but the conversion of live sheep into cooked mutton is difficult in the absence of firing. We bitterly regretted the Misses kosh, where a Willesden canvas tent and a good store of wood were securely packed in the cave. I even suggested crossing, but Zurfluh absolutely refused to have anything more to do with the séracs while the fog lasted. An hour later, however, our mourning was turned into joy, for we beheld the broad shoulders of the hunter, buried beneath a pile of wood, struggling up the grass slope. He had, it seems, on learning that there was no wood, concealed his baggage in a dry hole under a stone and crossed to the Misses kosh to fetch our supply from thence. A bold and kindly action, done without thought of reward, for men who had little or no claim upon him.

A lamb was promptly pursued and slain, and soon we were sitting round a roaring fire watching portions of the aforesaid lamb sizzling on long wooden spits. The contemplation of these succulent morsels shrined in a halo of dancing flame rapidly raised my spirits, and I regarded as inspired the hunter's favourable reply to my query as to the weather. Zurfluh, however, was not to be comforted . . . and cast bitter contempt on my efforts to speak the Tartar tongue.

The next morning his pessimism seemed justified, for the mist was thicker and wetter than ever. Yet the hunter still replied "Yak shi" to all inquiries, so, somewhat contrary to Zurfluh's wishes, the camp was packed, and about mid-day the hunter led us through the mist along an excellent path. The shepherd had also consented to join our party, so I had the rare and delightful privilege of walking unloaded. As we ascended, the source of Zurfluh's troubles on the previous day became obvious. The hunter had evidently wished him to ascend the glacier till beyond the séracs, and then to return to the kosh by the path we were now following. Zurfluh, however, recognising the fact that he was getting too far up the glacier, had turned to the right, and in the impenetrable fog forced the passage at the worst possible point. The hunter naturally refused to show the white feather before an unbeliever, and followed.

We walked past the séracs and reached the level glacier without difficulty. On the way across we picked up some fine horns—which had once belonged to a Tur—and which I believe now ornament Zurfluh's abode at Meiringen. After ascending the short slope that leads to the long level moraine which here forms the most convenient pathway, we halted whilst the hunter sought to rearrange his footgear. This latter was, however, hopelessly worn out by our previous expeditions, and the contemplation of his bleeding feet roused him to much wrath. Finally he chucked the *débris* of his hide sandals into a crevasse and expressed his intention of returning home. I confess he had reason on his side; I have known a moraine try the temper even of a well-shod member of the Alpine Club, what then could be expected from a "poor benighted heathen"? We endeavoured to coax him forward, but he was obdurate to the most artful flattery—possibly because he could not understand a word we said. The suggestion, conveyed by appropriate gestures and an occasional word, that he would not be paid if he did not do the work merely elicited the reply, also expressed by gestures and a large mass of wholly unintelligible sound, that he did not at all expect to be. These conversational efforts proved unsatisfactory to all concerned and consumed much time. It was in consequence a good deal past four before the luggage was redistributed. Happily the mists were by now obviously clearing, and through rifts and rents we could see the long ridges of Shkara glittering in cloudless sunshine.

Quitting the moraine, we swung round to our left and began ascending interminable slopes of séracs and stones. The shepherd here took pity on my struggles, and seizing my knapsack, insisted on adding it to the vast pile of luggage he was carrying. Despite his burden, he was still able to show us the way and strode upwards, a splendid picture of muscle and perfect balance. About six o'clock we reached the highest point at which it appeared likely we should find water. Above, long slopes of snow and screes led up to the little glacier which lies below the col separating the peak from the great buttress I had climbed two or three weeks before.

We dug out the screes with our axes and made an excellent plat-form for the tent, then the fire was lit and we rejoiced over hot soup, English biscuits, and Caucasian mutton. Before us was the great ice-embattled wall of Shkara and Janga, rising high into the warm tinted air, whilst below the silent glacier gloomed dark and cold, as the gathering mists of evening crawled slowly along its slopes. Behind our tent towered the great cliffs of Dych Tau. There is something in huge unclimbed peaks, especially when seen by the light of ebbing day, which is strangely solemn. Jest and joke are pushed aside as profanation, and one gazes on the tremendous cliffs with feelings closely akin to those with which the mediaeval pil-grim worshipped at some holy shrine. The lengthening shadows fell athwart its face and showed deep gullies and jagged ridges, ice-glazed rocks and vast pitiless slabs of unbroken granite. From crack to gully and gully to ridge, we traced a way till it emerged on a great smooth precipitous face where, as Zurfluh piously remarked, we must hope that "Der liebe Gott wird uns etwas helfen." We watched the last flicker of sunlight play round its topmost crags, and then crept into the shelter of tent and sleeping-bags. The hardier Tartar refused the proffered place beside us, and, having washed his head, his feet, and hands, in due accordance with the ritual of his creed, lay down in the open beside a great rock. . . . Zurfluh regarded these proceedings with much sad interest, feeling certain that the bitter wind would freeze him to death before morning.

At I A.M., Zurfluh, who had kept awake to bemoan the Tartar's slow and pitiable decease, crept out of the tent to investigate how this process was getting on. A few minutes later, with his teeth chattering, but none the less with real delight in face and voice, he told me that not merely was the Tartar still alive, but, bare feet and all, appeared to be enjoying a refreshing sleep! Zurfluh's mind relieved on this point, he engaged in a protracted struggle with the fire. The Bezingi wood always requires much coaxing, but at I A.M. it would try the patience of a saint and the skill of one of his Satanic majesty's most practised stokers. Unluckily the little stream, on which we had counted for a perennial supply of water, was frozen to its core, and the weary process of melting ice had to be undertaken. My boots were also frozen, and putting them on proved to be the most arduous and by far the most painful part of the expedition. However, these preliminary difficulties were at length overcome and we were able to rejoice over hot tea and biscuits in the warm shelter of the tent.

Soon after half-past two we began the ascent and tramped steadily up the crisp snow to the little glacier. We crossed it, and ascended the slopes to the col by the route I had previously taken when on the way to the south-western buttress. Reaching this we turned sharply to the right, and scrambling round one or two crumbling towers, were fairly launched on the face. Working upwards but bearing ever well to the right, we reached a shallow couloir still plastered in places by half-melted masses of snow. One of these, smitten by Zurfluh's axe, broke away bodily, striking me very severely on the head, knee, and hand. Luckily I was almost close to him, but even so, for a minute or two, I scarcely knew what had happened. Had there been three or four of us on the rope the results could scarcely have failed to be serious. I am aware that two men are usually regarded as constituting too small a party for serious mountain work. None the less, on rotten rocks, or where much frozen snow loosely adheres to the ledges and projecting crags, it has advantages which, so far as I am able to judge, make it almost an ideal number.

Happily, five minutes' rest restored my scattered senses, and we quitted this ill-behaved gully, bearing still further to the right over disintegrated rocks and loose stones. . . . Without halting we still pushed on, bearing ever to the right in order to reach the smaller of two long couloirs that had been very conspicuous from our camp. This couloir runs up the face of the peak towards the south-western ridge in the near neighbourhood of the summit. Zurfluh had, the previous evening, diagnosed its contents as snow, and the rocks being mostly ice-glazed and distinctly difficult, we thought it desirable to reach it as soon as possible. When we at length gained its brink we saw at a glance that it was much steeper than we had imagined, and that, if I may be pardoned the Irishism, the snow was ice. In consequence we clung to the rocks as long as any sort of decent progress could be made, and it was only when each foot of advance was costing precious minutes that we turned into the gully.

Hypercritical climbers have occasionally suggested that I am in the habit of cutting steps rather wide apart. I only wish these cavillers could have seen Zurfluh's staircase. He has a peculiar habit of only cutting steps for the left foot, his right having the faculty of adhering firmly to absolutely smooth ice and enabling him by a combination of jump and wriggle to lift his left foot from one secure step to another six feet above it. He kindly showed me how it was done and urged me to imitate his procedure, pointing out the great saving of time thus rendered possible. Since, however, any trifling error would have resulted in an undue acquaintance with the glacier below, I preferred to cut intervening steps; even then it was a most arduous gymnastic exercise to climb from one to another. Happily, some twenty minutes of these violent athletics brought us to a point where we could quit the gully for the slope on our right. Hard, solid rock then led us merrily upwards to a great secondary ridge. This ridge divides the south face of the peak into two well-marked divisions: to the east is the great couloir which reaches from the col between the two summits to the very base of the mountain, and beyond are the interminable series of buttresses and gullies that stretch away towards Mishirgi Tau; whilst to the west is the less broken cliff reaching to the south-western ridge. We worked up the secondary ridge, now on one side, now on the other, till we were pulled up at the point where it bulges outward and towers up into the great crag which, like the hand of some gigantic sun-dial, throws long shadows across the face of the mountain. It was evident that the work would now become very much more serious, so we halted and made a good meal. We packed the remainder of the provisions into the knapsack and stowed it away under a large stone.

After prospecting the cliff on our right, Zurfluh came to the conclusion that nothing could be done on that side. We therefore turned our attention to the rocks on our left, and were soon traversing a huge slab by the aid of various minute wrinkles and discolorations. Happily it soon became possible to turn upwards, and, trusting mainly to our finger tips and the sides of our boots, we forced our way back on to the ridge at the very top of the sun-dial projection. For a short distance it was almost horizontal and extraordinarily sharp. So much so, indeed, that we were fain to accept the attitude much affected by foreign climbers in foreign prints, and progress was made on our hands whilst a leg was slung over each side as a sort of balancing pole. A gap fifteen feet deep separated this razor edge from the mass of the mountain beyond. Zurfluh jumped down on to a convenient bed of snow and cheerily went on his way. Shortly afterwards I reached the gap, and, as I fondly imagined, similarly jumped, but the bed of snow did not take the impact kindly and slid away into the little couloir on my left, a more or less breathless Herr being left clinging to a sort of banister of rock which projected from the gap. Happily this incident escaped the notice of the professional member of the party. I say happily, because the *morale* of the leader is frequently a plant of tender growth, and should be carefully shielded from all adverse influences.

We were now on the final peak. Gestola, Tetnuld, and Janga were well below us, and even the corniced ridge of Shkara did not look as if it could give us much. Unluckily, over this great ridge an evil-looking mass of cloud had gathered, and from time to time shreds and strips were torn from it and whirled across the intervening space by a furious southerly gale. Some of these shreds and strips sailed high over our heads, shutting out the welcome warmth of the sun; others less aerially inclined now and again got tangled in the ridges below, blotting out their jagged spires and warning us that at any moment the cliffs around might be veiled in impenetrable mist.

The wall immediately above was evidently very formidable. Though I sought to keep up an affectation of assured success, I was quite unable to see how any further advance was to be made. Zurfluh, however, is a man who rises to such emergencies, and is moreover an exceptionally brilliant rock climber. He proved equal to the occasion, and vowed by the immortal gods that we would not be baffled a second time. Whilst he was looking for the most desirable line of attack, I replied to the shouts of the shepherd who had climbed to the col early in the morning, and, greatly interested in our proceedings, had spent the rest of the day on that bleak spot in a biting and furious wind.

Zurfluh, after a careful survey, determined that we must again traverse to our left. We crawled along the face of the great cliff, clinging to outward shelving and most unsatisfactory ledges, till we reached a place where strenuous efforts just enabled us to lift ourselves over a sort of bulge. Above this the angle was less steep, and a few cracks and splinters enabled us to get reliable hold. A short distance further, however, a second and, if possible, nastier bulge appeared. After contemplating Zurfluh's graceful attitudes and listening to his gasps as he battled with the desperate difficulty, it was "borne in upon me"—as the Plymouth Brethren say—that the second peak in the Caucasus ought not to be climbed by an unroped party. Would it not be contrary to all the canons laid down for the guidance of youth and innocence in the Badminton and All England series? [2] Might it not even be regarded as savouring of insult to our peak? I mildly suggested these fears to Zurfluh. He asked me whether I would come up for the rope or whether he should send the rope down to me. For some hidden reason a broad grin illuminated his face as he strongly recommended the former course,

[2] The Badminton Library of Sports and Pastimes, edited by the eighth Duke of Beaufort, was a series of books of instruction which appeared in the late nineteenth and early twentieth centuries.

pointing out that the ledge on which I was huddled was not a convenient place for roping operations. Despite this advice I unhesitatingly decided on the latter alternative, and when the rope came down, successfully grappled with the difficulty of putting it on. And now a strange phenomenon must be recorded: a moment earlier I could have sworn before any court—and been glad to do, provided the court was, as courts usually are, on level ground—that the cliff in front was absolutely perpendicular. Yet no sooner was the rope firmly attached than the cliff titled backwards till it barely exceeded a beggarly sixty degrees!

We were now able to get round the square corner of the peak on to the face fronting the lower summit, and could look across to the ice-swept cliffs of Koshtantau. The gap between the two peaks was well below us—indeed, we were almost level with the lower summit. I had always had misgivings about this section of the ascent and it was, therefore, with no small delight that I perceived a long crack up which a way could almost certainly be forced. Apart, however, from the accident of this crack or fault, I am not sure this wall could be ascended. With our elbows and backs against one side and our knees against the other, we worked our way quickly upwards. The lower peak sank rapidly, and the appearance of distant snows above its crest was hailed with triumphant shouts. Then Zurfluh dived into a dark hole behind a stone that had wedged itself in our narrow path, and desperate were the wriggles and squeezings necessary to push his body through the narrow aperture. Then we had to quit the crack for a yard or two and scramble up a great slab at its side. Once more we got back into our crack and on and ever upwards till at length we emerged on the ridge. On the ridge do I say? No; on the very summit itself. Every peak in Europe, Elbruz [3] alone excepted, was below us, and from our watchtower of 17,054 feet we gazed at the rolling world. Turning to the left, a few steps brought me to the culminating point, and I sat down on its shattered crest. Huge clouds were by now wrapping Shkara in an ever darkening mantle, and the long ridge of Janga was buried in dense, matted banks of vapour white and brilliant above, but dark and evil along their ever lowering under-edges. Koshtantau shone in its snowy

[3] 18,481 feet.

armour, white against black billows of heaped-up storm. Elbruz alone was clear and spotless, and its vastness made it look so close that Zurfluh laughed to scorn my statement that our passes from Mujal to the Bashil Su were between us and it. He maintained and still believes that Elbruz is situated close to Tiktengen, and I defy all the surveyors of the Holy Russian Empire to convince him of error. A yellow look about the snow suggested, it is true, considerable distance, but the huge size and height of the enormous mass so dwarfed the intervening space that I am not surprised at his mistake.

As I declined to give up my seat on the highest point, Zurfluh was constrained to build the cairn, on which his heart was set, on a point slightly lower. Under his fostering care this point grew and waxed strong till it looked proudly over the crest of its rival that, for the last few thousand years, had topped it by a foot. After three-quarters of an hour's halt the furious blasts of the hurricane made us quite willing to move, and at 11.30 A.M. we left the summit. We rattled down the crack, and got back on to the south face without much trouble. Then, however, I distinguished myself by losing the way, and was relegated to the nominally more important post of last man. Zurfluh with brilliant skill picked up the line of ledges and cracks by which we had ascended, and we duly reached the horizontal ridge. Elated by our success we strode boldly along its narrow edge instead of adopting the undignified procedure of the morning. Shortly afterwards Zurfluh imitated my bad example and lost the right line of descent. We could see the rock by which our knapsack was securely stowed, and our footprints were on a small patch of snow just above the wall, but we could not discover the line by which we had connected these two points. Ultimately we were compelled to make a sensational descent by a tiny cleft or crack just wide enough for toes and fingers. Its lower end opened into space, and a long sideways jump was requisite to reach footing. Zurfluh, aided by the rope, got across, and said he could catch and steady me as I came over. I have a keen remembrance of descending the crack, of leaning forwards and down as far as I could reach, and just being able to rest the point of my axe on a small excrescence; then leaning my weight upon it, I swung over sideways towards Zurfluh. An instant later he was clasping my knees with such devout enthusiasm that I felt like a holy prophet ejected from the shining mountain into the arms of some faithful devotee.

This practically ended our difficulties. A few minutes later we reached the knapsack and soon demolished its contents. Our porter was still sitting on the col watching us, and Zurfluh, mindful of the habits of the Swiss when in high places, averred that he would certainly have finished every scrap of provision in the camp. None the less we greeted his shouts with loud yodels and much triumphant brandishing of ice-axes. Our lunch being brought to a summary conclusion by the total exhaustion of the supplies, we stuffed the rope into the empty knapsack and turned once more to the descent. We got on rapidly till we reached the couloir. The ice was here so rotten, and much of it so ill-frozen to the rocks and underlying ice, and the whole gully was so obviously swept by falling stones, that we unanimously refused to follow our morning's track. My own impression is that, apart from other objections, even Zurfluh did not quite like descending the remarkable staircase by which we had scrambled up. Crossing the couloir we struck on to the rocks, and soon discovered some precipitous ice-glazed chimneys down which we managed to crawl. Regaining our route of the morning, we sped merrily downwards to the belt of red rocks. The summit of a new peak in one's pocket lends strength and swiftness even to the clumsy, and I shuffled after Zurfluh in most active fashion. Our porter soon came to the conclusion that the interest of the play was over, and we saw him pick himself up and go warily down the slopes. A little later, Zurfluh, perceiving that even a Herr could not go much astray, was seized with a desire to show the Tartar how easy slopes should be traversed, and dashed towards the col with the speed and graceful ease of the well-practised chamois hunter. When a man is being hopelessly outpaced by his companion, he always experiences great pleasure in seeing that same companion miss the easiest line of descent. This pleasure I experienced on seeing Zurfluh, after reaching the col, keep to the line by which we had come in the morning. My previous exploratory climb had made me aware of a convenient snow-filled gully in which an exceedingly rapid standing glissade was possible. Reaching this highway, I spun down to the little glacier. Having run across this, I sat myself comfortably on my hat, and slid down the long slopes almost into the tent, where Zurfluh was still busy emptying the snow from his pockets. . . .

We soon discovered that, instead of consuming the whole of our provisions, the porter had not even had a crust of bread. We urged him to take a preliminary lunch, or rather breakfast, while the soup was cooking, but he refused, and seemed in no hurry for dinner. He manipulated the fire with much skill, making the vile wood burn in a really creditable manner, and only pausing from his efforts to award me an occasional appreciative slap on the back. It being early, 4 P.M., Zurfluh expressed a strong desire to strike camp and descend; but the delights of the kosh did not rouse my enthusiasm and I refused to move. Indeed, it is one of the great pleasures of Caucasian travelling that the weary tramp over screes, uneven glacier, the horrors of the moraine, and, too frequently, the reascent to the hotel, are unknown. A camp at one spot is practically as comfortable as at any other, and in consequence, so soon as one feels inclined to sit down and laze, the day's work is over and one postpones the screes and moraines to the sweet distance of to-morrow. It is, indeed, a rare delight to sit at one's ease in the early afternoon and gaze at the huge cliffs amongst which one has been wandering, free from all the thought of hurry, of moraines, or of darkness.

Towards evening the gathering clouds burst in thunder, and the screes below us, right down to the glacier, were powdered with hail and snow. As the moon rose, however, the curtain was rent apart, and the great ridges, shining in the brilliant whiteness of fresh-fallen snow, gazed at us across the dark gulf of the Bezingi Glacier. The evening, being windless, was comparatively warm, and it was nearly midnight before Zurfluh's peaceful slumbers were disturbed by the struggles of a shivering Herr with his sleeping-bag.

The next morning we went down the glacier to the Misses kosh, packed up our belongings, and tramped to Tubeneli. Fresh stores had arrived from Naltcik and the old chief feasted us on chicken and cakes, but these delights failed to comfort the melancholy Zurfluh, and he flatly refused to do aught but return straight home. On Dych Tau the excitement of the climb had aroused all the vigour and strength he possessed, but now that the spurt was over he broke down completely. He was undoubtedly very poorly, and looked the mere ghost, and a most thin and melancholy ghost, of his former self. "Es gefällt mir nicht," may be good philosophy, but it undoubtedly tends to a pre-Raphaelite condition of body.

SIR HALFORD JOHN MACKINDER

1861–1947

SIR HALFORD MACKINDER's career began early and auspiciously. A paper, presented in 1887, on "The Scope and Methods of Geography" so impressed the Council of the Royal Geographical Society that the Society agreed to subsidize a readership in the subject at Oxford. He thus became the university's second reader in geography; the first was the Elizabethan, Richard Hakluyt. Mackinder remained active in education as Principal of University College, Reading, 1892–1903; Professor of Geography at the University of London, 1900–1925; and Director of the London School of Economics and Political Science, 1903–1908. Throughout his life he insisted, against opposition and indifference, on the indispensability of a knowledge of geography to all who would understand history, politics, and human society. He served as a Member of Parliament from 1910 to 1922, as British High Commissioner for South Russia from 1919 to 1920, as chairman of the Imperial Shipping Committee from 1920 to 1945 and of the Imperial Economic Committee from 1926 to 1931, and as a member of several royal commissions. He was knighted in 1920.

Mackinder's principal contribution to the interpretation of history and to prophecy is contained in essence in his paper "The Geographical Pivot of History" (*The Geographical Journal*, XXIII, April, 1904, 421–37) and his book *Democratic Ideals and Reality* (1919). He contends that with the ending of the "Columbian epoch" of maritime expansion, roughly from 1500 to 1900, continued acceptance of the doctrine of the supremacy of sea-power has become a source of false security. A more comprehensive view of history reveals to him that the crucial area is the great land-mass of Eurasia, which he called the Heartland, control of which is potentially decisive. Mackinder's formulation has become classic: "Who rules East Europe commands the Heartland; who rules the Heartland commands the World-Island [Europe, Asia, and Africa considered as a geographical unit]; who rules the World-Island commands The World." Elsewhere he states that "the grouping of lands and seas, and of fertility and natural pathways, is such as to lend itself to the growth of empires, and in the end of a single world-empire." Thus he saw the significant part of the First World War—after the collapse of Russia and the entrance of the United States—as actually a duel between land-power and sea-power, in which the wielders of sea-power temporarily saved themselves. He urged the peacemakers of 1919 to recognize "these geographical realities," and though no advocate of iron suppression, warned that the revival of German military potential, and, even worse, an effective and enduring alliance of Germany and Russia might another time prove unconquerable. Mackinder's warning was generally unheeded, except in Germany, for twenty years.

Mackinder's ascent of Mount Kenya—the first—was undertaken largely for pleasure. Even so, the report which he made to the Royal Geographical Society, only a part of which is given here, reveals a talent for observation and a passion for detailed knowledge.

The following selection is reprinted from H. J. Mackinder, "A Journey to the Summit of Mount Kenya . . . ," *The Geographical Journal*, XV (May, 1900), 453–76, by permission of The Royal Geographical Society.

A Journey to the Summit of Mount Kenya

IN EAST AFRICA stand two snow-capped mountains, extinct volcanic cones, whose names have been known for fifty years— Kilimanjaro and Kenya. They are about 200 miles apart, due north and south of one another, the equator crossing Kenya, the more northern of the two. It was the missionary Rebmann of Mombasa who, in 1848, first reported the existence of Kilimanjaro. In the following year his colleague, Krapf, saw Kenya from Kitui, a spot 90 miles south-east of the peak. Since that time Kilimanjaro is said to have been visited by more than a hundred Europeans, and both the British and the German Governments have now established stations in its immediate proximity. Its summit was conquered in 1889 by Dr. Hans Meyer. Kenya, on the other hand, being further inland, and for other reasons less accessible, has been more rarely visited. It was seen, for the second time only, in 1883 by Joseph Thomson, when he crossed the plateau of Laikipia, out of which rise the north-western slopes of the mountain. In 1887 Count Teleki penetrated the forest girdle of Kenya, and succeeded in reaching an elevation of nearly 14,000 feet. Six years later Dr. Gregory attained to a height probably about 2000 feet greater. Both of these attempts were on the south-western quadrant of the mountain. Captain Dundas had previously failed to emerge from the forests of the southern slope, but Dr. Kolb at a later time reached the open "alp" above the eastern forest. It appeared, therefore, that when the Uganda railway had reduced the distance from the coast to Kenya by two-thirds, it should be possible with no great expenditure of time, to convey a well-equipped expedition in a state of European health to the foot of the mountain, and that such an expedition would have a reasonable chance of completing the revelation of its alpine secrets.

Rail-head having arrived at the requisite point in the summer of last year [1898], our party, consisting of six Europeans, left Marseilles on June 10 [1899]. My colleagues were Mr. C. B. Hausburg, who shared with me the expense of the expedition; Mr. E. H. Saunders, a collector; Mr. C. F. Camburn, a taxidermist; César Ollier, an Alpine guide from Courmayeur; and Joseph Brocherel, a porter from the same village. We were aided by a grant from this Society. Mr. Hausburg was good enough to act, not merely as photographer, but also as camp-master, thus leaving me free for observation and survey. The most important item in our equipment was a series of forty boxes, tin-lined, each weighing 25 lbs., and containing a day's complete rations for six white men. Two of these boxes were a man's load, and we carried them to the mountain, where food could not be obtained. They served our purpose admirably, and in a year of unusual drought were the basis of our success. By any other method of packing, theft and waste would have compelled retreat long before our work was accomplished.

We reached Zanzibar on June 28, and, warned by a telegram from Mombasa informing us that other caravans were about to set out for the interior, and that porters were in unusual demand, we asked for and obtained the kind permission of General Matthews, the Sultan's first minister, to recruit Swahilis in Zanzibar. On July 4 we landed in Mombasa, where famine-stricken Wanyika were engaged on relief works, and small-pox was prevalent. We therefore arranged with Major Souttar, to whom our thanks are due, that the fifty-nine Zanzibaris, who arrived on the 6th, should march to the fort and be isolated for the night. On the following morning they were placed in the train and sent to rail-head, then to Nairobi, a three days' journey from Mombasa. Mr. Hausburg took charge of them, and with him there went the other four Europeans, while I remained at Mombasa until the 12th, completing our arrangements. . . .

The last detachment of the caravan left the railway on July 26, and marched to our first camp on the Nairobi river, 9 miles from the station. There we concentrated, and after a day's delay commenced our journey to Kenya in the morning mist of the 28th. All told we were 170 strong—six Europeans, sixty-six Swahilis, two tall Masai guides and the remainder naked Wakikuyu. For four days we crossed the Kapoti plains, steering by Donyo Sabuk, the "great mountain" of the Masai. The plains are treeless and carpeted with sweet grass, which at this season was burned brown and crumbled under the foot. In addition to the Nairobi, we crossed three considerable streams—the Ruiru, the Daruku, and the Thika—whose waters, thigh-deep, are drawn from the slopes of Kikuyu away to the north-west. Their winding valleys are trenched into the plateau, and along the bottoms a continuous belt of tree and bush overarches the river channel. There was evidence of lions at the river-banks, but game was not very abundant in this part of the plain, although we had seen herds of 1500 zebra, wildebeeste, and hartebeeste, at a distance of 20 or 30 miles to southward beyond the Nairobi station. Rhinoceros were the most striking tenants of the waste. On two occasions, when we went more than usually near to them, they charged into the caravan, fortunately without serious effect. . . .

On July 31 we made a march of 15 miles from the Athi to Muluka, Mbuthia's [1] village. Our way lay over the plain and across the Thika river into a country set thinly with scraggy trees, like a great apple orchard with drought-burned grass. This is the marchland between the grassy plain of the Masai and the cultivated hills and valleys of the Wakikuyu. Gradually the grass became longer and greener, until at last it was shoulder-high and seed-topped. Then we came suddenly to the brink of the deep valley of the Thuge brook, along which, in the bottom, wound a strip of irrigated cornland. On the

[1] Mbuthia was a Kikuyu chief.

opposite side, in a glade of the bush which ran up the slope, we pitched our camp in close neighbourhood to Muluka.

Here our troubles began, for our Kikuyu headmen came to us with strong expressions of distrust as to the intentions of their countryman, Mbuthia. It took some diplomacy to secure peace, and that evening we for the first time put a boma or fence round the camp, and the white men took turn in keeping guard. Next day we made a state entry into Muluka, photographed Mbuthia and his wives, and shifted camp across the ridge on which the village is placed, into the next valley—that of the Ilula brook. It was in this district that Mr. Haslam, one of the Protectorate officers, had been murdered a short time before, and here a neighbour of Mbuthia's, Mudiu of Katumba, a man of singularly deceitful and repellent countenance, intrigued with the Wakikuyu of our caravan, trying to make them desert us, in the hope, no doubt, of looting what we could not carry without their aid. In the evening, by fire-light, our Kikuyu headmen endeavoured to counteract his and similar influences by orations, whose resounding periods and eloquent vowel sounds were seductive even to those of us who could not understand a word that was spoken. As the peroration was reached the orator put questions to the crowd, who replied unanimously, with an effect which resembled the rapid recital of the Church Litany, punctuated by the loud grunting responses of the congregation. These Kikuyu headmen behaved well on the whole, and were loyal to us in spite of considerable temptations. Next morning, however, the whole body of Kikuyu porters attempted to desert, and were only checked by a display of firearms. . . .

On August 6 we marched out of the hill country of Kikuyu which is a trenched and denuded lava plateau—over the brow of the gneissic hill Kandundu, with an extensive view upon plains to eastward, and then through the gap between the gneissic hills, Kamuti and Kambijo, across the Sagana, to the plain which is the beginning of Meranga. Here we pitched camp and stayed for three days. In the last two marches we had again had to deal with rivers rather than brooks, and of these the Maragua, the Kaiahue, and the Mathioya are worthy of mention.

Meranga is a country about 30 miles across, extending from the

Sagana northward to the edge of the Kenya forests. It has very definite limits. We entered it when we crossed the Sagana; we left it when we crossed the Ragati. It is part of Kikuyu, and yet very distinct from the remainder of that land. It appears to be ruled by a system of informal meetings, or shauris, of elders, who sit on little stools in a great ring. Such a shauri was held within sight of our camp on the day of our arrival, summoned, no doubt, by Magonie, the elder of the neighbouring village, with whom we had made friends. Through our glasses we watched one orator after another address the assembly, and daylight was failing before the interpreter came to announce that "the rich men of Meranga," as he put it, had come to visit us. The shauri had, in fact, adjourned to our camp, and when the ring had been re-established, and when Hausburg and I had joined it, and Magonie had made speeches, we were informed that the Wameranga were our friends, and would do all they could for us. Then the fifty Wazee rose, and, shaking hands with us, filed away each to his own village, or, in the case of the more remote, to stay the night with Magonie. . . .

We left Magonie's on August 10, our guides being three Wazee—Kamanga, Kerrerri, and Magonie. Kamanga was an important elder verging on old age, a pleasant man, but of no strength of character. Magonie was a pushing, boisterous individual, friendly enough, but rather oppressive. We were told that he was a notorious drunkard. Kerrerri was a young man of somewhat Japanese countenance, very pleasant and intelligent, but of slippery character. I learned a great deal from him, but found it necessary to verify everything by the cross-examination of more stupid persons. A young friend of his who joined us later was the handsomest man I saw in Africa. . . .

For 7 miles from Magonie's our way was over the plain through fields of maize and maize stubble, and past banana groves. For the first time since we left the mango trees of the coast, we saw really fine spreading trees of the general appearance of walnut-trees, with large dark foliage—the remainder, no doubt, of the forest which seems to have clothed the greater part of the Kikuyu country at no distant date. The hedges between the fields were mostly of wild tomato, and bore both fruit and flowers. Beans, sweet potatoes, yams, and gourds were abundant. Narrow paths of greasy red soil traversed the country in all directions, crossing the streams by bridges formed of felled trees, the trunks of which are cleft down the centre, the flat surface being upturned. The paths were usually fenced in, and wild flowers grew along their edges. We saw evidence of the use of manure.

Towards the end of this march we entered a hill country, but the cultivation became if anything more extensive and more continuous, and the crops more luxuriant, for we had now come to that part of Kikuyu in which it appears to rain almost daily. From August 7 to the 15th, it rained every day from midnight, or earlier, until noon or later. We travelled under the most depressing conditions, drenched to the skin from the moment that we rose, making short marches over slippery paths, and pitching our camp on wet ground. Yet the aspect of the country was something never to be forgotten. Here, in the heart of Africa, in a region previously approached by half a dozen white men at most, we traversed square miles of standing maize, neatly divided by slight furrows into rectangular half-acre plots, each, we were told, valued for sale at the price of a goat, and we had to pitch camp in a market-place strewn with corn-cobs, or to march for several miles to the next vacant space. As we approached the end of Meranga, however, a singular change took place in the aspect of the people. At Magonie's on the Sagana, they had worn cloth, and friendship once established, had come freely into our camp, maintaining a day-long market outside it. Here as we approached the borders of Wangombe and of the dreaded Watumutumu, even the chiefs wore skins, and for hours we marched over a land heavy with crops, and yet saw neither man nor woman. Again and again Kerrerri asked me to prevent our Swahilis from shouting and singing, in order that the inhabitants might not be frightened, and that he might have an opportunity of establishing relations with them.

Through Meranga we followed the valley of the Ragati, an important tributary of the Sagana not marked on the maps, which descends due southwards from Kenya. On August 12 and 13 we crossed the upper basin, where a number of streams from the Kenya forests converge to form the Ragati proper. Here the higher grounds rise above the cultivation and have the aspect of a rough English

common, of the kind that would there be overgrown with gorse and
bracken. Both the uplands and the stream-edges were brilliant with
flowers; indeed, the whole of the upper part of Meranga is a paradise of wildflowers.

On August 13 we crossed the Ragati and entered the little country of Kaleti. . . . We now marched for two days through a forest
containing many elephants, whose paths we followed. The flowers
were here rarer, but of the same species as in the cultivated country.
The most singular point, however, was the almost complete absence
of winged insects, at any rate in the day-time. Song birds, on the
other hand, were abundant. The lofty trees were hung with beard-
moss. Here and there we traversed green glades, from which conical
hills, clothed with forest, could be seen to rise from among the
trees in our neighbourhood. Niana and Kerhari, the most prominent
of these hills, became important landmarks at a later stage of our
journey.

The rain now ceased, though it obviously persisted in the country
that we had traversed. Ahead, to northward, was a great arch of
blue sky, a clearing which had been seen at times, low on the horizon,
from so distant a point as Magonie's. The relation of wind, rain, and
land-relief was, in fact, strikingly illustrated by our experiences.
The south-east monsoon was blowing strongly without depositing
rain on the plains of the Athi and Sagana, whose elevation is about
5000 feet. When it struck the slope of Kikuyu, which rises gradually
from 5000 feet to about 7000 feet, it drenched the whole country
side. The high plains of Laikipia, which surmount the slope at an
elevation of about 7000 feet, were dry. So sudden is the change from
Kikuyu to Laikipia, that in the course of a single march of about 9
miles we left a dripping forest and came to a land which was the
scene during the next few weeks, not merely of prairie fires, but also
of forest fires. Yet in the presence of these fires we could see the
heavy bank of clouds close at hand, driving up over the brink of the
plateau and melting into thin air.

It was on the afternoon of August 15 that we emerged from the
forest of Kikuyu, and crossing the Sagana again, here flowing to
southwestward as a brawling mountain stream, we pitched the camp
which was to be the base of our operations on Kenya. The site was

a high one, and gave a wide view over the brown steppe of Laikipia to the distant curves of the Aberdare range. That evening the setting sun lit up the peak and snows of Kenya, which rose abruptly above the forest curtain of the mountain, at whose edge, splayed out for some distance on to the plain, we had now arrived. . . .

Next day, August 18, two parties left the camp—the one, under Sulimani, our Swahili headman, returned to Wangombe's to buy more food; the other was the mountain party in my own charge. Hausburg stayed in camp until the return of Sulimani, and was then to join me. Of the porters going to the mountain, twelve were equipped to remain there for some time, old Metropolitan police coats, boots, and extra blankets being served out to them.

On the evening of the 18th my party made a short march to a point at the forest edge, close to that by which Gregory entered it. Next day we commenced what we expected to be a tedious passage of perhaps three days. César and Joseph, woodmen as well as ice-men, led on what the guides christened "la grande route du Mont Kenya." Our work was eased by availing ourselves of elephant-paths and by keeping steadily to the ridge, thus avoiding the tangle by the streams. There was hoar-frost on the ground as we passed through the portal of the first trees in the early morning. Within, tall straight branchless conifers supported a dark roof of foliage with frequent gaps to the sky. The undergrowth was at first of laurel-like shrub and of tall stinging-nettles, and here green parrots flew screeching in flocks just above the treetops. Presently tufts of bamboo appeared, and then bamboo ousted all growth but the conifers, the ground-weeds, and the rope and string-like creepers. Hour after hour we forged onward, and after a time upward also, until with unexpected progress we grew ambitious of making the passage of the forest-zone in a single day. And this we accomplished, with one hour to spare before the inexorable tropical nightfall. We camped in a glade, part of the glade-maze which runs along the upper edge of the forest, and above us, comparatively close, was the green treeless shoulder of the mountain, hiding the central peak.

The next day we reconnoitred upward with a view to finding a site for the standing camp, which was to be the halfway shelter between the base of the mountain and the foot of the central peak, and in the afternoon we moved the tents to the spot selected. It was at an elevation of about 10,300 feet, and commanded a view over the forest slopes, across the Laikipian steppes, to Sattima and Nandarua, the twin heights of the Aberdare range. The phenomena of wind and cloud were of unceasing interest as watched from this position. At the camp itself even the lightest wind was rare, yet the drift of the smoke from the fires below showed the constant strength of the monsoon on the plain which we had left. A vast stratum of cloud hung day and night over the rainy slope by which we had ascended to the plain, and this we came to call the "cloud roof of Kikuyu." On one occasion I looked over its upper surface, across 80 miles of white woolly cloud, to the peaks of Donyo Lamuyu emerging like an island from a sea. Especially in the early morning, a tongue of cloud extended from the Kikuyu roof along the eastern foot of Sattima, thus masking from us the western half of Laikipia. At sunrise the summits of Nandarua and Sattima stood out cold and hard against the western sky, but as the morning advanced clouds capped the heights—clouds, however, of quite independent origin from the Kikuyu roof below, or its Laikipian tongue.

On August 21, César, Joseph, and I went up to what proved to be Gregory's Höhnel valley, and here for the first time we saw the extraordinary vegetation of the alpine zone of the mountain. The unbroken side of the valley, crowned with owl-haunted crags, has a moist peaty soil, in which are set yard-broad hemispherical tufts of wiry grass, each tuft having a moist rotten centre. Well-beaten rat-paths ramify in all directions between the tufts, while every here and there are groups of cactus-like giant lobelia, of which some send up tall spikes bearing the flowers. In general appearance very like the lobelia, except as regards the flower, is a species of giant groundsel with silvery leaves; but the greatest curiosity of all is the tree groundsel, with a thick dark trunk 8 or 10 feet high, surmounted by a cactus-like head of green leaves, beneath which is pendant a mass of dead leaves, dry as tinder towards their tips, but moist and rotten near the trunk. Occasionally a tall spike, several feet in height, bearing yellow grounded flowers and fluffy seeds, stands erect above the leaf-head, or broken and leaning gauntly to one side. In other spots are yellow composites, something like dandelions, but with blossoms sessile on the ground, and bushy everlasting flowers. Beautiful sunbirds with lark-like song fly from lobelia to lobelia.

That evening, as we were on the point of returning to the camp, a lighted match was dropped, for it never occurred to us that where the ground was boggy to the tread any special precaution was needful against fire. But the fire spread behind us with alarming rapidity, feeding on the surface of the grass tufts and the dry ends of the dead groundsel leaves. Next morning, when we set out with eight porters to carry stores up to form a depot, a great column of smoke rose in front of us, and above it was a white cloud drifting away to north-west, as though the volcano were once more in activity. Fortunately the men had boots with them, and beating an entry through the hissing line of red flames, which broke into a roar as they grasped a tree groundsel or shrub heath, we raced for 50 yards through the acrid smoke. It was fully a quarter of a mile before we could see and breathe freely again, and then we were in a new land. The mountain-side was black, covered with velvety mounds which had once been grass tufts, but set with thousands of gleaming points—the silvery groundsels, which had been protected by the moisture cupped in their broad leaves. Presently we realized that we were within a vast circle of fire, and that the whole of the collecting-ground convenient to our middle camp was endangered. We determined to preserve the upper Höhnel valley, and fought the fire for two hours, at last with success, though a long watch was still necessary to check the flames which every now and again broke from the border of the smouldering area. The sun went down that evening amid smoke-banks of mauve and orange, the orb itself changing from blood-red to a glorious ruddy gold, while above were roseate and pale green clouds. The after-glow was of copper. As night settled down the ruddy glare rose high over the edges of the deep black valley, and the silver groundsel gleamed weirdly in the diffused light; but in the rear—to eastward—was the cold dark valley head, the reward of our struggle in the afternoon.

The next morning we went up to the col above us and looked across the Teleki valley—in and from which Teleki and Gregory reached their highest points—on to the rocks and glacier of the central peak. We chose, from a distance, the position of our topmost camp, a mile from the foot of the ice, and then returned to our tents by the rushing Höhnel stream, to receive a further relay of stores and to prepare for the final advance on the following day. But that afternoon a message came up from Hausburg, who had just arrived at the middle camp, to the effect that two of our Swahilis had been murdered, and that the base camp was nearly devoid of supplies. I immediately left the two guides where they were, and joined Hausburg at sunset.

It appeared that the food caravan sent out on the 18th, in charge of Sulimani, had duly arrived at Wangombe's, and that the porters had bought food for themselves, and also a small quantity to be added to our store. Wangombe then said that he could not get much more in his village, and asked that men should be sent with him to make purchases in another village. This Sulimani refused to arrange, but Sudullah, an energetic and favourite askari, insisted on going, and five others volunteered to go with him. Wangombe and many of his men accompanied them. While passing through a banana shamba, our party was attacked with arrows and spears by a force in ambush, led, apparently, by Wangombe's brother. A fight ensued, in which two men fell on our side, and, it was reported, five on that of the enemy. The remainder of our men got back to camp, bringing with them the weapons of their slain adversaries, but Sudullah was unfortunately one of the killed. Wangombe came to Sulimani that evening, asking him to stay where he was, as he wished for a shauri in the morning; but Sulimani struck camp at midnight, and returned to Hausburg on the morning of the 21st. On the 22nd Hausburg dispatched Sulimani with thirty-five men, including the two Masai guides, to buy food at the Government station on Lake Naivasha, and leaving the base camp, now protected by a good boma, in charge of Ali, the interpreter, himself came up the mountain to consult with me.

On August 24 Hausburg and I went down again to the base, taking Saunders with us and all the food that could be spared. After going carefully through our stock, we determined to divide everything eatable between the men who still remained at the camp, and to dispatch them in Sulimani's track towards Naivasha. They refused to stir without a white man to lead them, and we had reluctantly to give the charge to our collector, Mr. Saunders. The Masai guides had gone with the previous party, and Saunders had to undertake the crossing of an untraversed country with no better guide than a pocket-compass and an envelope bearing approximate directions. On the evening of the 25th, having accompanied the caravan a short distance on the way, Hausburg and I turned aside to shelter for the night under the lee of a valley brink, with feelings of no little anxiety for the fate both of Sulimani and Saunders. The garrison on the mountain had food for about three weeks.

The next day we returned through the forest to the middle camp, and, while Hausburg helped Camburn to collect there and in the Höhnel valley, I rejoined César and Joseph in the Teleki valley, where they had established our top camp and built a stone hut. Thence, in the early morning of the 30th, we set out on our first attempt to climb the peak.

The central peak of Kenya is a pyramid of highly crystalline rock, cleft at the summit into two points, standing north-west and south-east of one another, the north-western being some 30 or 40 feet higher than the other, and the two perhaps 1000 feet higher than any other point on the mountain. The Masai have a legend that they had their origin on Kenya, and I propose that the twin points should be named after the great Masai chief, Batian, and Nelion, his brother. I owe the suggestion to Mr. S. L. Hinde. Nearly three-quarters of a mile to south-eastward an ice-clad peak, visible from the plains of Laikipia, rises to about 16,300 feet, and for this I suggest the name of the living Masai chief, Lenana. Between Lenana and the central peak are glacier passes from which descend to northward and southward, respectively, the two chief glaciers of Kenya, which have been named after Gregory and Lewis. As the word *Kenya* is probably a corruption of the Masai word signifying "mist," it seems appropriate, on that as well as physical grounds, to describe the notch in the summit between Batian and Nelion as the "Gate of the Mist."

Our way led up the left lateral moraine of the Lewis glacier, then diagonally across the glacier to a snow-filled couloir near its north-western corner. A short distance up the couloir we turned to the left and climbed the eastern face of the southern *arête* of the peak. We were here delayed by three *mauvais pas* and the treacherous nature of the fissured rock. On the ridge we were further delayed by the broken character of the edge, which compelled frequent traverses, so that night fell upon us at the foot of the point Nelion. We therefore sought a slab of rock just below the *arête* on its western side, and, after such food as could be afforded, tied ourselves to the rocks and prepared for the twelve hours of equatorial darkness. We were at an elevation of about 16,800 feet, but the cold was fortunately less than at the camp in the hollow of the head of the Teleki valley. It was not until 2 A.M. that the east wind, which had been moaning and screaming through the chinks of the rock-wall behind us, began to reach over and to stroke us with paws of cold air, making us draw close together and beat our knees. The sky was cloudless, and the stars, shining like lamps without twinkling, shed light enough to reveal the lakelets on the Two Tarn col to west of us. At 3 P.M. the moon rose, casting a cold light over the vast cloud roof of Kikuyu, and by diffused illumination making clear the surface of the Darwin glacier in the shadow of the precipice, 1500 feet beneath us. In the morning we climbed a little higher, aiming at the point Nelion, but were speedily brought up by a cleft cut completely through the peak, dividing the southern *arête* from Nelion. We had no alternative but to abandon the effort and return to our camp.

Hausburg and I now changed places, and while he and the two guides took the photographic camera, in one long day, completely round the foot of the peak, I went down on to the Laikipian plain to watch for the return of our caravans. I had to traverse the smouldering remains of a fire, which had seized the lower edge of the Kenya forest where it was crossed by our path.

As the days went by, spent chiefly in scanning the plain with a glass, and no one approached us, my wait became an anxious one; and on September 5, being the fifteenth day since the departure of Sulimani and the eleventh since that of Saunders, I had to send word for all to come down from the mountain in order to start for Naivasha on the 7th, lest starvation should overtake us. On the day arranged Hausburg duly conducted the retreat, to the bitter chagrin of César who had again been defeated by the peak. He and Joseph had laboriously cut their way up the Darwin glacier, and, bad weather intervening, could neither mount higher nor yet return by the dangerous way that they had come. They managed, however, to effect a traverse to the south *arête*, and returned by the route which we had followed in the first attempt.

Most fortunately, however, some two hours before Hausburg's arrival, Sulimani and Saunders marched in, and with them Captain Gorges, who commands at Naivasha. Sulimani had reached Naivasha, and after three days, consumed by an official correspondence, Captain Gorges had obtained leave to return with him to the foot of Kenya. They took local Masai guides, and followed an important native track over the Aberdare range to the north of Sattima, a track apparently unrecorded except in the native itineraries. . . . By an extraordinary chance, Saunders, who had made a difficult and toilsome journey over the shoulders of Sattima through trackless ravines choked with bush, struck the path which Gorges was following just half an hour before the caravan from Naivasha came up, two days out from the station. Thus it happened that our whole force was once more concentrated, and reinforced by the men belonging to Gorges. On the following day it was decided that Hausburg should lead the majority of our caravan back in company with Gorges, and that I should return to the mountain with four white and fifteen picked black men to make one more endeavour to solve its problems. Hausburg and Gorges left within six hours of our decision.

I now determined to move our base camp some 3 miles into the forest, and to leave Saunders and Camburn there, on a new collecting-ground. Our little force could not effect the removal of our stores at a single journey, and, following a practice which we had hitherto found successful, a portion of them was hidden in the bush. . . .

At last, on September 12, César, Joseph, and I left our top camp at noon to make the final attempt to reach the summit. The journey round the peak, made by Hausburg, had clearly shown that no way was practicable up the northern precipice, and we had already failed twice on the southern side, once on rock and once on ice. We now planned a route partly over rock and partly over ice. We followed our first track up and across the Lewis glacier, and up the face of the southern *arête*, near the top of which we spent the night under a Mummery tent.[2] We were up at earliest dawn, and away as soon as the sun rose out of the cloud roof to eastward, thawing our hands so that we could grasp the rocks. A traverse, with steps across the head of the Darwin glacier, brought us to a rocky rib descending from the western corner of Nelion, and up this we crept for a short way. We then decided to cross the glacier which hangs from the Gate of the Mist between the two points, and drains by a couloir into the Darwin glacier below. It proved very steep and intensely hard, so that three hours were consumed in cutting steps on a traverse which we had hoped to make in twenty minutes. A final rock scramble enabled us to set foot on the summit of Batian precisely at noon on September 13. The view from the Gate of the Mist had been magnificent. At the summit we were a few moments too late, for the mist, driving up, gave only momentary glimpses into the valleys beneath.

The mountain-top is like a stunted tower rising from among ruins and crowned by three or four low turrets, upon which we sat, feet inward. There was no snow there, and the thermometer slung in the air gave a temperature of 40 Fahr., while several kinds of lichen grew on the rocks. We dared, however, stay only forty minutes—time enough to make observations and to photograph—and then had to descend, not from any physical inconvenience due to the elevation, but for fear of the afternoon storm. We made our way downward from step to step cautiously in the mist, and reached our sleeping-place of the previous night at sunset; but we continued down the rocks by the moonlight, and arrived in camp after 10 P.M., exhausted, but victorious. We supped by the fire at midnight, with the sound of the Nairobi torrent ringing on the rocks and swelling and falling in the breeze, and from time to time with the hoot of an owl or bark of a leopard, yet none of them seeming to break the silence of the great peak which rose among the stars, sternly graceful, in the cold light of the sinking moon.

[2] See p. 152.

EVELYN WAUGH

BORN 1903

With *Decline and Fall* (1928), *Vile Bodies* (1930), *Black Mischief* (1932), *A Handful of Dust* (1934), and *Scoop* (1938), Evelyn Waugh established his preeminence among the novelists who responded with satire to the aberration and extravagance of the years between two wars. His special target was the barbarism of modern civilization, to a minor manifestation of which he returned in *The Loved One* (1948). Less well known are several unconventional and incisive books resulting from travels undertaken privately and as a journalist. *Labels* (1930) recounts a Mediterranean journey; *Remote People* (1930), travels in eastern Africa and southern Arabia; *Ninety-Two Days* (1934), an expedition to Brazil; and *Waugh in Abyssinia* (1936), some experiences while he was reporting Mussolini's Ethiopian campaign for the *Daily Express*. A selection from these books was published in 1947 under the title *When the Going Was Good*. Actually his novels and books of travel are noticeably complementary. The tropical settings prominent in *Black Mischief*, *A Handful of Dust*, and *Scoop* are imaginative projections of experience recorded in the travel books and emphasize the frenzy, depravity, and emptiness of modern sophistication. The anti-romance adumbrates the satire of the novels. A grotesque and occasionally "sick-making" humor is part of the method in both.

The selection presented here is taken from the part of *Remote People* which deals with southern Arabia and particularly Aden, which Waugh visited by "pure mischance" and expected to dislike. Instead, he enjoyed himself. Likewise his climb on the cliffs near Aden was something of a misadventure which resulted in amusement. The tone of mockery in his account of the exploit differs from the note struck by the professed partisans of mountaineering, who predominate in this anthology. Inevitably, most of the writers represented here would not hold such an attitude, but the humorously dissident viewpoint of Evelyn Waugh may provide a brief tonic of contrast.

A Tricky Bit

Nothing in my earlier acquaintance with Mr. Leblanc had given me any reason to suspect what I was letting myself in for when I accepted his invitation to join him in his little walk over the rocks. He was a general merchant, commercial agent, and shipowner of importance, the only European magnate in the Settlement; they said of him that he thrived on risk and had made and lost more than one considerable fortune in his time. I met him dining at the Residency, on my first evening in Aden. He talked of Abyssinia, where he had heavy business undertakings, with keen sarcasm; he expressed his contempt for the poetry of Rimbaud; he told me a great deal of very recent gossip about people in Europe; he produced, from the pocket of his white waistcoat, a Press-cutting about Miss Rebecca West's marriage; after dinner he played some very new gramophone records he had brought with him. . . .

A day or two afterwards he invited me to dinner at his house in Crater.[1] A smart car with a liveried Indian chauffeur came to fetch me. We dined on the roof; a delicious dinner; iced *vin-rosé*—"It is not a luxurious wine, but I am fond of it; it grows on a little estate of my own in the South of France"—and the finest Yemen coffee. With his very thin gold watch in his hand, Mr. Leblanc predicted the rising of a star—I forget which. Punctual to the second, it appeared, green and malevolent, on the rim of the hills; cigars glowing under the night sky; from below the faint murmur of the native streets; all infinitely smooth and civilised.

At this party a new facet was revealed to me in the character of my host. Mr. Leblanc the man of fashion I had seen. Here was Mr. Leblanc the patriarch. The house where we sat was the top story of his place of business; at the table sat his daughter, his secretary, and three of his "young men." The young men were his clerks, learning the business. One was French, the other two English lately down from Cambridge. They worked immensely hard—often, he told me,

[1] Waugh describes Aden as divided into two towns—Steamer Point and Crater Town, "the original nucleus of the settlement."

ten hours a day; often half way through the night, when a ship was in. They were not encouraged to go to the club or to mix in the society of Steamer Point. They lived together in a house near Mr. Leblanc's; they lived very well and were on terms of patriarchal intimacy with Mr. Leblanc's family. "If they go up to Steamer Point, they start drinking, playing cards, and spending money. Here, they work so hard that they cannot help saving. When they want a holiday they go round the coast visiting my agencies. They learn to know the country and the people; they travel in my ships; at the end of a year or two they have saved nearly all their money and they have learned business. For exercise we take little walks over the rocks together. Tennis and polo would cost them money. To walk in the hills is free. They get up out of the town into the cool air, the views are magnificent, the gentle exercise keeps them in condition for their work. It takes their minds, for a little, off business. You must come with us one day on one of our walks."

I agreed readily. After the torpid atmosphere of Aden it would be delightful to take some gentle exercise in the cool air. And so it was arranged for the following Saturday afternoon. When I left, Mr. Leblanc lent me a copy of Gide's *Voyage au Congo*.

Mr. Leblanc the man of fashion I knew, and Mr. Leblanc the patriarch. On Saturday I met Mr. Leblanc the man of action, Mr. Leblanc the gambler.

I was to lunch first with the young men at their "mess"—as all communal *ménages* appear to be called in the East. I presented myself dressed as I had seen photographs of "hikers," with shorts, open shirt, stout shoes, woollen stockings, and large walking-stick. We had an excellent luncheon, during which they told me how, one evening, they had climbed into the Parsees' death-house, and what a row there had been about it. Presently one of them said, "Well, it's about time to change. We promised to be round at the old man's at half-past."

"Change?"

"Well, it's just as you like, but I think you'll find those things rather hot. We usually wear nothing except shoes and shorts. We leave our shirts in the cars. They meet us on the bathing-beach. And if you've got any rubber-soled shoes I should wear them. Some of the rocks are pretty slippery." Luckily I happened to have some rubber shoes. I went back to the chaplain's house, where I was then living, and changed. I was beginning to be slightly apprehensive.

Mr. Leblanc looked magnificent. He wore newly creased white shorts, a silk openwork vest, and white *espadrilles* laced like a ballet dancer's round his ankles. He held a tuberose, sniffing it delicately. "They call it an Aden lily sometimes," he said. "I can't think why."

There was with him another stranger, a guest of Mr. Leblanc's on a commercial embassy from an oil firm. "I say, you know," he confided in me, "I think this is going to be a bit stiff. I'm scarcely in training for anything very energetic."

We set out in the cars and drove to a dead end at the face of the cliffs near the ancient reservoirs. I thought we must have taken the wrong road, but everyone got out and began stripping off his shirt. The Leblanc party went hatless; the stranger and I retained our topees.

"I should leave those sticks in the car," said Mr. Leblanc.

"But shan't we find them useful?" (I still nursed memories of happy scrambles in the Wicklow hills.)

"You will find them a great nuisance," said Mr. Leblanc.

We did as we were advised.

Then the little walk started. Mr. Leblanc led the way with light, springing steps. He went right up to the face of the cliff, gaily but purposefully, as Moses may have approached the rocks from which he was about to strike water. There was a little crack running like fork-lightning down the blank wall of stone. Mr. Leblanc stood below it, gave one little skip, and suddenly, with great rapidity and no apparent effort, proceeded to ascend the precipice. He did not climb; he rose. It was as if someone were hoisting him up from above and he had merely to prevent himself from swinging out of the perpendicular, by keeping contact with rocks in a few light touches of foot and hand.

In just the same way, one after another, the Leblanc party were whisked away out of sight. The stranger and I looked at each other. "Are you all right?" came reverberating down from very far ahead. We began to climb. We climbed for about half an hour up the cleft in the rock. Not once during that time did we find a place where it was possible to rest or even to stand still in any normal attitude. We just went on from foothold to foothold; our topees made it impossible to see more than a foot or two above our heads. Suddenly we came on the Leblanc party sitting on a ledge.

"You look hot," said Mr. Leblanc. "I see you are not in training. You will find this most beneficial."

As soon as we stopped climbing, our knees began to tremble. We sat down. When the time came to start again, it was quite difficult to stand up. Our knees seemed to be behaving as they sometimes do in dreams. . . .

"We thought it best to wait for you," continued Mr. Leblanc, "because there is rather a tricky bit here. It is easy enough when you know the way, but you need someone to show you. I discovered it myself. I often go out alone in the evenings finding tricky bits. Once I was out all night, quite stuck. I thought I should be able to find a way when the moon rose. Then I remembered there was no moon that night. It was a very cramped position."

The tricky bit was a huge overhanging rock with a crumbling flaky surface.

"It is really quite simple. Watch me and then follow. You put your right foot here . . ."—a perfectly blank, highly polished surface of stone—". . . then rather slowly you reach up with your left hand until you find a hold. You have to stretch rather far . . . so. Then you cross your right leg under your left—this is the difficult part—and feel for a footing on the other side. . . . With your right hand you just steady yourself . . . so." Mr. Leblanc hung over the abyss partly out of sight. His whole body seemed prehensile and tenacious. He *stood* there like a fly on the ceiling. "That is the position. It is best to trust more to the feet than the hands—push up rather than pull down . . . you see the stone here is not always secure." By way of demonstration he splintered off a handful of apparently solid rock from above his head and sent it tinkling down to the road below. "Now all you do is to shift the weight from your left foot to your right, and swing yourself round . . . so." And Mr. Leblanc disappeared from view.

Every detail of that expedition is kept fresh in my mind by recurrent nightmares. Eventually after about an hour's fearful climb

we reached the rim of the crater. The next stage was a tramp across
the great pit of loose cinders; then the ascent of the other rim, to the
highest point of the peninsula. Here we paused to admire the view,
which was indeed most remarkable; then we climbed down to the
sea. Variety was added to this last phase by the fact that we were
now in the full glare of the sun which had been beating on the cliffs
from noon until they were blistering hot.

"It will hurt the hands if you hang on too long," said Mr. Leblanc.
"One must jump on the foot from rock to rock like the little goats."

At last, after about three hours of it, we reached the beach. Cars
and servants were waiting. Tea was already spread; bathing-dresses
and towels laid out.

"We always bathe here, not at the club," said Mr. Leblanc. "They
have a screen there to keep out the sharks—while in this bay, only
last month, two boys were devoured."

We swam out into the warm sea. An Arab fisherman, hopeful of
a tip, ran to the edge of the sea and began shouting to us that it was
dangerous. Mr. Leblanc laughed happily and, with easy, powerful
strokes, made for the deep waters. We returned to shore and
dressed. My shoes were completely worn through, and there was
a large tear in my shorts where I had slipped among the cinders
and slid some yards. Mr. Leblanc had laid out for him in the car a
clean white suit, a shirt of green crêpe-de-Chine, a bow tie, silk
socks, buckskin shoes, ivory hairbrushes, scent spray, and hair lo-
tion. We ate banana sandwiches and drank very rich China tea.

For a little additional thrill on the way back, Mr. Leblanc took
the wheel of his car. I am not sure that that was not the most hair-
raising experience of all.

CHARLES FRANCIS MEADE

BORN 1881

C. F. MEADE has enjoyed a life-long passion for snow mountains, conceived when as a boy of twelve he went with his father to the Italian Piedmont and saw the peaks of the Levanna. His most active climbing was done during the years 1900 to 1930, in the mountains of Corsica, throughout the complex system of the Alps, and in the Garhwal Himalaya. His achievements include the first descent of the Jungfraujoch ridge of the Jungfrau, the second winter ascent of the Matterhorn, and a new route to the summit of the Guglia di Brenta in the Dolomites. The three seasons which he spent in exploring the wilderness of rock and ice around Kamet, in the Garhwal Himalaya, yielded much knowledge of the peaks and passes of that hitherto inaccurately mapped district. Although Mr. Meade himself was denied final victory on Kamet, information gathered by him contributed to the later success of an expedition led by Frank Smythe. Mr. Meade served as Vice-President of the Alpine Club in 1934 and 1935 and as a member of the Everest Committee in 1921 and 1922.

It was his fortune to climb with several of the great guides. He served his Alpine apprenticeship under the fearsome J. M. Blanc, usually known as le Greffier or Blanc Greffier, patriarch of a family of guides. With Pierre Blanc, son of the former, he climbed during his whole mountaineering career in Europe and Asia. Franz Lochmatter, who performed the miracles recounted by Geoffrey Winthrop Young in "A Memory of the Mischabel," also accompanied Mr. Meade on his second expedition to the Himalaya, as did Justin Blanc. The excellences of these men, particularly of le Greffier, are more conspicuously recorded in Mr. Meade's essays than are his own achievements.

Since 1930 Mr. Meade has written numerous articles on mountaineering, which have appeared in such periodicals as *Blackwood's, Spectator, Cornhill, Quarterly Review,* and *Fortnightly.* Some of these present narrative selected from his own experience; others examine critically the ideals and practices of modern mountaineers, particularly the Nazi *enfants perdus* of the 1930's. These essays, supplemented by new material, were published in 1940 under the title *Approach to the Hills.* Mr. Meade is currently writing a book which, according to his own description, will deal with "the psychology of mountaineers and mountain-lovers."

The following selection is reprinted from *Approach to the Hills*, by Charles Francis Meade, published by E. P. Dutton & Co., Inc., New York.

Kamet

THE GREAT Himalayan summit, Kamet, known to Tibetans as Kangmen, a name signifying "huge grandmother of the sacred snow-chain," was not discovered till 1848. In that year the surveyor, [Richard] Strachey, measuring the peaks in the tangled panorama of mountains visible from a view-point near the hill-station of Naini-Tal, found that one among them, a hundred miles away, was more than 25,000 feet high, surpassed all its neighbours by more than a thousand feet, and was only inferior by a couple of hundred feet to Nanda Devi herself, the highest mountain in British territory.[1]

The peak was given the name of Kamet, and twenty years later, the German brothers [Adolph and Hermann] Schlagintweit, pioneers far in advance of their time, attempted to climb it, approaching from the northern side in Tibet, and reaching a height of 22,239 feet. It is a curious fact, only discovered some forty years later, that this remarkable feat, brilliant though it was, had not really taken place on Kamet at all, but on Eastern Ibi Gamin, a neighbouring peak of 24,170 feet, which the climbers had not realized lay between them and their objective. It is curious, too, that several subsequent parties should have made exactly the same mistake.

The next explorers after the Schlagintweits were Longstaff, Bruce and Mumm with Alpine guides. They came from the Indian side in 1907, and reconnoitred both the eastern and western approaches. The result of their researches was that the great thoroughfare of the Kamet Glacier, affording the only means of access from the east, was condemned as dangerous on account of the ice-avalanches which appeared to fall right across it from both sides. Judging by the map,

[1] See p. 205. Today, of course, Nanda Devi is not in British territory.

therefore, a western glacier, named Khaiam, now seemed to offer the most hopeful alternative.

Accordingly in 1910, with Pierre Blanc and the Italian guide, Alexis Brocherel, I reconnoitred this glacier, hoping that it might provide a level highway, and afford a safer approach to the citadel than the route up the Kamet Glacier was said to do.

Well I remember the sanguine hopes with which we set out to ascend the glacier, after camping below it on the river flowing from the Mana Pass. Our camp was only a couple of marches above Mana, which is the last Indian village on the west side of the mountain, and 11,000 feet above sea-level.

But the Himalaya, unlike more sophisticated ranges, provides constant surprises for its explorers. We found that the glacier that we were ascending, instead of affording the easy, gradual approach that the map had encouraged us to hope for, not only turned out to be short and steep, but was shut in at its head by a ridge about 20,000 feet high, which prevented us from seeing any farther. As there was a depression in the ridge that was obviously accessible, and looked like a convenient pass, we pushed on hopefully. After walking half-way up the glacier, we could at first see nothing beyond the ridge that formed the horizon above our heads, but as we approached the supposed pass, there gradually rose above and beyond it the rocky dome of what was evidently a very big peak. Could it be Kamet? When at length we reached the gap there was no longer any doubt. The big peak was indeed Kamet, but unfortunately it was three or four miles from the saddle on which we stood, and in addition, it was cut off from us by a vast gulf, two or three thousand feet deep. In the bottom of the gulf an enormous glacier, not marked on any map, and coming from the foot of Kamet, flowed smoothly away out of sight in the direction of the Ganges and the Indian plain.

This *dénouement* closed our proceedings for 1910. The great unknown glacier that we had discovered appeared to be the missing highway that we had hoped to find, for it came from the actual foot of the peak. It was falsely shown on the map as quite a small ice-stream emerging from the Mana valley near a camping ground called Ghastole. If the map had been correct, this Ghastole Glacier (as it might be called) should have been enclosed at its head by a semi-circular mountain-range completely cutting it off from Kamet.

However, the mystery of this glacier was soon to be cleared up. In the following year, 1911, I was not in India, but Captain Morris Slingsby made an attempt on Kamet, and, acting on my advice, traveled up the Ghastole Glacier. As was expected the map was wrong, the glacier was twice as long as indicated, and the journey up the ice led Slingsby right round the actual foot of the mountain, ultimately enabling him to climb to a height of more than 22,000 feet.

In 1912, the Blanc brothers, Franz Lochmatter, Johann Perren and I followed in Slingsby's footsteps, and in our turn had the satisfaction of realizing our anticipations. After walking up the first four miles of ice, as shown on the map, we reached the point where the map marked a *cul-de-sac.* Here, looking round a corner of the mountains north of us, we saw as we had expected another four miles of unmapped glacier emerging from behind the foot of the huge precipitous pyramid of Kamet, towering 7,000 feet into the sky. So the facts had conclusively contradicted the map, and these upper reaches of the glacier, where we were standing, were the same that we had looked down upon from the Khaiam Saddle in 1910, and as we had supposed, here was the hoped-for highway that led to the foot of the mountain. Whether the latter could be climbed or not was another matter.

To clear up this point it was necessary to camp higher up the Ghastole Glacier, near its head. One long march took us up its entire length, and we pitched an advanced base-camp at 18,000 feet. To get to this camp we had to circumvent the foot of a great spur that descended from Kamet, and was crowned with jagged minor summits that were heavily snow-clad. Behind this spur we found ourselves in the innermost recesses of an arctic landscape built on a colossal scale, and entirely cut off from the every-day world like that wonderfully isolated "Jardin" in the upper region of the Mer-de-glace at Chamonix. Our position was close to the base of a wide and lofty rock-wall or curtain of precipice which united the main mass of Kamet with the superb double-headed rock-peak of Kamet's principal satellite, Western Ibi Gamin, 24,200 feet high, and like

Kamet, situated on the Tibetan frontier. The depression between the two mountain-masses appropriately came to be known as Slingsby's Saddle, for it was the point that he had reached and passed during his attempt in 1911.

Our world, however, as is so often the case among these vast mountains, was a world of illusions. For instance, for anyone in search of a route up the satellite, Western Ibi Gamin, there appeared to be a magnificent, easy rock-ridge ascending in one continuous sweep from the level of the glacier right up to the summit of this peak. Again, another great *arête* ascended from the point where the curtain of precipice was joined to the main mass of Kamet; apparently it led right to the top of the latter mountain with hardly a break anywhere. Half-way up this inviting *arête* a single rock-tower seemed to be the only obstacle, and to climb over it or cross its face looked feasible. It was this *arête* that Slingsby, encouraged by the convenient approach up the Ghastole Glacier, had chosen for his attempt on Kamet the previous year.

Yet the fact was that the friendly appearance of each of these two great ridges was utterly deceptive, and neither Western Ibi Gamin or Kamet was accessible in the way that we supposed. The attractive route up Western Ibi Gamin, as we subsequently discovered when viewing it in profile, was intersected by a huge vertical step, at least a thousand feet in height, and, in the case of the other ridge, the rock-tower that we took to be a mere tooth on the way up Kamet, was in reality the other great satellite of Kamet, namely Eastern Ibi Gamin, a peak 24,170 feet high, at least a mile distant from the greater mountain, and completely cutting us off from it.

Slingsby still believed after his attempt in 1911 that Kamet could be climbed by this route, but after my party had made two attempts by it in 1912, one of them failing at a height of 23,000 feet in bad weather, we became convinced that any attack on the mountain from this side would either involve us in the hopeless task of crossing the intervening summit of Eastern Ibi Gamin in the way, or else in the equally hopeless effort of traversing horizontally the precipitous face of this peak. Actually, both Slingsby's party and mine had been repeating the original mistake made by the Schlagintweits in their ascent more than forty years previously, and it is a remarkable fact that none of the attacks on Kamet from this side ever took place on the mountain, but all came to an end on the slopes of Eastern Ibi Gamin. It must be admitted that even a long experience in the Alps is insufficient to prepare one for the bewildering vastness of scale and complexity of topography that is characteristic of the Himalaya.

Later in the same year, when we realized the uselessness of making further attempts on the west side, we crossed the range to Niti, in order to investigate Kamet thoroughly from the east. It was only then that we explored the easy eastern approach up the Kamet Glacier, and discovered that the route which had been rejected was by no means as dangerous in respect of avalanches as had been supposed. In fact there could be no doubt that the Kamet Glacier was the key to the ascent.

Such, then, were the reasons that had caused us to return to the east side of Kamet in 1913, and to find ourselves once more on the Kamet Glacier, established in our advance base-camp, as I have already described.

It was the 20th of June. The bad weather had come to an end at last, and that morning a blazing sun drove us out of our tents at half-past six. There was evidently a prospect of a day or two of fine weather, so we busied ourselves packing loads for a move to higher camps. To have started at once would have been useless, as the fresh snow everywhere had not yet had time to settle. To wade up the glacier through unconsolidated snow would have been prohibitively exhausting, and higher up, where the slopes were steeper there would have been danger from avalanches. That evening we went to bed in broad daylight to the accompaniment of the Bhotias' [2] singing. As we lay listening in our sleeping-bags the concert was interrupted by the roar of a big rock-fall not far from the camp. In the Himalaya avalanches make one jumpy; one never seems very far from the reach of them, and their frequency is a sign that the mountains are still young, and have not yet reached the degree of stability of other ranges like the Alps. In the Alps, wherever there is danger, it is usually sufficiently obvious to the experienced eye, so that it can generally be avoided, but in the Himalaya experience is no guarantee of security, and often, when the camp-site seems quite safe, there is

[2] Bhotias are natives of southern Tibet, often hired as porters.

still a lurking sense of anxiety. The Himalayan scale, too, is so gigantic that it is difficult to gauge the limits of the avalanches.

At one o'clock in the morning of June the 21st we were off. There was a crystal-clear quality in the moonlight, and the snow was sparkling like diamonds in its rays. The Bhotias were bubbling with energy and high spirits; like us they were relieved that the long period of waiting was over. Marching up the upper part of the Kamet Glacier to its head, we pitched a light camp, consisting of one tent for Pierre and myself, and a second tent for seven Bhotias. Our altitude was probably 20,000 feet, and the camp was on a rock-ridge, so close underneath Kamet that the upper regions of the mountain were hidden from sight by the steepness of the precipice immediately above us. The Kamet Glacier that day was so easy to walk on that we had already established ourselves in camp by ten o'clock in the morning. I took some photographs of the magnificent sweep of the glacier, looking like a great frozen high-road, and winding away below us down the valley in symmetrical curves till it disappeared round a mountain-corner to join the Raikana Glacier and feed the headwaters of the Ganges.

On the way up during the morning I had found myself gasping for breath most uncomfortably. It is common on these mountains to suffer acutely from mountain-sickness at a relatively low elevation, and to feel discouraged in consequence, because one hastily assumes that the symptoms are bound to get worse as one goes higher. But this is not the case, for the attack wears off as often as not, and probably does not recur till a much greater height is reached. Today we were unlucky, for the weather was unfavourable; it was just the sort of day that is most trying, hot and cloudy without any breeze, and although we both felt well when we arrived, we soon had splitting head-aches. This year's experience confirmed our conviction that much of mountain-sickness in this district, at any rate, is caused by the sun shining with terrific force through still air that is not dense enough to give adequate protection. The Bhotias' habit of lying flat on their faces fast asleep in the sun probably accounts for a good deal of the discomfort from which several of them were now suffering. Our head-man, Alam Singh, was in a state of collapse. The thought of a meal made me feel sick, and the light seemed murderous in its intensity. It was not merely the direct rays of the sun, for even the glare inside the tent was intolerable, and I could well believe that sunstroke can attack one through the eyes. The extremes of heat and cold were astonishing; at almost any moment of the day sunstroke and frostbite were equally likely contingencies. I was conscious, too, of the effect that altitude has on the mind. As we climbed higher into the unknown, and penetrated farther into the secret and untrodden regions of this great mountain, the commonplace reality of every-day life faded from the landscape, while the sense of romance and mystery deepened. It was as if a gradually thickening veil was dimming our memories of the ordinary world. In the strange new world that we seemed to be partially conscious of, the fierceness of the sun's rays, the blinding light reflected from the snow, the savage cold, the clearness of the deep blue sky, combined to produce an impression of the most fantastic unreality. Yet at times a different impression prevailed. It was as if our normal sea-level consciousness were acting as a veil of illusion, so that only at great altitudes, in such places as this, did the veil of illusion become thin enough for the true reality to begin to shine through it, supernatural, incredible and incomprehensible.

At such a moment we seemed, as in the fairy-story, to have climbed the miraculous bean-stalk, so that we were beginning to explore the magical country beyond it, and just as it must have seemed to the hero of that romantic tale, the inspiring adventure was both nightmare and fairy-story combined. Perhaps this strange experience, painful though it was in many respects, had in it some of the quality of ecstasy, and perhaps it was this peculiarity that gave it its irresistible appeal. Indeed, whatever agonies and miseries the sufferer may endure on his pilgrimage to the heights, and however often he may swear never to return there, the longing to do so is certain to recur.

The ridge on which we were now camped ran into the base of a broad snow-covered precipice supporting a saddle-shaped glacier-plateau which formed a depression between Kamet and its nearest great neighbour, Eastern Ibi Gamin, the peak of 24,170 feet that had frustrated us when we were attacking from the west. The precipice so dominated the camp that it concealed the saddle from view. It was necessary to climb the precipice in order to camp on the plateau, if we were to have any chance of getting up the final portion of Kamet, where the upper slopes rose from the saddle in a continuous sweep of pure ice and snow for 2,000 feet at an angle of 45 degrees. As the recent bad weather had loaded all the rocks above the camp with fresh snow, we decided definitely that we must wait for daylight before starting, since with heavily-laden porters it would be too dangerous to climb by moonlight. We had noticed that the forehead of the precipice 1,000 feet above our heads, and just below the plateau, consisted of a steep slope of snow, or perhaps of ice. If it were ice, of course, it might require prolonged step-cutting, a formidable job when one is above 22,000 feet.[3]

On June the 23rd, at three in the morning we emerged reluctantly from the tent to inspect the weather. The long ice-valley of the Kamet Glacier below us was packed tight with dense white clouds, and a haze almost concealed the moon. These banks of fog were obviously the approaching monsoon, and all the way down the valley we could see the clouds waiting patiently in queues, ready for the monsoon wind to give them another push, and sweep them over the passes into Tibet. There among the bleak parched plateaux and immense roundheaded hills they would be dissolved in the thin, dry air. But it was too cold to linger outside the tent, and we quickly came to a decision to wait till the afternoon, so that if the weather became at all possible, we would try the ascent of the rocks and the snow-slope so as to pitch a camp on the plateau. It was meanwhile a considerable relief to be able to get back into one's sleeping-bag.

Curiously enough, we were now free from the attacks of breathlessness that affected us so unpleasantly, and for one obvious cause, several thousand feet below this camp. However, we felt bad enough in other respects, and although my head-ache had vanished after a night's rest, perhaps owing to a dose of bromide, I did not feel at all

---

[3] The Kamet Glacier up which we had come is formed at its head by the junction of two great ice-streams pouring down in ice-falls from either side of Kamet, to unite at the foot of the peak. One of them flows from the depression between Kamet and Mana Peak, and the other comes down from the ice-fields of the saddle that we hoped to reach, between Kamet and Eastern Ibi Gamin. This latter glacier is split into ice-falls by the rock cliffs which we had to climb on our way to the plateau. [Author's note.]

fit. Later during the day I was able to eat a small slice of barhal [4] venison, slightly flavoured with petrol from a leaky tin. Probably our state of acclimatization was not sufficiently advanced to justify us in making such long stages between camps, as we were now doing.

Next morning, the 23rd, we dozed uneasily till nine o'clock, and then began the struggle with a defective smoky primus stove, a miserable performance which seemed to occupy most of the day. In fact, primus stoves react to altitude badly, much as climbers do. It was a wretched day, and as I crawled panting into my sleeping-bag for the night I noticed it was snowing and consoled myself with the reflection that it was not very likely in view of the weather that we should have to turn out in the small hours in order to toil farther up the mountain.

Nevertheless, on the 24th of June, Pierre woke me at one o'clock in the morning with the news that it was gloriously fine, a clear moonlight night, and that we must start immediately. I at once reminded him that we had agreed already that the thousand feet of rock above the camp were in too bad condition to be safe for a night march with our laden men. So we got back into bed and remained in a state of coma, hardly to be described as sleep, till we eventually succeeded in setting out at 5.30 A.M., after eating an insignificant meal.

We soon found the ascent of the precipice trying owing to the quantities of fresh snow lying all over the rocks. Bhotias are in their element wherever there are crags to be climbed, but snow-covered rock is not what they are accustomed to, and consequently we had some anxious moments when the men launched themselves on to this snow-bound face, heavily laden as they were. A slip would have been fatal, and yet, such is the lethargic state of mind induced by altitude, that we neglected the elementary precaution of roping the party on these very treacherous cliffs. However, all the men climbed admirably, and at last we found ourselves on the supreme promontory of the precipice, where it abutted on the snow- or ice-slope that formed a sort of forehead just underneath the spacious plateau leading to the saddle, as we had noticed from the camp.

It was disconcerting when we came to the "forehead" to find that

[4] Also transliterated as burrhel or bharal. A wild sheep of the Himalaya.

it was a slope of steep, tough ice. Pierre, however, rapidly hacked a staircase up it in a style that perhaps only the best professionals can achieve. When prolonged step-cutting is required at such heights as this, the leader must be able to cut quickly, and balance himself in mere scratches in the ice. Time and energy are lacking for carving out the elegant "soup-plate" steps, such as a talented guide will prepare for his clients in the Alps, and when at last the leader was up he was glad to recuperate for a while. Later, he threw down a combination of all the available ropes as a hand-rail to help the rest of the party to follow in their turn.

At the top of the "forehead" began the lofty glacier-plateau sloping at an easy angle up to the high saddle between Kamet and Eastern Ibi Gamin. We were now in a strange paradoxical world, where the ordinary laws of nature do not seem to work. Snow here is soft, not because it is melted in the sun, but because it is frozen into fine dust by the intense cold. Here it is the relatively warm monsoon wind that brings the snow, and it is not the sun's warmth, but the icy northerly winds that remove it again. If the cold in such places begins to overwhelm the climber, it is useless for him to hasten the pace. On the contrary, he had better slow down, in order to diminish the rate of his breathing, for it is not inactivity on his part, but the violent gasping for breath in the thin cold air, that may dangerously deplete the vital store of warmth on which his life depends.

The endless monotony of toiling up the bleak slopes of this ghastly plateau through an increasing depth of powdery snow, and under a burning sun became a torment. When at last we camped it was only eleven o'clock in the morning, but I felt incapable of moving another yard.

We were now wearing extra-dark snow-spectacles, our faces were smothered in yellow grease, to keep off the blistering sunshine reflected from the dazzling fresh snow, and we had specially large boots to allow room for numerous socks and stockings as protection against the arctic cold. Yet when I sat in the entrance of the tent, half in sun and half in shade, I felt myself grilling and freezing simultaneously. Our camp here seemed to be at the foot of the final ice- and snow-slopes of the peak, and I estimated that we were three or four hundred feet below the high gap between Kamet and Eastern

Ibi Gamin, so that our height must have been about 23,000 feet, two thousand feet or more below the top of the mountain. The altitude was certainly very noticeable. Crawling into our sleeping-bags caused violent palpitations and fits of gasping. Any mild exertion brought on breathlessness and dizziness, with a curious empty feeling at the pit of the stomach. Probably we were insufficiently acclimatized to undertake an ascent of 7,000 feet in only two stages.

On the 25th of June there was intense and increasing cold towards the small hours of the morning, with a wind causing a horrid flapping of the tent. Our hot-water bottles had lost what little warmth they had, and the cold was depressing to our lowered circulations. We seemed too feeble to resist these low temperatures. It was difficult to produce hot water, for water no longer boils at a reasonable temperature at this height, and tea has to be stewed to extract any flavour from it. We dared not start before dawn for fear of getting frozen. To add to our discomfort the Bhotias had jammed the screw of the primus cooking-stove, so that it was almost dawn when Pierre at length succeeded in boiling some water for a refill of the hot-water bottles. Unfortunately with the arrival of daylight there was nothing for it but to get up.

As I poked my head out of the tent into the revoltingly cold air of early dawn, I observed seas of cold grey cloud lying in the valleys, but the far peaks were all clear, especially the gigantic Gurla Mandata, 25,000 feet high, rising into the Tibetan sky in superb isolation, a hundred miles away. The divine Nanda Devi, the only superior to Kamet, now showed her true height, and completely dwarfed the usually magnificent peak of Dunagiri which now seemed to crouch at the goddess's feet. The glittering ice-crest of the principal Mana Peak looked as if it were on our level, and its minor summits were obviously beneath us.

We stumbled unwillingly out of the tent, after much shouting to rouse the poor mountain-sick Bhotias who had been vomiting during the night. Starting at once with three men who seemed to be less ill than the others, we put one of them in front to make the track by stamping his way through the deep fresh snow. He was to take it in turn with the others, and we hoped that when they became exhausted we should be able to continue without them. I soon noticed, however, that the snow was getting deeper, and I realized from the state of my exhaustion at starting that it was a hopeless job, for I kept stopping to rest every hundred yards, sinking down in the snow, or leaning gasping and bent double over my ice-axe used as a support. At last, before we reached the top of the plateau, Pierre, at my suggestion, left me and went on with two Bhotias, while I turned back with Shyamu. Pierre and his men then got as far as the foot of the ridge that ascends from the saddle to the top of Kamet. Here they tried the ridge and found snow above their knees, and the gallant Bhotias, who were still doing the leading began to stagger in their tracks. Further progress was impossible. Higher up it might have been necessary to take to the face where the slopes appeared to be in a dangerous state from avalanches, and Pierre decided to follow me back to the 23,000-feet camp, where he joined me about an hour after my return. From the saddle he had had a magnificent view over Tibet towards the north, apparently much the same panorama that we had seen from our highest points on the other side of Kamet during the previous year; a limpid brown landscape bright in the sun, containing hundreds of miles of rolling mountains like gigantic downs, and on the horizon a chain of snows. This peaceful undulating Tibetan country formed a striking contrast with the stormy sea of savage peaks which we looked back upon whenever we turned our eyes towards the Indian valleys, where the threatening monsoon-clouds were beginning their advance once more.

On the return of Pierre's party, Shyamu prepared some tinned fruit for all of us. On the previous day we had only eaten a few water-biscuits and drunk some cocoa. The plan of ascending by forced marches had not been a success, and we determined to get down to our advanced base at 16,000 feet as quickly as possible.

As soon as we had swallowed the fruit we began the descent. Fearing that the steps cut that morning in the ice-slope of the "forehead" might have melted in the sun, we were tempted to try the descent of a broad easy couloir on our left. We had shunned this route on the way up because of its dangerous appearance, and now one glance at the various potential missiles lying about the brink of it convinced us that we had been right. So we made back to the "forehead," and descended its steeply sloping ice with all our ropes tied together to form a balustrade, fixed to an ice-axe planted upright in a snow-drift, Pierre remaining behind to extricate the axe, and descend by his own unaided exertions. Pierre, on these occasions, seems to master any really formidable obstacles by means of a skilfully planned series of bold and determined dashes, on the principle recommended for cavalry action according to the drill-book, that is to say progression in a series of bounds. In this manner, therefore, he had soon descended to our level. But he was still separated from us by a precipitous ice-gully, and, to enable him to reach us, Alam and Shyamu, after many unsuccessful attempts, managed to throw him the end of a rope. Then, crossing the forbidding-looking gully in two or three deft and strenuous jumps, he rejoined us at the base of the "forehead." Thereupon, hurriedly coiling the spare rope, we embarked on the descent of the snow-covered precipice beneath. On these treacherous rocks I dreaded a slip on the part of our exhausted porters, but nothing happened, and we all reached the 20,000-feet camp without mishap.

The following day we descended to the advance base-camp on our way back to the plains and Bombay, where, a month after our defeat on Kamet [5] we took ship for England. . . .

[5] Kamet was climbed in 1931 by an expedition under the leadership of Frank Smythe. See his book *Kamet Conquered* (1932).

THE SIKONG EXPEDITION

1932

MINYA KONKA, the White Ice Mountain of Minyag, stands in Sikong province of China about thirty miles south of Tatsienlu (Kangting). Although long known to the sparse native population as a holy mountain, it did not become an object of scientific and sporting interest until 1879, when a group led by Count Bela Szechenyi explored its environs. Theodore Roosevelt, Jr., and his brother Kermit, in search of the giant panda in 1929, passed near by and guessed its elevation to be 30,000 feet. Other parties and lone explorers from time to time attempted the mountain without success.

In 1932 an expedition sponsored by the American Alpine Club and assisted by the American Geographical Society set out for Minya Konka. The principal members were Arthur B. Emmons, Terris Moore, Jack Theodore Young, and Richard L. Burdsall; all but Burdsall were students. Their stated objectives were simple and demanding: (1) to determine the altitude of the mountain, (2) to reconnoiter and, if possible, reach its summit, (3) to bring back small collections of bird and animal life. They were successful in all three and acquired as well much new information about the mountain and the surrounding territory. Thus the climbers of the Sikong Expedition made the highest complete ascent (24,891 feet) ever achieved by Americans. Of peaks successfully attacked the only one higher is the Himalayan Nanda Devi (25,661 feet), which was climbed by a predominantly British party in 1936. The greatest of the giants—Everest, K2 (Mount Godwin-Austen), and Kanchenjunga—are yet unconquered.

Like the ascent itself, the book entitled *Men against the Clouds*, which reported the results of the expedition, was the joint labor of the four principal members. Of the selection given here the major part was written by Emmons and the account of reaching the summit itself by Moore, who was recently appointed president of the University of Alaska.

The following selection is reprinted from *Men against the Clouds*, by Richard L. Burdsall and Arthur B. Emmons, 3rd. Copyright, 1935, by Harper and Brothers.

The Conquest of Minya Konka

Moore and I [Emmons] had the base camp to ourselves, the porters having returned to the valley. For two delightfully warm days we lay in the grass about the fire and exulted in the caress of the warm sunshine, a scene such as to gladden the heart of any bucolic muse.

Occasionally the distant mumuring rumble of an avalanche drew our attention to the silvery bulk of the Konka rising over ten thousand feet above us, straight into the blue smiling sky.

We could hear the far-off roar of the wind along the ridge, two miles away—a low monotone—and enjoyed the more our seclusion. Otherwise, we forgot the stern, grim fight of the past three weeks, and exulted in the present relaxation and a well-earned rest. Life seemed like one long pleasant dream from which we would fain not be awakened—the more so because of the hard work which lay ahead. . . .

On the second day of our sojourn at the base we were joined by Young from Camp I. During our absence higher up he and Burdsall, with the two high [altitude] porters, Chingwa and Chelay, had moved some two hundred and fifty pounds of stores to 18,000 feet, each night returning to the base. When everything had gone up, including new stocks of provisions from Tatsienlu, the porters were sent down, while Burdsall and Young moved to Camp I to acclimatize and await our return from the upper regions.

Young now joined us to confer about the porters. The men were too untrained and without discipline to be of much use without supervision. It seemed essential that one of us should remain at the base camp or at the monastery to hold the men in readiness should an emergency demand their immediate services. Also, when the campaign was over we should need them to help in the speedy evacuation of the mountain.

Young realized that he was the best qualified to assume this all-important post as head of the support party, both through his knowledge of the language and his previous experience with the natives.

He also felt that his physical reaction to the altitude thus far had been less encouraging than might have been expected, and that his lack of mountain experience would tend to lessen the chances of success for the rest of the party.

To be sure, his record both on the reconnaissance and thus far on the ascent did not altogether bear out such a premise, for in both cases he had done much excellent work. He had, however, suffered more from the effects of altitude than the rest, and I think, on the whole, his choice was a wise one. He generously resigned his place in the summit party and volunteered to take charge of the porters. . . .

The last phase of the assault began. We now knew the strength and deadliness of the weapons with which the Konka could defend itself. It was to be the last dire thrust we could make at the heart of our gigantic adversary. Were we beaten back, there could be no rallying. Defeat and possible disaster would be the result. It was now a case of risking everything in one last supreme effort, an effort requiring every atom of skill and strength we could muster. We were going the limit.

October 20th saw a renewal of the activity. Moore left the base camp at an early hour to join Burdsall at Camp I and push on through to Camp II on the spur the same day. I remained until late in the afternoon to cut some willow sticks to be used as trail markers.

It was after three before I started for Camp I. On reaching the Crampon Place in the gully, darkness descended, but I climbed steadily to where the original Camp I had been. From here it was only a matter of seventy yards to the present location of the tent, but a damp mist enveloped everything, making the intervening distance hazardous going in the dark. I nearly stumbled over the tent without seeing it.

As I half expected, both Moore and Burdsall were in residence. The threatening weather had made their continuing on to 19,800 feet inadvisable. The present situation was awkward because three of us must somehow cook our meals and sleep in a tent scarcely large enough for two. To further complicate matters, it began to snow, rendering some one's suggestion to sleep outside impossible. Somehow we all managed to get inside, though the walls bulged alarmingly. The tent was wide enough to allow one foot eight inches to a man, and we slept with shoulders overlapping. Apparently we all slept soundly!

Nearly a foot of snow fell during the night, and higher up considerably more. Getting away at 8.30 A.M., we shouldered forty-five-pound loads. The going was heavy indeed, and it was slow work breaking the track. Ten steps and rest. Ten steps and rest. One hundred and change the lead. All three of us took turns at plowing up through a heartbreaking mass of clinging snow. Crampons clogged. Footsteps gave way. On we fought. Three hours to reach the halfway point. Yet Camp II still seemed infinitely far away.

To our relief, we found that in the zone above the wind had done its work. The area above the crevasses had been blown clear and the footing became firm once more. Our pace remained the same, however, for by now we were so badly worn that each step required a tremendous amount of our failing energy.

It was late afternoon before we attained Camp II. Only the top two feet of the tent showed above the snow! It was hopelessly buried, so we merely dumped the loads alongside and started back for 18,000 feet and a second night wedged into the two-man tent there.

We took pains to climb carefully and deliberately at all times, especially while descending, for then it is that by far the greater proportion of mountaineering accidents occur. It is desperately hard, if not impossible, when one's knees are fairly caving in with weariness, not to relax for an instant, and such relaxation sometimes proves fatal.

The two-man tent was left at Camp I and stocked with provisions and a double sleeping-bag in case a hurried retreat became necessary. The three of us the next day again started up for the spur. The tent at [Camp] II having been so badly snowed under, we decided to finesse it entirely and go on through to Camp III in a single day. Our present loads would complete the stock of necessities for all camps, including the establishment of a fourth one on the main northwest ridge itself. Thus until the Konka campaign was over, Camp I would see no more of us.

The day was perfect, and although we had a great distance to cover, we did not hurry. The light conditions were excellent and our cameras got plenty of use. Until now we had been so absorbed in merely consolidating our various camps that little attempt had been made to make a photographic record of our surroundings.

We had no moving-picture equipment, for which we were doubly thankful, both because of the considerable additional weight involved and because of the expenditure of time and energy required in the exposure of film where conditions made such an undertaking extremely difficult. To film such a climb properly there must be one man whose sole responsibility is to do nothing but "shoot" the film. Our personnel was far too limited for any such extravagance. Moreover, we were there to climb the Konka, not to take pictures of it. Hence a few characteristic "stills" for purposes of record had to suffice.

A couple of hours were spent at Camp II in digging down to the tent door and in readjusting loads. Once the door had been cleared, I crawled inside to retrieve the remainder of the food and unexposed film. There was barely room to squeeze in, and I noticed that, although the canvas remained untorn by the weight of snow, the pole had snapped, leaving the surrounding drift still supporting the walls to which it had frozen.

We continued on up the spur that afternoon. Now our shortage of equipment and man-power made itself markedly evident. By the time Camp III was reached, we were all utterly worn, especially Burdsall, who, through poor acclimatization, felt badly exhausted. This was his first experience above 20,000 feet. All day the thin air had sapped his strength, and though we repeatedly demanded that he share part of his load with us, he grimly and steadfastly refused.

Had he had the acclimatization and orientation which Moore and I had gained on our high reconnaissance, he would have been as fit as either of us in all probability. If we had had sufficient tents, equipment, and personnel to accommodate a corps of high-altitude porters above Camp I, he could have become inured to the present severe conditions less rapidly and more completely by being able to work at a slower pace. In this way a self-sufficient party is usually handicapped at high altitudes by lack of porters.

We all felt the unspoken realization that we were rapidly nearing the end of our tether, though not one of us would ever have admitted it, even to himself. It was touch and go as to whether we should be able to carry a camp up the steep summit ridge to 22,000 or 23,000 feet, and from there force our way through unknown obstacles to the summit. Trivial happenings at such extreme altitudes take on a new significance and can have the most decisive and overwhelming influence where a man is reaching the outer fringes of his endurance. The breaks must be with us, and by far the most important of these was the weather—an uncertain quantity at best in these ranges. If the weather held, then, it might be possible—just possible— to win through to the summit. We found Camp III in order, and, after setting up the tent, crawled wearily inside, but not before the stakes had been reinforced with all available ice-axes. . . .

It was estimated that six more loads remained at 19,800 feet. These could be brought to Camp II in two relays in a single day. By tomorrow night we should be fully consolidated here at 20,700, and ready to carry on with Camp IV on the northwest *arête*.

Next morning, Moore started ahead for [Camp] II to dig out the tent there if that were again necessary. It was our custom to go unroped over this section, and Burdsall and I followed him at a more leisurely pace.

The day was cloudless and almost without wind. As we strode down along the spur, a sense of well-being pervaded me. The rarefied air no longer laid a heavy hand on body and mind. I felt exhilarated by a strong sense of superiority lent by the tremendous height of the spur, as I glanced contemptuously down across the vast tableland of Tibet, spreading off to that distant gray line where earth and sky met.

Exalted lords of the earth we were until, turning to see how Burdsall was progressing, I gazed up across the savage cliffs that dropped away with magnificent symmetry from a bastioned ice-bound summit, a long silvery pennant of snow whipping from it to the northeast. For there, nearly a mile above me, was the goal we had set out to win. I felt subdued and oppressed by its huge and awful presence— this Holy Mountain of Minya. How utterly futile it seemed to match one's pitiful strength against so relentless a foeman.

And yet one felt irresistibly drawn towards a thing of such utter beauty and majesty whose moods and changes were never the same. One sympathized with those untutored, simple-minded Tibetans that here was a Being to be at once feared and loved. How incomparably glorious it looked in the morning light!

We met Moore just leaving Camp II with his first load. He reported that there were only four loads left, which on later consideration we narrowed to three and a half. Burdsall and I decided we might stretch a point and clean up the lot, obviating a second trip. When the loads had been made up I found that mine was in excess of fifty pounds, and Burdsall's somewhat less. Camp II was officially "closed for the season."

I began strongly to regret my exuberance as I swung up the pack, but to save my face I could say nothing. As we started upward our pace was funereal, and we made up our minds to taking the whole afternoon to cover the distance to Camp III. Again, however, once a rhythm was well established in our respiration as well as our stride, the loads seemed miraculously pounds lighter, though still a crushing weight to lift uphill at over 20,000 feet.

Having climbed seven hundred feet, we met Moore returning for his second installment. When he was informed that there was nothing left, he was at first incredulous, then righteously indignant that we had been such fools as to overload ourselves in this fashion, when we had all agreed to make two trips and take equal amounts. To soothe his injured feelings we shared part of our packs with him. And so the Camp by the Hump was reestablished.

On October 24th a much-begrudged day off was taken on our meager food supply, a windy day along the spur with clouds enveloping everything so thickly that visibility was literally zero. A prolonged game of chess consumed whatever of the day was not occupied in cooking and eating our two meals. To cheer lagging appetites we made up a hypothetical list of "The Most Luxurious Foods One Could Possibly Take on a Canoe Trip!" a pastime in our present situation we felt to be slightly irrelevant, but entertaining withal. Much interest and amusement was also found in reading all the labels and directions on our various tins of food. . . .

Our appetites above 20,000 feet were never strong. Eating became rather an onerous duty than a pleasure. The diet consisted largely of concentrated foods, and was high in sugar. The sugar had an undeniable taste of gasoline, but was just as welcome. Among the things obtainable in Tatsienlu were eggs. These eggs, though three weeks old, were nonetheless considered as a great delicacy. They had been solidly frozen for days, and one could shell them raw as though they had been hard boiled.

We used to make an egg soufflé which would make any Waldorf chef wilt with envy. Two of the aforementioned three-weeks-old eggs were peeled and fried in yak butter in an aluminum bowl. The whites would have been long since cooked before the yolks had even melted, a condition which, though inconvenient, did not seem to spoil the taste. The whole was then beaten up with granulated yak cheese into a delicious concoction—my mouth waters yet at the thought! But we survived and liked to tell the tale.

The *pièce de resistance* of our diet consisted of three-minute oatmeal which invariably took at least twenty minutes to cook. So low was the temperature of boiling water at 21,000 feet that one could plunge one's hand into it without suffering undue discomfort. We tried to disguise the oatmeal in various ways with malted milk, sugar, and butter, but its flavor was not to be thus easily defied. Oatmeal was oatmeal, and before long we became so inordinately tired of this food that a solemn oath was sworn whereby, once away from the mountain, we could never be coerced or cajoled into touching it again. Once back in Tatsienlu, however, this resolution died a premature death, for when a bowl of Mrs. Cunningham's steaming Scotch porridge was set before us, there was no resisting it. We ate it prayerfully, joyfully, and with great gusto.

Each man was allowed but one spoon and one aluminum bowl. With these implements, a pocket knife, and any accessories nature provided, he had to eat and drink everything that came his way, and be as merry as he might. There was no water to spare in which to wash dishes—water meant fuel—and fuel here was more precious than fine gold. He simply used the Tibetan system of licking his bowl clean with his tongue before the next course, or cleaned it with snow.

On the morning of the 25th we recorded 5 F. at 9 A.M. as we started for the Gap with substantial loads of food and extra clothes. The steps around the Hump were filled and took some time to clear. . . . The southwest gale was on the job as always, and so battered and bullied us that we felt almost bruised by its impacts. The skirts of our parkas flapped viciously about our knees. Flying snow particles clung to our clothes in a white rime. Icicles formed on our eyebrows and beards. Again and again we were beaten from our tracks despite thirty-pound loads. Balance regained, again the slow rhythm of our feet timed to our breathing, the trip-hammer pounding of heart against ribs, as we labored on.

Short rests to lean, gasping, over one's ice-ax, back to the wind. Stamping of feet to keep them alive. Pauses that seemed like heaven itself as long as one were only not moving upward. Then the response of tortured lungs as we struggled on again.

Five hours of steady plugging and we breasted a sharp rise at 21,700 feet to throw off our packs and lie panting in the snow. My feet began to ache with the cold and grew steadily colder despite my efforts to revive them.

Another hour we fought our way upward and finally sank to rest behind a low ice bastion at 22,000 feet. By this time my feet were becoming numb, and I told the men that I was worried about them. It was well along in the afternoon and we had reached the point of exhaustion where to continue much higher would not have been possible. Furthermore, here occurred about the only place on the ridge so far which offered even a vestige of shelter or of a level spot for a tent. Within three thousand feet of the top we considered that we had a fighting chance of making the climb from here, though we had hoped to put the camp five hundred feet higher.

All things taken into account, it was decided that our present elevation would have to suffice. We might possibly have to advance our position higher, but only after a determined try at the summit from here.

Leaving our loads securely placed, we made a quick descent to Camp III. My feet recovered on the way down, accompanied by the painful return of circulation. Once in the tent, I removed boots and socks. One or two toes seemed a little white, but a massage soon brought back good color and sensation. I spent a very comfortable night.

October 26th saw the dismantling of Camp III, for we had need of the tent above. Leaving a small cache of extra fuel, clothes, and exposed film, the climbing party again turned its collective face toward the ridge.

The thermometer hovered around zero, and as we entered the Gap the wind again struck us with numbing force. This day was a repetition of the previous one, save that there was no return to Camp III.

When we reached the 22,000-foot level and the site of Camp IV, my feet were again giving trouble. After a prolonged rest in the lee of the ridge, we attacked the lower lip of a small snow-filled bergschrund with our ice-axes, hewing a platform from the living ice.

The top half of the 'schrund protected the tent in some measure from the battering of the wind, and the snow-filled crack, when augmented by part of its lower lip, made a space just large enough for the tent. It was an hour and a half of hard work before the platform was ready. Its architectural points, to be sure, would not have evoked much praise from a landscape gardener, and it had a very decided outward tilt not conducive to a feeling of security. Nevertheless, we had to make the best of it, so eyes were cut from the solid ice at great labor, large enough to admit tent ropes, and the tent was literally tied to the mountain. Still, it was "home," and after putting the finishing touches on Camp IV, we crawled thankfully inside.

That evening the discussion revolved about the next phase of the campaign. Burdsall was in poor condition through lack of sleep and acclimatization, but both Moore and I were feeling perfectly fit. In view of these circumstances, Moore and I decided on the morrow to scout a route up through the first band of rocks, cutting steps where necessary and marking the route. We hoped with luck to force our way through to about 24,000 feet. While we were thus engaged, Burdsall was going to take a day of rest in Camp IV to recover some of his strength. On the first good day thereafter the three of us together would make a determined attempt at the summit.

Scarcely had this plan of action been evolved when I attempted to slice a frozen biscuit with my pocket knife. The biscuit was tough and its frozen interior yielded but little to my efforts. Suddenly it gave way and the knife broke through, cutting a deep gash in the palm of my left hand nearly two inches long. The wound was so deep that a number of the sensory nerves in the two little fingers were severed.

I sat and dazedly watched the thick drops of blood ooze out and drip slowly onto my sleeping-bag. Suddenly the significance of what had happened penetrated my altitude-benumbed consciousness. Moore assisted me in sterilizing the cut and adjusting a tight compress.

Now at the eleventh hour fate had struck us a dire blow. Our plans had to be changed. We knew from what we had already seen of the final fifteen hundred feet of the ridge that its ascent, if possible at all, would exact the last atom of skill and strength from every man. The climbers would be taxed to the very limit of their endurance. If indeed it were possible to win a way through the various obstacles, we fully expected to encounter some very ticklish pieces of ice-work and even a bit of rock-climbing might be expected. My left hand would be of little use to me in holding a rope or ax, with two fingers partly paralyzed. Furthermore, both the wound and its tight compress would so tend to cut off the circulation from the two injured fingers that there was almost a certainty of freezing them on such exposure as the ascent entailed.

At the high camp there was hardly enough food for another five days. It was scarcely conceivable to us that the summit could be reached on the first try. Burdsall, though suffering badly from altitude, stubbornly insisted that he was fit to carry on. There was no time to be lost in making the first assault. Therefore, with the keenest pang of disappointment I made the decision to remain in Camp IV in reserve while the other two made the attempt. If they failed, then perhaps I could join them in a second attempt when the hand had been given more time to recover.

The reconnaissance was abandoned, and on the following day the entire party rested out of deference to Burdsall's condition. We felt our quest but the forlornest of hopes, and watched with despair our hard-won victory slipping through our fingers. . . .

That evening breakfast was cooked for the following morning, to save time in getting off. Moore and Burdsall talked over the plans for the climb in every detail. The items to be taken to the summit were placed in two rucksacks. These included emergency rations, a flashlight, cameras and film, a compass, and American and Chinese flags. Preparations complete, we all set our mental alarm clocks for 3.30 A.M. . . .

At 3.40 on the morning of October 28th, Camp IV was astir. Moore looked out through the door and proclaimed the stars were shining brightly and that there were no clouds visible. The wind still blew out of the west, sending showers of fine powdered snow sifting into the tent. Our day had come!

I reheated the frozen blocks of oatmeal and brewed a pot of hot malted milk, while the two climbers busied themselves in dressing. Four o'clock in the morning was a deadly hour at which to do anything save sleep at 22,000 feet on a cold morning. The work of dressing was almost more than human patience would stand.

It was an hour before the men were ready and fed. Then they crawled out into the black night, and I could hear them grumbling as they tried to adjust frozen crampon bindings in the dark with numb but mittened hands.

It was just five o'clock when I wished them good luck and a safe return. Moore took the lead and, with a perfunctory wave of his flashlight, was swallowed up in the frozen darkness, his only link to his companion a strand of flaxen rope paying out slowly through Burdsall's finger. When fifty feet of it had slipped away, Burdsall drew his parka hood closer about his face and with a brief salute he too disappeared into the gloom.

I was alone!

It was a bitter pill being thus relegated to a passive rôle when my two companions were fighting their way up along that ridge, some-where "out there." I had grave and not unfounded misgivings about ever seeing them again. One slip on the part of either man on those upper slopes and only a miracle could save them—places where one must walk with the nicety of a ballet dancer while fighting for breath and keeping one's balance against a lashing gale. It was not hard to conjure up pictures of disaster under such circumstances, though I had great faith in their ability and judgment. . . .

As to what actually befell Moore and Burdsall on that fateful 28th of October, I will quote the following from an account of Terris Moore:

As we left the tent and Emmons, there was yet no suggestion of dawn. The stars burned from a black sky down to the eastern horizon. The lightness of the snow, however, faintly revealed our frosty crampons biting into the hard-packed névé. I led the way with a tiny flashlight, occasionally coming upon one of our old tracks in its pencil of light. The snow rose steeply, and Dick [Burdsall] crawled along slowly at the end of the fifty-foot line, at times feeling for the steps with his heavily mittened hands. At intervals I drew from a fold in my parka one of a small bundle of willow sticks and drove it upright in the snow to mark the trail.

Traveling in this fashion, we had risen some two hundred feet when, topping a sharp rise we found the first light of dawn illuminating the upper slopes. Here we rested in glad anticipation of the sun's warmth.

Not a cloud could be seen in the entire sky of our upper world. A deep purple line marked the rim of the horizon one hundred and fifty miles away in Tibet. Jupiter still glowed brightly above and to the east of the summit. The wind swept us powerfully in isolated gusts. It was getting lighter and the flashlight was no longer necessary. As I adjusted my goggles, my leather face mask, temporarily pushed up over my forehead, was seized by the wind and whisked away across the smooth slopes below and disappeared. Its loss was a serious matter, but there was no returning for another. We pushed on.

The sun began to rise, though we still climbed in the shadow of the peak, its great purple outline lying at our feet across the brown hills of Tibet. It receded with visible rapidity as the sun lifted higher above the horizon. Gazing down at the vast territory still blanketed by the mountain's shadow made me at this moment peculiarly aware of our great height.

We continued on slowly, rising at an average rate of three hundred feet an hour. The brilliant edge of the sun pushed above the shoulder as we approached the highest point reached by Emmons and me ten days before.

Here the smooth rounded contours of the ridge were broken by a series of frost-smothered rocks. Burdsall and I climbed upward through them cautiously, moving with one man continually belayed, the ax driven well into snow-filled cracks and the rope paid out from a turn about its head. The angle of the ridge increased very considerably, and every care was used to prevent a slip. Our crampons held beautifully in the firm crust, and we rejoiced that it was not necessary to waste precious time and energy in cutting steps.

Having surmounted this first band of rocks by a small snow couloir, we found ourselves at the foot of another open slope. Above this, however, we were disconcerted to see that the ridge narrowed sharply and was topped by a number of unpleasant-looking surface features. What lay beyond was hidden behind this maze of snow blocks and cornices.

A slight mistake now in our choice of route might easily spell defeat, for while it would soon become evident upon advancing higher, it might cause a delay in retracing our steps—a delay so disastrous that there would not be time to reach the summit and yet leave a safe margin for the descent.

I therefore had to rely solely upon my memory as to the tentative route traced through these intricacies with the field-glasses from below on our reconnaissance, when we had obtained a composite though distorted view of the terrain.

We advanced upward at a slow, steady pace calculated to produce a minimum of fatigue. Our altitude was by now nearly 24,000 feet, and all the other peaks in the range had sunk into insignificance below the line of the horizon. I was surprised to find myself not much more affected by breathlessness and lassitude than on the two days of carrying loads to 22,000 feet. Probably the greater altitude was compensated for by the day of acclimatization at Camp IV and by the absence of packs. Burdsall, too, seemed better than before and climbed splendidly.

The sun was just leaving the meridian as we encountered the first of the broken ice. We wound our way up through the tangle of towering pinnacles and top-heavy blocks of ice. Although able to see ahead but a short distance, we felt the top was not far off. We spurred ourselves on to greater effort, though our pace was scarcely more than a slow crawl. A few steps and we would pause to lean panting with bent heads over our ice-axes. Looking back and down between my feet along the length of the rope, it appeared impossible that I had taken such a very long time to climb those few steps from where Burdsall stood.

We found, to our dismay, that what we had taken for the summit was in reality just another bump on the ridge. On reaching it I traversed to the right out on to the huge western face, while Burdsall held me carefully belayed. The view thus afforded showed me what was unmistakably the summit some three hundred feet above; obviously there was nothing to be gained by continuing in this direction. I retraced my steps and we changed our course more to the left.

At last, cutting steps up over a low wall, I saw that our present position was connected with the summit by a very narrow though unbroken crest. Though it appeared but a short distance above, it was fully an hour before we stood at 2.40 P.M. on the highest point after nine and a half hours of steady climbing.

There were three small summit platforms grouped close together. These we ascended in turn and sank down thankfully in the snow on the third. Here we had some protection from the wind, which apparently came from below, most of its force shooting well above our heads.

This was the first time we had really had an opportunity to view our surroundings at leisure, so engrossed had we been in the struggle to reach this point.

The horizon surrounded us in one unbroken ring. No mountain massifs nor even clouds relieved the vast expanse of blue-black sky. At such great height the visible horizon is seen at some considerable distance below the true horizon. Its depression was very evident and I fancied I could actually see the curvature of the earth. The panorama of tremendous snow peaks, which had so dominated the sky at our 19,800-foot camp, had now dwindled to a series of mere white patches against the brown plain.

Rested, we rose and warily approached the eastern edge of the summit, fearing cornices. At our feet, nearly three miles below, the great sea of clouds lapped at the bases of the peaks. As the eye traveled eastward it moved away across the endless plains of China to the distant line where earth and sky met. Here and there rugged black islands of rock protruded through the mists in bold relief.

North and south the entire range lay at our feet. To the west stretched the vast undulating plateau of Tibet, broken here and there by isolated snow ranges, mysterious and remote.

We spoke of Emmons lying in his blankets below, and heartily wished him with us to share in this moment of victory.

Despite the intense cold, the sun exerted a real force in this thin air, which could scarcely, however, be described as heat. We tried to converse above the rushing of the wind, but the thin atmosphere only weakly conveyed our shouts to muffled ears. Cameras were got into action to perpetuate these fleeting moments. I removed two of the three layers of my mittens to operate mine, but I saw, to my consternation, that Dick had bared his hands completely to adjust some small mechanism. We exposed some twenty negatives, including a complete panorama of the distant horizon and the serrated topography beneath it.

Flag-waving was certainly not one of the purposes of this expedition, yet, since this was the highest point of land (24,900 feet) which Americans had ever reached, we flew the American flag for a few brief seconds from my inverted ice-ax while Dick photographed it. The same courtesy was shown the Chinese emblem because of the many kindnesses extended to us by that country whose guests we were.

The sun was sinking well into the west before we abandoned the summit. We found, to our dismay, that these simple operations had consumed over an hour, and we began the descent immediately.

As we crept down along the narrow crest just below the top, the wind mounted to truly alarming proportions, certainly the worst in any of my experience. The loss of my face mask earlier in the day had painful results, for I now found it almost impossible to face unprotected the devastating blast that swept up along the ridge.

It was necessary to negotiate these ticklish bits with face averted, clinging desperately to maintain my balance. The parka hood beat about my ears with a noise not unlike gunfire, and the air was charged with a sandblast of driven snow.

As we gradually attained a lower altitude, however, the wind abated somewhat and we could proceed with some semblance of comfort and assurance. Once clear of the upper difficulties of the ridge, our descent, though still requiring extreme care, was more rapid.[1]

The sun was well down on the western horizon and my watch read six o'clock. Still no sign of the returning climbers, and my apprehension for their safety increased with each fleeting minute of the time for their safe return.

Then above the clamor of the wind I heard a faint shout. Hastily I undid the door, just in time to see Burdsall come stumbling down the slope, closely followed by Moore.

Both men presented a weird appearance, their beards and eyebrows a mass of ice and their clothes sheathed in a white rime of frost. They sank exhausted in the snow, unable for the moment to rise or remove the rope. Moore looked the more done in of the pair, but his recovery was more rapid than Burdsall's.

Unable to restrain myself longer, I posed the momentous question, "Well, what luck?" Moore smiled wearily and said simply, "We made it." Made it! The thrill was electric! What an eloquent story those three words told. We had traveled over halfway around the globe, spent nearly a year in attaining our present position, and now at last the Konka had fallen!

My own feelings were somewhat confused. Great elation that we had at last triumphed over the Konka, a tremendous feeling of relief that the men were safely back, the job finished, and that we could now go down and leave these inhospitable surroundings, and a gnawing disappointment that I had been *hors de combat* for so glorious an exploit.

Burdsall complained of a numbness in some of his fingers and on inspection found that seven of the tips were suspiciously white. After massaging his hands, the color returned a little, but on the

[1] Here the passage from Moore's diary ends, and Emmons's narrative continues.

following morning the tips began to turn black and swell. It was frostbite acquired when his mittens had been removed to take photographs on the summit, where only a few seconds of exposure to the air had been sufficient to do the harm.

One might say that logically the story should end here, our goal having been won. Did this story deal with fiction, not fact, such a happy ending might be all in good order. Unhappily, that was not the case.

For one of our number, at least, the sequel to this tale of high adventure was fraught with events which to him, anyway, presented no anticlimax whatsoever. The Konka had gone down in defeat, but it still had power to strike back—and did.

The strain, physical and mental, to which we had all been subjected began to manifest itself in an all-consuming desire to get down and away from the mountain as far as ever we could, now that the campaign was over. This desire was augmented by the depleted condition of the stores in our high camps. At Camp IV there remained but two or three days' food. Should a severe winter storm beset us, our predicament might be serious in the extreme. We therefore determined to quit Camp IV and strike out for the base the very day following the climb.

A late start was made in demolishing Camp IV. All items were jettisoned which could not be carried down in one trip. Those removed included only things of some intrinsic value or items which would be necessary on the trek back across the Tibetan uplands to Tatsienlu. . . .

We started down about noon, and, descending slowly, took two hours to reach the Gap, and from there another to the cache at 20,700 feet.

Here the party unroped in order that each man might choose his own pace to Camp II.

Moore went ahead, accompanied by Burdsall, to dig out Camp II and salvage some film and a camera that had been left there. I stopped to pack up several things at the cache.

It was there that I first began to feel sharp jabbing pains in my right foot, though at the time I thought little about them. On carrying my load a few yards farther, the pain increased to such an extent that I sat down before long to have a look. It was so swollen that I had difficulty in removing my boot, and further inspection revealed that the entire foot was nearly double its size and had turned a purplish black nearly to the instep—a rather unpleasant sight with which to be suddenly confronted. Then it was that I realized with a shock that both my feet must have been numb for several days at least without my having realized the fact.

The left foot was still without sensation, and I did not have to look at it to know its condition. In desperation I replaced my socks and boot. The others were far ahead along the spur and could not hear my shouts. I was alone at 21,000 feet with a pair of frozen feet.

My pack, fortunately, contained a sleeping-bag which might possibly save my life should I be forced to bivouac, so I dared not leave the load behind. With each passing minute the pain in my foot increased until to place my weight on it became almost unbearable torture.

Luckily for me the left foot remained numb and I knew that my salvation lay in keeping it so until I could get off the mountain or at least join the other men. Using my ax as a cane, I managed to hobble along, and after two hours reached Camp II just behind Burdsall.

I began to experience that feeling of resignation which has led more than one man to a death in the snow. But Camp II was completely buried and I *had* to go on. Moore had been forced to cut the peak from the tent and fish out the contents from its dark interior with an ice-ax!

Realizing that in my unstable condition I could never negotiate the steep slopes below the spur with a pack, I threw it down on the shelf, where it undoubtedly remains to this day. We roped and climbed over the brink of the slope. Moore anchored, being the only fit member of the party, for Burdsall's fingers were giving him trouble. He was also decidedly unwell and our progress was reduced to a snail's pace.

I soon saw that if my other foot thawed out up here, I would not only place myself, but the rest of the party, in a very grave position. Knowing that, unencumbered as I was, I could make better time alone than if I stayed on the rope, I removed it and struck out by myself in a last desperate effort to reach the base camp, though both Moore and Burdsall were reluctant to let me do so. In any event, they would be following in case I got into difficulty.

Much fresh snow had fallen and it was a delicate job maneuvering through the hidden crevasses I recalled from our previous trips. Once free of these, I glissaded slopes which anyone in his right mind might have shunned for their steepness.

Luck favored me and I made famous time to Camp I, experiencing difficulty in only one or two places. I arrived here just as a golden sunset flamed across Tibet, and scrawled a large "O.K.—Art" in the snow beside the tent, which they later found.

Then began the descent into the gully, and there my troubles began in earnest. While I was on the snow its softness acted as a cushion for the feet. The hard rock, however, gave me the full benefit of my painful condition. My left foot, moreover, had also begun to thaw out, and I found it well-nigh impossible to stand up. Reaching the Crampon Place at the snow line, I discarded my crampons for the last time with a thankful sigh, and then began to hitch myself slowly down the gully in a sitting position.

During our absence high up, the sun had got in its work here at 18,000 feet. Many rocks had melted free of the snow and were hanging precariously balanced. Several came crashing down the gully, narrowly missing me in the dusk.

I had got fairly beneath the menacing wall of ice which had always made this route so hazardous, when the tottering mass cracked like a pistol-shot. Six times I could hear the ice being split asunder from within. By the time the last report had died away I was scrambling well up the opposite wall of the gully, the pain of my frozen feet forgotten in the presence of this new peril.

I sat for perhaps fifteen minutes perched on a ledge, waiting to see the huge bulk of ice crash down across the track below.

Nothing happened. The silence was unbroken save by the trickle of running water somewhere beneath the ice and the tinkle of an icicle as it fell and broke in some rift in the glacier wall.

Darkness was upon me and I had no time to lose, so screwing up my courage, I scrambled on down, feeling the glacier's icy breath upon me and glancing up fearfully at the one-hundred-foot front of ice as it glinted evilly in the evening light.

The short pitch of steep rock at the lower end of the gully gave me considerable trouble, but I managed it somehow, feeling for hand and footholds in the darkness.

At last, after what seemed an eternity, but in reality could not have been more than fifteen minutes, I rounded the corner where the Dump lay protected by the abrupt cliffs of the Pyramid.

I contemplated spending the night here, and I would have been wise had I done so. To be sure there was nothing here save a leaking tin of gasoline and several pairs of crampons, but it was a sheltered nook and I would have been assured of seeing Moore and Burdsall, for they must of necessity pass this point.

The idea of trying to reach the base camp still predominated, though by now all I could do was to stumble from boulder to boulder, using my hands for support as much as I could.

I blundered on in the semi-darkness over the loose rocks of the moraine which punished my feet cruelly. It took me an hour to descend another four hundred feet to the lower portion of the glacier. By now only the light of the stars faintly illumined the confused desolation of rocks over which the path led. The pain in my feet was fast becoming unendurable and the base camp was still far away.

Seeing the folly of trying to proceed farther, when I reached the glacier floor at 17,000 feet I made for a point several hundred yards away, out towards the center of the ice where I could hear running water. It was desirable to have water should I be marooned here for some time.

Half walking, half crawling, I at last reached a small trickle on the surface of the ice, though it was fast freezing up with the evening chill.

Not having eaten since morning, I consumed several of my few remaining malted-milk tablets—the only sustenance I would have until I should be rescued, which might be a day or two. I had therefore religiously to conserve my supply.

A sudden realization came upon me that in leaving the trail I had placed myself in an even more serious position. After taking a prolonged drink of water, my last for a good many hours, I tried to retrace my steps to a point where the trail skirted close beneath a shoulder of the Pyramid.

To my dismay, my feet and legs refused to function. It was rather a dismal feeling to know that I was helpless here alone at 17,000 feet on a remote Tibetan peak, a week's travel across the mountains to the first outpost of civilization, over two weeks from the nearest doctor, and probably two thousand miles through war-torn China to the nearest railhead.

But I think I can say, without boasting, that I rather enjoyed the novelty and sheer drama of the situation. At any rate, I was stimulated by it to the point of yodeling at the black empty cliffs above. Perhaps the triumph of yesterday had something to do with this exuberance now that the stress of the recent struggle was over. Certainly the relief brought by being no longer on those deadly white snowfields, but on terra firma again, had a decided influence. It may have been that I was beginning to crack under the strain of the last few weeks and hours, but if so, at least I felt in a joyful mood about it.

On one good hand and my knees I crawled back over the moraine, hitching myself up one side of mound after mound of broken boulders and slithering down the other. After what seemed an interminable period I again reached the trail, where I stretched out on a rock, worn out. My knees were so cut and bruised that this form of locomotion was no longer possible. I had come to the end of my tether. As to whether I were rescued I was too exhausted at the moment to care. The Konka had been climbed, so what else mattered.

It was too cold to sleep and far too uncomfortable. The feet mercifully regained some of their former numbness, and I had not the strength of will to try to revive them. I sat through the long weary hours, occasionally shifting my position on the boulder, which soon became uncommonly hard, and stared up at the stars. The Pleiades were setting behind the dark bulk of a mountain ridge, and moved with painful slowness. The night dragged on its interminable length.

A low dank cloud came sweeping up from the valley below, and whatever its clammy fringes touched became coated with frost. Nor was I spared. Before long my clothes were sheathed with frost crystals. Fortunate it was that my stanch high-altitude clothes were warm enough to keep me from freezing.

I wondered how Moore and Burdsall had fared and whether they had reached Camp I. If not, would they descend and find me on the morrow? I was not at all sure I wanted to face another two days and a night of exposure without food, water, or shelter.

I was awakened from such reveries by the reverberating roar of an avalanche. I turned just in time to see a large section of the glacier front under which I had passed but a few hours before, topple and cascade down over the track below like a mammoth waterfall. Huge blocks of ice were hurled into the air as they bounded down the slopes to land far out on the glacier below. Our route beneath was white with shattered ice in the dim starlight.

Though I was half a mile away and out of danger, the ground shook with the concussion and several stones came tumbling down from the shoulder not far from me. It was certainly one of the largest falls of ice I had ever seen, and its sinister possibilities made me shiver. At least Burdsall and Moore would have little to fear from it within the next day or so. Its bolt was spent.

The night wore on. Though it was not excessively cold, I was thoroughly chilled. Centuries passed in marshaled array. There was no sleep. Oh, if the dawn would only come!

When hope had been given up of ever seeing the sun again, an almost imperceptible lightening of the highest snowfields heralded the dawn. No Mayan sun-worshiper ever greeted the sun with more ecstasy!

By nine o'clock the sunlight found and bathed the slopes below me and soon its warmth crept to where I lay. Tying a white handkerchief to the shaft of my ice-ax as a flag, I propped it up and then fell asleep.

When I awoke several hours later I was so warm that I peeled off two layers of sweaters. I tried a halloo, but it brought only answering echoes. I was reasonably sure, however, that the men had not passed me on their way down.

I ate three more of my malted-milk tablets to ease a ravenous hunger. There were six left. A strong thirst assailed me, engendered by the hot sun. About every fifteen minutes I gave a shout, hoping that Moore and Burdsall were on their way down. Three short blasts on a police whistle was our signal for help, but even these brought no response.

Two hours passed. The sun began to sink towards the mountain across the valley. My apprehension about the two climbers grew as the day wore on. The base of the gully was visible from where I lay, but it revealed no signs of the men. Perhaps they had passed me when I slept. At any rate, on not finding me at the base camp, I knew they would instigate a search.

Then in response to one of my shouts came an answer—but from *below*. In a few moments a shaggy Tibetan head appeared above a mound of moraine, closely followed by a second. Here were Chingwa and Chelay. They ran forward on seeing me, and their faces broke into delighted smiles as they greeted "Ngan Hsien Sheng," as they called me.

I inquired as to the whereabouts of Young, and they pointed towards the lamasery. Then I remembered that this was the tenth day after our parting, the day on which we had hoped to return. The two porters had been sent ahead to look for signs of us. Young himself had remained at the Gompa [2] to engage an aggregation of men to dismantle the base camp. Neither Burdsall nor Moore had yet made an appearance.

These two stalwart porters took turns carrying me on their backs down over the precipitous slopes of loose rocks and underlying ice with never a false step. On some of the steeper bits I sat down and, grasping my legs, they towed me along, to the decided detriment of my trousers.

At 5 P.M. we reached the base camp. Never was there a more welcome sight than the cheery fire of juniper in front of the tent.

Moore came in with a load twenty minutes later, having spent the night at Camp I, and reported that Burdsall was following at a slower pace. They had been rather anxious as to my fate, especially when they came upon the débris-littered slopes below the ice wall, and he expressed relief at finding me safely in the valley.

[2] The Konka Gompa, a lamasery in the village of Tsemei, headquarters of the expedition.

I soaked my feet in ice water. They appeared in such poor condition that both Moore and I felt it imperative that they should have medical attention without delay before any serious complications should set in. Accordingly, Moore at once set out for the lamasery to seek Young and engage horses and a retinue for the trip to Tatsienlu. He was benighted half-way down and spent a supperless night beneath a boulder, arriving at the lamasery at an early hour on the following morning.

Burdsall came in at dusk with his load, very tired. His fingers, though not seriously frozen, had developed painful blisters. But the last of the expedition was safely off the mountain, so no one complained.

It snowed six inches that night. The wood became wet and our fire was decidedly sickly the next morning. We attempted to construct a stretcher from a folding camp cot, but its folding propensities were too pronounced and the idea had to be abandoned. By lashing two cross-bars on to a pack-board, a system was evolved that proved more successful. I sat on the lower bar, straddling the pack-board, and hung my arms over the upper one, thus maintaining balance.

Chingwa and Chelay once more shared the work of carrying my 170 pounds, only this time under less difficult circumstances.

I bade farewell to Burdsall, who stayed behind to assist in demolishing the base camp. For ten hours the two Tibetans took turn and turn about at carrying me down over as rough a five miles of country as one could find; so rugged was the trail that no horse or yak could ever have made the trip.

When it came time to ford the stream, my two hardy men hesitated. And well they might, for in the late afternoon the icy water was waist deep and of terrifying swiftness as it boiled along the boulder-strewn bed. I climbed as high on my improvised sedan chair as I could without overbalancing, in an attempt to keep my feet dry.

The stocky Chelay was carrying me at the time and he looked like a small terrier beneath my relatively huge bulk. Chingwa took his hand to steady him and together they stepped into the milky water. At times we balanced on the edge of one submerged boulder for an interminable period before stepping to the next. Disaster seemed impending. At last the men climbed safely out on the farther bank, dripping and shivering, but smiling as ever.

It was not until dark that they staggered up the steep trail to the door of the lamasery, where I was enthusiastically welcomed by Young and Moore.

Horses had been engaged for the morrow, and it was planned that Moore and I should make the trip out to Tatsienlu with all possible speed, accompanied by Gaomo, leaving Young and Burdsall with the porters to bring the remaining gear down to the lamasery.

Young had shot a large grizzly of a little known species while we were making the ascent. In addition to the bear, he had bagged several pheasants, and that evening we dined royally on roast pheasant and bear's paws. The latter are reputed to have brought two hundred dollars a plate in New York restaurants! To cap the climax, home mail had just come in by courier. Frozen feet, aches and pains, hardship and high altitudes, were nearly, if not quite, forgotten as we sat around the fire in the smoke-filled lamasery kitchen and swapped tales with Young of the events of the past ten days.

The lamas seemed incredulous when we told them we had scaled their Holy Mountain to its summit. Still more incredulous were they when, asking if we had brought back the lump of gold, we replied that it had been left there, being too heavy. The story of our porters, however, that they had seen us descending one of the high ridges lent our tale considerable prestige. At any rate, our hosts looked upon me and my misfortunes as a horrid example of what befalls a man who is indiscreet enough to tamper with the awful power of Dorjelutru. Perhaps they were right, but despite my offense, they felt I had been punished severely enough and did everything they could to make me comfortable.

Both Chingwa and Chelay were rewarded with ten rupees apiece for their fine work, a sum which to them constituted a small fortune. Such good friends had we become that they asked me to take them with me to America, which they supposed to be a mere two weeks' travel down the river!

CLARENCE KING

1842–1901

HENRY ADAMS observed that Clarence King "had in him something of the Greek—a touch of Alcibiades or Alexander." The comparison aptly suggests an amazing combination of qualities—talent, charm, energy, shrewdness, and prodigality—which gave to their careless possessor a unique place in American cultural life. "One Clarence King only existed in the world."

Having graduated from the Sheffield Scientific School of Yale University, young Clarence King went west in 1863. Aboard the Sacramento-to-San Francisco boat, he fell into conversation with W. H. Brewer, then an assistant in the geological survey of California. With typical *élan* King volunteered his services and thereby commenced an eminent career as a geologist. Three years later he successfully presented to Congress a plan for a full survey of the Fortieth Parallel across the Cordilleran ranges from eastern Colorado to the California boundary. The project was executed under the administrative control of General A. A. Humphreys of the Corps of Engineers, but the moving spirit was Clarence King. Largely as a result of this project Congress in 1878 united several independent agencies into the United States Geological Survey and appointed King as head. In 1881 he resigned to enter private practice as a mining engineer. During his remaining years he made and lost a fortune, spent several months in a mental hospital, and died alone of tuberculosis in Phoenix, Arizona.

The sketches published as *Mountaineering in the Sierra Nevada* record observations and experiences during King's early years in California, while participating in expeditions led by Brewer and J. D. Whitney. The manuscripts came to the *Atlantic Monthly* in 1871. They captured the attention of William Dean Howells, then the assistant editor. Their appearance in the pages of the *Atlantic* was the occasion of excitement; in book form they were highly successful. Immediately King achieved literary reputation and entrée into the society of the learned and the cultivated, which he enjoyed easily and unself-consciously. Despite great talent his strictly literary output was slight. Friends have recorded that King seemed to prefer conversation to writing, that in the course of an evening's gaiety he would expend in talk the material for a book. Literature was to him chiefly a recreation; having achieved eminence which he did not earnestly seek, he felt no compulsion to confirm it by labor.

Much the same casual spirit motivated King's few ascents. Like John Muir, he climbed simply because he wished to, and like Muir he relied more on natural ingenuity and verve than on orthodox mountain craft. Judged by modern standards his ascents were not impressive and his accounts were exaggerated. Nonetheless, as Francis P. Farquhar has pointed out in his recent edition of *Mountaineering in the Sierra Nevada*, King contributed conspicuously not only to the literature of mountaineering but also to the nascence of the sport in America.

The following selection is reprinted from Clarence King, *Mountaineering in the Sierra Nevada*, Boston, James R. Osgood & Co., 1872. The title of the selection has been supplied.

Mount Tyndall, 1864

MORNING DAWNED BRIGHTLY upon our bivouac among a cluster of dark firs in the mountain corridor opened by an ancient glacier of King's River into the heart of the Sierras. It dawned a trifle sooner than we could have wished, but Professor Brewer and Hoffmann had breakfasted before sunrise, and were off with barometer and theodolite upon their shoulders, purposing to ascend our amphitheatre to its head and climb a great pyramidal peak [1] which swelled up against the eastern sky, closing the view in that direction.

We who remained in camp spent the day in overhauling campaign materials and preparing for a grand assault upon the summits. For a couple of hours we could descry our friends through the field-glasses, their minute black forms moving slowly on among piles of giant *débris;* now and then lost, again coming into view, and at last disappearing altogether.

It was twilight of evening and almost eight o'clock when they came back to camp, Brewer leading the way, Hoffmann following; and as they sat down by our fire without uttering a word, we read upon their faces terrible fatigue.

So we hastened to give them supper of coffee and soup, bread and

[1] Mount Brewer, elevation 13,557 feet.

venison, which resulted, after a time, in our getting in return the story of the day.

For eight whole hours they had worked up over granite and snow, mounting ridge after ridge, till the summit was made about two o'clock.

These snowy crests bounding our view at the eastward we had all along taken to be the summits of the Sierra, and Brewer had supposed himself to be climbing a dominant peak, from which he might look eastward over Owens Valley and out upon leagues of desert. Instead of this a vast wall of mountains, lifted still higher than his peak, rose beyond a tremendous cañon which lay like a trough between the two parallel ranks of peaks. Hoffmann showed us on his sketch-book the profile of this new range, and I instantly recognized the peaks which I had seen from Mariposa, whose great white pile had led me to believe them the highest points of California.

For a couple of months my friends had made me the target of plenty of pleasant banter about my "highest land," which they lost faith in . . . ; but now that the truth had burst upon Brewer and Hoffmann they could not find words to describe the terribleness and grandeur of the deep cañon, nor for picturing those huge crags towering in line at the east. Their peak, as indicated by the barometer, was in the region of thirteen thousand four hundred feet, and a level across to the farther range showed its crests to be at least fifteen hundred feet higher. They had spent hours upon the summit scanning the eastern horizon, and ranging downward into the labyrinth of gulfs below, and had come at last with reluctance to the belief that to cross this gorge and ascend the eastern walls of peaks was utterly impossible.

Brewer and Hoffmann were old climbers, and their verdict of impossible oppressed me as I lay awake thinking of it; but early next morning I had made up my mind, and, taking Cotter [2] aside, I asked him in an easy manner whether he would like to penetrate the Terra Incognita with me at the risk of our necks, provided Brewer should consent. In a frank, courageous tone he answered after his usual mode, "Why not?" Stout of limb, stronger yet in heart, of iron

[2] Richard D. Cotter, a packer employed by the expedition.

endurance, and a quiet, unexcited temperament, and, better yet, deeply devoted to me, I felt that Cotter was the one comrade I would choose to face death with, for I believed there was in his manhood no room for fear or shirk.

It was a trying moment for Brewer when we found him and volunteered to attempt a campaign for the top of California, because he felt a certain fatherly responsibility over our youth, a natural desire that we should not deposit our triturated remains in some undiscoverable hole among the feldspathic granites; but, like a true disciple of science, this was at last over-balanced by his intense desire to know more of the unexplored region. He freely confessed that he believed the plan madness, and Hoffmann, too, told us we might as well attempt to get on a cloud as to try the peak.

As Brewer gradually yielded his consent, I saw by his conversation that there was a possibility of success; so we spent the rest of the day in making preparations.

Our walking-shoes were in excellent condition, the hobnails firm and new. We laid out a barometer, a compass, a pocket-level, a set of wet and dry thermometers, note-books, with bread, cooked beans, and venison enough to last a week, rolled them all in blankets, making two knapsack-shaped packs strapped firmly together with loops for the arms, which, by Brewer's estimate, weighed forty pounds apiece.

Gardner declared he would accompany us to the summit of the first range to look over into the gulf we were to cross, and at last Brewer and Hoffmann also concluded to go up with us.

Quite too early for our profit we all betook ourselves to bed, vainly hoping to get a long refreshing sleep from which we should arise ready for our tramp.

Never a man welcomed those first gray streaks in the east gladder than I did, unless it may be Cotter, who has in later years confessed that he did not go to sleep that night. Long before sunrise we had done our breakfast and were under way, Hoffmann kindly bearing my pack, and Brewer Cotter's.

Our way led due east up the amphitheatre and toward Mount Brewer, as we had named the great pyramidal peak.

Awhile after leaving camp, slant sunlight streamed in among

gilded pinnacles along the slope of Mount Brewer, touching here and there, in broad dashes of yellow, the gray walls which rose sweeping up on either hand like the sides of a ship.

Our way along the valley's middle ascended over a number of huge steps, rounded and abrupt, at whose bases were pools of transparent snow-water edged with rude piles of erratic glacier blocks, scattered companies of alpine firs, of red bark and having cypress-like darkness of foliage, with fields of snow under sheltering cliffs, and bits of softest velvet meadow clouded with minute blue and white flowers.

As we climbed, the gorge grew narrow and sharp, both sides wilder; and the spurs which projected from them, nearly overhanging the middle of the valley, towered above us with more and more severe sculpture. We frequently crossed deep fields of snow, and at last reached the level of the highest pines, where long slopes of *débris* swept down from either cliff, meeting in the middle. Over and among these immense blocks, often twenty and thirty feet high, we were obliged to climb, hearing far below us the subterranean gurgle of streams.

Interlocking spurs nearly closed the gorge behind us; our last view was out a granite gateway formed of two nearly vertical precipices, sharp-edged, jutting buttress-like, and plunging down into a field of angular boulders which fill the valley bottom.

The eye ranged out from this open gateway overlooking the great King's Cañon with its moraine-terraced walls, the domes of granite upon Big Meadows, and the undulating stretch of forest which descends to the plain.

The gorge turning southward, we rounded a sort of mountain promontory, which, closing the view behind us, shut us up in the bottom of a perfect basin. In front lay a placid lake reflecting the intense black-blue of the sky. Granite, stained with purple and red, sank into it upon one side, and a broad spotless field of snow came down to its margin upon the other.

From a pile of large granite blocks, forty or fifty feet up above the lake margin, we could look down fully a hundred feet through the transparent water to where boulders and pebbles were strewn upon the stone bottom. We had now reached the base of Mount

Brewer and were skirting its southern spurs in a wide open corridor surrounded in all directions by lofty granite crags from two to four thousand feet high; above the limits of vegetation, rocks, lakes of deep heavenly blue, and white trackless snows were grouped closely about us. Two sounds, a sharp little cry of martens, and occasional heavy crashes of falling rock, saluted us.

Climbing became exceedingly difficult, light air—for we had already reached twelve thousand five hundred feet—beginning to tell upon our lungs to such an extent that my friend, who had taken turns with me in carrying my pack, was unable to do so any longer, and I adjusted it to my own shoulders for the rest of the day.

After four hours of slow laborious work we made the base of the *débris* slope which rose about a thousand feet to a saddle pass in the western mountain wall, that range upon which Mount Brewer is so prominent a point. We were nearly an hour in toiling up this slope over an uncertain footing which gave way at almost every step. At last, when almost at the top, we paused to take breath, and then all walked out upon the crest, laid off our packs, and sat down together upon the summit of the ridge, and for a few moments not a word was spoken.

The Sierras are here two parallel summit ranges. We were upon the crest of the western ridge, and looked down into a gulf five thousand feet deep, sinking from our feet in abrupt cliffs nearly or quite two thousand feet, whose base plunged into a broad field of snow lying steep and smooth for a great distance, but broken near its foot by craggy steps often a thousand feet high.

Vague blue haze obscured the lost depths, hiding details, giving a bottomless distance out of which, like the breath of wind, floated up a faint tremble, vibrating upon the senses, yet never clearly heard.

Rising on the other side, cliff above cliff, precipice piled upon precipice, rock over rock, up against sky, towered the most gigantic mountain-wall in America, culminating in a noble pile of Gothic-finished granite and enamel-like snow. How grand and inviting looked its white form, its untrodden, unknown crest, so high and pure in the clear strong blue! I looked at it as one contemplating the purpose of his life; and for just one moment I would have rather liked to dodge that purpose, or to have waited, or have found some excellent reason why I might not go; but all this quickly vanished, leaving a cheerful resolve to go ahead.

From the two opposing mountain-walls, singular, thin, knife-blade ridges of stone jutted out, dividing the sides of the gulf into a series of amphitheatres, each one a labyrinth of ice and rock. Piercing thick beds of snow, sprang up knobs and straight isolated spires of rock, mere obelisks curiously carved by frost, their rigid, slender forms casting a blue, sharp shadow upon the snow. Embosomed in depressions of ice, or resting on broken ledges, were azure lakes, deeper in tone than the sky, which at this altitude, even at midday, has a violet duskiness.

To the south, not more than eight miles, a wall of peaks stood across the gulf, dividing the King's, which flowed north at our feet, from the Kern River, that flowed down the trough in the opposite direction.

I did not wonder that Brewer and Hoffmann pronounced our undertaking impossible; but when I looked at Cotter there was such complete bravery in his eye that I asked him if he was ready to start. His old answer, "Why not?" left the initiative with me; so I told Professor Brewer that we would bid him good by. Our friends helped us on with our packs in silence, and as we shook hands there was not a dry eye in the party. Before he let go of my hand Professor Brewer asked me for my plan, and I had to own that I had but one, which was to reach the highest peak in the range.

After looking in every direction I was obliged to confess that I saw as yet no practicable way. We bade them a "good by," receiving their "God bless you" in return, and started southward along the range to look for some possible cliff to descend. Brewer, Gardner, and Hoffmann turned north to push upward to the summit of Mount Brewer, and complete their observations. We saw them whenever we halted, until at last, on the very summit, their microscopic forms were for the last time discernible. With very great difficulty we climbed a peak which surmounted our wall just to the south of the pass, and, looking over the eastern brink, found that that the precipice was still sheer and unbroken. In one place, where the snow lay against it to the very top, we went to its edge and contemplated the slide. About three thousand feet of unbroken white, at a fearfully steep angle, lay below us. We threw a stone over and watched it bound until it was lost in the distance; after fearful leaps we could only detect it by the flashings of snow where it struck, and as these were, in some instances, three hundred feet apart, we decided not to launch our own valuable bodies, and the still more precious barometer, after it.

There seemed but one possible way to reach our goal; that was to make our way along the summit of the cross ridge which projected between the two ranges. This divide sprang out from our Mount Brewer wall, about four miles to the south of us. To reach it we must climb up and down over the indented edge of the Mount Brewer wall. In attempting to do this we had a rather lively time scaling a sharp granite needle, where we found our course completely stopped by precipices four and five hundred feet in height. Ahead of us the summit continued to be broken into fantastic pinnacles, leaving us no hope of making our way along it; so we sought the most broken part of the eastern descent, and began to climb down. The heavy knapsacks, beside wearing our shoulders gradually into a black-and-blue state, overbalanced us terribly, and kept us in constant danger of pitching headlong. At last, taking them off, Cotter climbed down until he had found a resting-place upon a cleft of rock, then I lowered them to him with our lasso, afterwards descending cautiously to his side, taking my turn in pioneering downward, receiving the freight of knapsacks by lasso as before. In this manner we consumed more than half the afternoon in descending a thousand feet of broken, precipitous slope; and it was almost sunset when we found ourselves upon the fields of level snow which lay white and thick over the whole interior slope of the amphitheatre. The gorge below us seemed utterly impassable. At our backs the Mount Brewer wall either rose in sheer cliffs or in broken, rugged stairway, such as had offered us our descent. From this cruel dilemma the cross divide furnished the only hope, and the sole chance of scaling that was at its junction with the Mount Brewer wall. Toward this point we directed our course, marching wearily over stretches of dense frozen snow, and regions of *débris*, reaching about sunset the last alcove of the amphitheatre, just at the foot of the Mount Brewer wall. It was evidently impossible for us to attempt to climb it that evening, and we looked about the desolate recesses for a sheltered camping-spot. A high granite wall surrounded us upon three sides, recurring to the southward in long elliptical curves; no part of the summit being less than two thousand feet above us, the higher crags not unfrequently reaching three thousand feet. A single field of snow swept around the base of the rock, and covered the whole amphitheatre, except where a few spikes and rounded masses of granite rose through it, and where two frozen lakes, with their blue ice-disks, broke the monotonous surface. Through the white snow-gate of our amphitheatre, as through a frame, we looked eastward upon the summit group; not a tree, not a vestige of vegetation in sight—sky, snow, and granite the only elements in this wild picture.

After searching for a shelter we at last found a granite crevice near the margin of one of the frozen lakes—a sort of shelf just large enough for Cotter and me—where we hastened to make our bed, having first filled the canteen from a small stream that trickled over the ice, knowing that in a few moments the rapid chill would freeze it. We ate our supper of cold venison and bread, and whittled from the sides of the wooden barometer-case shavings enough to warm water for a cup of miserably tepid tea, and then, packing our provisions and instruments away at the head of the shelf, rolled ourselves in our blankets and lay down to enjoy the view.

After such fatiguing exercises the mind has an almost abnormal clearness: whether this is wholly from within, or due to the intensely vitalizing mountain air, I am not sure; probably both contribute to the state of exaltation in which all alpine climbers find themselves. The solid granite gave me a luxurious repose, and I lay on the edge of our little rock niche and watched the strange yet brilliant scene.

All the snow of our recess lay in the shadow of the high granite wall to the west, but the Kern divide which curved around us from the southeast was in full light; its broken sky-line, battlemented and adorned with innumerable rough-hewn spires and pinnacles, was a mass of glowing orange intensely defined against the deep violet sky. At the open end of our horseshoe amphitheatre, to the east, its floor of snow rounded over in a smooth brink, overhanging precipices that sank two thousand feet into the King's Cañon. Across the gulf rose the whole procession of summit peaks, their lower halves rooted in a deep sombre shadow cast by the western wall, the heights bathed in a warm purple haze, in which the irregular marbling of snow burned with a pure crimson light. A few fleecy clouds, dyed fiery orange, drifted slowly eastward across the narrow zone of sky which stretched from summit to summit like a roof. At times the sound of waterfalls, faint and mingled with echoes, floated up through the still air. The snow near by lay in cold ghastly shade, warmed here and there in strange flashes by light reflected downward from drifting clouds. The sombre waste about us; the deep violet vault overhead; those far summits, glowing with reflected rose; the deep impenetrable gloom which filled the gorge, and slowly and with vapor-like stealth climbed the mountain wall extinguishing the red light, combined to produce an effect which may not be described; nor can I more than hint at the contrast between the brilliancy of the scene under full light, and the cold, deathlike repose which followed when the wan cliffs and pallid snow were all overshadowed with ghostly gray.

A sudden chill enveloped us. Stars in a moment crowded through the dark heaven, flashing with a frosty splendor. The snow congealed, the brooks ceased to flow, and, under the powerful sudden leverage of frost, immense blocks were dislodged all along the mountain summits and came thundering down the slopes, booming upon the ice, dashing wildly upon rocks. Under the lee of our shelf we felt quite safe, but neither Cotter nor I could help being startled and jumping just a little, as these missiles, weighing often many tons, struck the ledge over our heads and whizzed down the gorge, their stroke resounding fainter and fainter, until at last only a confused echo reached us.

The thermometer at nine o'clock marked twenty degrees above zero. We set the "minimum" and rolled ourselves together for the night. The longer I lay the less I liked that shelf of granite; it grew hard in time, and cold also, my bones seeming to approach actual contact with the chilled rock; moreover, I found that even so vigorous a circulation as mine was not enough to warm up the ledge to anything like a comfortable temperature. A single thickness of blanket is a better mattress than none, but the larger crystals of orthoclase, protruding plentifully, punched my back and caused me to revolve on a horizontal axis with precision and frequency. How I loved Cotter! How I hugged him and got warm, while our backs gradually petrified, till we whirled over and thawed them out together! The slant of that bed was diagonal and excessive; down it we slid till the ice chilled us awake, and we crawled back and chocked ourselves up with bits of granite inserted under my ribs and shoulders. In this pleasant position we got dozing again, and there stole over me a most comfortable ease. The granite softened perceptibly. I was delightfully warm and sank into an industrious slumber which lasted with great soundness till four, when we rose and ate our breakfast of frozen venison.

The thermometer stood at two above zero; everything was frozen tight except the canteen, which we had prudently kept between us all night. Stars still blazed brightly, and the moon, hidden from us by western cliffs, shone in pale reflection upon the rocky heights to the east, which rose, dimly white, up from the impenetrable shadows of the cañon. Silence—cold, ghastly dimness, in which loomed huge forms—the biting frostiness of the air, wrought upon our feelings as we shouldered our packs and started with slow pace to climb toward the "divide."

Soon, to our dismay, we found the straps had so chafed our shoulders that the weight gave us great pain, and obliged us to pad them with our handkerchiefs and extra socks, which remedy did not wholly relieve us from the constant wearing pain of the heavy load.

Directing our steps southward toward a niche in the wall which bounded us only half a mile distant, we travelled over a continuous snow-field frozen so densely as scarcely to yield at all to our tread, at the same time compressing enough to make that crisp frosty sound which we all used to enjoy even before we knew from the books that it had something to do with the severe name of regelation.

As we advanced, the snow sloped more and more steeply up toward the crags, till by and by it became quite dangerous, causing us to cut steps with Cotter's large bowie-knife—a slow, tedious operation, requiring patience of a pretty permanent kind. In this way we spent a quiet social hour or so. The sun had not yet reached us, being shut out by the high amphitheatre wall; but its cheerful light reflected downward from a number of higher crags, filling the recess with the brightness of day, and putting out of existence those shadows which so sombrely darkened the earlier hours. To look back when we stopped to rest was to realize our danger—that smooth swift slope of ice carrying the eye down a thousand feet to the margin of a frozen mirror of ice; ribs and needles of rock piercing up through the snow, so closely grouped that, had we fallen, a miracle only might save us from being dashed. This led to rather deeper steps, and greater care that our burdens should be held more nearly over the centre of gravity, and a pleasant relief when we got to the top of the snow and sat down on a block of granite to breathe and look up in search of a way up the thousand-foot cliff of broken surface, among the lines of fracture and the galleries winding along the face.

It would have disheartened us to gaze up the hard, sheer front of precipices, and search among splintered projections, crevices, shelves, and snow-patches for an inviting route, had we not been animated by a faith that the mountains could not defy us.

Choosing what looked like the least impossible way, we started; but, finding it unsafe to work with packs on, resumed the yesterday's plan—Cotter taking the lead, climbing about fifty feet ahead, and hoisting up the knapsacks and barometer as I tied them to the end of the lasso. Constantly closing up in hopeless difficulty before us, the way opened again and again to our gymnastics, till we stood together upon a mere shelf, not more than two feet wide, which led diagonally up the smooth cliff. Edging along in careful steps, our backs flattened upon the granite, we moved slowly to a broad platform where we stopped for breath.

There was no foothold above us. Looking down over the course we had come, it seemed, and I really believe it was, an impossible descent; for one can climb upward with safety where he cannot downward. To turn back was to give up in defeat; and we sat at least half an hour, suggesting all possible routes to the summit, accepting none, and feeling disheartened. About thirty feet directly over our heads was another shelf, which, if we could reach, seemed to offer at least a temporary way upward. On its edge were two or three spikes of granite; whether firmly connected with the cliff, or merely blocks of *débris*, we could not tell from below. I said to Cotter, I thought of but one possible plan: it was to lasso one of these blocks, and to climb, sailor-fashion, hand over hand, up the rope. In the lasso I had perfect confidence, for I had seen more than one Spanish bull throw his whole weight against it without parting a strand. The shelf was so narrow that throwing the coil of rope was a very difficult undertaking. I tried three times, and Cotter spent five minutes vainly whirling the loop up at the granite spikes. At last I made a lucky throw, and it tightened upon one of the smaller protuberances. I drew the noose close, and very gradually threw my hundred and fifty pounds upon the rope; then Cotter joined me, and, for a moment, we both hung our united weight upon it. Whether the rock moved slightly or whether the lasso stretched a little we were unable to decide; but the trial must be made, and I began to climb slowly. The smooth precipice-face against which my body swung offered no foothold, and the whole climb had therefore to be done by the arms, an effort requiring all one's determination. When about half-way up I was obliged to rest, and, curling my feet in the rope, managed to relieve my arms for a moment. In this position I could not resist the fascinating temptation of a survey downward.

Straight down, nearly a thousand feet below, at the foot of the rocks, began the snow, whose steep, roof-like slope, exaggerated into an almost vertical angle, curved down in a long white field, broken far away by rocks and polished, round lakes of ice.

Cotter looked up cheerfully and asked how I was making it; to which I answered that I had plenty of wind left. At that moment when hanging between heaven and earth, it was a deep satisfaction to look down at the wild gulf of desolation beneath, and up to unknown dangers ahead, and feel my nerves cool and unshaken.

A few pulls hand over hand brought me to the edge of the shelf, when, throwing an arm around the granite spike, I swung my body upon the shelf and lay down to rest, shouting to Cotter that I was all right, and that the prospects upward were capital. After a few moments' breathing I looked over the brink and directed my comrade to tie the barometer to the lower end of the lasso, which he did, and that precious instrument was hoisted to my station, and the lasso sent down twice for knapsacks, after which Cotter came up the rope in his very muscular way without once stopping to rest. We took our loads in our hands, swinging the barometer over my shoulder, and climbed up a shelf which led in a zig-zag direction upward and to the south, bringing us out at last upon the thin blade of a ridge which connected a short distance above with the summit. It was formed of huge blocks, shattered, and ready, at a touch, to fall.

So narrow and sharp was the upper slope, that we dared not walk, but got astride, and worked slowly along with our hands, pushing the knapsacks in advance, now and then holding our breath when loose masses rocked under our weight.

Once upon the summit, a grand view burst upon us. Hastening to step upon the crest of the divide, which was never more than ten feet wide, frequently sharpened to a mere blade, we looked down the other side, and were astonished to find we had ascended the gentler slope, and that the rocks fell from our feet in almost vertical precipices for a thousand feet or more. A glance along the summit toward the highest group showed us that any advance in that direction was impossible, for the thin ridge was gashed down in notches three or four hundred feet deep, forming a procession of pillars, obelisks, and blocks piled upon each other, and looking terribly insecure.

We then deposited our knapsacks in a safe place, and, finding that it was already noon, determined to rest a little while and take a lunch at over thirteen thousand feet above the sea.

West of us stretched the Mount Brewer wall with its succession of smooth precipices and amphitheatre ridges. To the north the great gorge of the King's River yawned down five thousand feet. To the south the valley of the Kern, opening in the opposite direction, was broader, less deep, but more filled with broken masses of granite. Clustered about the foot of the divide were a dozen alpine lakes; the higher ones blue sheets of ice, the lowest completely melted. Still lower in the depths of the two cañons we could see groups of forest trees; but they were so dim and so distant as never to relieve the prevalent masses of rock and snow. Our divide cast its shadow for a mile down King's Cañon in dark blue profile upon the broad sheets of sunny snow, from whose brightness the hard splintered cliffs caught reflections and wore an aspect of joy. Thousands of rills poured from the melting snow, filling the air with a musical tinkle as of many accordant bells. The Kern Valley opened below us with its smooth oval outline, the work of extinct glaciers, whose form and extent were evident from worn cliff-surface and rounded wall; snow-fields, relics of the former *névé*, hung in white tapestries around its ancient birthplace; and, as far as we could see, the broad, corrugated valley, for a breadth of fully ten miles, shone with burnishings wherever its granite surface was not covered with lakelets or thickets of alpine vegetation.

Through a deep cut in the Mount Brewer wall we gained our first view to the westward, and saw in the distance the wall of the South King's Cañon, and the granite point which Cotter and I had climbed a fortnight before. But for the haze we might have seen the plain; for above its farther limit were several points of the Coast Ranges, isolated like islands in the sea.

The view was so grand, the mountain colors so brilliant, immense snow-fields and blue alpine lakes so charming, that we almost forgot we were ever to move, and it was only after a swift hour of this delight that we began to consider our future course.

The King's Cañon, which headed against our wall, seemed untraversable—no human being could climb along the divide; we had then but one hope of reaching the peak, and our greatest difficulty lay at the start. If we could climb down to the Kern side of the divide, and succeed in reaching the base of the precipices which fell from our feet, it really looked as if we might travel without difficulty among the *roches moutonnées* to the other side of the Kern Valley, and make our attempt upon the southward flank of the great peak. One look at the sublime white giant decided us. We looked down over the precipice, and at first could see no method of descent. Then we went back and looked at the road we had come up, to see if that were not possibly as bad; but the broken surface of the rocks was evidently much better climbing-ground than anything ahead of us. Cotter, with danger, edged his way along the wall to the east, and I to the west, to see if there might not be some favorable point; but we both returned with the belief that the precipice in front of us was as passable as any of it. Down it we must.

After lying on our faces, looking over the brink, ten or twenty minutes, I suggested that by lowering ourselves on the rope we might climb from crevice to crevice; but we saw no shelf large enough for ourselves and the knapsacks too. However, we were not going to give it up without a trial; and I made the rope fast round my breast, and, looping the noose over a firm point of rock, let myself slide gradually down to a notch forty feet below. There was only room beside me for Cotter, so I made him send down the knapsacks first. I then tied these together by the straps with my silk handkerchiefs, and hung them off as far to the left as I could reach without losing my balance, looping the handkerchiefs over a point of rock. Cotter then slid down the rope, and, with considerable difficulty, we whipped the noose off its resting-place above, and cut off our connection with the upper world.

"We're in for it now, King," remarked my comrade, as he looked aloft, and then down; but our blood was up, and danger added only an exhilarating thrill to the nerves.

The shelf was hardly more than two feet wide, and the granite so smooth that we could find no place to fasten the lasso for the next descent; so I determined to try the climb with only as little aid as possible. Tying it round my breast again, I gave the other end into Cotter's hands, and he, bracing his back against the cliff, found for himself as firm a foothold as he could, and promised to give me all the help in his power. I made up my mind to bear no weight unless it was absolutely necessary; and for the first ten feet I found cracks and protuberances enough to support me, making every square inch of surface do friction duty, and hugging myself against the rocks as tightly as I could. When within about eight feet of the next shelf, I twisted myself round upon the face, hanging by two rough blocks of protruding feldspar, and looked vainly for some further hand-hold; but the rock, beside being perfectly smooth, overhung slightly, and my legs dangled in the air. I saw that the next cleft was over three feet broad, and I thought, possibly, I might, by a quick slide, reach it in safety without endangering Cotter. I shouted to him to be very careful and let go in case I fell, loosened my hold upon the rope, and slid quickly down. My shoulder struck against the rock and threw me out of balance; for an instant I reeled over upon the verge, in danger of falling, but, in the excitement, I thrust out my hand and seized a small alpine gooseberry-bush, the first piece of vegetation we had seen. Its roots were so firmly fixed in the crevice that it held my weight and saved me.

I could no longer see Cotter, but I talked to him, and heard the two knapsacks come bumping along till they slid over the eaves above me, and swung down to my station, when I seized the lasso's end and braced myself as well as possible, intending, if he slipped, to haul in slack and help him as best I might. As he came slowly down from crack to crack, I heard his hobnailed shoes grating on the granite; presently they appeared dangling from the eaves above my head. I had gathered in the rope until it was taut, and then hurriedly told him to drop. He hesitated a moment, and let go. Before he struck the rock I had him by the shoulder, and whirled him down upon his side, thus preventing his rolling overboard, which friendly action he took quite coolly.

The third descent was not a difficult one, nor the fourth; but when we had climbed down about two hundred and fifty feet, the rocks were so glacially polished and water-worn that it seemed impossible to get any farther. To our right was a crack penetrating the rock perhaps a foot deep, widening at the surface to three or four inches, which proved to be the only possible ladder. As the chances seemed rather desperate, we concluded to tie ourselves together, in order to share a common fate; and with a slack of thirty feet between us, and our knapsacks upon our backs, we climbed into the crevice, and began descending with our faces to the cliff. This had to be done with unusual caution, for the foothold was about as good as none, and our fingers slipped annoyingly on the smooth stone; besides, the knapsacks and instruments kept a steady backward pull, tending to overbalance us. But we took pains to descend one at a time, and rest whenever the niches gave our feet a safe support. In this way we got down about eighty feet of smooth, nearly vertical wall, reaching the top of a rude granite stairway, which led to the snow; and here we sat down to rest, and found to our astonishment that we had been three hours from the summit.

After breathing a half-minute we continued down, jumping from rock to rock, and, having, by practice, become very expert in balancing ourselves, sprang on, never resting long enough to lose the *aplomb,* and in this manner made a quick descent over rugged *débris* to the crest of a snow-field, which, for seven or eight hundred feet more, swept down in a smooth, even slope, of very high angle, to the borders of a frozen lake.

Without untying the lasso which bound us together, we sprang upon the snow with a shout, and glissaded down splendidly, turning now and then a somersault, and shooting out like cannon-balls almost to the middle of the frozen lake; I upon my back, and Cotter feet first, in a swimming position. The ice cracked in all directions. It was only a thin, transparent film, through which we could see deep into the lake. Untying ourselves, we hurried ashore in different directions, lest our combined weight should be too great a strain upon any point.

With curiosity and wonder we scanned every shelf and niche of the last descent. It seemed quite impossible we could have come down there, and now it actually was beyond human power to get back again. But what cared we? "Sufficient unto the day—" We were bound for that still distant, though gradually nearing, summit; and we had come from a cold shadowed cliff into deliciously warm sunshine, and were jolly, shouting, singing songs, and calling out the companionship of a hundred echoes. Six miles away, with no grave danger, no great difficulty, between us, lay the base of our grand mountain. Upon its skirts we saw a little grove of pines, an ideal bivouac, and toward this we bent our course.

After the continued climbing of the day, walking was a delicious rest, and forward we pressed with considerable speed, our hobnails giving us firm footing on the glittering glacial surface. Every fluting of the great valley was in itself a considerable cañon, into which we descended, climbing down the scored rocks, and swinging from block to block, until we reached the level of the pines. Here, shel-

tered among *roches moutonnées*, began to appear little fields of
alpine grass, pale yet sunny, soft under our feet, fragrantly jewelled
with flowers of fairy delicacy, holding up amid thickly clustered
blades chalices of turquoise and amethyst, white stars, and fiery little
globes of red. Lakelets, small but innumerable, were held in glacial
basins, the striae and grooves of that old dragon's track ornamenting
their smooth bottoms.

One of these, a sheet of pure beryl hue, gave us much pleasure
from its lovely transparency, and because we lay down in the neck-
lace of grass about it and smelled flowers, while tired muscles relaxed upon warm beds of verdure, the pain in our burdened shoulders
went away, leaving us delightfully comfortable.

After the stern grandeur of granite and ice, and with the peaks
and walls still in view, it was relief to find ourselves again in the
region of life. I never felt for trees and flowers such a sense of intimate relationship and sympathy. When we had no longer excuse
for resting, I invented the palpable subterfuge of measuring the
altitude of the spot, since the few clumps of low, wide-boughed
pines near by were the highest living trees. So we lay longer with
less and less will to rise, and when resolution called us to our feet
the getting-up was sorely like Rip Van Winkle's in the third act.

The deep glacial cañon-flutings across which our march then lay
proved to be great consumers of time; indeed it was sunset when
we reached the eastern ascent, and began to toil up through scattered pines, and over trains of moraine rocks, toward the great peak.
Stars were already flashing brilliantly in the sky, and the low glowing
arch in the west had almost vanished when we reached the upper
trees, and threw down our knapsacks to camp. The forest grew on
a sort of plateau-shelf with a precipitous front to the west—a level
surface which stretched eastward and back to the foot of our mountain, whose lower spurs reached within a mile of camp. Within the
shelter lay a huge fallen log, like all these alpine woods one mass of
resin, which flared up when we applied a match, illuminating the
whole grove. By contrast with the darkness outside, we seemed to
be in a vast, many-pillared hall. The stream close by afforded water
for our blessed teapot; venison frizzled with mild, appetizing sound
upon the ends of pine sticks; matchless beans allowed themselves to

become seductively crisp upon our tin plates. That supper seemed to me then the quintessence of gastronomy, and I am sure Cotter and I must have said some very good *après-dîner* things, though I long ago forgot them all. Within the ring of warmth, on elastic beds of pine-needles, we curled up, and fell swiftly into a sound sleep.

I woke up once in the night to look at my watch, and observed that the sky was overcast with a thin film of cirrus clouds to which the reflected moonlight lent the appearance of a glimmering tent, stretched from mountain to mountain over cañons filled with impenetrable darkness, only the vaguely lighted peaks and white snow-fields distinctly seen. I closed my eyes and slept soundly until Cotter woke me at half past three, when we arose, breakfasted by the light of our fire, which still blazed brilliantly, and, leaving our knapsacks, started for the mountain with only instruments, canteens, and luncheon.

In the indistinct moonlight climbing was very difficult at first, for we had to thread our way along a plain which was literally covered with glacier boulders, and the innumerable brooks which we crossed were frozen solid. However, our march brought us to the base of the great mountain, which, rising high against the east, shut out the coming daylight, and kept us in profound shadow. From base to summit rose a series of broken crags, lifting themselves from a general slope of *débris*. Toward the left the angle seemed to be rather gentler, and the surface less ragged; and we hoped, by a long *détour* round the base, to make an easy climb up this gentler face. So we toiled on for an hour over the rocks, reaching at last the bottom of the north slope. Here our work began in good earnest. The blocks were of enormous size, and in every stage of unstable equilibrium, frequently rolling over as we jumped upon them, making it necessary for us to take a second leap and land where we best could. To our relief we soon surmounted the largest blocks, reaching a smaller size, which served us as a sort of stairway.

The advancing daylight revealed to us a very long, comparatively even snow-slope, whose surface was pierced by many knobs and granite heads, giving it the aspect of an ice-roofing fastened on with bolts of stone. It stretched in far perspective to the summit, where already the rose of sunrise reflected gloriously, kindling a fresh enthusiasm within us.

Immense boulders were partly embedded in the ice just above us, whose constant melting left them trembling on the edge of a fall. It communicated no very pleasant sensation to see above you these immense missiles hanging by a mere band, and knowing that, as soon as the sun rose, you would be exposed to a constant cannonade.

The east side of the peak, which we could now partially see, was too precipitous to think of climbing. The slope toward our camp was too much broken into pinnacles and crags to offer us any hope, or to divert us from the single way, dead ahead, up slopes of ice and among fragments of granite. The sun rose upon us while we were climbing the lower part of this snow, and in less than half an hour, melting, began to liberate huge blocks, which thundered down past us, gathering and growing into small avalanches below.

We did not dare climb one above another, according to our ordinary mode, but kept about an equal level, a hundred feet apart, lest, dislodging the blocks, one should hurl them down upon the other.

We climbed alternately up smooth faces of granite, clinging simply by the cracks and protruding crystals of feldspar, and then hewed steps up fearfully steep slopes of ice, zigzagging to the right and left to avoid the flying boulders. When midway up this slope we reached a place where the granite rose in perfectly smooth bluffs on either side of a gorge—a narrow cut, or walled way, leading up to the flat summit of the cliff. This we scaled by cutting ice steps, only to find ourselves fronted again by a still higher wall. Ice sloped from its front at too steep an angle for us to follow, but had melted in contact with it, leaving a space three feet wide between the ice and the rock. We entered this crevice and climbed along its bottom, with a wall of rock rising a hundred feet above us on one side, and a thirty-foot face of ice on the other, through which light of an intense cobalt-blue penetrated.

Reaching the upper end, we had to cut our footsteps upon the ice again, and, having braced our backs against the granite, climb up to the surface. We were now in a dangerous position: to fall into the crevice upon one side was to be wedged to death between rock and ice; to make a slip was to be shot down five hundred feet, and then hurled over the brink of a precipice. In the friendly seat which this wedge gave me, I stopped to take wet and dry observations with the thermometer—this being an absolute preventive of a scare—and to enjoy the view.

The wall of our mountain sank abruptly to the left, opening for the first time an outlook to the eastward. Deep—it seemed almost vertically—beneath us we could see the blue water of Owens Lake, ten thousand feet down. The summit peaks to the north were piled in titanic confusion, their ridges overhanging the eastern slope with terrible abruptness. Clustered upon the shelves and plateaus below were several frozen lakes, and in all directions swept magnificent fields of snow. The summit was now not over five hundred feet distant, and we started on again with the exhilarating hope of success. But if Nature had intended to secure the summit from all assailants, she could not have planned her defences better; for the smooth granite wall which rose above the snow-slope continued, apparently, quite round the peak, and we looked in great anxiety to see if there was not one place where it might be climbed. It was all blank except in one place; quite near us the snow bridged across the crevice, and rose in a long point to the summit of the wall—a great icicle-column frozen in a niche of the bluff—its base about ten feet wide, narrowing to two feet at the top. We climbed to the base of this spire of ice, and, with the utmost care, began to cut our stairway. The material was an exceedingly compacted snow, passing into clear ice as it neared the rock. We climbed the first half of it with comparative ease; after that it was almost vertical, and so thin that we did not dare to cut the footsteps deep enough to make them absolutely safe. There was a constant dread lest our ladder should break off, and we be thrown either down the snow-slope or into the bottom of the crevasse. At last, in order to prevent myself from falling over backwards, I was obliged to thrust my hand into the crack between the ice and the wall, and the spire became so narrow that I could do this on both sides; so that the climb was made as upon a tree, cutting mere toeholes, and embracing the whole column of ice in my arms. At last I reached the top, and, with the greatest caution, wormed my body over the brink, and, rolling out upon the smooth surface of the granite, looked over and watched Cotter make his climb. He came steadily up, with no sense of nervousness, until he got to the narrow part of the ice, and here he stopped and looked up with a forlorn face to me; but as he climbed up over the edge the broad smile came back to his face, and he asked me if it had occurred to me that we had, by and by, to go down again.

We now had an easy slope to the summit, and hurried up over rocks and ice, reaching the crest at exactly twelve o'clock. I rang my hammer upon the topmost rock; we grasped hands, and I reverently named the grand peak MOUNT TYNDALL.[3]

To our surprise, upon sweeping the horizon with my level, there appeared two peaks equal in height with us, and two rising even higher. That which looked highest of all was a cleanly cut helmet of granite upon the same ridge with Mount Tyndall, lying about six miles south, and fronting the desert with a bold square bluff which rises to the crest of the peak, where a white field of snow trims it gracefully.

Mount Whitney, as we afterwards called it in honor of our chief, is probably the highest land within the United States.[4] Its summit looked glorious, but inaccessible.

The general topography overlooked by us may be thus simply outlined. Two parallel chains, enclosing an intermediate trough, face each other. Across this deep enclosed gulf, from wall to wall, juts the thin, but lofty and craggy ridge, or "divide," before described, which forms an important water-shed, sending those streams which enter the chasm north of it into King's River, those south forming the most important sources of the Kern, whose straight, rapidly deepening valley stretches south, carved profoundly in granite, while the King's, after flowing longitudinally in the opposite course for eight or ten miles, turns abruptly west around the base of Mount Brewer, cuts across the western ridge, opening a gate of its own, and carves a rock channel transversely down the Sierra to the California plain.

Fronting us stood the west chain, a great mural ridge watched over

[3] Presumably in honor of the English physicist and mountaineer John Tyndall (1820–93), author of *Hours of Exercise in the Alps.*
[4] Elevation 14,495 feet. King's surmise is correct.

by two dominant heights, Kaweah Peak and Mount Brewer, its wonderful profile defining against the western sky a multitude of peaks and spires. Bold buttresses jut out through fields of ice, and reach down stone arms among snow and *débris*. North and south of us the higher, or eastern, summit stretched on in miles and miles of snowpeaks, the farthest horizon still crowded with their white points. East the whole range fell in sharp, hurrying abruptness to the desert, where, ten thousand feet below, lay a vast expanse of arid plain intersected by low parallel ranges, traced from north to south. Upon the one side a thousand sculptures of stone, hard, sharp, shattered by cold into infiniteness of fractures and rift, springing up, mutely severe, into the dark, austere blue of heaven; scarred and marked, except where snow or ice, spiked down by ragged granite bolts, shields with its pale armor these rough mountain shoulders; storm-tinted at summit, and dark where, swooping down from ragged cliff, the rocks plunge over cañon-walls into blue, silent gulfs.

Upon the other hand, reaching out to horizons faint and remote, lay plains clouded with the ashen hues of death; stark, wind-swept floors of white, and hill-ranges, rigidly formal, monotonously low, all lying under an unfeeling brilliance of light, which, for all its strange, unclouded clearness, has yet a vague half-darkness, a suggestion of black and shade more truly pathetic than fading twilight. No greenness soothes, no shadow cools the glare. Owen's Lake, an oval of acrid water, lies dense blue upon the brown sage-plain, looking like a plate of hot metal. Traced in ancient beach-lines, here and there upon hill and plain, relics of ancient lake-shore outline the memory of a cooler past—a period of life and verdure when the stony chains were green islands among basins of wide, watery expanse.

The two halves of this view, both in sight at once, express the highest, the most acute, aspects of desolation—inanimate forms out of which something living has gone forever. From the desert have been dried up and blown away its seas. Their shores and white, salt-strewn bottoms lie there in the eloquence of death. Sharp white light glances from all the mountain-walls, where in marks and polishings has been written the epitaph of glaciers now melted and vanished into air. Vacant cañons lie open to the sun, bare, treeless, half shrouded with snow, cumbered with loads of broken *débris*, still as graves, except when flights of rocks rush down some chasm's throat, startling the mountains with harsh, dry rattle, their fainter echoes from below followed too quickly by dense silence.

The serene sky is grave with nocturnal darkness. The earth blinds you with its light. That fair contrast we love in lower lands between bright heavens and dark cool earth here reverses itself with terrible energy. You look up into an infinite vault, unveiled by clouds, empty and dark, from which no brightness seems to ray, an expanse with no graded perspective, no tremble, no vapory mobility, only the vast yawning of hollow space.

With an aspect of endless remoteness burns the small white sun, yet its light seems to pass invisibly through the sky, blazing out with intensity upon mountain and plain, flooding rock details with painfully bright reflections, and lighting up the burnt sand and stone of the desert with a strange blinding glare. There is no sentiment of beauty in the whole scene; no suggestion, however far remote, of sheltered landscape; not even the air of virgin hospitality that greets us explorers in so many uninhabited spots which by their fertility and loveliness of grove or meadow seem to offer man a home, or us nomads a pleasant camp-ground. Silence and desolation are the themes which nature has wrought out under this eternally serious sky. A faint suggestion of life clings about the middle altitudes of the eastern slope, where black companies of pine, stunted from breathing the hot desert air, group themselves just beneath the bottom of perpetual snow, or grow in patches of cloudy darkness over the moraines, those piles of wreck crowded from their pathway by glaciers long dead. Something there is pathetic in the very emptiness of these old glacier valleys, these imperishable tracks of unseen engines. One's eye ranges up their broad, open channel to the shrunken white fields surrounding hollow amphitheatres which were once crowded with deep burdens of snow—the birthplace of rivers of ice now wholly melted; the dry, clear heavens overhead, blank of any promise of ever rebuilding them. I have never seen Nature when she seemed so little "Mother Nature" as in this place of rocks and snow, echoes and emptiness. It impresses me as the ruins of some bygone geological period, and no part of the present order, like a specimen of chaos which has defied the finishing hand of Time.

Of course I see its bearings upon climate, and could read a lesson quite glibly as to its usefulness as a condenser, and tell you gravely how much California has for which she may thank these heights, and how little Nevada; but looking from this summit with all desire to see everything, the one overmastering feeling is desolation, desolation!

Next to this, and more pleasing to notice, is the interest and richness of the granite forms; for the whole region, from plain to plain, is built of this dense solid rock, and is sculptured under chisel of cold in shapes of great variety, yet all having a common spirit, which is purely Gothic.

In the much discussed origin of this order of building, I never remember to have seen, though it can hardly have escaped mention, any suggestion of the possibility of the Gothic having been inspired by granite forms. Yet, as I sat on Mount Tyndall, the whole mountains shaped themselves like the ruins of cathedrals—sharp roof-ridges, pinnacled and statured; buttresses more spired and ornamented than Milan's; receding doorways with pointed arches carved into blank façades of granite, doors never to be opened, innumerable jutting points with here and there a single cruciform peak, its frozen roof and granite spires so strikingly Gothic I cannot doubt that the Alps furnished the models for early cathedrals of that order. . . .

All the while I made my instrumental observations, the fascination of the view so held me that I felt no surprise at seeing water boiling over our little fagot blaze at a temperature of one hundred and ninety-two degrees F., nor in observing the barometrical column stand at 17.99 inches; and it was not till a week or so after that I realized we had felt none of the conventional sensations of nausea, headache, and I don't know what all, that people are supposed to suffer at extreme altitudes; but these things go with guides and porters, I believe, and with coming down to one's hotel at evening there to scold one's picturesque *aubergiste* in a French which strikes upon his ear as a foreign tongue; possibly all that will come to us with advancing time, and what is known as "doing America." They are already shooting our buffaloes; it cannot be long before they will cause themselves to be honorably dragged up and down our Sierras, with perennial yellow gaiter, and ostentation of bath-tub.

Having completed our observations, we packed up the instruments, glanced once again around the whole field of view, and descended to the top of our icicle ladder. Upon looking over, I saw to my consternation that during the day the upper half had broken off. Scars traced down upon the snow-field below it indicated the manner of its fall, and far below, upon the shattered *débris*, were strewn its white relics. I saw that nothing but the sudden gift of wings could possibly take us down to the snow-ridge. We held council and concluded to climb quite round the peak in search of the best mode of descent.

As we crept about the east face, we could look straight down upon Owen's Valley, and into the vast glacier gorges, and over piles of moraines and fluted rocks, and the frozen lakes of the eastern slope. When we reached the southwest front of the mountain we found that its general form was that of an immense horseshoe, the great eastern ridge forming one side, and the spur which descended to our camp the other, we having climbed up the outer part of the toe. Within the curve of the horseshoe was a gorge, cut almost perpendicularly down two thousand feet, its sides rough-hewn walls of rocks and snow, its narrow bottom almost a continuous chain of deep blue lakes with loads of ice and *débris* piles. The stream which flowed through them joined the waters from our home grove, a couple of miles below the camp. If we could reach the level of the lakes, I believed we might easily climb round them, and out of the upper end of the horseshoe, and walk upon the Kern plateau round to our bivouac.

It required a couple of hours of very painstaking deliberate climbing to get down the first descent, which we did, however, without hurting our barometer, and fortunately without the fatiguing use of the lasso; reaching finally the uppermost lake, a granite bowlful of cobalt-blue water, transparent and unrippled. So high and enclosing were the tall walls about us, so narrow and shut in the cañon, so flattened seemed the cover of sky, we felt oppressed after the expanse and freedom of our hours on the summit.

The snow-field we followed, descending farther, was irregularly honeycombed in deep pits, circular or irregular in form, and melted to a greater or less depth, holding each a large stone embedded in the bottom. It seems they must have fallen from the overhanging heights with sufficient force to plunge into the snow.

Brilliant light and strong color met our eyes at every glance— the rocks of a deep purple-red tint, the pure alpine lakes of a cheerful sapphire blue, the snow glitteringly white. The walls on either side for half their height were planed and polished by glaciers, and from the smoothly glazed sides the sun was reflected as from a mirror.

Mile after mile we walked cautiously over the snow, and climbed around the margins of lakes, and over piles of *débris* which marked the ancient terminal moraines. At length we reached the end of the horseshoe, where the walls contracted to a gateway, rising on either side in immense vertical pillars a thousand feet high. Through this gateway we could look down the valley of the Kern, and beyond to the gentler ridges where a smooth growth of forest darkened the rolling plateau. Passing the last snow, we walked through this gateway and turned westward round the spur toward our camp. The three miles which closed our walk were alternately through groves of *Pinus flexilis* and upon plains of granite. . . .

The sun was still an hour high when we reached camp, and with a feeling of relaxation and repose we threw ourselves down to rest by the log, which still continued blazing. We had accomplished our purpose.

During the last hour or two of our tramp Cotter had complained of his shoes, which were rapidly going to pieces. Upon examination we found to our dismay that there was not over half a day's wear left in them, a calamity which gave to our difficult homeward climb a new element of danger. The last nail had been worn from my own shoes, and the soles were scratched to the quick, but I believed them stout enough to hold together till we should reach the main camp.

We planned a pair of moccasins for Cotter, and then spent a pleasant evening by the camp-fire, rehearsing our climb to the detail, sleep finally overtaking us and holding us fast bound until broad daylight next morning, when we woke with a sense of having slept for a week, quite bright and perfectly refreshed for our homeward journey.

After a frugal breakfast, in which we limited ourselves to a few cubic inches of venison, and a couple of stingy slices of bread, with a single meagre cup of diluted tea, we shouldered our knapsacks, which now sat lightly upon toughened shoulders, and marched out upon the granite plateau.

We had concluded that it was impossible to retrace our former way, knowing well that the precipitous divide could not be climbed from this side; then, too, we had gained such confidence in our climbing powers, from constant victory, that we concluded to attempt the passage of the great King's Cañon, mainly because this was the only mode of reaching camp, and since the geological section of the granite it exposed would afford us an exceedingly instructive study.

The broad granite plateau which forms the upper region of the Kern Valley slopes in general inclination up to the great divide. This remarkably pinnacled ridge, where it approaches the Mount Tyndall wall, breaks down into a broad depression where the Kern Valley sweeps northward, until it suddenly breaks off in precipices three thousand feet down into the King's Cañon.

The morning was wholly consumed in walking up this gently inclined plane of granite, our way leading over the glacier-polished foldings and along graded undulations among labyrinths of alpine garden and wildernesses of erratic boulders, little lake-basins, and scattered clusters of dwarfed and sombre pine.

About noon we came suddenly upon the brink of a precipice which sunk sharply from our feet into the gulf of the King's Cañon. Directly opposite us rose Mount Brewer and up out of the depths of those vast sheets of frozen snow swept spiry buttress-ridges, dividing the upper heights into those amphitheatres over which we had struggled on our outward journey. Straight across from our point of view was the chamber of rock and ice where we had camped on the first night. The wall at our feet fell sharp and rugged, its lower two-thirds hidden from our view by the projections of a thousand feet of crags. Here and there, as we looked down, small patches of ice, held in rough hollows, rested upon the steep surface, but it was too abrupt for any great fields of snow. I dislodged a boulder upon the edge and watched it bound down the rocky precipice, dash over eaves a thousand feet below us, and disappear; the crash of its fall coming up to us from the unseen depths fainter and fainter, until the air only trembled with confused echoes.

A long look at the pass to the south of Mount Brewer, where we had parted from our friends, animated us with courage to begin the descent, which we did with utmost care, for the rocks, becoming more and more glacier-smoothed, afforded us hardly any firm footholds. When down about eight hundred feet we again rolled rocks ahead of us, and saw them disappear over the eaves, and only heard the sound of their stroke after many seconds, which convinced us that directly below lay a great precipice.

At this juncture the soles came entirely off Cotter's shoes, and we stopped upon a little cliff of granite to make him moccasins of our provision bags and slips of blanket, tying them on as firmly as we could with the extra straps and buckskin thongs.

Climbing with these proved so insecure that I made Cotter go behind me, knowing that under ordinary circumstances I could stop him if he fell.

Here and there in the clefts of the rocks grew stunted pine bushes, their roots twisted so firmly into the crevices that we laid hold of them with the utmost confidence whenever they came within our reach. In this way we descended to within fifty feet of the brink, having as yet no knowledge of the cliffs below, except our general memory of their aspect from the Mount Brewer wall.

The rock was so steep that we descended in a sitting posture, clinging with our hands and heels.

I heard Cotter say, "I think I must take off these moccasins and try it barefooted, for I don't believe I can make it." These words were instantly followed by a startled cry, and I looked round to see him slide quickly toward me, struggling and clutching at the smooth granite. As he slid by I made a grab for him with my right hand, catching him by the shirt, and, throwing myself as far in the other direction as I could, seized with my left hand a little pine tuft, which held us. I asked Cotter to edge along a little to the left, where he could get a brace with his feet and relieve me of his weight, which he cautiously did. I then threw a couple of turns with the lasso round the roots of the pine bush, and we were safe, though hardly more than twenty feet from the brink. The pressure of curiosity to get a look over that edge was so strong within me, that I lengthened out sufficient lasso to reach the end, and slid slowly to the edge, where, leaning over, I looked down, getting a full view of the wall for miles. Directly beneath, a sheer cliff of three or four hundred feet stretched down to a pile of *débris* which rose to unequal heights along its face, reaching the very crest not more than a hundred feet south of us. From that point to the bottom of the cañon broken rocks, ridges rising through vast sweeps of *débris*, tufts of pine and frozen bodies of ice, covered the farther slope.

I returned to Cotter, and, having loosened ourselves from the pine bush, inch by inch crept along the granite until we supposed ourselves to be just over the top of the *débris* pile, where I found a firm brace for my feet, and lowered Cotter to the edge. He sang out "All right!" and climbed over on the uppermost *débris*, his head only remaining in sight of me; when I lay down upon my back, making knapsack and body do friction duty, and, letting myself move, followed Cotter and reached his side.

From that point the descent required us two hours of severe constant labor, which was monotonous of itself, and would have proved excessively tiresome but for the constant interest of glacial geology beneath us. When at last we reached bottom and found ourselves upon a velvety green meadow, beneath the shadow of wide-armed pines, we realized the amount of muscular force we had used up, and threw ourselves down for a rest of half an hour, when we rose, not quite renewed, but fresh enough to finish the day's climb.

In a few minutes we stood upon the rocks just above King's River—a broad white torrent fretting its way along the bottom of an impassable gorge. Looking down the stream, we saw that our right bank was a continued precipice, affording, so far as we could see, no possible descent to the river's margin, and indeed, had we gotten down, the torrent rushed with such fury that we could not possibly have crossed it. To the south of us, a little way up stream, the river flowed out from a broad oval lake, three quarters of a mile in length, which occupied the bottom of the granite basin. Unable to cross the torrent, we must either swim the lake or climb round its head. Upon our side the walls of the basin curved to the head of the lake in sharp smooth precipices, or broken slopes of *débris;* while on the opposite side its margin was a beautiful shore of emerald meadow, edged with a continuous grove of coniferous trees. Once upon this other side, we should have completed the severe part of our journey, crossed the gulf, and have left all danger behind us; for the long slope of granite and ice which rose upon the west side of the cañon and the Mount Brewer wall opposed to us no trials save those of simple fatigue.

Around the head of the lake were crags and precipices in singu-larly forbidding arrangement. As we turned thither we saw no possible way of overcoming them. At its head the lake lay in an angle of the vertical wall, sharp and straight like the corner of a room; about three hundred feet in height, and for two hundred and fifty feet of this, a pyramidal pile of blue ice rose from the lake, rested against the corner, and reached within forty feet of the top. Looking into the deep blue water of the lake, I concluded that in our exhausted state it was madness to attempt to swim it. The only other alternative was to scale that slender pyramid of ice and find some way to climb the forty feet of smooth wall above it; a plan we chose perforce, and started at once to put into execution, de-termined that if we were unsuccessful we would fire a dead log which lay near, warm ourselves thoroughly, and attempt the swim. At its base the ice mass overhung the lake like a roof, under which the water had melted its way for a distance of not less than a hundred feet, a thin eave overhanging the water. To the very edge of this I cautiously went, and, looking down into the lake, saw through its beryl depths the white granite blocks strewn upon the bottom at least one hundred feet below me. It was exceedingly transparent, and, under ordinary circumstances, would have been almost tempt-ing for a dive; but at the end of our long fatigue, and with the still unknown tasks ahead, I shrunk from a swim in such a chilly tem-perature.

We found the ice-angle difficultly steep, but made our way suc-cessfully along its edge, clambering up the crevices melted between its body and the smooth granite to a point not far from the top, where the ice had considerably narrowed, and rocks overhanging it encroached so closely that we were obliged to leave the edge and make our way with cut steps out upon its front. Streams of water, dropping from the overhanging rock-eaves at many points, had worn circular shafts into the ice, three feet in diameter and twenty feet in depth. Their edges offered us our only foothold, and we climbed from one to another, equally careful of slipping upon the slope itself, or falling into the wells. Upon the top of the ice we found a narrow, level platform, upon which we stood together, resting our backs in the granite corner, and looked down the awful pathway of King's Cañon, until the rest nerved us up enough to turn our eyes upward at the forty feet of smooth granite which lay between us and safety.

Here and there were small projections from its surface, little protruding knobs of feldspar, and crevices riven into its face for a few inches.

As we tied ourselves together, I told Cotter to hold himself in readiness to jump down into one of these in case I fell, and started to climb up the wall, succeeding quite well for about twenty feet. About two feet above my hands was a crack, which, if my arms had been long enough to reach, would probably have led me to the very top; but I judged it beyond my powers, and, with great care, descended to the side of Cotter, who believed that his superior length of arm would enable him to make the reach.

I planted myself against the rock, and he started cautiously up the wall. Looking down the glare front of ice, it was not pleasant to consider at what velocity a slip would send me to the bottom, or at what angle, and to what probable depth, I should be projected into the ice-water. Indeed, the idea of such a sudden bath was so annoying that I lifted my eyes toward my companion. He reached my farthest point without great difficulty, and made a bold spring for the crack, reaching it without an inch to spare, and holding on wholly by his fingers. He thus worked himself slowly along the crack toward the top, at last getting his arms over the brink, and gradually drawing his body up and out of sight. It was the most splendid piece of slow gymnastics I ever witnessed. For a moment he said nothing; but when I asked if he was all right cheerfully repeated, "All right." It was only a moment's work to send up the two knapsacks and barometer, and receive again my end of the lasso. As I tied it round my breast, Cotter said to me, in an easy, confident tone, "Don't be afraid to bear your weight." I made up my mind, however, to make that climb without his aid, and husbanded my strength as I climbed from crack to crack. I got up without difficulty to my former point, rested there a moment, hanging solely by my hands, gathered every pound of strength and atom of will for the reach, then jerked myself upward with a swing, just getting the tips of my fingers into the crack. In an instant I had grasped it with my right hand also. I felt the sinews of my fingers relax a little, but the picture of the slope of ice and the blue lake affected me so strongly that I redoubled my grip, and climbed slowly along the crack until I reached the angle and got one arm over the edge as Cotter had done. As I rested my body upon the edge and looked up at Cotter, I saw that, instead of a level top, he was sitting upon a smooth roof-like slope, where the least pull would have dragged him over the brink. He had no brace for his feet, nor hold for his hands, but had seated himself calmly, with the rope tied round his breast, knowing that my only safety lay in being able to make the climb entirely unaided; certain that the least waver in his tone would have disheartened me, and perhaps made it impossible. The shock I received on seeing this affected me for a moment, but not enough to throw me off my guard, and I climbed quickly over the edge. When we had walked back out of danger we sat down upon the granite for a rest.

In all my experience of mountaineering I have never known an act of such real, profound courage as this of Cotter's. It is one thing, in a moment of excitement, to make a gallant leap, or hold one's nerves in the iron grasp of will, but to coolly seat one's self in the door of death, and silently listen for the fatal summons, and this all for a friend—for he might easily have cast loose the lasso and saved himself—requires as sublime a type of courage as I know.

But a few steps back we found a thicket of pine overlooking our lake, by which there flowed a clear rill of snow-water. Here, in the bottom of the great gulf, we made our bivouac; for we were already in the deep evening shadows, although the mountain-tops to the east of us still burned in the reflected light. It was the luxury of repose which kept me awake half an hour or so, in spite of my vain attempts at sleep. To listen for the pulsating sound of waterfalls and arrowy rushing of the brook by our beds was too deep a pleasure to quickly yield up.

Under the later moonlight I rose and went out upon the open rocks, allowing myself to be deeply impressed by the weird Dantesque surroundings—darkness, out of which to the sky towered stern, shaggy bodies of rock; snow, uncertainly moonlit with cold pallor; and at my feet the basin of the lake, still, black, and gemmed with reflected stars, like the void into which Dante looked through the bottomless gulf of Dis. A little way off there appeared upon the brink of a projecting granite cornice two dimly seen forms; pines I knew them to be, yet their motionless figures seemed bent forward, gazing down the cañon; and I allowed myself to name them Mantuan and Florentine, thinking at the same time how grand and spacious the scenery, and how powerful their attitude, how infinitely more profound the mystery of light and shade, than any of those hard, theatrical conceptions with which Doré has sought to shut in our imagination. That artist, as I believe, has reached a conspicuous failure from an overbalancing love of solid, impenetrable darkness. There is in all his Inferno landscape a certain sharp boundary between the real and unreal, and never the infinite suggestiveness of great regions of half-light, in which everything may be seen, nothing recognized. Without waking Cotter, I crept back to my blankets, and to sleep.

The morning of our fifth and last day's tramp must have dawned cheerfully; at least, so I suppose from its aspect when we first came back to consciousness, surprised to find the sun risen from the eastern mountain-wall and the whole gorge flooded with its direct light. Rising as good as new from our mattress of pine twigs, we hastened to take breakfast, and started up the long, broken slope of the Mount Brewer wall. To reach the pass where we had parted from our friends required seven hours of slow, laborious climbing, in which we took advantage of every outcropping spine of granite and every level expanse of ice to hasten at the top of our speed. Cotter's feet were severely cut; his tracks upon the snow were marked by stains of blood, yet he kept on with undiminished spirit, never once complaining. The perfect success of our journey so inspired us with happiness that we forgot danger and fatigue, and chatted in liveliest strain.

It was about two o'clock when we reached the summit and rested a moment to look back over our new Alps, which were hard and distinct under direct unpoetic light; yet with all their dense gray and white reality, their long, sculptured ranks, and cold, still summits, we gave them a lingering farewell look, which was not without its deep fulness of emotion, then turned our backs and hurried down the *débris* slope into the rocky amphitheatre at the foot of Mount Brewer, and by five o'clock had reached our old campground. We found here a note pinned to a tree informing us that the party had gone down into the lower cañon, five miles below, that they might camp in better pasturage.

The wind had scattered the ashes of our old campfire, and banished from it the last sentiment of home. We hurried on, climbing among the rocks, which reached down to the crest of the great lateral moraine, and then on in rapid stride along its smooth crest, riveting our eyes upon the valley below, where we knew the party must be camped.

At last, faintly curling above the sea of green tree-tops, a few faint clouds of smoke wafted upward into the air. We saw them with a burst of strong emotion, and ran down the steep flank of the moraine at the top of our speed. Our shouts were instantly answered by the three voices of our friends, who welcomed us to their camp-fire with tremendous hugs.

After we had outlined for them the experience of our days, and as we lay outstretched at our ease, warm in the blaze of the glorious camp-fire, Brewer said to me, "King, you have relieved me of a dreadful task. For the last three days I have been composing a letter to your family, but somehow I did not get beyond 'It becomes my painful duty to inform you.'"

JOHN MUIR

1838–1914

In "Explorations in the Great Tuolumne Cañon" (*Overland Monthly*, XI, August, 1873, 146), an article on what is now part of Yosemite National Park, John Muir wrote, "The life of a mountaineer is favorable to the development of soul-life, as well as limb-life, each receiving abundance of exercise and abundance of food." Almost all of John Muir's activities, during a varied and vigorous life, contributed to the formation of a man highly developed in limb and soul alike. Reared on a farm in Wisconsin, he began early a never-ended course of self-education. In 1863 he left the University of Wisconsin without a degree and, supporting himself by casual employment, made a series of walking tours through the middle-western states and Canada. The climax was his "thousand-mile walk" from Southen Indiana to the Gulf of Mexico. During this exploit and others he kept a scientific and philosophical journal and left some seventy notebooks of observations on his travels. In 1868 he reached California, spent six years in the Yosemite country, then traveled through Nevada, Utah, the Northwest, and Alaska. Returning to California he operated from 1881 to 1891 a successful fruit ranch in the Alhambra Valley. He sold the ranch, traveled more, and devoted himself increasingly to the writing of popular educational articles on Western forests and scenery and to crusading for conservation of natural resources. With Robert Underwood Johnson, one of the editors of *Century*, he initiated a campaign for preservation of the Yosemite country from exploitation; in 1890 Congress established Yosemite National Park. Muir vehemently denounced the predatory interests which wished to nullify the effect of Grover Cleveland's actions in setting aside forest preserves. In 1903 he and Theodore Roosevelt camped together; within a short time thereafter large areas of California were brought under the protection of the United States Forest Service.

Muir probably did not think of climbing as a sport separate from routine employment. Indeed, because of his passionate and adventurous temper, he never experienced the enslavement of routine. His whole life was given to learning by experience all aspects of physical nature which came within his view. The mountains were a part of nature; hence to be studied, climbed, and extolled in writing.

The following selection is reprinted from *The Mountains of California,*

A Near View of the High Sierra

EARLY ONE BRIGHT MORNING in the middle of Indian summer, while the glacier meadows were still crisp with frost crystals, I set out from the foot of Mount Lyell, on my way down to Yosemite Valley, to replenish my exhausted store of bread and tea. I had spent the past summer, as many preceding ones, exploring the glaciers that lie on the head waters of the San Joaquin, Tuolumne, Merced, and Owen's rivers; measuring and studying their movements, trends, crevasses, moraines, etc., and the part they had played during the period of their greater extension in the creation and development of the landscapes of this alpine wonderland. The time for this kind of work was nearly over for the year, and I began to look forward with delight to the approaching winter with its wondrous storms, when I would be warmly snow-bound in my Yosemite cabin with plenty of bread and books; but a tinge of regret came on when I considered that possibly I might not see this favorite region again until the next summer, excepting distant views from the heights about the Yosemite walls.

To artists, few portions of the High Sierra are, strictly speaking, picturesque. The whole massive uplift of the range is one great picture, not clearly divisible into smaller ones; differing much in this respect from the older, and what may be called, riper mountains of the Coast Range. All the landscapes of the Sierra, as we have seen, were born again, remodeled from base to summit by the developing icefloods of the last glacial winter. But all these new landscapes were not brought forth simultaneously; some of the highest, where the ice lingered longest, are tens of centuries younger than those of the warmer regions below them. In general, the younger the mountain-landscapes—younger, I mean, with reference to the time of their emergence from the ice of the glacial period—the less separable are they into artistic bits capable of being made into warm, sympathetic, lovable pictures with appreciable humanity in them.

Here, however, on the head waters of the Tuolumne, is a group of wild peaks on which the geologist may say that the sun has but just begun to shine, which is yet in a high degree picturesque, and in its main features so regular and evenly balanced as almost to appear conventional—one somber cluster of snow-laden peaks with gray pine-fringed granite bosses braided around its base, the whole surging free into the sky from the head of a magnificent valley, whose lofty walls are beveled away on both sides so as to embrace it all without admitting anything not strictly belonging to it. The foreground was now aflame with autumn colors, brown and purple and gold, ripe in the mellow sunshine; contrasting brightly with the deep, cobalt blue of the sky, and the black and gray, and pure, spiritual white of the rocks and glaciers. Down through the midst, the young Tuolumne was seen pouring from its crystal fountains, now resting in glassy pools as if changing back again into ice, now leaping in white cascades as if turning to snow; gliding right and left between granite bosses, then sweeping on through the smooth meadowy levels of the valley, swaying pensively from side to side with calm, stately gestures past dipping willows and sedges, and around groves of arrowy pine; and throughout its whole eventful course, whether flowing fast or slow, singing loud or low, ever filling the landscape with spiritual animation, and manifesting the grandeur of its sources in every movement and tone.

Pursuing my lonely way down the valley, I turned again and again to gaze on the glorious picture, throwing up my arms to inclose it as in a frame. After long ages of growth in the darkness beneath the glaciers, through sunshine and storms, it seemed now to be ready and waiting for the elected artist, like yellow wheat for the reaper; and I could not help wishing that I might carry colors and brushes with me on my travels and learn to paint. In the mean time I had to be content with photographs on my mind and sketches in my note-books. At length, after I had rounded a precipitous headland that puts out from the west wall of the valley, every peak vanished from sight, and I pushed rapidly along the frozen meadows, over the divide between the waters of the Merced and Tuolumne, and down through the forests that clothe the slopes of Cloud's Rest, arriving in Yosemite in due time—which with me, is *any* time. And, strange to say, among the first people I met here were two artists who, with letters of introduction, were awaiting my return. They inquired whether in the course of my explorations in the adjacent mountains I had ever come upon a landscape suitable for a large painting; whereupon I began a description of the one that had so lately excited my admiration. Then, as I went on further and further into details, their faces began to glow, and I offered to guide them to it, while they declared that they would gladly follow, far or near, whithersoever I could spare the time to lead them.

Since storms might come breaking down through the fine weather at any time, burying the colors in snow, and cutting off the artists' retreat, I advised getting ready at once.

I led them out of the valley by the Vernal and Nevada Falls, thence over the main dividing ridge to the Big Tuolumne Meadows, by the old Mono trail, and thence along the upper Tuolumne River to its head. This was my companions' first excursion into the High Sierra, and as I was almost always alone in my mountaineering, the way that the fresh beauty was reflected in their faces made for me a novel and interesting study. They naturally were affected most of all by the colors—the intense azure of the sky, the purplish grays of the granite, the red and browns of dry meadows, and the translucent purple and crimson of huckleberry bogs; the flaming yellow of aspen groves, the silvery flashing of the streams, and the bright green and blue of the glacier lakes. But the general expression of the scenery—rocky and savage—seemed sadly disappointing; and as they threaded the forest from ridge to ridge, eagerly scanning the landscapes as they were unfolded, they said: "All this is huge and sublime, but we see nothing as yet at all available for effective pictures. Art is long, and art is limited, you know; and here are foregrounds, middle-grounds, backgrounds, all alike; bare rock-waves, woods, groves, diminutive flecks of meadow, and strips of glittering water." "Never mind," I replied, "only bide a wee, and I will show you something you will like."

At length, toward the end of the second day, the Sierra Crown began to come into view, and when we had fairly rounded the projecting headland before mentioned, the whole picture stood revealed in the flush of the alpenglow. Their enthusiasm was excited beyond bounds, and the more impulsive of the two, a young Scotchman, dashed ahead, shouting and gesticulating and tossing his arms in the air like a madman. Here, at last, was a typical alpine landscape.

After feasting awhile on the view, I proceeded to make camp in a sheltered grove a little way back from the meadow, where pine-boughs could be obtained for beds, and where there was plenty of dry wood for fires, while the artists ran here and there, along the river-bends and up the sides of the canon, choosing foregrounds for sketches. After dark, when our tea was made and a rousing fire had been built, we began to make our plans. They decided to remain several days, at the least, while I concluded to make an excursion in the mean time to the untouched summit of [Mount] Ritter.

It was now about the middle of October, the springtime of snow-flowers. The first winter-clouds had already bloomed, and the peaks were strewn with fresh crystals, without, however, affecting the climbing to any dangerous extent. And as the weather was still profoundly calm, and the distance to the foot of the mountain only a little more than a day, I felt that I was running no great risk of being storm-bound.

Mount Ritter is king of the mountains of the middle portion of the High Sierra, as Shasta of the north and Whitney of the south sections. Moreover, as far as I know, it had never been climbed. I had explored the adjacent wilderness summer after summer, but my studies thus far had never drawn me to the top of it. Its height above sea-level is about 13,300 feet, and it is fenced round by steeply inclined glaciers, and canons of tremendous depth and ruggedness, which render it almost inaccessible. But difficulties of this kind only exhilarate the mountaineer.

Next morning, the artists went heartily to their work and I to mine. Former experiences had given good reason to know that passionate storms, invisible as yet, might be brooding in the calm sungold; therefore, before bidding farewell, I warned the artists not to be alarmed should I fail to appear before a week or ten days, and advised them, in case a snow-storm should set in, to keep up big fires and shelter themselves as best they could, and on no account to become frightened and attempt to seek their way back to Yosemite alone through the drifts.

My general plan was simply this: to scale the cañon wall, cross over to the eastern flank of the range, and then make my way south-ward to the northern spurs of Mount Ritter in compliance with the intervening topography; for to push on directly southward from camp through the innumerable peaks and pinnacles that adorn this portion of the axis of the range, however interesting, would take too much time, besides being extremely difficult and dangerous at this time of year.

All my first day was pure pleasure; simply mountaineering in-dulgence, crossing the dry pathways of the ancient glaciers, tracing happy streams, and learning the habits of the birds and marmots in the groves and rocks. Before I had gone a mile from camp, I came to the foot of a white cascade that beats its way down a rugged gorge in the cañon wall, from a height of about nine hundred feet, and pours its throbbing waters into the Tuolumne. I was acquainted with its fountains, which, fortunately, lay in my course. What a fine traveling companion it proved to be, what songs it sang, and how passionately it told the mountain's own joy! Gladly I climbed along its dashing border, absorbing its divine music, and bathing from time to time in waftings of irised spray. Climbing higher, higher, new beauty came streaming on the sight: painted meadows, late-blooming gardens, peaks of rare architecture, lakes here and there, shining like silver, and glimpses of the forested middle region and the yellow lowlands far in the west. Beyond the range I saw the so-called Mono Desert, lying dreamily silent in thick purple light—a desert of heavy sun-glare beheld from a desert of ice-burnished granite. Here the waters divide, shouting in glorious enthusiasm and falling eastward to vanish in the volcanic sands and dry sky of the Great Basin, or westward to the Great Valley of California, and thence through the Bay of San Francisco and the Golden Gate to the sea.

Passing a little way down over the summit until I had reached an elevation of about 10,000 feet, I pushed on southward toward a group of savage peaks that stand guard about Ritter on the north and west, groping my way, and dealing instinctively with every obstacle as it presented itself. Here a huge gorge would be found cutting across my path, along the dizzy edge of which I scrambled until some less precipitous point was discovered where I might safely venture to the bottom and then, selecting some feasible portion of the opposite wall, reascend with the same slow caution. Massive, flat-topped spurs alternate with the gorges, plunging abruptly from the shoulders of the snowy peaks, and planting their feet in the warm desert. These were everywhere marked and adorned with characteristic sculptures of the ancient glaciers that swept over this entire region like one vast ice-wind, and the polished surfaces produced by the ponderous flood are still so perfectly preserved that in many places the sunlight reflected from them is about as trying to the eyes as sheets of snow.

God's glacial-mills grind slowly, but they have been kept in motion long enough in California to grind sufficient soil for a glorious abundance of life, though most of the grist has been carried to the lowlands, leaving these high regions comparatively lean and bare; while the post-glacial agents of erosion have not yet furnished sufficient available food over the general surface for more than a few tufts of the hardiest plants, chiefly carices and eriogonae. And it is interesting to learn in this connection that the sparseness and repressed character of the vegetation at this height is caused more by want of soil than by harshness of climate; for, here and there, in sheltered hollows (countersunk beneath the general surface) into which a few rods of well-ground moraine chips have been dumped, we find groves of spruce and pine thirty to forty feet high, trimmed around the edges with willow and huckleberry bushes, and oftentimes still further by an outer ring of tall grasses, bright with lupines, larkspurs, and showy columbines, suggesting a climate by no means repressingly severe. All the streams, too, and the pools at this elevation are furnished with little gardens wherever soil can be made to lie, which, though making scarce any show at a distance, constitute charming surprises to the appreciative observer. In these bits of leafiness a few birds find grateful homes. Having no acquaintance with man, they fear no ill, and flock curiously about the stranger, almost allowing themselves to be taken in the hand. In so wild and so beautiful a region was spent my first day, every sight and sound inspiring, leading one far out of himself, yet feeding and building up his individuality.

Now came the solemn, silent evening. Long, blue, spiky shadows crept out across the snow-fields, while a rosy glow, at first scarce discernible, gradually deepened and suffused every mountain-top, flushing the glaciers and the harsh crags above them. This was the alpenglow, to me one of the most impressive of all the terrestrial manifestations of God. At the touch of this divine light, the mountains seemed to kindle to a rapt, religious consciousness, and stood hushed and waiting like devout worshippers. Just before the alpenglow began to fade, two crimson clouds came streaming across the summit like wings of flame, rendering the sublime scene yet more impressive; then came darkness and the stars.

Icy Ritter was still miles away, but I could proceed no farther that night. I found a good campground on the rim of a glacier basin about 11,000 feet above the sea. A small lake nestles in the bottom of it, from which I got water for my tea, and a stormbeaten thicket near by furnished abundance of resiny fire-wood. Somber peaks, hacked and shattered, circled half-way around the horizon, wearing a savage aspect in the gloaming, and a waterfall chanted solemnly across the lake on its way down from the foot of a glacier. The fall and the lake and the glacier were almost equally bare; while the scraggy pines anchored in the rock-fissures were so dwarfed and shorn by storm-winds that you might walk over their tops. In tone and aspect the scene was one of the most desolate I ever beheld. But the darkest scriptures of the mountains are illumined with bright passages of love that never fail to make themselves felt when one is alone.

I made my bed in a nook of the pine-thicket, where the branches were pressed and crinkled overhead like a roof, and bent down around the sides. These are the best bedchambers the high mountains afford—snug as squirrel-nests, well ventilated, full of spicy odors, and with plenty of wind-played needles to sing one asleep. I little expected company, but, creeping in through a low side-door, I found five or six birds nestling among the tassels. The night-wind began to blow soon after dark; at first only a gentle breathing, but increasing toward midnight to a rough gale that fell upon my leafy roof in ragged surges like a cascade, bearing wild sounds from the crags overhead. The waterfall sang in chorus, filling the old ice-fountain with its solemn roar, and seeming to increase in power as the night advanced—fit voice for such a landscape. I had to creep out many times to the fire during the night, for it was biting cold and I had no blankets. Gladly I welcomed the morning star.

The dawn in the dry, wavering air of the desert was glorious. Everything encouraged my undertaking and betokened success. There was no cloud in the sky, no storm-tone in the wind. Breakfast of bread and tea was soon made. I fastened a hard, durable crust to my belt by way of provision, in case I should be compelled to pass a night on the mountain-top; then, securing the remainder of my little stock against wolves and wood-rats, I set forth free and hopeful.

How glorious a greeting the sun gives the mountains! To behold this alone is worth the pains of any excursion a thousand times over. The highest peaks burned like islands in a sea of liquid shade. Then the lower peaks and spires caught the glow, and long lances of light, streaming through many a notch and pass, fell thick on the frozen meadows. The majestic form of Ritter was full in sight, and I pushed rapidly on over rounded rock-bosses and pavements, my iron-shod shoes making a clanking sound, suddenly hushed now and then in rugs of bryanthus, and sedgy lake-margins soft as moss. Here, too, in this so-called "land of desolation," I met cassiope, growing in fringes among the battered rocks. Her blossoms had faded long ago, but they were still clinging with happy memories to the evergreen sprays, and still so beautiful as to thrill every fiber of one's being. Winter and summer, you may hear her voice, the low, sweet melody of her purple bells. No evangel among all the mountain plants speaks Nature's love more plainly than cassiope. Where she dwells, the redemption of the coldest solitude is complete. The very rocks and glaciers seem to feel her presence, and become imbued with her own fountain sweetness. All things were warming and wakening. Frozen rills began to flow, the marmots came out of their nests in boulder-piles and climbed sunny rocks to bask, and the dun-headed sparrows were flitting about seeking their breakfasts. The lakes seen from every ridge-top were brilliantly

rippled and spangled, shimmering like the thickets of the low Dwarf
Pines. The rocks, too, seemed responsive to the vital heat—rock-
crystals and snow-crystals thrilling alike. I strode on exhilarated,
as if never more to feel fatigue, limbs moving of themselves, every
sense unfolding like the thawing flowers, to take part in the new
day harmony.

All along my course thus far, excepting when down in the canons,
the landscapes were mostly open to me, and expansive, at least on
one side. On the left were the purple plains of Mono, reposing
dreamily and warm; on the right, the near peaks springing keenly
into the thin sky with more and more impressive sublimity. But
these larger views were at length lost. Rugged spurs, and moraines,
and huge, projecting buttresses began to shut me in. Every feature
became more rigidly alpine, without, however, producing any
chilling effect; for going to the mountains is like going home. We
always find that the strangest objects in these mountain wilds are
in some degree familiar, and we look upon them with a vague sense
of having seen them before.

On the southern shore of a frozen lake, I encountered an extensive
field of hard, granular snow, up which I scampered in fine tone, intending to follow it to its head, and cross the rocky spur against
which it leans, hoping thus to come direct upon the base of the main
Ritter peak. The surface was pitted with oval hollows, made by
stones and drifted pine-needles that had melted themselves into the
mass by the radiation of absorbed sun-heat. These afforded good
footholds, but the surface curved more and more steeply at the
head, and the pits became shallower and less abundant, until I found
myself in danger of being shed off like avalanching snow. I persisted, however, creeping on all fours, and shuffling up the smoothest
places on my back, as I had often done on burnished granite, until,
after slipping several times, I was compelled to retrace my course
to the bottom, and make my way around the west end of the lake,
and thence up to the summit of the divide between the head waters
of Rush Creek and the northernmost tributaries of the San Joaquin.

Arriving on the summit of this dividing crest, one of the most
exciting pieces of pure wilderness was disclosed that I ever discovered
in all my mountaineering. There, immediately in front, loomed the

majestic mass of Mount Ritter, with a glacier swooping down its face nearly to my feet, then curving westward and pouring its frozen flood into a dark blue lake, whose shores were bound with precipices of crystalline snow; while a deep chasm drawn between the divide and the glacier separated the massive picture from everything else. I could see only the one sublime mountain, the one glacier, the one lake; the whole veiled with one blue shadow—rock, ice, and water close together without a single leaf or sign of life. After gazing spellbound, I began instinctively to scrutinize every notch and gorge and weathered buttress of the mountain, with reference to making the ascent. The entire front above the glacier appeared as one tremendous precipice, slightly receding at the top, and bristling with spires and pinnacles set above one another in formidable array. Massive lichen-stained battlements stood forward here and there, hacked at the top with angular notches, and separated by frosty gullies and recesses that have been veiled in shadow ever since their creation; while to right and left, as far as I could see, were huge, crumbling buttresses, offering no hope to the climber. The head of the glacier sends up a few finger-like branches through narrow *couloirs;* but these seemed too steep and short to be available, especially as I had no ax with which to cut steps, and the numerous narrow-throated gullies down which stones and snow are avalanched seemed hopelessly steep, besides being interrupted by vertical cliffs; while the whole front was rendered still more terribly forbidding by the chill shadow and the gloomy blackness of the rocks.

Descending the divide in a hesitating mood, I picked my way across the yawning chasm at the foot, and climbed out upon the glacier. There were no meadows now to cheer with their brave colors, nor could I hear the dun-headed sparrows, whose cheery notes so often relieve the silence of our highest mountains. The only sounds were the gurgling of small rills down in the veins and crevasses of the glacier, and now and then the rattling report of falling stones, with the echoes they shot out into the crisp air.

I could not distinctly hope to reach the summit from this side, yet I moved on across the glacier as if driven by fate. Contending with myself, the season is too far spent, I said, and even should I be successful, I might be storm-bound on the mountain; and in the cloud-darkness, with the cliffs and crevasses covered with snow, how could I escape? No; I must wait till next summer. I would only approach the mountain now, and inspect it, creep about its flanks, learn what I could of its history, holding myself ready to flee on the approach of the first storm-cloud. But we little know until tried how much of the uncontrollable there is in us, urging across glaciers and torrents, and up dangerous heights, let the judgment forbid as it may.

I succeeded in gaining the foot of the cliff on the eastern extremity of the glacier, and there discovered the mouth of a narrow avalanche gully, through which I began to climb, intending to follow it as far as possible, and at least obtain some fine wild views for my pains. Its general course is oblique to the plane of the mountain-face, and the metamorphic slates of which the mountain is built are cut by cleavage planes in such a way that they weather off in angular blocks, giving rise to irregular steps that greatly facilitate climbing on the sheer places. I thus made my way into a wilderness of crumbling spires and battlements, built together in bewildering combinations, and glazed in many places with a thin coating of ice, which I had to hammer off with stones. The situation was becoming gradually more perilous; but, having passed several dangerous spots, I dared not think of descending; for, so steep was the entire ascent, one would inevitably fall to the glacier in case a single misstep were made. Knowing, therefore, the tried danger beneath, I became all the more anxious concerning the developments to be made above, and began to be conscious of a vague foreboding of what actually befell; not that I was given to fear, but rather because my instincts, usually so positive and true, seemed vitiated in some way, and were leading me astray. At length, after attaining an elevation of about 12,800 feet, I found myself at the foot of a sheer drop in the bed of the avalanche channel I was tracing, which seemed absolutely to bar further progress. It was only about forty-five or fifty feet high, and somewhat roughened by fissures and projections; but these seemed so slight and insecure, as footholds, that I tried hard to avoid the precipice altogether, by scaling the wall of the channel on either side. But, though less steep, the walls were smoother than the obstructing rock, and repeated efforts only showed that I must either go right ahead or turn back. The tried dangers beneath seemed even greater than that of the cliff in front; therefore, after scanning its face again and again, I began to scale it, picking my holds with intense caution. After gaining a point about halfway to the top, I was suddenly brought to a dead stop, with arms outspread, clinging close to the face of the rock, unable to move hand or foot either up or down. My doom appeared fixed. I *must* fall. There would be a moment of bewilderment, and then a lifeless rumble down the one general precipice to the glacier below.

When this final danger flashed upon me, I became nerve-shaken for the first time since setting foot on the mountains, and my mind seemed to fill with a stifling smoke. But this terrible eclipse lasted only a moment, when life blazed forth again with preternatural clearness. I seemed suddenly to become possessed of a new sense. The other self, bygone experiences, Instinct, or Guardian Angel— call it what you will—came forward and assumed control. Then my trembling muscles became firm again, every rift and flaw in the rock was seen as through a microscope, and my limbs moved with a posi- tiveness and precision with which I seemed to have nothing at all to do. Had I been borne aloft upon wings, my deliverance could not have been more complete.

Above this memorable spot, the face of the mountain is still more savagely hacked and torn. It is a maze of yawning chasms and gullies, in the angles of which rise beetling crags and piles of detached boulders that seem to have gotten ready to be launched below. But the strange influx of strength I had seemed inexhaustible. I found a way without effort, and soon stood upon the topmost crag in the blessed light.

How truly glorious the landscape circled around this noble sum- mit!—giant mountains, valleys innumerable, glaciers and meadows, rivers and lakes, with the wide blue sky bent tenderly over them all. But in my first hour of freedom from that terrible shadow, the sunlight in which I was laving seemed all in all.

Looking southward along the axis of the range, the eye is first caught by a row of exceedingly sharp and slender spires, which rise openly to a height of about a thousand feet, above a series of short, residual glaciers that lean back against their bases; their fantastic sculpture and the unrelieved sharpness with which they spring out of the ice rendering them peculiarly wild and striking. These are "The Minarets." Beyond them you behold a sublime wilderness of mountains, their snowy summits towering together in crowded abundance, peak beyond peak, swelling higher, higher as they sweep on southward, until the culminating point of the range is reached on Mount Whitney, near the head of the Kern River, at an elevation of nearly 14,700 feet above the level of the sea.[1]

Westward, the general flank of the range is seen flowing sublimely away from the sharp summits, in smooth undulations; a sea of huge gray granite waves dotted with lakes and meadows, and fluted with stupendous canons that grow steadily deeper as they recede in the distance. Below this gray region lies the dark forest zone, broken here and there by upswelling ridges and domes; and yet beyond lies a yellow, hazy belt, marking the broad plain of the San Joaquin, bounded on its farther side by the blue mountains of the coast.

Turning now to the northward, there in the immediate foreground is the glorious Sierra Crown, with Cathedral Peak, a temple of marvelous architecture, a few degrees to the left of it; the gray, massive form of Mammoth Mountain to the right; while Mounts Ord, Gibbs, Dana, Conness, Tower Peak, Castle Peak, Silver Mountain, and a host of noble companions, as yet nameless, make a sublime show along the axis of the range.

Eastward, the whole region seems a land of desolation covered with beautiful light. The torrid volcanic basin of Mono, with its one bare lake fourteen miles long; Owen's Valley and the broad lava table-land at its head, dotted with craters, and the massive Inyo Range, rivaling even the Sierra in height; these are spread, map-like, beneath you, with countless ranges beyond, passing and overlapping one another and fading on the glowing horizon.

At a distance of less than 3,000 feet below the summit of Mount Ritter you may find tributaries of the San Joaquin and Owen's rivers, bursting forth from the ice and snow of the glaciers that load its flanks; while a little to the north of here are found the highest affluents of the Tuolumne and Merced. Thus, the fountains of four

[1] See p. 253.

of the principal rivers of California are within a radius of four or five miles.

Lakes are seen gleaming in all sorts of places—round, or oval, or square, like very mirrors; others narrow and sinuous, drawn close around the peaks like silver zones, the highest reflecting only rocks, snow, and the sky. But neither these nor the glaciers, nor the bits of brown meadow and moorland that occur here and there, are large enough to make any marked impression upon the mighty wilderness of mountains. The eye, rejoicing in its freedom, roves about the vast expanse, yet returns again and again to the mountain peaks. Perhaps some one of the multitude excites special attention, some gigantic castle with turret and battlement, or some Gothic cathedral more abundantly spired than Milan's. But, generally, when looking for the first time from an all-embracing standpoint like this, the inexperienced observer is oppressed by the incomprehensible grandeur, variety, and abundance of the mountains rising shoulder to shoulder beyond the reach of vision; and it is only after they have been studied one by one, long and lovingly, that their far-reaching harmonies become manifest. Then, penetrate the wilderness where you may, the main telling features, to which all the surrounding topography is subordinate, are quickly perceived, and the most complicated clusters of peaks stand revealed harmoniously correlated and fashioned like works of art—eloquent monuments of the ancient ice-rivers that brought them into relief from the general mass of the range. The canons, too, some of them a mile deep, mazing wildly through the mighty host of mountains, however lawless and ungovernable at first sight they appear, are at length recognized as the necessary effects of causes which followed each other in harmonious sequence—Nature's poems carved on tables of stone—the simplest and most emphatic of her glacial compositions.

Could we have been here to observe during the glacial period, we should have overlooked a wrinkled ocean of ice as continuous as that now covering the landscapes of Greenland; filling every valley and canon with only the tops of the mountain peaks rising darkly above the rock-encumbered ice-waves like islets in a stormy sea—those islets the only hints of the glorious landscapes now smiling in the sun. Standing here in the deep, brooding silence all the wilderness seems motionless, as if the work of creation were done. But in the midst of this outer steadfastness we know there is incessant motion and change. Ever and anon, avalanches are falling from yonder peaks. These cliff-bound glaciers, seemingly wedged and immovable, are flowing like water and grinding the rocks beneath them. The lakes are lapping their granite shores and wearing them away, and every one of these rills and young rivers is fretting the air into music, and carrying the mountains to the plains. Here are the roots of all the life of the valleys, and here more simply than elsewhere is the eternal flux of nature manifested. Ice changing to water, lakes to meadows, and mountains to plains. And while we thus contemplate Nature's methods of landscape creation, and, reading the records she has carved on the rocks, reconstruct, however imperfectly, the landscapes of the past, we also learn that as these we now behold have succeeded those of the pre-glacial age, so they in turn are withering and vanishing to be succeeded by others yet unborn.

But in the midst of these fine lessons and landscapes, I had to remember that the sun was wheeling far to the west, while a new way down the mountain had to be discovered to some point on the timber line where I could have a fire; for I had not even burdened myself with a coat. I first scanned the western spurs, hoping some way might appear through which I might reach the northern glacier, and cross its snout; or pass around the lake into which it flows, and thus strike my morning track. This route was soon sufficiently unfolded to show that, if practicable at all, it would require so much time that reaching camp that night would be out of the question. I therefore scrambled back eastward, descending the southern slopes obliquely at the same time. Here the crags seemed less formidable, and the head of a glacier that flows northeast came in sight, which I determined to follow as far as possible, hoping thus to make my way to the foot of the peak on the east side, and thence across the intervening canons and ridges to camp.

The inclination of the glacier is quite moderate at the head, and, as the sun had softened the névé, I made safe and rapid progress, running and sliding, and keeping up a sharp outlook for crevasses. About half a mile from the head, there is an ice-cascade, where the glacier pours over a sharp declivity and is shattered into massive blocks separated by deep, blue fissures. To thread my way through the slippery mazes of this crevassed portion seemed impossible, and I endeavored to avoid it by climbing off to the shoulder of the mountain. But the slopes rapidly steepened and at length fell away in sheer precipices, compelling a return to the ice. Fortunately, the day had been warm enough to loosen the ice-crystals so as to admit of hollows being dug in the rotten portions of the blocks, thus enabling me to pick my way with far less difficulty than I had anticipated. Continuing down over the snout, and along the left lateral moraine, was only a confident saunter, showing that the ascent of the mountain by way of this glacier is easy, provided one is armed with an ax to cut steps here and there.

The lower end of the glacier was beautifully waved and barred by the outcropping edges of the bedded ice-layers which represent the annual snowfalls, and to some extent the irregularities of structure caused by the weathering of the walls of crevasses, and by separate snowfalls which have been followed by rain, hail, thawing and freezing, etc. Small rills were gliding and swirling over the melting surface with a smooth, oily appearance, in channels of pure ice—their quick, compliant movements contrasting most impressively with the rigid, invisible flow of the glacier itself, on whose back they all were riding.

Night drew near before I reached the eastern base of the mountain, and my camp lay many a rugged mile to the north; but ultimate success was assured. It was now only a matter of endurance and ordinary mountain-craft. The sunset was, if possible, yet more beautiful than that of the day before. The Mono landscape seemed to be fairly saturated with warm, purple light. The peaks marshaled along the summit were in shadow, but through every notch and pass streamed vivid sunfire, soothing and irradiating their rough, black angles, while companies of small, luminous clouds hovered above them like very angels of light.

Darkness came on, but I found my way by the trends of the canons and the peaks projected against the sky. All excitement died with the light, and then I was weary. But the joyful sound of the waterfall across the lake was heard at last, and soon the stars were seen reflected in the lake itself. Taking my bearings from these, I discovered the little pine thicket in which my nest was, and then I had a rest such as only a tired mountaineer may enjoy. After lying loose and lost for a while, I made a sunrise fire, went down to the lake, dashed water on my head, and dipped a cupful for tea. The revival brought about by bread and tea was as complete as the exhaustion from excessive enjoyment and toil. Then I crept beneath the pine-tassels to bed. The wind was frosty and the fire burned low, but my sleep was none the less sound, and the evening constellations had swept far to the west before I awoke.

After thawing and resting in the morning sunshine, I sauntered home—that is, back to the Tuolumne camp—bearing away toward a cluster of peaks that hold the fountain snows of one of the north tributaries of Rush Creek. Here I discovered a group of beautiful glacier lakes, nestled together in a grand amphitheater. Toward evening, I crossed the divide separating the Mono waters from those of the Tuolumne, and entered the glacier basin that now holds the fountain snows of the stream that forms the upper Tuolumne cascades. This stream I traced down through its many dells and gorges, meadows and bogs, reaching the brink of the main Tuolumne at dusk.

A loud whoop for the artists was answered again and again. Their camp-fire came in sight, and half an hour afterward I was with them. They seemed unreasonably glad to see me. I had been absent only three days; nevertheless, though the weather was fine, they had already been weighing chances as to whether I would ever return, and trying to decide whether they should wait longer or begin to seek their way back to the lowlands. Now their curious troubles were over. They packed their precious sketches, and next morning we set out homeward bound, and in two days entered the Yosemite Valley from the north by way of Indian Canon.

JOHN CHARLES FRÉMONT

1813–1890

It is not necessary here to attempt a judgment of Frémont's character or of the effect of his total career on American expansion. That part of his life of which one triumph is recounted in the following selection preceded the long history of ambiguous glory, dissipated favors of fortune, and unfulfilled promise which puzzled his friends and enemies alike and led Josiah Royce to conclude that he "possessed all the qualities of genius except ability."

The circumstances attending Frémont's expedition of 1842, to South Pass and the Wind River Mountains of Wyoming, were altogether fortunate. He had recently married Jessie Benton and enjoyed the powerful support of her father, Thomas Hart Benton, Senator from Missouri. Though not yet thirty, Frémont was well trained in exploration and topographical engineering and was ready for his first command. The territory which he would traverse was not completely unknown; it was his task to map and to collect information. His party was well equipped. Its personnel was competent, particularly the guides and *voyageurs*, most famous of whom was Kit Carson.

Setting out in June, 1842, the expedition followed first the Kansas River valley, then the Platte River, which provided a route to the Rockies. Early in August it reached South Pass, the major objective, where Frémont was astonished to find the rise gradual and the actual "culminating point" almost undistinguishable. The ascent of Frémont's Peak, made a week later, marked the westernmost reach of the expedition, which returned to Missouri in October.

Frémont hurried to Washington and set to organizing the findings of the expedition. The composition of the report soon became a task of collaboration between Frémont and his talented, well-educated wife. The result was a narrative both detailed and vivid, even occasionally flamboyant, which quickly became popular reading and helped elevate Frémont to the position of popular hero.

Like most of the American pioneers in climbing, Frémont was neither a professed nor a technically skillful mountaineer. The peak which he ascended is not now considered formidable. But he felt its challenge keenly, and acting "beyond the strict order of our instructions" he climbed it, to his own exaltation.

The following selection is reprinted from John Charles Frémont, *Report of the Exploring Expedition to the Rocky Mountains in the Year 1842 . . . ,*

Washington, Blair and Reeves, Printers, 1845. The title of the selection has been supplied.

Frémont's Peak

AUGUST 10.—The air at sunrise is clear and pure, and the morning extremely cold, but beautiful. A lofty snow peak of the mountain is glittering in the first rays of the sun, which has not yet reached us. The long mountain wall to the east, rising two thousand feet abruptly from the plain, behind which we see the peaks, is still dark, and cuts clear against the glowing sky. A fog, just risen from the river, lies along the base of the mountain. A little before sunrise, the thermometer was at 35°, and at sunrise 33°. Water froze last night, and fires are very comfortable. The scenery becomes hourly more interesting and grand, and the view here is truly magnificent; but, indeed, it needs something to repay the long prairie journey of a thousand miles. The sun has just shot above the wall, and makes a magical change. The whole valley is glowing and bright, and all the mountain peaks are gleaming like silver. Though these snow mountains are not the Alps, they have their own character of grandeur and magnificence, and will doubtless find pens and pencils to do them justice. In the scene before us, we feel how much wood improves a view. The pines on the mountain seemed to give it much additional beauty. I was agreeably disappointed in the character of the streams on this side of the ridge. Instead of the creeks, which description had led me to expect, I find bold, broad streams, with three or four feet of water, and a rapid current. The fork on which we are encamped is upwards of a hundred feet wide, timbered with groves or thickets of the low willow. We were now approaching the loftiest part of the Wind river chain; and I left the valley a few miles from our encampment, intending to penetrate the mountains as far as possible with the whole party. We were soon involved in very broken ground, among long ridges covered with fragments of granite. Winding our way up a long ravine, we came unexpectedly in view of a most beautiful lake, set like a gem in the mountains. The sheet of water lay transversely across the direction we had been pursuing; and, descending the steep, rocky ridge, where it was necessary to lead our horses, we followed its banks to the southern extremity. Here a view of the utmost magnificence and grandeur burst upon our eyes. With nothing between us and their feet to lessen the effect of the whole height, a grand bed of snow-capped mountains rose before us, pile upon pile, glowing in the bright light of an August day. Immediately below them lay the lake, between two ridges, covered with dark pines, which swept down from the main chain to the spot where we stood. Here, where the lake glittered in the open sunlight, its banks of yellow sand in the light foliage of aspen groves contrasted well with the gloomy pines. "Never before," said Mr. Preuss, "in this country or in Europe, have I seen such magnificent, grand rocks." I was so much pleased with the beauty of the place, that I determined to make the main camp here, where our animals would find good pasturage, and explore the mountains with a small party of men. Proceeding a little further, we came suddenly upon the outlet of the lake, where it found its way through a narrow passage between low hills. Dark pines, which overhung the stream, and masses of rock, where the water foamed along, gave it much romantic beauty. Where we crossed, which was immediately at the outlet, it is two hundred and fifty feet wide, and so deep, that with difficulty we were able to ford it. Its bed was an accumulation of rocks, boulders, and broad slabs, and large angular fragments, among which the animals fell repeatedly.

The current was very swift, and the water cold, and of a crystal purity. In crossing this stream, I met with a great misfortune in having my barometer broken. It was the only one. A great part of the interest of the journey for me was in the exploration of these mountains, of which so much had been said that was doubtful and contradictory; and now their snowy peaks rose majestically before me, and the only means of giving them authentically to science, the object of my anxious solicitude by night and day, was destroyed. We had brought this barometer in safety a thousand miles, and broke it almost among the snow of the mountains. The loss was felt by the whole camp—all had seen my anxiety, and aided me in preserving it. The height of these mountains, considered by the hunters and traders the highest in the whole range, had been a theme of constant discussion among them; and all had looked forward with pleasure to the moment when the instrument, which they believed to be true as the sun, should stand upon the summits, and decide their disputes. Their grief was only inferior to my own.

This lake is about three miles long, and of very irregular width, and apparently great depth, and is the head water of the third New Fork, a tributary to Green river, the Colorado of the west. On the map and in the narrative, I have called it Mountain Lake. I encamped on the north side, about three hundred and fifty yards from the outlet. This was the most western point at which I obtained astronomical observations, by which this place, called Bernier's encampment, is made in 110° 08′ 03″ west longitude from Greenwich, and latitude 43° 49′ 49″. The mountain peaks, as laid down, were fixed by bearings from this and other astronomical points. We had no other compass than the small ones used in sketching the country; but from an azimuth, in which one of them was used, the variation of the compass is 18° east. The correction made in our field work by the astronomical observations indicates that this is a very correct observation.

As soon as the camp was formed, I set about endeavoring to repair my barometer . . . a standard cistern barometer, of Troughton's construction. The glass cistern had been broken about midway; but as the instrument had been kept in a proper position, no air had found its way into the tube, the end of which had always remained covered. I had with me a number of vials of tolerably thick glass, some of which were of the same diameter as the cistern, and I spent the day in slowly working on these, endeavoring to cut them of the requisite length; but, as my instrument was a very rough file, I invariably broke them. A groove was cut in one of the trees, where the barometer was placed during the night, to be out of the way of any possible danger, and in the morning I commenced again. Among the powder horns in the camp, I found one which was very transparent, so that its contents could be almost as plainly seen as through glass. This I boiled and stretched on a piece of wood to the requisite diameter, and scraped it very thin, in order to increase to the utmost its transparency. I then secured it firmly in its place on the instrument, with strong glue made from a buffalo, and filled it with mercury, properly heated. A piece of skin, which had covered one of the vials, furnished a good pocket, which was well secured with strong thread and glue, and then the brass cover was screwed to its place. The instrument was left some time to dry; and when I reversed it, a few hours after, I had the satisfaction to find it in perfect order; its indications being about the same as on the other side of the lake before it had been broken. Our success in this little incident diffused pleasure throughout the camp; and we immediately set about our preparations for ascending the mountains.

As will be seen on reference to a map, on this short mountain chain are the head waters of four great rivers of the continent; namely, the Colorado, Columbia, Missouri, and Platte Rivers.[1] It had been my design, after having ascended the mountains, to continue our route on the western side of the range, and crossing through a pass at the northwestern end of the chain, about thirty miles from our present camp, return along the eastern slope, across the heads of the Yellowstone river, and join on the line to our station of August 7, immediately at the foot of the ridge. In this way, I should be enabled to include the whole chain, and its numerous waters, in my survey; but various considerations induced me, very reluctantly, to abandon this plan.

I was desirous to keep strictly within the scope of my instructions; and it would have required ten or fifteen additional days for the accomplishment of this object; our animals had become very much worn out with the length of the journey; game was very scarce; and . . . the spirits of the men had been much exhausted by the hardships and privations to which they had been subjected. Our provisions had well-nigh all disappeared. Bread had been long out of the question; and of all our stock, we had remaining two or three

[1] See also p. 300. The headwaters of these rivers are actually located as follows: the Colorado in north central Colorado, the Columbia in the Kootenay district of British Columbia, the Missouri in southwestern Montana, the North Platte in the North Park district of Colorado and the South Platte in the South Park district of the same state.

pounds of coffee, and a small quantity of maccaroni, which had been husbanded with great care for the mountain expedition we were about to undertake. Our daily meal consisted of dry buffalo meat, cooked in tallow; and, as we had not dried this with Indian skill, part of it was spoiled; and what remained of good, was as hard as wood, having much the taste and appearance of so many pieces of bark. Even of this, our stock was rapidly diminishing in a camp which was capable of consuming two buffaloes in every twenty-four hours. These animals had entirely disappeared; and it was not probable that we should fall in with them again until we returned to the Sweet Water.

Our arrangements for the ascent were rapidly completed. We were in a hostile country, which rendered the greatest vigilance and circumspection necessary. The pass at the north end of the mountain was generally infested by Blackfeet; and immediately opposite was one of their forts, on the edge of a little thicket, two or three hundred feet from our encampment. We were posted in a grove of beech, on the margin of the lake, and a few hundred feet long, with a narrow *prairillon* on the inner side, bordered by the rocky ridge. In the upper end of this grove we cleared a circular space about forty feet in diameter, and, with the felled timber and interwoven branches, surrounded it with a breastwork five feet in height. A gap was left for a gate on the inner side, by which the animals were to be driven in and secured, while the men slept around the little work. It was half hidden by the foliage; and, garrisoned by twelve resolute men, would have set at defiance any band of savages which might chance to discover them in the interval of our absence. Fifteen of the best mules, with fourteen men, were selected for the mountain party. Our provisions consisted of dried meat for two days, with our little stock of coffee, and some maccaroni. In addition to the barometer and a thermometer, I took with me a sextant and spy glass, and we had of course our compasses. In charge of the camp I left Bernier, one of my most trustworthy men, who possessed the most determined courage.

AUGUST 12.—Early in the morning we left the camp, fifteen in number, well armed, of course, and mounted on our best mules. A pack animal carried our provisions, with a coffee pot and kettle, and three or four tin cups. Every man had a blanket strapped over his saddle, to serve for his bed, and the instruments were carried by turns on their backs. We entered directly on rough and rocky ground; and, just after crossing the ridge, had the good fortune to shoot an antelope. We heard the roar, and had a glimpse of a water-fall as we rode along; and, crossing on our way two fine streams, tributary to the Colorado, in about two hours' ride we reached the top of the first row or range of the mountains. Here, again, a view of the most romantic beauty met our eyes. It seemed as if, from the vast expanse of uninteresting prairie we had passed over, Nature had collected all her beauties together in one chosen place. We were overlooking a deep valley, which was entirely occupied by three lakes, and from the brink the surrounding ridges rose precipitously five hundred and a thousand feet, covered with the dark green of the balsam pine, relieved on the border of the lake with the light foliage of the aspen. They all communicated with each other; and the green of the waters, common to mountain lakes of great depth, showed that it would be impossible to cross them. The surprise manifested by our guides when these impassable obstacles suddenly barred our progress proved that they were among the hidden treasures of the place, unknown even to the wandering trappers of the region. Descending the hill, we proceeded to make our way along the margin to the southern extremity. A narrow strip of angular fragments of rock sometimes afforded a rough pathway for our mules, but generally we rode along the shelving side, occasionally scrambling up, at a considerable risk of tumbling back into the lake.

The slope was frequently 60°; the pines grew densely together, and the ground was covered with the branches and trunks of trees. The air was fragrant with the odor of the pines; and I realised this delightful morning the pleasure of breathing that mountain air which makes a constant theme of the hunter's praise, and which now made us feel as if we had all been drinking some exhilarating gas. The depths of this unexplored forest were a place to delight the heart of a botanist. There was a rich undergrowth of plants, and numerous gay-colored flowers in brilliant bloom. We reached the outlet at length, where some freshly barked willows that lay in the water showed that beaver had been recently at work. There were some small brown squirrels jumping about in the pines, and a couple of large mallard ducks swimming about in the stream.

The hills on this southern end were low, and the lake looked like a mimic sea, as the waves broke on the sandy beach in the force of a strong breeze. There was a pretty open spot, with fine grass for our mules; and we made our noon halt on the beach, under the shade of some large hemlocks. We resumed our journey after a halt of about an hour, making our way up the ridge on the western side of the lake. In search of smoother ground, we rode a little inland; and, passing through groves of aspen, soon found ourselves again among the pines. Emerging from these, we struck the summit of the ridge above the upper end of the lake.

We had reached a very elevated point; and in the valley below, and among the hills, were a number of lakes at different levels; some two or three hundred feet above others, with which they communicated by foaming torrents. Even to our great height, the roar of the cataracts came up, and we could see them leaping down in lines of snowy foam. From this scene of busy waters, we turned abruptly into the stillness of a forest, where we rode among the open bolls of the pines, over a lawn of verdant grass, having strikingly the air of cultivated grounds. This led us, after a time, among masses of rock which had no vegetable earth but in hollows and crevices, though still the pine forest continued. Toward evening, we reached a defile, or rather a hole in the mountains, entirely shut in by dark pine-covered rocks.

A small stream, with a scarcely perceptible current, flowed through a level bottom of perhaps eighty yards width, where the grass was saturated with water. Into this the mules were turned, and were neither hobbled nor picketed during the night, as the fine pasturage took away all temptation to stray; and we made our bivouac in the pines. The surrounding masses were all of granite. While supper was being prepared, I set out on an excursion in the neighborhood, accompanied by one of my men. We wandered about among the crags and ravines until dark, richly repaid for our walk by a fine collection of plants, many of them in full bloom. Ascending a peak to find the place of our camp, we saw that the little defile in which we lay communicated with the long green valley of some stream, which, here locked up in the mountains, far away to the south, found its way in a dense forest to the plains.

Looking along its upward course, it seemed to conduct, by a smooth gradual slope, directly toward the peak, which, from long consultation as we approached the mountain, we had decided to be the highest of the range. Pleased with the discovery of so fine a road for the next day, we hastened down to the camp, where we arrived just in time for supper. Our table service was rather scant; and we held the meat in our hands, and clean rocks made good plates, on which we spread our maccaroni. Among all the strange places on which we had occasion to encamp during our long journey, none have left so vivid an impression on my mind as the camp of this evening. The disorder of the masses which surrounded us; the little hole through which we saw the stars overhead; the dark pines where we slept; and the rocks lit up with the glow of our fires, made a night picture of very wild beauty.

AUGUST 13.—The morning was bright and pleasant, just cool enough to make exercise agreeable, and we soon entered the defile I had seen the preceding day. It was smoothly carpeted with a soft grass, and scattered over with groups of flowers, of which yellow was the predominant color. Sometimes we were forced, by an occasional difficult pass, to pick our way on a narrow ledge along the side of the defile, and the mules were frequently on their knees; but these obstructions were rare, and we journeyed on in the sweet morning air, delighted at our good fortune in having found such a beautiful entrance to the mountains. This road continued for about three miles, when we suddenly reached its termination in one of the grand views which, at every turn, meet the traveller in this magnificent region. Here the defile up which we had travelled opened out into a small lawn, where, in a little lake, the stream had its source.

There were some fine *asters* in bloom, but all the flowering plants appeared to seek the shelter of the rocks, and to be of lower growth than below, as if they loved the warmth of the soil, and kept out of the way of the winds. Immediately at our feet a precipitous descent led to a confusion of defiles, and before us rose the mountains. . . . It is not by the splendor of far-off views, which have lent such a glory to the Alps, that these impress the mind; but by a gigantic disorder of enormous masses, and a savage sublimity of naked rock, in wonderful contrast with innumerable green spots of a rich floral beauty, shut up in their stern recesses. Their wildness seems well suited to the character of the people who inhabit the country.

I determined to leave our animals here, and make the rest of our way on foot. The peak appeared so near, that there was no doubt of our returning before night; and a few men were left in charge of the mules, with our provisions and blankets. We took with us nothing but our arms and instruments, and, as the day had become warm, the greater part left our coats. Having made an early dinner, we started again. We were soon involved in the most ragged precipices, nearing the central chain very slowly, and rising but little. The first ridge hid a succession of others; and when, with great fatigue and difficulty, we had climbed up five hundred feet, it was but to make an equal descent on the other side; all these intervening places were filled with small deep lakes, which met the eye in every direction, descending from one level to another, sometimes under bridges formed by huge fragments of granite, beneath which was heard the roar of the water. These constantly obstructed our path, forcing us to make long *détours;* frequently obliged to retrace our steps, and frequently falling among the rocks. Maxwell was precipitated toward the face of a precipice, and saved himself from going over by throwing himself flat on the ground. We clambered on, always expecting, with every ridge that we crossed, to reach the foot of the peaks, and always disappointed, until about 4 o'clock, when, pretty well worn out, we reached the shore of a little lake, in which there was a rocky island. . . . We remained here a short time to rest, and continued on around the lake, which had in some places a beach of white sand, and in others was bound with rocks, over which the way was difficult and dangerous, as the water from innumerable springs made them very slippery.

By the time we had reached the further side of the lake, we found ourselves all exceedingly fatigued, and, much to the satisfaction of the whole party, we encamped. The spot we had chosen was a broad flat rock, in some measure protected from the winds by the surrounding crags, and the trunks of fallen pines afforded us bright fires. Near by was a foaming torrent, which tumbled into the little

lake about one hundred and fifty feet below us, and which, by way
of distinction, we have called Island lake. We had reached the upper
limit of the piney region; as, above this point, no tree was to be seen,
and patches of snow lay everywhere around us on the cold side of
the rocks. The flora of the region we had traversed since leaving
our mules was extremely rich, and, among the characteristic plants,
the scarlet flowers of the *dodecatheon dentatum* everywhere met the
eye in great abundance. A small green ravine, on the edge of which
we were encamped, was filled with a profusion of alpine plants in
brilliant bloom. From barometrical observations, made during our
three days' sojourn at this place, its elevation above the Gulf of
Mexico is 10,000 feet. During the day, we had seen no sign of animal
life; but among the rocks here, we heard what was supposed to be the
bleat of a young goat, which we searched for with hungry activity,
and found to proceed from a small animal of a gray color, with short
ears and no tail—probably the Siberian squirrel. We saw a considerable number of them, and, with the exception of a small bird
like a sparrow, it is the only inhabitant of this elevated part of the
mountains. On our return, we saw, below this lake, large flocks of
the mountain goat. We had nothing to eat to-night. Lajeunesse, with
several others, took their guns and sallied out in search of a goat; but
returned unsuccessful. At sunset, the barometer stood at 20.522;
the attached thermometer 50°. Here we had the misfortune to break
our thermometer, having now only that attached to the barometer.
I was taken ill shortly after we had encamped, and continued so until
late in the night, with violent headache and vomiting. This was
probably caused by the excessive fatigue I had undergone, and want
of food, and perhaps, also, in some measure, by the rarity of the air.
The night was cold, as a violent gale from the north had sprung up
at sunset, which entirely blew away the heat of the fires. The cold,
and our granite beds, had not been favorable to sleep, and we were
glad to see the face of the sun in the morning. Not being delayed
by any preparation for breakfast, we set out immediately.

On every side as we advanced was heard the roar of waters, and
of a torrent, which we followed up a short distance, until it expanded
into a lake about one mile in length. On the northern side of the
lake was a bank of ice, or rather of snow, covered with a crust of ice.

[Kit] Carson had been our guide into the mountains, and, agreeably to his advice, we left this little valley, and took to the ridges again; which we found extremely broken, and where we were again involved among precipices. Here were ice fields; among which we were all dispersed, seeking each the best path to ascend the peak. Mr. Preuss attempted to walk along the upper edge of one of these fields, which sloped away at an angle of about twenty degrees; but his feet slipped from under him, and he went plunging down the plane. A few hundred feet below, at the bottom, were some fragments of sharp rock, on which he landed; and though he turned a couple of somersets, fortunately received no injury beyond a few bruises. Two of the men, Clement Lambert and Descoteaux, had been taken ill, and lay down on the rocks a short distance below; and at this point I was attacked with headache and giddiness, accompanied by vomiting, as on the day before. Finding myself unable to proceed, I sent the barometer over to Mr. Preuss, who was in a gap two or three hundred yards distant, desiring him to reach the peak, if possible, and take an observation there. He found himself unable to proceed further in that direction, and took an observation, where the barometer stood at 19.401; attached thermometer 50°, in the gap. Carson, who had gone over to him, succeeded in reaching one of the snowy summits of the main ridge, whence he saw the peak towards which all our efforts had been directed, towering eight or ten hundred feet into the air above him. In the mean time, finding myself grow rather worse than better, and doubtful how far my strength would carry me, I sent Basil Lajeunesse, with four men, back to the place where the mules had been left.

We were now better acquainted with the topography of the country, and I directed him to bring back with him, if it were in any way possible, four or five mules, with provisions and blankets. With me were Maxwell and Ayer; and after we had remained nearly an hour on the rock, it became so unpleasantly cold, though the day was bright, that we set out on our return to the camp, at which we all arrived safely, straggling in one after the other. I continued ill during the afternoon, but became better towards sundown, when my recovery was completed by the appearance of Basil and four men, all mounted. The men who had gone with him had been too much fatigued to return, and were relieved by those in charge of the horses; but in his powers of endurance Basil resembled more a mountain goat than a man. They brought blankets and provisions, and we enjoyed well our dried meat and a cup of good coffee. We rolled ourselves up in our blankets, and with our feet turned to a blazing fire, slept soundly until morning.

AUGUST 15.—It had been supposed that we had finished with the mountains; and the evening before, it had been arranged that Carson should set out at daylight, and return to breakfast at the Camp of the Mules, taking with him all but four or five men, who were to stay with me and bring back the mules and instruments. Accordingly, at the break of day they set out. With Mr. Preuss and myself remained Basil Lajeunesse, Clement Lambert, Janisse, and Descoteaux. When we had secured strength for the day by a hearty breakfast, we covered what remained, which was enough for one meal, with rocks, in order that it might be safe from any marauding bird; and, saddling our mules, turned our faces towards the peaks. This time we determined to proceed quietly and cautiously, deliberately resolved to accomplish our object if it were within the compass of human means. We were of opinion that a long defile which lay to the left of yesterday's route would lead us to the foot of the main peak. Our mules had been refreshed by the fine grass in the little ravine at the Island camp, and we intended to ride up the defile as far as possible, in order to husband our strength for the main ascent. Though this was a fine passage, still it was a defile of the most rugged mountains known, and we had many a rough and steep slippery place to cross before reaching the end. In this place the sun rarely shone; snow lay along the border of the small stream which flowed through it, and occasional icy passages made the footing of the mules very insecure, and the rocks and ground were moist with the trickling waters in this spring of mighty rivers. We soon had the satisfaction to find ourselves riding along the huge wall which forms the central summits of the chain. There at last it rose by our sides, a nearly perpendicular wall of granite, terminating 2,000 to 3,000 feet above our heads in a serrated line of broken, jagged cones. We rode on until we came almost immediately below the main peak, which I denominated the Snow peak, as it exhibited more snow to the eye than any of the neighboring summits. Here were three small lakes of a green color, each of perhaps a thousand yards in diameter, and apparently very deep. These lay in a kind of chasm; and, according to the barometer, we had attained but a few hundred feet above the Island lake. The barometer here stood at 20.450, attached thermometer 70°.

We managed to get our mules up to a little bench about a hundred feet above the lakes, where there was a patch of good grass, and turned them loose to graze. During our rough ride to this place, they had exhibited a wonderful surefootedness. Parts of the defile were filled with angular, sharp fragments of rock, three or four and eight or ten feet cube; and among these they had worked their way, leaping from one narrow point to another, rarely making a false step, and giving us no occasion to dismount. Having divested ourselves of every unnecessary encumbrance, we commenced the ascent. This time, like experienced travellers, we did not press ourselves, but climbed leisurely, sitting down so soon as we found breath beginning to fail. At intervals we reached places where a number of springs gushed from the rocks, and about 1,800 feet above the lakes came to the snow line. From this point our progress was uninterrupted climbing. Hitherto I had worn a pair of thick moccasins, with soles of *parflèche;* but here I put on a light thin pair, which I had brought for the purpose, as now the use of our toes became necessary to a further advance. I availed myself of a sort of comb of the mountain, which stood against the wall like a buttress, and which the wind and the solar radiation, joined to the steepness of the smooth rock, had kept almost entirely free from snow. Up this I made my way rapidly. Our cautious method of advancing in the outset had spared my strength; and, with the exception of a slight disposition to headache, I felt no remains of yesterday's illness. In a few minutes we reached a point where the buttress was overhanging, and there was no other way of surmounting the difficulty than by passing around one side of it, which was the face of a vertical precipice of several hundred feet.

Putting hands and feet in the crevices between the blocks, I succeeded in getting over it, and, when I reached the top, found my companions in a small valley below. Descending to them, we continued climbing, and in a short time reached the crest. I sprang upon the summit, and another step would have precipitated me into an immense snow field five hundred feet below. To the edge of this field was a sheer icy precipice; and then, with a gradual fall, the field sloped off for about a mile, until it struck the foot of another lower ridge. I stood on a narrow crest, about three feet in width, with an inclination of about 20° N. 51° E. As soon as I had gratified the first feelings of curiosity, I descended, and each man ascended in his turn; for I would only allow one at a time to mount the unstable and precarious slab, which it seemed a breath would hurl into the abyss below. We mounted the barometer in the snow of the summit, and, fixing a ramrod in a crevice, unfurled the national flag to wave in the breeze where never flag waved before. During our morning's ascent, we had met no sign of animal life, except the small sparrow-like bird already mentioned. A stillness the most profound and a terrible solitude forced themselves constantly on the mind as the great features of the place. Here, on the summit, where the stillness was absolute, unbroken by any sound, and the solitude complete, we thought ourselves beyond the region of animated life; but while we were sitting on the rock, a solitary bee (*bromus, the humble bee*) came winging his flight from the eastern valley, and lit on the knee of one of the men.

It was a strange place, the icy rock and the highest peak of the Rocky mountains,[2] for a lover of warm sunshine and flowers; and we pleased ourselves with the idea that he was the first of his species to cross the mountain barrier—a solitary pioneer to foretell the advance of civilization. I believe that a moment's thought would have made us let him continue his way unharmed; but we carried out the law of this country, where all animated nature seems at war; and, seizing him immediately, put him in at least a fit place— in the leaves of a large book, among the flowers we had collected on our way. The barometer stood at 18.293, the attached thermometer at 44°; giving for the elevation of this summit 13,570 feet above the Gulf of Mexico, which may be called the highest flight of the bee. It is certainly the highest known flight of that insect. . . .

[2] The elevation of Frémont's Peak is 13,730 feet. Gannett's Peak, five miles to the north, is somewhat higher. In Colorado there are fifty-four peaks higher than 14,000 feet.

The day was sunny and bright, but a slight shining mist hung over the lower plains, which interfered with our view of the surrounding country. On one side we overlooked innumerable lakes and streams, the spring of the Colorado of the Gulf of California; and on the other was the Wind river valley, where were the heads of the Yellowstone branch of the Missouri; far to the north, we just could discover the snowy heads of the *Trois Tetons*, where were the sources of the Missouri and Columbia rivers; and at the southern extremity of the ridge, the peaks were plainly visible, among which were some of the springs of the Nebraska or Platte river. Around us, the whole scene had one striking main feature, which was that of terrible convulsion. Parallel to its length, the ridge was split into chasms and fissures; between which rose the thin lofty walls, terminated with slender minarets and columns. . . . According to the barometer, the little crest of the wall on which we stood was three thousand five hundred and seventy feet above that place, and two thousand seven hundred and eighty above the little lakes at the bottom, immediately at our feet. Our camp at the Two Hills (an astronomical station) bore south 3° east, which, with a bearing afterward obtained from a fixed position, enabled us to locate the peak. The bearing of the *Trois Tetons* was north 50° west, and the direction of the central ridge of the Wind river mountains south 39° east. The summit rock was gneiss, succeeded by sienitic gneiss. Sienite and feldspar succeeded in our descent to the snow line, where we found a feldspathic granite. I had remarked that the noise produced by the explosion of our pistols had the usual degree of loudness, but was not in the least prolonged, expiring almost instantaneously. Having now made what observations our means afforded, we proceeded to descend. We had accomplished an object of laudable ambition, and beyond the strict order of our instructions. We had climbed the loftiest peak of the Rocky mountains, and looked down upon the snow a thousand feet below, and, standing where never human foot had stood before, felt the exultation of first explorers. It was about 2 o'clock when we left the summit; and when we reached the bottom, the sun had already sunk behind the wall, and the day was drawing to a close. . . .

THE FITZGERALD EXPEDITION

1897

DURING A LIFE generally devoted to the occupations of a gentleman of means and to inconspicuous military service, Edward FitzGerald twice emerged into public prominence. He financed, organized, led, and reported on two mountaineering expeditions—to the New Zealand Alps in 1895 and to the Andes of Chile and Argentina in 1897.

His aspiration to be the first to climb Aorangi or Mount Cook in New Zealand was frustrated by alert South Island mountaineers. In the Andes he had better fortune, for the highest peak in the Western Hemisphere, Aconcagua (22,835 feet), was ascended for the first time by a member of his party, although not by FitzGerald himself. Much valuable information was collected concerning climate, topography, geology, and botany.

Previously the Andes had received considerable exploratory attention and some literary celebration. Baron Alexander von Humboldt in 1803 had unsuccessfully attempted Chimborazo, which was finally climbed by Edward Whymper in 1880. Both men published widely read records, respectively *Ansichten der Natur* (1808) and *Travels amongst the Great Andes of the Equator* (1892). In 1835 Charles Darwin crossed from Valparaiso to Mendoza over the Portillo Pass and returned by way of the Cumbre Pass. This and other Andean travels are related in *The Voyage of the Beagle* (1845). Later Dr. Paul Güssfeldt, a German geographer, reached the summit of Maipo alone, and in 1883 very nearly conquered Aconcagua, again virtually alone.

Besides FitzGerald, the prominent members of the 1897 expedition were Stuart Vines, surveyor and chief assistant; the naturalist Philip Gosse, son of Sir Edmund Gosse; A. E. Lightbody, a photographer; and Mattias Zurbriggen, a guide experienced in the Alps and the Himalaya. The party was expensively equipped and provisioned; the Chilean government gave generous support. The first ascent of Aconcagua was accomplished by Zurbriggen alone, FitzGerald having become ill en route. Almost simultaneously climbers from the German *Turnverein* of Santiago, eager to forestall the Englishmen and to complete the triumph almost achieved by Güssfeldt, failed to exceed 21,000 feet. A second ascent of Aconcagua, for purposes of surveying, was made by Zurbriggen and Vines, who also, after three failures, climbed Tupungato (21,490 feet). The account of the latter success, which is presented here, was written by Vines.

The following selection is reprinted from E. A. FitzGerald [*et al.*], *The Highest Andes* . . . , London, Methuen & Co., Ltd., 1899, by permission of Methuen & Co., Ltd.

Tupungato Ascended

OUR FOURTH ATTEMPT on Tupungato was made on 12th April [1897]. The night had been bitterly cold, and none of us slept very well. The small Mummery tent,[1] in which I was packed with Zurbriggen and Joseph Pollinger, was now pitched in a safer position, where there was no danger of rocks from above falling on us, yet the ground underneath was still so near the ice that it chilled us to the bone as we lay down. During the night the thermometer sank to 24 below freezing, but fortunately there was no wind—a great improvement on the zero with a hurricane of four nights before. Remembering our experience of frost-bite on Aconcagua in the early morning, we decided to risk nothing by climbing before sunrise. We had two alternatives before us, either to crawl out of our tent and start in the night-hours before sunrise, thereby spoiling a good night's rest, greatly needed, if not an absolute necessity for a day's work at such high altitudes, with the additional hardship of the cold of the early morning, and the risk this involved; or, on the other hand, to start, after taking something hot, at daybreak, and reach a height of 21,000 feet at one or two o'clock, the warmest time of the day, fortified by a good night's rest for that terrible last thousand feet, with the disadvantage, and risk, no doubt, of a descent after sunset, exhausted by the ascent. It was the cold and the wind we dreaded, especially so late in the season, and the cold was far less after sunset than before sunrise; therefore I think we pursued the least risky course, and the one most likely to lead to success, in starting late. It was half-past six before we crawled out of the tent, and there was no guessing what sort of weather was in store for us, as the

[1] See p. 152.

western horizon, which always gave the best indication, was completely shut out from our view by the great wall of the spur under which we were encamped. . . . At seven we made a start. It was still intensely cold, and Zurbriggen and I set out in our ponchos—garments far better adapted for riding than for climbing. In selecting the route, our chief thought was how best to avoid the broken and crumbling surface over which we had already toiled.

This was now our third ascent of the spur. The first had been made by the broken slope on the northern side, which we had found very fatiguing, and the second by the rocks nearer to the actual dome of Tupungato, where the rope had been needed. Zurbriggen led us now by fairly firm ground half-way between the two previous lines of ascent, I came next, and Joseph Pollinger brought up the rear. This order was maintained during the greater part of the day. I knew well enough that this would be our last attack on the mountain —it was now or never. The season was already so far advanced that the rigours of winter were beginning to be felt, and the danger of frost-bite at these high altitudes had determined us, whatever might be the result of the fourth attempt, to leave Tupungato, and return to Vacas as soon as possible.

Nothing of any importance happened until we reached the top of the spur. Although we had chosen a fresh line of ascent, the soil underfoot was still much the same as before. There was the same dreary slipping on the rotten ground, the same relief when the ground was firm. As we ascended, the necessity for halts became gradually more frequent. It was at half-past nine, when we were some fifteen hundred feet above our camping-ground, that we reached the summit of the ridge, about 18,500 feet above sea-level. After ascending another five hundred feet, thinking it better to take a long rest before going farther, we sat down under a boulder and tried to make a meal. . . .

When we reached the summit of the ridge, we were able to take stock of the weather. It was a perfect day without a cloud in the sky. Even the hilltops on the Pacific coast were entirely free from haze. Nothing could have been more encouraging, for it was from that quarter that all the storms that had hitherto assailed us had come. The wind was as before in the north-west, and still very cold; but it was as nothing compared with the hurricane from which we had suffered on the second attempt. These signs cheered us greatly, and we started again at ten o'clock, feeling more hopeful of success than ever before. Zurbriggen now proposed a new route. Instead of turning towards the south and ascending the gentle slope of the ridge to the dome—as we had done on the two former occasions—he pointed out that we should gain relief from the wearisome monotony of tramping up the débris-covered surface of the spur, by making our way to the ridge of rocks on the western or Santiago side, leading towards the summit, where we should have a firm foothold. As we marched on in that direction, I noticed that many of the stones in my path were covered with a white deposit. In some cases it nearly enveloped them in a thin layer, but elsewhere, it lay over them in lumps, and I even found pieces of this superficial deposit lying loose. It seemed to be a white mineral of some kind. Many of the stones on the surface of the spur were hollowed out in the centre, and cup-shaped. Professor Bonney, after hearing my description of them, has suggested that they were probably volcanic bombs thrown from the prehistoric crater of Tupungato, twisted into this peculiar cup-like shape by their flight through the air and sudden cooling. Unfortunately, I could not find a specimen small enough to carry away with me. . . .

At half-past ten we reached the rocks on the western side of the spur, and began to climb them. . . . The scramble up the rocks was most interesting; these did not present any great difficulty, and we were able to dispense with the rope. In spite of the fact that the ascent was more abrupt than by the former route, and required more exertion, none of us seemed at this time to be much affected, though we were considerably more than 19,000 feet above the sea. I always look back upon this part of our ascent of Tupungato with particular pleasure. It was before our troubles began, and while we still happily imagined that we should reach the summit about two o'clock. The rocks we were climbing formed a narrow ridge, like a balustrade between the spur and the dome of the mountain, rising about eighty to a hundred feet from it on one hand, and descending in sheer precipice some four thousand feet to the valley on the Chilian side. As we ascended, the view was superb, for we looked right over the edge of the rocks into the valley beneath us, and far away to the west. At our feet, as it seemed, was spread out a wide plain intersected by rivers; beyond was a great range of hills running north and south, which could hardly have been less than 12,000 feet high. This immense line of cliffs, about twenty miles from Tupungato, diminished in height towards the north, but not very far from this extremity was a sight that instantly arrested our attention. It was nothing less than a volcano in full eruption. The discovery took my breath away, for I had always understood that there was no volcano in these regions, dormant or active, except the lofty San José, due south of Tupungato. We halted and looked at the volcano long and intently. The clearness of the atmosphere at this time in the morning—it wanted yet half an hour to noon—enabled us to observe its features with accuracy. The whole structure of the crater was peculiar. There was no cone, and the opening was not in the summit alone, but an enormous V-shaped aperture, tapering towards the bottom, seemed to run from the top of the cliffs to their very base. In the distance it had the appearance of an immense grey talus turned upside down. From the top of this opening there poured forth vast volumes of dark brown steam, which floated away through the air for a dozen miles towards the south-east. . . . Zurbriggen was as much struck as myself by the remarkable sight, and declared that, though in the jet of steam it bore resemblance to the numerous volcanoes he had seen in New Zealand, its shape and structure were entirely different. I proposed photographing it at once, and taking bearings, which would probably have involved a delay of more than half an hour. Zurbriggen pointed out, however, that we could not be more than two hours from the summit, and that as the day was clear and settled, we should get an even finer view of it from above. We all felt in good condition, and not in need of a rest; so we pressed on, and I contented myself for the moment with making a very rough sketch of the volcano in my notebook. Two hours had been spent in coming up these rocks, and at 12.30 we left them for a wide couloir filled with snow, which we imagined would shortly bring us to the summit. We cut a few steps in the snow here and there, and sometimes returned to the rocks, where they afforded an easier route. In this way we ascended for an hour, with frequent halts, and were now at an altitude of 20,000 feet.

We had felt comparatively little fatigue while moving over easier ground and at a lower level. But at so great a height every increase in altitude tells at once, and exhaustion now began to come quickly upon us. My legs moved heavily, and I made the sides of the couloir re-echo with my heavy breathing. No one spoke a word. Zurbriggen strode on in front of me, and frequently looked impatiently ahead, evidently expecting to see the summit of the mountain loom up every moment over the brow of the slope we were ascending. We had had ample opportunity of examining the nature of this slope from different points of view to the north, and we were convinced that the highest point lay on this, the northern side of Tupungato. Two days before, when I had taken photographs of the mountain from a point nine miles away in the valley, whence we could see the several peaks rising above the circle of the dome, Zurbriggen and I had fully discussed the matter and concluded that, unless the mountain stretched away a great distance to the south, the northern peak must be the highest. The moment was at hand when we should know whether our conjecture was right. As we marched on, I looked time after time at Zurbriggen, and admired the steady pace he was keeping, wondering whether the heaviness of my legs would increase, and how long I should be able to follow him. Joseph Pollinger was behind me, and I fancied he must be watching my efforts with feelings in which admiration had a very small part. He was an excellent guide, and, although I did not know how he had done on Aconcagua, as he was never with me on that mountain, he had always lasted out well on Tupungato. Suddenly, about half-past one, we all three paused by common consent. One of us had stopped abruptly, and the others stopped too, without a word being uttered. Zurbriggen and I turned round and looked at Pollinger, who was lying flat on his face and groaning. He was suffering violent pains in the abdomen, and he declared between his gasps that he felt very sick and ill, and could not go another step higher. We were anxious to take him with us, so I tried to persuade him that he would be all right after a short rest, and proposed that Zurbriggen and I should divide his pack between us, so as to make things as easy as possible for him. But, as he still insisted that he felt far too ill to go on, and seemed to have a great desire to descend as soon as possible, we gave up trying to persuade him. "Let me get down lower! For God's sake let me descend! I shall die if I stop here!" was his only answer to us. Yes, he was right. The only remedy for his illness was to descend with all speed to a lower altitude; he would be well if only he could get down a thousand feet or more. I then discussed the matter with Zurbriggen, and determined on the route he should take. If he descended by the couloir, and walked along the whole length of the spur until he came above the camp, and then turned to the right and descended to it, he would be able to gain shelter without risk. He would find Lanti there, and could wait for us, or go down still farther, as he felt inclined. We had always found descending such an efficient remedy for the sickness, that we felt confident he would be all right again at 18,000 feet. I divided his pack with Zurbriggen, and we decided to leave everything that we should not absolutely need, including a rucksack, behind. Pollinger said he felt much better already, and would wait a little longer and rest where he was. As we could watch him for a considerable distance, we continued the ascent, telling him to signal if he did not feel all right. Then we went on our way, and looking back from time to time, we were thankful to find that he made encouraging signals, and that his pace increased until we lost sight of him on the distant declivity of the mountain.

I was now feeling in no very good condition myself, as the difficulty of getting enough oxygen out of the rarefied atmosphere became every moment greater. My breathing grew at every step more and more laboured. The sides of the couloir which we were still traversing seemed like prison walls to my lungs. It would be a stretch of imagination to suppose for one moment that there was less air in such a place. But I had suffered far more from breathlessness in the couloirs and enclosed places on Aconcagua, and instinctively felt that my breathlessness at this moment was due to the same causes. The air seemed "flat" to my thirsty lungs, where it was not stirred and freshened by the wind. It is interesting to note what Mr. Freshfield says on this subject of the "stagnation of the air" in his account of the ascent of Mount Elbruz. "The gale which nearly defeated us saved us from mountain-sickness. I have compared the accounts of many mountain travellers, and it seems apparent that those who suffer from 'rarity of the air' do so mostly on still days and in hollows rather than on ridges. From De Saussure's time 'the stagnation of the air' has been complained of. I have myself been on Mont Blanc three times, and once only, the day being perfectly still, did I suffer in any degree from nausea and headache. On that occasion I had been living at 6000 feet for some weeks previously, and was in exceptionally good training. Two years later I came straight out from England and felt no inconvenience of any kind, although the pace from the Cabane Vallot to the top was hurried." [2] This is particularly interesting as it coincides exactly with my own experiences when we reached the great arête of Aconcagua, and still more with those I am about to relate.

Gradually we began to emerge from the couloir, and, looking ahead, beheld at last what we had so long desired to see. It was the northernmost peak on the dome of Tupungato, which, according to our calculations, ought to be the very highest point on the mountain, and this peak was the one we had selected when looking from below. It was nearly two o'clock, the hour at which we had calculated to reach the summit. We felt confident that in half an hour we should be rewarded for three weeks of struggle and hardship, and should have hours before us to look upon one of the finest views ever beheld by man, for the sky was absolutely cloudless. Slowly, and with short steps we tramped on, our eyes turned towards the summit, when suddenly, without a moment's warning, Zurbriggen sat down on the ground and exclaimed, "I am finished—I go no farther!" Fearing that the strain had been too much for his heart, I was greatly alarmed, but when I asked what was the matter he only pointed in the direction of the peak, and declared that he could go no farther.

I saw in a moment the cause of his collapse. Looming up beyond the nearest peak, which we had expected to be the highest, was another peak far to the south, and certainly higher by a good two hundred feet. "That point," said Zurbriggen, pointing a dismal finger at it, "is an hour away from where we are, and I cannot do it." In the

[2] Douglas W. Freshfield, *The Exploration of the Caucasus* (1902), II, 168–69.

greatest anxiety I asked him to tell me his symptoms. It appeared, however, that there was nothing more the matter than exhaustion, and the effects of sudden disappointment. "It's my legs!" he answered. "They will not carry me a step farther." I tried to persuade him that the southern peak was scarcely half an hour away from us, though I knew only too well that he had probably underestimated the distance, although in the clear air it looked only a few steps. He was not to be persuaded, however, that the distance was less than he knew it to be. I thought it possible, nevertheless, that after a rest and some stimulant he might be able to resume the ascent. Half a bottle of wine had been reserved for the summit, but I now gave it to him, and said, "Look here, Mattias, if you sit down behind this rock sheltered from the wind and take twenty minutes' rest, and promise me to drink the whole of this wine, I am convinced you will reach the summit. I will take your rucksack, the camera, and things, and go on a bit to see how the land lies." Leaving him behind me, I turned my steps with bitter feelings once more towards the summit. For nearly a month we had tried together to conquer this hoary-headed giant; we had made four separate attempts and had suffered severe privations and many disappointments; and now, when success lay almost within our grasp, I felt that I was likely to reach the summit alone, and I seemed to have no heart left in me for the task.

Zurbriggen's exhaustion was not hard to account for. He had led the way all day, and had tired himself out by doing so; for the labour of the leader of a party up these slopes is very much greater than that of any of his companions. At these altitudes every step must be made with the view of expending as little exertion as possible. Those who follow have not the trouble of selecting the footholds, and can mark where the man in front has slipped, and profit by his experience. Moreover, his foot by slipping makes in the loose ground a firm place for the next man to step in; so that the man behind gains as much as the leader loses. After I had gone thirty or forty yards, I hesitated, and then stopped. It was painful for me to go on without Zurbriggen, and I almost decided to wait for him. But on looking back I saw that he seemed to be doing better, and was now seated under the shelter of the rock, solacing himself with a pipe. After all, I reflected, I could do no good by waiting for him, and probably he would make a greater effort if I left him and pushed on. So I resumed my way alone and strode out as vigorously as I could.

I was now well free of the stifling couloir, and there was a cold wind blowing which seemed to refresh me, while with each step that brought me nearer to my goal, I gained new energy, and my excitement rose. Between the northern peak—the cause of our first disappointment—and the higher peak which I was now making for, there was a wide bed of black volcanic scoria, across which I moved at a pace which fairly astonished me. Amidst the general gray, pink and brown colour of the mountain surface, and the patches of white snow which lay here and there, this black volcanic bed stood out in marked and peculiar contrast, looking for all the world as if it had been brought there in cart-loads to fill up the depression. Having crossed it, I came to the base of a ridge leading to the peak. I even increased my speed—I knew my legs ached and that my breathing was laboured, but I did not heed the suffering and it did not prevent me from rushing on at what seemed at this height a mad pace. The steep slope of the ridge made no difference. I stopped for rest and breath as often as before, but between the halts the pace was maintained. It was shortly after three o'clock when I reached the summit of this peak.

Alas, another disappointment was in store. As I set my foot at last upon the highest point and looked eagerly around, a most unwelcome sight presented itself. Far away on the southern edge of the mountain-top, which until now I had never seen, another peak rose up, and seemed to challenge supremacy with that on which I stood. Between me and it was a wide depression. I brought my Abney level to bear upon it, and my fears were realised. I was not yet on the top of Tupungato: the new peak was considerably higher than the one I had surmounted. I felt that it would probably take me an hour to reach it, but I believed myself quite equal to the new task. I looked back. Zurbriggen was still sitting on the very spot where I had left him, and I had small expectation that he would ever reach the summit of the mountain. This was very disheartening, but there was nothing for it, and without halt or rest I set out for the third peak.

In front of me to the left lay a great field of snow, and to the right a rock arête. Either might be selected as the route, but I did not know the condition of the snow, and considered that the safer way lay by the rocks. With more haste than prudence I scrambled down them, elated by the view which every moment widened out before my gaze, for I was crossing the western side of the dome, and each step increased my first sight of the outlook to the south. I reached the end of the rock arête, and, without resting, hurried across the bed of the depression and began at once the ascent of the opposite slope. I had at least four hundred feet to climb, but I kept up the same pace until at last I gained the top.

It was 3.45, nearly two hours later than the time at which we had expected to be upon the summit. I had surmounted the third of those baffling peaks, but were my labours really at an end, or was fresh and fatal disappointment in store? It was almost with a sinking heart that I looked around. But one desperately anxious glance told me enough. No other and loftier peak rose before me. Everything was beneath my feet, and at last I stood on the highest point of Tupungato.

I was on the summit of Tupungato at last, and all my efforts and disappointments were more than repaid. I stood on a great mound, in shape like a pyramid with a blunted top some two yards wide, rising several hundred feet above the general surface of the dome. Its whole surface was entirely free from snow and covered with loose rocks and débris, though this débris, from the appearance of things, was a mere superficial deposit, close beneath which lay a solid rock foundation. I picked up the highest piece of rock, the veritable tip of the mountain, which lay loose on the ground and was an excellent example of the stones that lay around. As this, however, was far too large for me to carry down, I flung it to the earth, when it broke in half and disclosed a hollow inside, in which was a quantity of a substance like glue or gum, transparent, hard and brittle, probably fused matter and glass. The half I brought away with me proved, on examination, to be a very fine specimen of andesite, riddled with fulgurites, or tubes melted out by lightning. Having thus examined my foothold and secured the fallen monster's head, I threw down the rucksack, and without the loss of a moment set to work to commemorate the ascent by a stone man—a cairn that would be a sufficient memorial of the FitzGerald Expedition to future climbers of Tupungato. But though they were interesting and valuable from a geological point of view, the stones on the summit did not lend themselves well to the construction of a stone man. The larger and heavier ones were frozen to the ground, and most of them, resembling pumice in structure, were much too light and brittle for the substantial edifice I wished to erect, for was I not standing on the very spot where the storm-fiends of the Andes gathered daily for their wildest orgies? I had, therefore, to descend ten or twenty feet every now and then to bring up more durable material. It was hard work, but I went at it with an energy that surprised me, and, though panting for breath, I was not seriously distressed. I felt fit and well, and was satisfied I was doing an immense amount of work. After some considerable time spent at high altitudes, one becomes so accustomed to working slowly and deliberately that the fact that one is doing very little at the cost of much labour does not strike one very forcibly. It was only by comparison, therefore, that I felt I was working quickly, for the excitement and the glorious circumstances of the situation kept me going. Secondly, there was no longer any necessity for me to husband my strength. The highest point had been reached: I could now let myself go. The disproportion between the labour and its results only became evident to me afterwards when I calculated and summed up the outcome of my labours on the summit of Tupungato. The exertion of gathering and piling up the heaviest stones I could find kept me warm, which was very necessary, for there was a strong wind blowing, and the thermometer registered 19° of frost.

I had scarcely been working for more than ten minutes when I heard a shout, and looking up saw Zurbriggen on the northern peak I had just left. As I afterwards learnt, he had felt so much revived by the rest and the wine I made him drink, that not long after I had disappeared from view on the peak he pulled himself together and decided to follow me, thinking I had already reached the summit. He got there only to find himself again disappointed, but seeing me already on the last peak, and engaged in the work I have spoken of, he promptly followed. I waved my arms in answer to his shout, and went on with my task. As he began the descent towards me, I had hopes that it would ease and rest him for the ascent of the final few hundred feet. Not many minutes after I saw him he was descending the snow slope at a great pace. It was a shorter and quicker route than the rock arête that I had followed, and in a very short space of time he was within fifty feet of me. I ran down to meet him, and grasped his hands. Now that we stood on the summit together, I felt at last that Tupungato had really been ascended. As soon as he had breath enough to speak, he turned to me with a smile, and said, "Now I'm off to Mendoza to settle my book, and make those men pay for doubting the FitzGerald Expedition. . . ." He was quite his old self again. The wine, the rest, and the pipe had worked wonders, otherwise the fresh disappointment that awaited him on surmounting the second peak must have made him give up the attempt. He helped me to put the finishing touches to the cairn, which, when completed, was a solid and substantial erection, about four feet high, that might even bid defiance for many years to Tupungato's furious storms.

It was now half-past four, and no time was to be lost. I wrote on one side of my card, "FitzGerald Expedition"; and on the other:—

"Stuart Vines, with Mattias Zurbriggen, Swiss guide, made the ascent of this mountain on 12th April 1897, after three attempts, being stopped by storms."

Also the following words upon a leaf of my notebook:—

"Joseph Pollinger came with us from our bivouac, about 17,000 feet, below ridge on north side of mountain, but turned back sick about 1000 feet from the summit. Temp. 13 Fahr. Zurbriggen and I reached the summit at 3.45."

My card and the piece of paper I enclosed in a wine bottle which Zurbriggen placed at the base of the cairn and carefully covered over with stones.

In spite of all the bad weather we had suffered from throughout our work—and indeed the weather experienced during this summer was described by the Meteorological Office in Santiago as without a record—we had no cause to complain on the days of the two chief ascents. The circumstances were very similar. Both summits were reached about an hour and a half before sunset. But the 12th of April even surpassed the 13th of February, the day of my ascent of Aconcagua; for now in the whole expanse of sky around, over ocean and land, I could not discern a single cloud. Only in the direction of the Pacific a haze hung over the mountains, and to my great disappointment, I could gain no further view of the volcano seen earlier in the day. I accounted for this by supposing that the haze which hid it from sight was probably caused by the smoke of the volcano itself, the wind having shifted and dropped, so that the vapours now hung in a cloudy form around the mountain. This haze was not due, I thought, to the weather, for in all other directions the view was magnificently clear. In the brilliant air the spectacle that lay before us was one of extraordinary extent and grandeur. Range beyond range of mountains stretched away towards the great plain of Santiago, forty miles to the west. Far away, beyond the hills that almost seemed to lie at our feet, stretched the great waters of the Pacific, a tract of blue ocean sparkling to the horizon, and clearly visible, although the distance from Tupungato to the sea-coast is not less than 130 miles. The view from the top of Tupungato is in many ways even finer than that obtained from Aconcagua. The expanse of ocean visible towards the west is less vast, but there is ample compensation in the outlook over the great unending plains on the eastern side. The pampas of Argentina stretched almost without a break from our very feet to the South Atlantic Ocean. The position of Tupungato could be very clearly defined: it forms part of the great frontier barrier between Chile and Argentina, which is also the waterparting of all the rivers to the Pacific and Atlantic. I could see those glittering rivers winding like ribbons through the pampas, spreading fertility around them, and scattering plenty through the land—a sight which contrasted strikingly with the turbulent and unending array of rugged peaks and ridges that surrounded me on every side but this. Though Aconcagua lies in Argentina, yet the view from its summit towards the west over Chile is far more interesting than that to the east. From the summit of Tupungato the conditions are reversed—Aconcagua seems to belong to the Chilians, Tupungato to the Argentines; and in order to gain a really perfect idea of the Cordilleras of the Andes at this latitude, one ascent does not complete the picture without the other.

The Andes seem to rise up from Santiago in ever-ascending gradation, until at last they culminate in the immense mass of Tupungato; beyond, they fall abruptly away; mountains disappear; and a country almost fen-like in its monotonous flatness succeeds. Our nearest neighbour on the Argentine side was the pyramid of the Cerro de la Plata, not more than twenty miles to the north-east. It seems to rise from a mass of high mountains surrounding it on every side and merging imperceptibly into it, so that it possesses no well-marked or definite base of its own. Its height has been estimated at 19,200 feet. The chain on which I stood, the frontier boundary between these two great States, ran southward towards the Peuquenes or Portillo Pass, trampled each year by the iron-shod feet of many thousand head of cattle passing from the rich pastures of the pampas to supply the mining settlements on the coast of northern Chile, and on to the volcano of San José, reckoned at some 19,500 feet, and Maipo, the scene of Güssfeldt's triumphs in 1883. On the Chilian side scores of dark rocks rear their heads, a sinister array of precipitous impossibilities from which any climber would turn away in despair. And to the north the same great barrier ran: at my feet the great mountain-spur on which we had suffered so many hardships and disappointments from wind and weather; beyond, a snow arête leading up to the steep walls of ice and rock that support the virgin cone of Pollera, in shape not unlike the Weisshorn, so well known to Zermatt climbers; and, towering above the Pollera, the pyramid of Navarro. Then in one great curve sweeping westward to the lofty glacier perched high between the two peaks of Juncal, and thence northward again, the clear-cut features of this immense ridge ran to the Cumbre Pass. . . .

The subject of Aconcagua as seen from Tupungato deters my pen. In our many struggles up its flanks, we had often gazed with ever-increasing wonder on the mighty contours that rose above our heads. I remember the first occasion we beheld it we all stood gazing at it in silence until one of the porters broke the spell by ejaculating, "What's that?" That Aconcagua was a high mountain we well knew.

We had all suffered from its height. But when near at hand it was quite impossible to realise the vastness of its proportions. Not so from where I now stood on a pinnacle sixty miles away. I had long known it was over four thousand feet higher than any mountain within thirty miles of it, but it looked ten thousand feet higher, as it reared its immense head and shoulders from amongst its neighbours, like some huge rock towering out of the waves of the sea. It stood before me without rival. Even the great crags of Juncal did not challenge it, though they were almost thirty miles nearer. Facing us was the wall of that enormous precipice. Dark and sinister it looked, for this southern face of almost perpendicular ice and rock seldom sees the sun. Behind Aconcagua, but almost forty miles farther and too far off for comparison, I could see the white slopes of Mercedario. Then I turned my eyes upon Tupungato itself and surveyed the surface of the dome, an undulating plateau at my feet covering an immense area. It is comparatively free from snow, except on the eastern side, where enormous snowfields fall over the precipice and sink down almost to the great moraine-filled valley beneath. On the plateau comparatively little solid rock appears above the surface, the same denuding agencies having been at work as on Aconcagua. Three peaks—or rather three huge débris-covered mounds—present themselves, one on the northern side, one to the east, and the highest to the south. I traversed the plateau from end to end, and, as on Aconcagua, discovered no traces whatever of a crater, though the nature of the rocks and the general shape of the summit tend to make one believe that its volcanic origin is of more recent date than that of Aconcagua. The peak on which I stood was as a mere excrescence on the enormous circle of the dome, whose sides, bellying at the top and falling sheer below, cut off all view of the valleys lying beneath the base of the mountain. This prevented me from seeing the nature of the southern and south-western face. Sixty-two years before, Charles Darwin beheld this side of Tupungato, when crossing the Portillo Pass on 22nd March 1835, and he says of it:—

"We had a fine view of a mass of mountain called Tupungato, the whole clothed with unbroken snow. From one peak my arriero said he had once seen smoke proceeding; and I thought I could distinguish the form of a large crater. In the maps Tupungato figures as a single mountain; this Chileno method of giving one name to a tract of mountains is a fruitful source of error. In the region of snow there was a blue patch which no doubt was glacier, a phenomenon that has been said not to occur in these mountains." [3]

It is extremely unlikely that there would be anything approaching a crater half-way down the southern slopes of the mountain. I presume, therefore, that Darwin thought he could discern the outlines of a crater in the three peaks rising above the dome, or perhaps in the rock arête by which I had reached the summit. As to the arriero's remark, it only shows that the mule-drivers of the Cordillera played with the truth sixty-two years ago as badly as they do today. It is a peculiar fact that right above the spot where Darwin made this observation, but behind him to the south, there is a great hanging glacier, which cloud must have prevented him from seeing.

I took the compass bearings of the principal surrounding heights, and then setting the little camera on the cairn, I took two views of Aconcagua, one of La Plata, and one of the eastern peak of Tupungato and the pampas. I would gladly have taken more, but we had now been more than an hour on the summit, and Zurbriggen, not without cause, became very impatient to go. It was nearly five o'clock, the sun was getting very low over the Pacific, and in less than an hour it would set. It was tempting Providence to remain.

During these seventy minutes on the summit I had worked as I never worked in my life. The cairn, the record, the bearings, the photographic views, the examination of the dome, formed my tale of work, and yet I had not half seen all there was to see. Why had I not time to wander at leisure over that great summit; select specimens from every one of the peaks; examine more carefully its contours, and try to form an opinion as to the reasons of the total obliteration of the ancient crater? This must be left to others. I hope to hear of the ascent of Tupungato by some geologist in the next few years. Let him start early in the season, and, apart from the altitude, all he will have to fear is the wind-storms. It has often

[3] Quoted from the first edition (1839) of the work commonly known as *The Voyage of the Beagle*. In the second edition (1845), the passage is cut to a single sentence and the suggestion of volcanic activity is omitted.

been remarked in mountaineering, since the first ascent of Mont Blanc, that the pioneers make far too much of the hardships they endured, and the difficulties of their ascents. It seems to me that those who come after do an injustice to those who have gone before. What one man has done, another can do, or feels confident that he can, and this confidence is itself a great factor of success at high altitudes. Dangers and difficulties seen and experienced for the first time always seem, nay, are more terrible than after they have been overcome and described. Mr. Leslie Stephen said of his first ascent of the Rothhorn, "The next traveller who makes the ascent will probably charge me with exaggeration. It is, I know, very difficult to avoid giving just cause for that charge. I must therefore apologise beforehand, and only beg my anticipated critic to remember two things: one, that on the first ascent a mountain, in obedience to some mysterious law, always is more difficult than at any succeeding ascent; secondly, that nothing can be less like a mountain at one time than the same mountain at another." [4]

Zurbriggen was right; it would be worse than foolish to wait a moment longer. We had no camp awaiting us at 19,000 as on Aconcagua, and the distance to our 17,000 foot bivouac was considerably greater than that which separated the camp on Aconcagua from the summit. At the high bivouac there was little food and no methylated spirits, so we planned to reach the base camp in the valley that night by pushing on in the moonlight, on which we could rely for the greater part of the descent. With much reluctance I shut up the camera, and put it in my pocket. As it was, I had given too much attention to my photographs and too little heed to surrounding conditions. To manipulate the camera properly gloves were out of the question, and photographing on Tupungato with 19° of frost and half a gale blowing is dangerous work—as I was quickly reminded by finding that two of my fingers were frost-bitten and lifeless. I showed them to Zurbriggen, who seized them in his powerful grasp and instantly started down, forcing me to follow. Down the slope of the peak and across the hard snow of the eastern slope we made our way hand in hand, Zurbriggen crunching my lifeless fingers in the most merciless manner as we went. He was

[4] See *The Playground of Europe*, edited by H. E. G. Tyndale (1936), pp. 40–41.

saving time as well as my fingers, for I was loth to leave the spot
so hurriedly, and tried vainly to snatch a specimen or two with the
other hand. The edge of the dome, eight hundred feet from the
summit, commanded a magnificent view over the mountains and valleys near, and I insisted on taking two more photographs, Zurbriggen waiting with impatience, and demanding after this delay
that we should press on with all possible speed. We plunged down
the couloir by which we had ascended, but the ground unfortunately
was very rotten, and we had not gone many yards when the pace
and the tired state we were in began to tell, and Zurbriggen, putting
his foot on a loose piece of rock, slipped and came down on his
back with great violence. Before leaving the summit of Tupungato
he had hastily packed away the monster's head—the topmost
rock—in the inside pocket at the back of his coat. It was on this
that he fell, and the top of Tupungato, as if in revenge for being
thus carried from its home, bit him badly in the back. A volley of
oaths rang over the mountain, and Zurbriggen lay on his back
writhing. Under ordinary circumstances it would be absurd to suppose two able-bodied men could not descend this couloir with care
in safety, but, now the excitement of the summit was over, we suddenly realised how tired and feeble we were, and the rotten state
of the ground became a real danger to us, for we stepped heavily,
and our foothold on the stone surface was uncertain. Zurbriggen
lay where he had fallen for some time groaning, but I, in my turn,
preached the necessity of pressing on unless we were to spend
another uncomfortable night at the 17,000 foot bivouac and he
pulled himself together once more. Straight down by the slopes of
snow from the dome, we at length reached the great spur, which,
with its gentle descent, afforded much relief to our weary limbs.
Night was closing in, and we determined to push on to the bivouac
by the route with which we were best acquainted—i.e. to descend
the spur for its full length and then turn sharply down the slope
on the right to the great snowfields which lie at its base. Owing to
the gathering darkness I was unable to collect any specimens. At
six o'clock we reached the point where the descent to the snow-
fields began. At last we must bid farewell to the great horizon line
of the Pacific, into which the sun was dipping, and we stood in

silence gazing westward, our faces suffused by the light of its last rays. It seemed impossible to tear ourselves away, but suddenly Zurbriggen turned to me and asked where I intended to sleep. It was quite enough—visions of comfort in the camp below, and dreary reminiscences of the lofty bivouac where we must stop unless we made haste, determined us to hurry on, so leaving the sunset behind us, we turned our backs on the west and dived down the long slope eastward.

I shall never forget the weary struggle down that steep declivity of broken stones and crumbling rock. The light had faded, and whether one hurried or went slowly it was impossible to avoid falls. Our arms were too tired for us to support ourselves by our axes, and soon we began to realise that we should never reach the main valley and its sheltering camp that night, even if it were possible to find the way by moonlight. I stumbled along, trying to remember what provisions for supper had been left at the bivouac. It was all that we had now to look forward to. Suddenly my attention was arrested by the magnificent spectacle of the afterglow following the sunset, as it hung in the eastern sky over the pampas. A line of fire, as it seemed, was spread across the heavens, slowly changing to colder tints. The rainbow of shifting colours that hung thus in the far-distant east in the twilight, was even more wonderful than the sunset we had seen from Aconcagua. The effect was extraordinary, for, the eye being unaided by any sight of foreground leading up to it, this fiery streak seemed assuredly some startling meteoric phenomenon. All objects at a great distance seen from a high mountain have, to the inexperienced eye, especially at first sight, the appearance of being lifted up too high. The observer looks down for the horizon,—and lo! it is high above. The higher one goes the greater is the illusion. This lasts only for a time, for the eye is led by the ground beneath, the slope of the mountain, the ranges and valleys between, up to the distant blue line, and the horizon humbles itself and resumes its proper place. Now here there was nothing to lead the eye or to teach it that this band of fire across the dark arc of heaven had any connection with the earth. I shall never forget its grandeur. The colours turned pale and faded out, night came on, but the moon shone brightly in the sky, and bathed the wide expanse of stone peaks and aiguilles beneath us in its sombre light.

At eight o'clock we heard a voice calling from below, a distant shout and then another. We soon recognised it as the voice of Lanti, and he came up to meet us and reported that he and Lochmatter had been at the bivouac since midday, and that Pollinger had arrived about three in the afternoon, seeming fairly well and strong. It seems that after we left him he had taken the descent very easily, and each step downwards had relieved his pains and given him fresh life, so that after two hours' rest and some food he had descended with Lochmatter to the valley camp. As soon as we reached the bivouac, Lanti tried to get us some supper, but nothing would induce the self-cooking tin lamps to work or the methylated spirits to burn, and we went supperless to bed. Thus ended one of the most eventful days of our work in the Andes, and of my life. . . .

HENRY DAVID THOREAU

1817–1862

IN JULY, 1845, Thoreau commenced his two-year life of self-dependence at Walden Pond. In the intensive self-cultivation which was his major purpose nothing was more important or exciting than physical nature, which he saw with the vision of a poet and the scrutiny of a gauger. His residence at Walden, however, was not continuous. In his recent biography of Thoreau Professor H. S. Canby suggests that, "having tasted wildness at the pond, he was no longer content with walks to Wachusett or the Catskills but must pry out the realities of the wilderness itself." Accordingly, late in August, 1846, he started with several companions for the Maine woods and Mount Katahdin.

The wilderness part of the trip was made by bateau *via* an inland waterway of lakes and streams to a point about fourteen miles southwest of Katahdin. Then Thoreau, "as the oldest mountain-climber" of the group, took the lead. They followed a straight course through rough and tangled forest and, after one night encamped, reached what is now Baxter Peak, the highest of the cirque called Mount Katahdin. The objective reached, they returned without delay to civilization. The whole expedition was conducted briskly, smoothly, and with relative comfort for all.

Thoreau's account of this journey, entitled simply "Ktaadn," was first printed separately in the *Union Magazine* in 1848, the sale having been arranged by Horace Greeley. Later it formed part of the volume known as *The Maine Woods*, in which his wilderness wanderings of 1853 and 1857 are also memorialized. Professor Canby describes *The Maine Woods* as "propaganda for the art of sauntering with an open eye, and for the proper use of leisure." The tendentiousness of *Walden* is largely lacking, only to be inferred from occasional shrewd comments and brief diatribes. As the narrative progresses even these occur less frequently, leaving the story of an observant, thoughtful, and intermittently poetic man on vacation.

A selection from "Ktaadn" proper for an anthology of the literature of mountaineering cannot be made without some violence to the continuity of a casual narrative-essay and to the spirit in which Thoreau traveled. Certainly he wished to stand on the summit of Katahdin, but the attainment of the peak was not the sole rationale of the journey. He devotes lengthy and delighted description to all other aspects and events of the trip. There is no change of tone in the paragraphs which recount the climb—no heightening or saved-up outburst of poetizing. Reaching the highest point was to Thoreau excellent and enjoyable, but not heroic or even climactic. He had a thoroughly amateur spirit about climbing and would have scorned as sharply as did John Ruskin the mere gymnast and the glory-seeker. Thoreau's narrative is in the great tradition of philosophical traveling.

The following selection is reprinted from Henry David Thoreau, *The Maine Woods*, Boston, Ticknor and Fields, 1864.

Ktaadn

At LENGTH we reached an elevation sufficiently bare to afford a view of the summit, still distant and blue, almost as if retreating from us. A torrent, which proved to be the same we had crossed, was seen tumbling down in front, literally from out of the clouds. But this glimpse at our whereabouts was soon lost, and we were buried in the woods again. The wood was chiefly yellow birch, spruce, fir, mountain-ash, or round-wood, as the Maine people call it, and moose-wood. It was the worst kind of travelling; sometimes like the densest scrub-oak patches with us. The cornel, or bunch-berries, were very abundant, as well as Solomon's seal and moose-berries. Blueberries were distributed along our whole route; and in one place bushes were drooping with the weight of the fruit, still as fresh as ever. It was the 7th of September. Such patches afforded a grateful repast, and served to bait the tired party forward. When any lagged behind, the cry of "blueberries" was most effectual to bring them up. Even at this elevation we passed through a moose-yard, formed by a large flat rock, four or five rods square, where they tread down the snow in winter. At length, fearing that if we held the direct course to the summit we should not find any water near our camping-ground, we gradually swerved to the west, till, at four o'clock, we struck again the torrent which I have mentioned, and here, in view of the summit, the weary party decided to camp that night.

While my companions were seeking a suitable spot for this purpose, I improved the little daylight that was left, in climbing the mountain alone. We were in a deep and narrow ravine, sloping up to the clouds, at an angle of nearly forty-five degrees, and hemmed in by walls of rock, which were at first covered with low trees, then with impenetrable thickets of scraggy birches and spruce-trees, and with moss, but at last bare of all vegetation but lichens, and almost continually draped in clouds. Following up the course of the torrent which occupied this—and I mean to lay some emphasis on this word *up*—pulling myself up by the side of perpendicular falls of twenty or thirty feet, by the roots of firs and birches, and then, perhaps, walking a level rod or two in the thin stream, for it took up the whole road, ascending by huge steps, as it were, a giant's stairway, down which a river flowed, I had soon cleared the trees, and paused on the successive shelves, to look back over the country. The torrent was from fifteen to thirty feet wide, without a tributary, and seemingly not diminishing in breadth as I advanced; but still it came rushing and roaring down, with a copious tide, over and amidst masses of bare rock, from the very clouds, as though a waterspout had just burst over the mountain. Leaving this at last, I began to work my way, scarcely less arduous than Satan's anciently through Chaos,[1] up the nearest, though not the highest peak. At first scrambling on all fours over the tops of ancient black spruce-trees (*Abies nigra*), old as the flood, from two to ten or twelve feet in height, their tops flat and spreading, and their foliage blue, and nipt with cold, as if for centuries they had ceased growing upward against the bleak sky, the solid cold. I walked some good rods erect upon the tops of these trees, which were overgrown with moss and mountain-cranberries. It seemed that in the course of time they had filled up the intervals between the huge rocks, and the cold wind had uniformly levelled all over. Here the principle of vegetation was hard put to it. There was apparently a belt of this kind running quite round the mountain, though, perhaps, nowhere so remarkable as here. Once, slumping through, I looked down ten feet, into a dark and cavernous region, and saw the stem of a spruce, on whose top I stood, as on a mass of coarse basket-work, fully nine inches in diameter at the ground. These holes were bears' dens, and the bears

[1] See Milton, *Paradise Lost*, II, ll. 871 ff.

were even then at home. This was the sort of garden I made my way *over*, for an eighth of a mile, at the risk, it is true, of treading on some of the plants, not seeing any path *through* it—certainly the most treacherous and porous country I ever travelled.

> Nigh foundered on he fares,
> Treading the crude consistence, half on foot,
> Half flying.[2]

But nothing could exceed the toughness of the twigs—not one snapped under my weight, for they had slowly grown. Having slumped, scrambled, rolled, bounced, and walked, by turns, over this scraggy country, I arrived upon a sidehill, or rather side-mountain, where rocks, gray, silent rocks, were the flocks and herds that pastured, chewing a rocky cud at sunset. They looked at me with hard gray eyes, without a bleat or a low. This brought me to the skirt of a cloud, and bounded my walk that night. But I had already seen that Maine country when I turned about, waving, flowing, rippling, down below.

When I returned to my companions, they had selected a camping-ground on the torrent's edge, and were resting on the ground; one was on the sick list, rolled in a blanket, on a damp shelf of rock. It was savage and dreary scenery enough; so wildly rough, that they looked long to find a level and open space for the tent. We could not well camp higher, for want of fuel; and the trees here seemed so evergreen and sappy, that we almost doubted if they would acknowledge the influence of fire; but fire prevailed at last, and blazed here, too, like a good citizen of the world. Even at this height we met with frequent traces of moose, as well as of bears. As here was no cedar, we made our bed of coarser feathered spruce; but at any rate the feathers were plucked from the live tree. It was, perhaps, even a more grand and desolate place for a night's lodging than the summit would have been, being in the neighborhood of those wild trees, and of the torrent. Some more aerial and finer-spirited winds rushed and roared through the ravine all night, from time to time arousing our fire, and dispersing the embers about. It was as if we lay in the very nest of a young whirlwind. At midnight, one of my

[2] *Ibid.*, ll. 940–42.

bedfellows, being startled in his dreams by the sudden blazing up to its top of a fir-tree, whose green boughs were dried by the heat, sprang up, with a cry, from his bed, thinking the world on fire, and drew the whole camp after him.

In the morning, after whetting our appetite on some raw pork, a wafer of hard bread, and a dipper of condensed cloud or water-spout, we all together began to make our way up the falls, which I have described; this time choosing the right hand, or highest peak, which was not the one I had approached before. But soon my companions were lost to my sight behind the mountain ridge in my rear, which still seemed ever retreating before me, and I climbed alone over huge rocks, loosely poised, a mile or more, still edging toward the clouds; for though the day was clear elsewhere, the summit was concealed by mist. The mountain seemed a vast aggregation of loose rocks, as if some time it had rained rocks, and they lay as they fell on the mountain sides, nowhere fairly at rest, but leaning on each other, all rocking-stones, with cavities between, but scarcely any soil or smoother shelf. They were the raw materials of a planet dropped from an unseen quarry, which the vast chemistry of nature would anon work up, or work down, into the smiling and verdant plains and valleys of earth. This was an undone extremity of the globe; as in lignite, we see coal in the process of formation.

At length I entered within the skirts of the cloud which seemed forever drifting over the summit, and yet would never be gone, but was generated out of that pure air as fast as it flowed away; and when, a quarter of a mile farther, I reached the summit of the ridge, which those who have seen in clearer weather say is about five miles long, and contains a thousand acres of table-land, I was deep within the hostile ranks of clouds, and all objects were obscured by them. Now the wind would blow me a yard of clear sunlight, wherein I stood; then a gray, dawning light was all it could accomplish, the cloud-line ever rising and falling with the wind's intensity. Sometimes it seemed as if the summit would be cleared in a few moments, and smile in sunshine; but what was gained on one side was lost on another. It was like sitting in a chimney and waiting for the smoke to blow away. It was, in fact, a cloud-factory—these were the cloud-works, and the wind turned them off done from the cool, bare rocks. Occasionally, when the windy columns broke in to me, I caught sight of a dark, damp crag to the right or left; the mist driving ceaselessly between it and me. It reminded me of the creations of the old epic and dramatic poets, of Atlas, Vulcan, the Cyclops, and Prometheus. Such was Caucasus and the rock where Prometheus was bound. Aeschylus had no doubt visited such scenery as this. It was vast, Titanic, and such as man never inhabits. Some part of the beholder, even some vital part, seems to escape through the loose grating of his ribs as he ascends. He is more lone than you can imagine. There is less of substantial thought and fair understanding in him, than in the plains where men inhabit. His reason is dispersed and shadowy, more thin and subtile, like the air. Vast, Titanic, inhuman Nature has got him at disadvantage, caught him alone, and pilfers him of some of his divine faculty. She does not smile on him as in the plains. She seems to say sternly, why came ye here before your time? This ground is not prepared for you. Is it not enough that I smile in the valleys? I have never made this soil for thy feet, this air for thy breathing, these rocks for thy neighbors. I cannot pity nor fondle thee here, but forever relentlessly drive thee hence to where I *am* kind. Why seek me where I have not called thee, and then complain because you find me but a stepmother? Shouldst thou freeze or starve, or shudder thy life away, here is no shrine, nor altar, nor any access to my ear.

> Chaos and ancient Night, I come no spy
> With purpose to explore or to disturb
> The secrets of your realm, but . . .
>   . . . as my way
> Lies through your spacious empire up to light.[3]

The tops of mountains are among the unfinished parts of the globe, whither it is a slight insult to the gods to climb and pry into their secrets, and try their effect on our humanity. Only daring and insolent men, perchance, go there. Simple races, as savages, do not climb mountains—their tops are sacred and mysterious tracts never visited by them. Pomola is always angry with those who climb to the summit of Ktaadn.[4]

According to [Charles T.] Jackson, who, in his capacity of geo-

---

[3] *Paradise Lost*, II, ll. 970–74.
[4] Pomola is the name of an irascible Indian devil who inhabits one of the peaks of Mount Katahdin. According to legend he can be appeased by a cask of rum.

logical surveyor of the State, has accurately measured it—the altitude
of Ktaadn is 5,300 feet, or a little more than one mile above the level
of the sea—and he adds, "It is then evidently the highest point in the
State of Maine, and is the most abrupt granite mountain in New
England." The peculiarities of that spacious table-land on which I
was standing, as well as the remarkable semi-circular precipice or
basin on the eastern side, were all concealed by the mist. I had
brought my whole pack to the top, not knowing but I should have
to make my descent to the river, and possibly to the settled portion of
the State alone, and by some other route, and wishing to have a
complete outfit with me. But at length, fearing that my companions
would be anxious to reach the river before night, and knowing that
the clouds might rest on the mountain for days, I was compelled to
descend. Occasionally, as I came down, the wind would blow me a
vista open, through which I could see the country eastward, boundless forests, and lakes, and streams, gleaming in the sun, some of them
emptying into the East. There were also new mountains in sight in
that direction. Now and then some small bird of the sparrow family
would flit away before me, unable to command its course, like a
fragment of the gray rock blown off by the wind.

I found my companions where I had left them, on the side of
the peak, gathering the mountain cranberries, which filled every
crevice between the rocks, together with blueberries, which had
a spicier flavor the higher up they grew, but were not the less agreeable to our palates. When the country is settled, and roads are made,
these cranberries will perhaps become an article of commerce. From
this elevation, just on the skirts of the clouds, we could overlook
the country, west and south, for a hundred miles. There it was, the
State of Maine, which we had seen on the map, but not much like
that—immeasurable forest for the sun to shine on, that eastern *stuff*
we hear of in Massachusetts. No clearing, no house. It did not look
as if a solitary traveler had cut so much as a walking-stick there.
Countless lakes—Moosehead in the southwest, forty miles long by
ten wide, like a gleaming silver platter at the end of the table;
Chesuncook, eighteen long by three wide, without an island; Mil-
linocket, on the south, with its hundred islands; and a hundred others
without a name; and mountains also, whose names, for the most part,

are known only to the Indians. The forest looked like a firm grass sward, and the effect of these lakes in its midst has been well compared, by one who has since visited this same spot, to that of a "mirror broken into a thousand fragments, and wildly scattered over the grass, reflecting the full blaze of the sun."

JOHN BEATTY

1828–1914

AT THE OUTBREAK of the Civil War, John Beatty was profitably established as co-owner of a private bank in Cardington, Ohio. He volunteered for service, campaigned without remission until 1864, and resigned from the army a brigadier-general. From 1868 to 1873 he represented the Eighth Ohio District in Congress. The remainder of his life he devoted to banking, to writing, and to participation in the public life of Ohio. His best-known book, *The Citizen-Soldier* (1879), is an unpretentious diary of his years in the Union Army, valuable for its honest presentation of everyday military life. It was reissued in 1946 as *Memoirs of a Volunteer*.

The mountain in West Virginia which Beatty climbed probably could not be identified, except as being near the Union Army encampment at Philippi. He himself enjoys no reputation as a climber and had no notion that he was engaging in a sport which would become famous. Yet, although he set out "for want of something better to do," he discovered several of the fundamental vexations and rewards of low-level mountaineering and in doing so plainly enjoyed himself. His account has the humorous veracity of a candid and observant man.

The following selection is reprinted from John Beatty, *The Citizen-Soldier* . . . , Cincinnati, Wilstach, Baldwin & Co., 1879. The title of the selection has been supplied.

Initiation

JULY] 30, [1861]. About two o'clock P.M., for want of something better to do, I climbed the high mountain in front of our camp. The side is as steep as the roof of a gothic house. By taking hold of bushes and limbs of trees, after a half hour of very hard work, I managed to get to the top, completely exhausted. The outlook was magnificent. Tygart's valley, the river winding through it, and a boundless succession of mountains and ridges, all lay before me. My attention, however, was soon diverted from the landscape to the huckleberries. They were abundant; and now and then I stumbled on patches of delicious raspberries. I remained on the mountain, resting and picking berries, until half-past four. I had to be in camp at six to post my pickets, but there was no occasion for haste. So, after a time, I started leisurely down, not the way I had come up but, as I supposed, down the eastern slope, a way, apparently, not so steep and difficult as the one by which I had ascended. I traveled on, through vines and bushes, over fallen timber and under great trees, from which I could scarcely obtain a glimpse of the sky, until finally I came to a mountain stream. I expected to find the road, not the stream, and began to be a little uncertain as to my whereabouts. After reflection, I concluded I would be most likely to reach camp by going up the stream, and so started. Trees in many places had fallen across the ravine, and my progress was neither easy nor rapid; but I pushed on as best I could. I never knew so well before what a mountain stream was. I scrambled over rocks and fallen trees and through thickets of laurel, until I was completely worn out. Lying down on the rocks, which in high water formed part of the bed of the stream, I took a drink, looked at my watch, and found it was half-past five. My pickets were to be posted at six. Having but a half hour left, I started on. I could see no opening yet. The stream twisted and turned, keeping no one general direction for twenty rods, and hardly for twenty feet. It grew smaller, and as the ravine narrowed the way became more difficult. Six o'clock had not come. I could not see the sun and only occasionally could get glimpses of the sky. I began to realize that I was lost, but concluded finally that I would climb the mountain again and ascertain, if I could, in what direction the camp lay. I have had some hard tramps, and have done some hard work, but never labored half so hard in a whole week as I did for one hour in getting up that mountain, pushing through vines, climbing over logs, breaking through brush. Three or four times I lay down out of breath, utterly exhausted, and thought I would proceed no further until morning; but when I thought of my pickets, and reflected that General Reynolds would not excuse a trip so foolish and untimely, I made new efforts and pushed on. Finally I reached the summit of the mountain, but found it not the one from which I had descended. Still higher mountains were around me. The trees and bushes were so dense I could hardly see a rod before me. It was now seven o'clock, an hour after the time when I should have been in camp. I lay down, determined to remain all night; but my clothing was so thin that I soon became chilly, and so got up and started on again. Once I became entangled in a wilderness of grapevines and briers, and had much difficulty in getting through them. It was now half-past seven and growing dark; but fortunately at this time I heard a dog bark, a good way off to the right, and, turning in that direction, I came to a cowpath. Which end of it should I take? Either end, I concluded, would be better than to remain where I was; so I worked myself into a dogtrot, wound down around the side of the mountain, and reached the road, a mile and a half south of camp, and went to my quarters as fast as my legs could carry me. I found my detail for picket duty waiting and wondering what could so detain the officer of the day.

CHARLES EDWARD MONTAGUE

THE FOLLOWING selection is reprinted from C. E. Montague, *Fiery Particles*, New York, Doubleday, Doran & Co., 1924. See also pp. 19–20.

In Hanging Garden Gully

To CLIMB UP ROCKS is like all the rest of your life, only simpler and safer. In all the rest of your life, any work you may do, by way of a trade, is a taking of means to some end. That end may be good. We all hope it is. But who can be sure? Misgiving is apt to steal in. Are you a doctor—is it your job to keep all the weak ones alive? Then are you not spoiling the breed for the future? Are you a parson or politician or some sort of public improver, always trying to fight evil down? May you not then be making a muff every day of somebody else who ought to have had his dragon to fight, with his own bow and spear, when you rushed in to rob him and the other little St. Georges of discipline and of victory? Anyhow, all the good ends seem a good long way off, and the ways to them dim. You may be old by the time you are there. The salt may have lost half its savour.

No such dangers or doubts perplex the climber on rocks. He deals, day by day, with the Ultimate Good, no doubt in small nips, but still authentic and not watered down. His senses thrill with delight to find that he is just the sum of his own simple powers. He lives on, from moment to moment, by early man's gleeful achievement of balance on one foot out of four. He hangs safe by a single hand that learnt its good grip in fifty thousand years of precarious dodging among forest boughs, with the hungry snakes looking up from the ground for a catch like the expectant fieldsmen in the slips. The next little ledge, the object of all human hope and desire, is only some twelve feet away—about the length of the last leap of that naked bunch of clenched and quivering muscles, from whom you descend, at the wild horse that he had stalked through the grass. Each time that you get up a hard pitch you have succeeded in life. Besides, no one can say you have hurt him.

Care will come back in the end: the clouds return after the rain; but for those first heavenly minutes of sitting secure and supreme at the top of Moss Ghyll or the Raven Crag Gully you are Columbus when he saw land from the rigging and Gibbon when he laid down his pen in the garden house at Lausanne. It's good for you, too; it makes you more decent. No one, I firmly believe, could be utterly mean on the very tip of the Weisshorn. I could, if I had known the way, have written a lyric about these agreeable truths as I sat by myself in the tiny inn at Llyn Ogwen where Telford's great London-to-Holyhead road climbs over a pass between three-thousand-foot Carnedds and Glyders. I was a convalescent then, condemned still to a month of rest cure for body and mind. But it was June, and fine weather. Rocks had lately become dry and warm.

There are places in Britain where rock-climbing cannot honestly be called a rest cure. I mean, for the body. Look at the Coolin—all the way that a poor invalid must tramp from Sligachan southward before he gets among the rough, trusty, prehensile gabbro, the best of all God's stones. Think of Scawfell Crag, the finest crag in the world, but its base cut off from the inn by all that Sisyphean plod up the heart-breaking lengths of Brown Tongue. From Ogwen you only need walk half an hour, almost on the flat, and then—there you are, at the foot of your climb. The more I considered the matter, the more distinctly could I perceive that my doctor, when saying "Avoid all violent exercise," meant that if ever I got such an opening as this for a little "steady six-furlong work," as it is called in the training reports, I ought to take care not to miss it.

But I was the only guest at the inn. And to climb alone is counted a sin against the spirit of the sport. All the early fathers of climbing held the practice heretical. Certainly some of them—Whymper, Tyndall, and others—climbed by themselves when they had a mind to. Thus did King David, on distinguished occasions, relax the general tensity of his virtue. But these exceptions could not obscure the general drift of the law and the prophets of mountaineering. Then came another pause-giving reflection. If, as the Greeks so delicately put it, anything incurable happens while you are climbing alone, your clay is exposed, defenceless and dumb, to nasty *obiter dicta* during the inquest. "Woe unto him," as Solomon says, "who is alone when he falleth!" Insensate rustic coroners and juries, well as they may understand that riding to hounds in a stone-wall country is one of the choicer forms of prudence, will prose and grumble over extinct mountaineers. Their favourite vein is the undesirable one of their brother, the First Clown in *Hamlet,* who thought it a shame that Ophelia (she seems to have slipped up while climbing a tree) "should have countenance in this world to drown or hang herself more than her even Christian." [1]

No mean impediments these to a sensitive, conscientious nature's design for seeking health and joy among the attractive gullies and slabs that surround Llyn Idwal. Against them I marshalled all that I could remember of St. Paul's slighting observations on the law; also any agility that I had gained in the Oxford Greats school in resolving disagreeable discords into agreeable higher harmonies. Black was certainly not white. Still, as the good Hegelian said, black might, after all, be an aspect of white. In time it was duly clear to my mind that sin lies not in the corporal act, but in the thoughts of the sinner. So long as the heart sincerely conversed with the beauty of the truths on which rested the rule of never climbing alone it mattered little what the mere legs did: your soul was not in your legs. One of casuistry's brightest triumphs had been fairly won, my liberty gained, my intellectual integrity saved, my luncheon sandwiches ordered for eight in the morning—when somebody else arrived at the inn.

He stood confessed a botanist—he had the large green cylindrical can of the tribe, oval in section and hung by a strap from the shoulder, like the traditional *vivandière's* little cask in French art. He was also, I found while we smoked through that evening together, a good fellow. He had, too, a good leg, if one only. The other

[1] Slightly misquoted. See Act V, scene 1, ll. 29–32.

was stiff and unbendable at the knee. He had broken it last year, he said, and the bones seemed to have set only too hard, or else Nature had gracelessly grudged to the mended knee-joint of her lover a proper supply of whatever substitute she uses for ball bearings.

His name was Darwin. "No relation, really," he humbly assured me. His father was only some obscure squire. The son's Christian name had been Charles at the font, but on coming of age the dear fellow had felt it immodest to prey any more than he need upon his eponymous hero's thrice-honoured names. So he had meekly converted the Charles by deed poll into Thomas. This lowly and beautiful gesture convinced me, as you may suppose, that here was the man to go climbing with. He was indeed one of the innocent, one-thoughted kind that wake up happy each day and never turn crusty, and always think you are being too good to them.

One lure alone had drawn him to these outworks of Snowdon. Some eccentric flower grew on these heights, and a blank page in one of his books of squashed specimens ached for it. Was it so lovely? I asked, like a goose. He was too gentle to snub me. But all that fellow's thoughts shone out through his face. Every flower that blew—to this effect did his soul mildly rebuke mine—was beauteous beyond Helen's eyes. All he said was: "No, not fair, perhaps, to outward view as many roses be; but, just think!—it grows on no patch of ground in the world but these crags!"

"It is not merely better dressed," said I, "than Solomon. It is wiser."

It was about then, I think, that the heart of the man who had gone mad on the green-stuff and that of the man who knew what was what, in the way of a recreation, rushed together like Paolo's and Francesca's. What had already become an *entente cordiale* ripened at tropical speed into alliance. Darwin had found a second, half-invalided perhaps, but still the holder of two unqualified legs, for to-morrow's quest of his own particular Grail. To me it now seemed to be no accident that Darwin had come to the inn: it was ordained, like the more permanent union of marriage, for a remedy against sin, and to avoid climbing alone.

We got down to business at once. A charming gully, I told him,

led right up to the big crag over Cwm Idwal. Not Twll Du, the
ill-famed Devil's Kitchen. That, I frankly said, was justly *detes-
tata matribus*—wet and rotten and lethal, and quite flowerless too.
My gully, though close to that man-eating climb, was quite another affair. Mine was the place for town children to spend a
happy day in the country: the very place also for starting the day's
search for the object of Darwin's desire. In saying this, too, I was
honest. Lots of plants grow in some gullies; ferns, mosses, grasses,
all sorts of greens flourish in a damp cleft, like hair in an armpit;
why not one kind of waste rabbit-food as well another? You see,
I had not been a casuist merely, before Darwin came. I had used
the eyes Heaven gave me, and reconnoitred the gully well from
below, and if any flower knew how to tell good from bad, in the
way of a scramble, it would be there. I ended upon a good note. The
place's name, I said impressively, was Hanging Garden Gully, no
doubt because of the rich indigenous flora.

His eyes shone at that, and we went straight to the kitchen to ask
Mrs. Jones for the loan of a rope. I had none with me that journey:
the sick are apt to relinquish improvidently these necessaries of a
perfect life. Now, in the classics of mountaineering the right thing
in such cases of improvised enterprise is that the landlady lends
you her second-best clothes-line. Far happier we, Mrs. Jones having
by her a 120-foot length of the right Alpine rope, with the red
worsted thread in its middle. It had been left in her charge by a
famous pillar of the Scottish Mountaineering Club till he should
come that way again. "The gentleman," Mrs. Jones told us, "said
I was always to let any climbing gentlemen use it." Heaven was
palpably smiling upon our attempt.

The sun smiled benedictively, too, on the halt and the sick as
they stood, about nine the next morning, roping up at the foot of
their climb. "A fisherman's bend," I took care to explain, as I knotted
one end of the rope round Darwin's chest.

"The botanical name," he replied—"did I tell you?—is Lloydia."
How some men do chatter when they are happy! Can't carry their
beans.

We were not likely to need the whole 120 feet of the rope. So I
tied myself on at its middle and coiled the odd 60 feet round my

shoulder. "A double overhand knot," I confessed, as I tightened it round me. "A bad knot, but for once it may do us no harm."

"The vernacular name," said the garrulous fellow, "is spider-wort."

"Tut, tut!" I inwardly said.

The lower half of that gully was easier than it had looked: just enough in it to loosen your muscles and make you want more. Higher up, the gully grew shallow and had greater interest. The top part of all, as I remember it now, might be called either a chimney or crack, being both. In horizontal section, it was a large obtuse angle indented into the face of the crag. The crag at this part, and the gully's bed with it, rose at an angle of some 60 degrees. Now, when you climb rock at an angle of 60 degrees the angle seems to be just 90. In early mountaineering records the pioneers often say, "Our situation was critical. Above us the crag rose verti-cal," or, "To descend was impossible now. But in front the rocky face, for some time perpendicular, had now begun to overhang." If you take a clinometer to the scenes of some of those literal esti-mates you blush for your kind. The slope of the steepest—and easiest—ridge of the three by which the Matterhorn is climbed is only 39 degrees. But this, though not purely digressive, is partly so. All that strictly had to be said was that an upright and very obtuse-angled trough in smooth rock that rises at 60 degrees cannot be climbed.

But in the very bed of our trough there had been eroded, from top to bottom, a deepish irregular crack in the rock. Into this crack, at most parts, you could stick a foot, a knee, or an arm. Also, the sides of the large obtuse angle, when you looked closely, were not utterly smooth. On the right wall, as we looked up, certain small wrinkles, bunions, and other minute but lovable diversities in the face of the stone gave promise of useful points of resistance for any right boot that might scrape about on the wall in the hope of exert-ing auxiliary lateral pressure, while the left arm and thigh, hard at work in the crack, wriggled you up by a succession of cater-pillarish squirms. This delectable passage was 80 feet high, as I measured it with my experienced eye. An inexperienced measuring-tape might have put it at fifty. To any new recruit to the cause—

above all, to one with a leg as inflexible as the stoniest stone that it pressed—I felt that the place was likely to offer all that he could wish in the line of baptisms of fire. Still, as the pioneers said, to descend was impossible now: the crack was too sweet to be left. And Darwin, thus far, had come up like a lamplighter, really. I told him so, frankly. Alpine guides are the men at psychology. Do they not get the best out of the rawest new client, in any hard place, by ceasing to hide the high estimate that they have formed of his natural endowment for the sport? *"Vous êtes—je vous dis franchement, monsieur—un chamois! Un véritable chat de montagne!"*

I was leading the party. I was the old hand. Besides, I could bend both my knees. Desiring Darwin to study my movements, so that he presently might—so far as comformity would not cramp his natural talents—copy them closely, I now addressed myself to the crack. When half-way up I heard the voice of a good child enduring, with effort, a painful call upon its patience. "Any Lloydia yet?" it wistfully said. Between my feet I saw Darwin below. Well, he was certainly paying the rope out all right, as I had enjoined; but he did it "like them that dream." His mind was not in it. All the time he was peering hungrily over the slabby containing walls of the gully, and now he just pawed one of them here and there with a tentative foot—you know how a puppy, when first it sees ice, paws the face of the pond. "These botanists!" I thought. "These fanatics!" You know how during a happy physical effort—a race or a hunt, a fight or a game—you think, with a sort of internal quiet, about a lot of old things. There came back to my mind the old lines that I had once had to make Latin verse of:

> How vainly men themselves amaze
> To win the palm, the oak, or bays,
> And their incessant labours see
> Crowned from some single herb or tree.[2]

Meanwhile I took a precaution. I first unroped myself. Then I passed the rope, from below, through the space behind a stone that was jammed fast in the crack. Then I roped myself on again, just at my old place on the rope. A plague of a job it was, too, with all

[2] Marvell, "The Garden," ll. 1–4. Slightly altered.

those 60 feet of spare rope to uncoil and re-coil. But you see how it worked: I had now got the enthusiast moored. Between him and me the rope went through the eye of a needle, so I could go blithely on. I went. In the top of the crack I found a second jammed stone. It was bigger than number one: in fact, it blocked the way and made you clamber round outside it rather interestingly; but it, too, had daylight showing through a hole behind it. Sounds from below were again improving my natural stock of prudence. You can't, I thought, be too safe. Once more I unroped, just under this chock-stone, and pushed the rope up through the hole at its back. When the rope fell down to me, outwards over the top of the stone, I tied on again, just as before, and then scrambled up over the outer side of the stone with an ecstatic pull on both arms, and sat on its top in the heaven that big-game hunters know when they lie up against the slain tiger and smoke.

If you have bent up your mind to take in the details, you will now have an imposing vision of the connections of Darwin and me with each other and with the Primary or Palaeozoic rocks of Cambria. From Darwin, tied on to its end, the rope ran, as freely as a bootlace runs through the eyelets, behind the jammed stone 30 feet above his head, and then again behind my present throne of glory at the top; then it was tied on to me; and then there were 60 feet, half its length, left over to play with.

Clearly Darwin, not being a thread, or even a rope, could not come up the way that the rope did, through the two needle-eyes. Nor did I care, he being the thing that he was, to bid him untie and then to pull up his end of the rope through the eyes, drop it down to him clear through the air, and tell him to tie on again. He was, as the Irish say of the distraught, "fit to be tied," and not at all fit for the opposite. If he were loose he might at any moment espy that Circe of his in some place out of bounds. There seemed to be only one thing to do. I threw down the spare 60 feet of the rope, and told him first to tie himself on to its end, and then, but not before, to untie himself from the other. I could not quite see these orders obeyed. A bulge of rock came between him and my eyes, but I was explicit. "Remember that fisherman's bend!" I shouted. Perhaps my voice was rather austere; but who would not forgive a wise virgin for saying, a little dryly, to one of the foolish, "Well, use your spare can"? As soon as he sang out "All right" I took a good haul on what was now the working half of the rope, to test his knot-making. Yes, he *was* all right. So I bade him come up, and he started. Whenever he looked up I saw that he had a wild, gadding eye; and whenever he stopped to breathe during the struggle he gasped, "I can't see it yet."

He came nearly half-way, and then he did see it. He had just reached the worst part. Oh, the Sirens know when to start singing! That flower of evil was far out of his reach, or of what his reach ought to have been. Some twelve feet away on his right it was rooted in some infinitesimal pocket of blown soil, a mere dirty thumb-nailful of clay. For a moment the lover eyed the beloved across one huge slab of steep stone with no real foothold or handhold upon it—only a few efflorescent minutiae small as the bubukles and whelks and knobs on the nose of some fossil Bardolph. The whole wall of the gully just there was what any man who could climb would have written off as unclimbable. Passion, however, has her own stand-ards, beyond the comprehension of the wise:

> His eye but saw that light of love,
> The only star it hailed above.

My lame Leander gave one whinny of desire. Then he left all and made for his Hero.

You know the way that a man, who has no idea how badly he bats, will sometimes go in and hit an unplayable bowler right out of the ground, simply because the batsman is too green to know that the bowler cannot be played. Perhaps that was the way. Or perhaps your sound climber, having his wits, may leave, at his boldest, a margin of safety, as engineers call it, so wide that a madman may cut quite a lot off its edge without coming surely to grief. Or was it only a joke of the gods among themselves over their wine? Or can it be that the special arrangements known to be made for the safety of sailors, when in their cups, are extended at times to cover the case of collectors overcome by the strong waters of the acquisitive in-stinct? Goodness knows! Whatever the powers that helped him, this crippled man, who had never tried climbing before, went skating off to his right flank, across that impossible slant, on one foot and one stilt, making a fool of the science of mountaineering.

I vetoed, I imprecated, I grew Athanasian. All utterly useless. As soon could you whistle a dog back to heel when he fleets off on fire with some fresh amour. I could only brace myself, take a good hold of the rope in both hands, and be ready to play the wild salmon below as soon as he slipped and the line ran out tight. While I waited I saw, for the first time, another piquant detail of our case. Darwin, absorbed in his greed, had never untied the other end of the rope. So he was now tied on both ends. The whole rope made a circle, a vicious circle. Our whole caravan was sewn on to the bony structure of Wales with two big stitches, one at each jammed stone.

You see how it would work. When Darwin should fall, as he must, and hang in the air from my hands, gravitation would swing him back into the centre of the chimney, straight below me, bashing him hard against the chimney's opposite wall. No doubt he would be stunned. I should never be able to hoist his dead weight through the air to my perch, so I should have to lower him to the foot of the chimney. That would just use up the full 60 feet of rope. It would run the two 60-foot halves of the rope so tight that I should never be able to undo the bad central knot that confined me. Could I but cut it when Darwin was lowered into provisional safety, and then climb down to see to him! No; I had lost my knife two days ago. I should be like a netted lion, with no mouse to bite through his cords: A Prometheus, bound to his rock.

But life spoils half her best crises. That wretch never slipped. He that by this time had no sort of right to his life came back as he went, treading on air, but now with that one bloom of the spider-wort in his mouth. Apologising for slowness, and panting with haste, he writhed up the crack till his head appeared over the chock-stone beside me. Then he gave one cry of joy, surged up over the stone, purring with pleasure, and charged the steep slope of slippery grass above the precipice we had scaled. "You never told me!" he cried; and then for the first time I noticed that up here the whole place was speckled with Lloydia. The next moment Darwin fell suddenly backwards, as if Lloyd himself or some demon gardener of his had planted a very straight one on the chin of the onrushing trespasser in his pleasance. You guess? Yes. One of his two tethers, the one coming up from behind the lower jammed stone, had run out; it had pulled him up short as he leapt upon the full fruition of his desire.

He was easy to field as he rolled down the grass. But his tug on the rope had worked it well into some crevice between the lower jammed stone and the wall of the crack. We were anchored now, good and fast, to that stone, more than three fathoms below. What to do now? Climb down and clear the jammed rope? Leave that lame voluptuary rioting upon a precipice's edge? Scarcely wise—would it have been? Puzzled and angry, I cast away shame. I knew well that as Spartan troops had to come back with their shields or upon them, or else have trouble with their mothers, a climber who leaves his tackle behind in a retreat is likely to be a scorn and a hissing. Still, I cast away shame. Ours was no common case; no common ethics would meet it. I untied us both, and threw both ends of the rope down the chimney; then I let Darwin graze for a minute; then I drove him relentlessly up the steep grass to the top of the crag, and round by the easy walking way down.

As we passed down the valley below, I looked up. The whole length of our chimney was visibly draped with the pendent double length of that honest Scots mountaineer's rope. "I don't really know how to thank you enough," Darwin was babbling beside me, "for giving me such a day!"

But I felt as if I were one of the villains in plays who compromise women of virtue and rank by stealing their fans and leaving them lying about in the rooms of bad bachelors. Much might be said for climbing alone, no matter what the authorities thought. A good time it would be, all to myself, when I came back to salvage that rope.

ERNEST A. BAKER

1869–1941

By PROFESSION Ernest A. Baker was a librarian and a student of English literature. As borough librarian of Woolwich and secretary of the Educational Committee of the British Library Association he won a reputation for energy and resourcefulness, so that when the School of Librarianship of the University of London was founded, he was the logical choice for director. He held this position from 1919 to 1934. His major work of literary scholarship is the ten-volume *History of the English Novel* (1924–1939), known to students of fiction as the most comprehensive treatment available. He is reputed to have read every important novel ever written in Europe, England, and America.

Baker hiked and climbed extensively in all the mountainous regions of Great Britain. The writer of his obituary in *The Times* mentions his unfailing youthfulness, and in *Who's Who* as late as 1940 Baker lists his recreations as climbing, cave-exploring, and fly-fishing. In the second of these, an unusual predilection for a mountaineer, he excelled and was for years regarded as one of the foremost speleologists in England. His numerous contributions to the literature of mountaineering are mainly modest, humorous narratives of his own exploits, which, while rarely startling, demanded the full ingenuity of a skilled rock-climber.

The following selection is reprinted from Ernest A. Baker, *The Highlands with Rope and Rucksack*, London, H. F. and G. Witherby, Ltd., 1923, by permission of H. F. and G. Witherby, Ltd.

A Scramble in Arran

BEN NUIS is the western terminal of the highest range in Arran,[1] of which the eastern end is Goat Fell. It is not a well-known peak, the

[1] An island off the west coast of Scotland.

aspect it presents towards the more frequented points of view lacking interest, though as seen from Brodick its horn-like summit is a graceful termination to the crumpled chain of ridges and rocky steeples. The name Ben Nuis is descriptive, meaning the face-mountain, for the great feature of the hill is the precipice on its eastern front. This sheer cliff, about five hundred feet high, and covered with "boiler-plates," has long been regarded by rock-climbers in Arran as a standard of comparison for anything unusually difficult. What is a "boiler-plate"? To explain this graphic metaphor will help to explain the difficulties of the Ben Nuis climb. A large part of this wall of cliff is faced with slabs of granite, smooth in the mass, though rough in surface, their joints overlapping except where they are flush, in either case offering hardly the vestige of a ledge between. Even when such slabs are inclined at a low angle they are exceedingly hard to climb; when they are steep, as here, they soon become unscalable. There is no way of ascending such a cliff except by a gully or similar fissure.

My companion, J. W. Puttrell, and I know a good deal more about boiler-plates and the idiosyncrasies of Arran climbing than we knew when we landed at Brodick after a choppy passage, and, looking up towards the sovereign heights of the island, beheld nothing but a turmoil of mist and cloud, out of which the rain descended as if to prohibit climbing for many days to come. We had never heard of Ben Nuis, though Goat Fell and C[h]ir Mhor were names full of meaning; but we had begged our entertainer, L. J. Oppenheimer, who was holidaying in Arran, to find us something fresh and sweet, and when a glorious day broke we set out full of faith in the unknown name. The burns were in spate; the Rosa River was brimfull, though clear as ever and alive with feeding trout. We quitted Glen Rosa just beyond the bridge over the Rough Burn, which mightily well deserved its name that day, for it tumbled and roared over the slabby bed in no pretty cascade, but in a tumult of foam. Breasting the steep brae, we ascended near the margin of the torrent to the boggy moor on the top.

Our party numbered six. Two of us had brought our wives, in anticipation of a day of easy and entertaining sport. The gentleman who became sixth, brother to our host and guide, had a camera;

but the part he was to act in the sequel had nothing to do with photography. Crossing bogs, wading through purple heather, leaping streams, and fording the Rough Burn, we came under the cliffs. At the head of a rocky cove was the Ben Nuis Chimney, the titbit that Oppenheimer had reserved for our refined palates. Was it easy or difficult? We could not make up our minds, but we inclined to the former opinion, and at all events were engrossed with the problem of what we would do afterwards. We were half-encircled by rocky peaks. There Ben Tarsuinn displayed a range of buttresses and chimneys, and sent down towards the glen a long, steep rift that suggested possibilities of all kinds. Between towered the pinnacles of A' Chir, Chir Mhor, and the rest. What a splendid ridge-walk for the ladies! And, when we had dispatched our chimney, there was an interesting cleft in the southern curtain of Ben Nuis—a sort of Doctor's Chimney, we called it, in recollection of the famous Lake District climb. We would do that in the afternoon; so we planned, while we sat at lunch round a bubbling source of delicious water below the chimney. We gave the trio of non-climbers rendezvous at the top; going round by the end of the cliffs, they would surely not be up very much sooner than we.

Our chimney runs from top to bottom of the crags a little south of the peak. Even at Brodick, the thin black line, four or five hundred feet long, is plainly visible, though one can hardly realise how profound is the fissure that it marks. The change in the angle of inclination halfway up is a feature that makes it easy to recognise. Scrambling up some steep grass, we came to the foot of our climb, and discovered at once the meaning of a musical murmuring that had tickled our ears—the gully was running with water. The pitch at the bottom was a water-slide about thirty-five feet high, with a thin stream spreading over a bed of rock a yard or two wide. But a drenching is the merest of trifles to our fugleman Puttrell when sport is in the wind, and light-heartedly and full of confidence he began to clamber up the watery slabs. Straightway, however, we received a lesson that might have taught us to leave such a climb alone, at least on the day after a downpour. Our leader strove in vain to establish any footing or handhold on the disintegrated granite—the rotten stuff crumbled at a touch. Time after time he endeavoured to advance; we each of us tried first one side of the slabs and then the other; we made hopeless attempts to scale the buttress to the right; but we succeeded only in getting well soaked, and tumbled back on one another in a heap. How these practically impossible things are ultimately done is not easy to explain. Neither Oppenheimer nor I succeeded finally in going up the water-slide without a certain measure of support from the rope; it would have wasted time to be too conscientious when once we had got a man on the top. But our leader by patient and plucky efforts won his way up, and was loudly cheered by us and by the friends watching from the fell-side. He managed to secure a grip, a sorry and doubtful grip it was, by standing on Oppenheimer's shoulders, who in turn was propped and steadied by me. Oppenheimer then held his foot while he struggled upwards an inch at a time, digging his toes into the mossy channel and spreading himself out so as to utilise every particle of friction. All this occupied an unconscionable length of time, and all the while the diverted stream was running through our comrade's clothes and bubbling out at his boots. From below, the rocks belied their nature. What looked like a handy knob proved to be a rounded corner impossible to grasp; it was so all the way up.

Above the water-slide a sharp slope of crumbling rock, down which, as the absence of loose fragments told us, a small torrent was wont to sweep in bad weather, led into a deep and gloomy recess, which a cluster of jammed blocks thirty feet up converted into a cave. This part of the chimney is not unlike the highest part of Moss Ghyll on Scawfell. The parallel walls are not quite vertical, so that one side overhangs, and a perpetual dropping of water sprinkled us bountifully. To propose climbing such a straight-walled cavern seemed absurd; its appearance was utterly forbidding. But Puttrell, with his usual alertness, saw a way up, and we trusted that fortune would make things easier beyond the natural bridge over the chasm. He mounted to this by his favourite method, back against one wall and feet against the other; we joined him, and sat on this curious perch for our first rest. A few feet higher a new difficulty begins, a pitch resembling the water-slide but much steeper. Two of us were not unwilling to beat a retreat when our leader's attempt to surmount this barrier failed; but he confronted it again, undaunted by the paucity of holds and the certainty of a disastrous fall if aught gave way. Once more he retired, and we had made up our minds to descend, when, moved by some reluctant impulse, he grappled with the obstacle again and, to our surprise, it yielded.

Beyond it we found ourselves in a deep and narrow cleft, with an inclined floor so slippery that we could maintain our position only by wedging with back and feet against the opposite walls. These walls streamed with moisture, which struck through and chilled us to the bone. A little way above us frowned an obstacle of a different kind. Massy fragments of rock had tumbled across and blocked up the chimney entirely, but for a hole in the roof of a funnel-shaped cave. Gazing upwards as well as we could in our constricted attitude, we saw our leading man climb laboriously to a point just under the cave, when he disappeared to one side. He was an extraordinary time making himself safe up there, and we began to wax impatient. His answer was to offer me the honour of leading straight up through the cave and the hole, as I was the slimmest of the three; this perilous course had no fascination. When, after a struggle, we joined him on a scanty ledge at the side, we found our situation critical. The chimney itself, in its wet condition, was too much for us; the great rock-masses enclosing it on this side were appallingly steep; the other side was a hopeless precipice. Could we retreat? We felt that such a course was hazardous in the extreme. The only way for the hindmost man, who of course could not be assisted by the rope, to return down the water-slide at the bottom was to slide—or tumble—down the slippery slope, trusting to luck for our catching him safely. And the water-slide, unfortunately, was not the most serious thing we had left in our rear.

We crept round a corner on to the face of the mountain. On a shelf overhung by the great rock buttressing the chimney we found a little plot of grass and bilberries, islanded amid the crags and hopelessly cut off from access in all directions save one. We sat down to divide our only refreshment, two tablets of chocolate; ate up the bilberries, and debated what was to be done. The painful feature of the situation was that our wives were on the fell-side yonder, and must by this time have surmised that something was amiss, since three or four hours had already elapsed and we were long overdue at the summit. They were visible as dots among the rocks and scree far down; we hoped the distance would save them from understanding how serious was our plight. One chance remained, but it was exceedingly hazardous and the issue uncertain. The rock overhanging the shelf where we sat had a steep corner at the side abutting on the chimney. Could we surmount this corner, we should at least get away from our shelf, and perchance the rocks would be easier above it. As a possible anchorage, a cleft was discovered going right through under the big rock, and having re-arranged the rope we threaded it here; I remained on the outside holding the rope, while the other two, being carefully secured, returned to the ledge on the inside wall. Puttrell now made a persevering attempt to climb the aforesaid corner, backed up by Oppenheimer. Twice he renewed the attempt, but was obliged at last to give it up. We scanned every inch of rock for the slightest possibility of another way over. No, there was absolutely nothing else to try. Were we to be driven to descend again by the chimney? Our hearts sank at the idea.

But I weighed a stone and a half less than Puttrell. Perhaps the two of them might support my weight a few inches higher on the corner, and so enable me to grasp some kind of hold. Once more the rope was re-arranged. Puttrell was lashed to the rock, while my rope was threaded through the hole and allowed to go out inch by inch as I ascended. I climbed on Puttrell's shoulders, then on to the steep corner, where he held my foot firmly against the rock while I stretched up towards a flimsy coating of grass and bilberry on the sloping top of the buttress. Would it hold even for a few moments while I scrambled across it? Spreading my body over the rock and digging both hands into the fibrous growth, I cautiously wriggled upwards and clutched an angle of the rock beyond. The first step was safely accomplished, but no direct advance was possible. The only hope was in a traverse out on the face of the cliff. Yet the outlook in that direction was far from inviting, overhanging blocks and steep slabs alternating with narrow strips of herbage; the holds were as scarce as ever. In a climb of any difficulty nothing is more disconcerting than a vegetable hold. I felt it was touch and go with me all the way; but at all events Oppenheimer with the threaded rope would be able to check me if I came off, the rocks were not jagged, and a fall would hardly be fatal. Nevertheless, I felt far from comfortable as I glanced down over some forty or fifty feet of boiler-plates to the grassy patch where my descent would probably end on the brink of a far deeper plunge. At one point, in balancing across a gap, with right foot on a sloping splinter and left hand pressed upon a rounded corner, I felt my fingers somehow come away. For the fraction of a second I thought myself gone; but regaining my balance, I shifted my weight across to the splinter, hardly daring to breathe, straddled the gap, and crept round the corner to a ledge. Thence, scrambling up a few feet, I worked my way slowly back to a point immediately above my two comrades, who of course were all the while concealed from view by the intervening rocks. The footing was bad, nothing but a yielding cushion of turf and bilberry; but it was wasting time to search for a rock-ledge. I must stand as firmly as possible and keep the rope taut as they came up, not giving them a chance to slip. It was an immense relief when Puttrell's head came into sight. With him safe, we both held the rope for Oppen-heimer.

And now we congratulated ourselves that the worst was over. Descending into our gully, we found we were on the roof of the cave that we dared not climb: after all these dangerous and com-plicated manoeuvres we had only ascended a few feet. But now, it seemed, everything changed for the better. Not only was the slope easier, but the tilt sideways, which had doubled the awkwardness of the lower portion, was not so acute. Heartened up by the prospect of a speedy escape, we went ahead again. It would be tedious to de-scribe the next few pitches in detail. They were neither so difficult as those we had climbed nor so exposed; better still, they were comparatively dry. After being converted into temporary water-courses, we felt this was something to be thankful for. Puttrell led up with his usual address, and all was going merrily, when he sud-denly looked back and informed us that we were stopped again. We hurried up to see what new monster stood in our path. We had reached a spot where the chimney expands into a wide cavity, with smooth walls on either hand, and, right in the angle, a deep, inner chimney continuing the line of the main fissure up and out of sight. This inner chimney overhung in one part, and here a mass of earth and ferns was lodged, resting apparently on a chock-stone. It was a complete barricade. We looked despairingly round. The right-hand buttress appeared unscalable. On the other side we were walled in by a cliff nearly sheer. It struck me that there was a bare possibility of a wary climber's finding a hard and dangerous way up it for some distance, but only in the last extremity; my suggestion met with no approval, and I was bound to confess that it looked a desperate venture.

Once more we climbed round the buttress on to the face. Here a grassy shelf extended for several yards, with a beetling wall above and a clear drop below strictly limiting our movements. It was an area as well defended against entrance or exit as the platform where we had been blockaded previously; and, to make it worse for any daring attempt of our leader to climb round the obstacles, there was no belay for the rope. Bitter was our disappointment. We had almost forgotten our friends on the hillside, who had been watching our proceedings all this while, and, though naturally too far away to see exactly what we were at, must naturally have been in a state of extreme disquietude. We could descry them on a curving shoulder of Ben Nuis that commanded a full-length view of the climb. We were on the stage, they in the dress-circle; and probably they were in momentary expectation of witnessing a tragedy. A shout came faintly on our ears, "How are you getting on?" Puttrell shouted in reply, "Only moderate." This was painting the situation in quiet colours. "Shall I go for a rope?" was the next message that we made out, after it had been twice repeated. We looked at each other, but no man assented to this extreme proposal, and the answer was, "Not yet."

We retired into the cavity. Puttrell tried the buttress, with very little hope of succeeding, by climbing on Oppenheimer's shoulders while I held them both with the rope; but the only result was that the human pyramid collapsed and Oppenheimer got his hand damaged. He tested the chimney, only to confirm his belief that it would not go. The outlook was as grim as grim could be. We held a few moments' debate. We had done our best, and there was no reasonable hope of extricating ourselves; we decided that a rope should be sent for. The necessary instructions were shouted to our friends, and Oppenheimer's brother at once started for Brodick to fetch a rescue party.

We had been in the chimney six hours. We were soaked to the skin, wretchedly cold, for the chimney looks north; we were as hungry as wolves. The rescuers would take hours to get here, they could not be expected till after nightfall; in all probability our deliverance could not be effected until dawn. Our faces grew rueful indeed when we thought of the night we were to spend in a place that had nothing to recommend it but its security. The novel and inglorious experience of being rescued had no charms. As a forlorn hope I went and examined the sheer left wall again. It was smooth and ledgeless except at the joints, where tufts of herbage sprouted, and here and there where the decayed rock left a crumbling corner sticking out that might lend a little support if handled gingerly. If it had to be tested, I was evidently the destined victim; both my comrades were too heavy to utilize such frail supports.

I was placed in the middle of the eighty-foot rope; they were at the ends. Oppenheimer stood well back in the recess, his duty being to jerk me in quickly in case of a fall. Puttrell stood further out, so as to catch me, if possible, in the descent. I crawled on to the lowest tuft with the utmost caution; it held whilst I brought all my weight up. Standing erect and scrambling on to the next tuft was an affair of nice balance. Once more I pulled myself cautiously erect. As I crept outwards and upwards, aslant, an uninterrupted view down the gully opened beneath me, and a touch on a flake of rock that had promised to be the key to the whole stratagem sent it clattering down the chasm. This forced me further to the right. One bigger flake, with a clump of vegetation wedged behind it, threatened to follow the other. There was no alternative—I had to embrace the possible foe; and it never budged while I swarmed on to the top, and there found myself at the end of my tether. With the hand disengaged I undid the rope, pulled it up, and tied myself on again at the end. Forty feet higher and seventy feet above my companions in adversity I found a safe stance, from which a plain and easy course appeared right to the summit. All shouted hilariously when I called out this cheering news. Puttrell came up in a few minutes, we let down the rope again for Oppenheimer; the tension was relaxed, and away we went up the hundred feet of rock and scree to the top. We came through a chaotic heap of boulders, with caves and dark passages between, beyond which we found the two ladies, who had stationed themselves to mark the spot for the rescuers. Their relief was not exceeded by ours, and, I need not say, we bitterly regretted the ordeal to which we had unwittingly condemned them. We had had the interest and excitement to sustain us; their suspense had not even had the relief of our transient successes. Thoroughly famished, we devoured the relics of the midday meal, and, still eating, set off rapidly towards the glen in the hope of forestalling the rescue party.

The sun set as we went down. Not only the forky pinnacles of Arran, but also the peaks of the mainland as far north as Ben Cruachan stood out against a sky of immaculate purity. Eastwards the cloudy outline of the Ayrshire hills marked, as it were, the boundaries of night. The encircling sea had the unearthly tints of evening; Ailsa Craig was a soft shadow floating on deep blues and violets; the stony crests all about us gleamed and flushed. What were physical discomforts and fatigue with such glories around us? The least beautiful side of Goat Fell, a wilderness of shapeless rock and scree, was radiant with light and colour, a splendid object rising out of the twilight depths of Glen Rosa. We dropped into the glen as darkness came on, and had not gone far when we met our friend coming up with a band of keepers, shepherds, and tourists, carrying lanterns, a long rope, and brandy. The last was the only succour of which we availed ourselves. We apologised for their disappointment; they congratulated us on our escape. The brandy came from a farm down the glen, and the farmer, we were told, though of the weaker sex, was man enough to promise us a horse-whipping as soon as she set eyes on us. No doubt we richly deserved it. Our own sufferings had some compensation afterwards, when we learned on sure authority that our climb had never been done before, and that several good men had been deterred by its ugly appearance. But the satisfaction was outweighed by the sense that our wives had suffered torments of anxiety through our rashness.

JOHN BUCHAN
(First Baron Tweedsmuir)

1875–1940

In his versatility John Buchan reminds one of his compatriot Sir Walter Scott. Like him Buchan was essentially a man of action, and the energy which characterized him as historian, biographer, novelist, publisher, politician, civil administrator, and traveler made him also a sportsman, equally interested in participation and reflection.

"Wood, sea, and hill," he wrote, "were the intimacies of my childhood, and they have never lost their spell for me." Doubtless these helped to determine his favorite sports—walking, fishing, deer-stalking, and climbing. He did not distinguish sharply among them and did not attempt the feats of the professional athlete. They were the recreations of a busy man of affairs and student. As a result of walking tours in Scotland while he was an undergraduate, he recalls in his autobiography, *Pilgrim's Way* (1940), that "the works of Aristotle are forever bound up for me with the smell of peat reek and certain stretches of granite and heather."

John Buchan climbed in South Africa, in the Dolomites, and on the Chamonix *aiguilles*, but early and late in life his primary field was Scotland, particularly the hills of the island of Skye, which he explored with unexampled thoroughness. Snow and ice did not strongly attract him, but rock-climbing he found an inexhaustible delight. Buchan himself states that after his marriage in 1907 he abandoned mountaineering "as scarcely a married man's game." This assertion must be taken advisedly, for he then concentrated on the slightly less arduous sport of deer-stalking. L. S. Amery, author of the obituary notice in *The Alpine Journal*, records that as late as 1937, when Buchan was Governor-General of Canada, he climbed the face of a severe cliff on the Mackenzie River.

Although his active participation in mountaineering undoubtedly declined with years, his interest in mountains remained vigorous. His direct contributions to the literature of mountaineering were few, but his novels generously provide descriptions vivid in themselves and often, as in the chapter from *The Three Hostages* given here, the scenes of exciting action. Although many of the place-names used are actual, the specific area can scarcely be identified.

The Three Hostages is a tale of adventure in which Sir Richard Hannay breaks up a gang of intriguers, led by Dominick Medina, who are trying to promote international chaos and war. Their chief tactical advantage is the custody of three young and high-born hostages. Sir Richard rescues all three and finally destroys the conspiracy. In the final chapter of the book, the defeated and unregenerate Medina seeks to revenge himself on Sir Richard.

The following selection is reprinted from John Buchan, *The Three Hostages*, Boston, Houghton Mifflin Co., 1924, by permission of the executors of the late John Buchan.

How I Stalked Wilder Game than Deer

I: 9 A.M. TO 2.15 P.M.

Obviously I could make no plan, and I had no clear idea in my head as to what kind of settlement I wanted with Medina. I was certain that I should find him somewhere on the hill, and that, if he got a chance, he would try to kill me. The odds were, of course, against his succeeding straight off, but escape was not what I sought—I must get rid of this menace forever. I don't think that I wanted to kill him, but indeed I never tried to analyse my feelings. I was obeying a blind instinct, and letting myself drift on the tides of fate.

Corrie-na-Sidhe is an upper corrie, separated from the Aicill valley by a curtain of rock and scree which I daresay was once the moraine of a glacier and down which the Alt-na-Sidhe tumbled in a fine chain of cascades. So steep is its fall that no fish can ascend it, so that, while at the foot it is full of sizable trout, in the corrie itself it holds nothing, as Greenslade reported, but little dark fingerlings. It was very warm as we mounted the chaos of slabs and boulders, where a very sketchy and winding track had been cut for bringing down the deer. Only the toughest kind of pony could make that ascent. Though the day was young the heat was already great, and the glen behind us swam in a glassy sheen. Kennedy, as usual, mopped his brow and grunted, but the lean Angus strode ahead as if he were on the flat.

At the edge of the corrie we halted for a spy. Deep hollows have a trick of drawing the wind, and such faint currents of air as I could detect seemed to be coming on our left rear from the north-east. Angus was positive, however, that though the south had gone out of the wind, it was pretty well due east, with no north in it, and maintained that when we were farther up the corrie we would have it fair on our left cheek. We were not long in finding beasts. There was a big drove of hinds on the right bank of the burn, and another lot, with a few small stags, on the left bank, well up on the face of Bheinn Fhada. But there was nothing shootable there.

"The big stags will be all on the high tops," said Angus. "We must be getting up to the burnhead."

It was easier said than done, for there were the hinds to be cir-cumvented, so we had to make a long circuit far up the hill called Clonlet, which is the westernmost of the Machray tops south of the Aicill. It was rough going, for we mounted to about the three thousand feet level, and traversed the hill-side just under the upper scarp of rock. Presently we were looking down upon the cup which was the head of the corrie, and over the col could see the peak of Stob Coire Easain and the ridge of Stob Ban, both on Haripol and beyond the Reascuill. We had another spy, and made out two small lots of stags on the other side of the Alt-na-Sidhe. They were too far off to get a proper view of them, but one or two looked good beasts, and I decided to get nearer.

We had to make a cautious descent of the hill-side in case of deer lying in pockets, for the place was seamed with gullies. Before we were halfway down I got my telescope on one of the lots, and picked out a big stag with a poor head, which clearly wanted shooting. Angus agreed, and we started down a sheltering ravine to get to the burnside. The sight of a quarry made me forget everything else, and for the next hour and a half I hadn't a thought in the world except how to get within range of that beast. One stalk is very much like another, and I am not going to describe this. The only trouble came from a small stag in our rear, which had come over Clonlet and got the scent of our track on the hill-face. This unsettled him and he went off at a great pace towards the top of the burn. I thought at first that the brute would go up Bheinn Fhada and carry off our lot with him, but he came to a halt, changed his mind, and made for the Haripol march and the col.

After that it was plain sailing. We crawled up the right of the Alt-na-Sidhe, which was first-class cover, and then turned up a tributary gully which came down from Bheinn Fhada. Indeed the whole business was too simple to be of much interest to any one, except the man with the rifle. When I judged I was about the latitude of my stag, I crept out of the burn and reached a hillock from which I had a good view of him. The head, as I suspected, was poor—only nine points, though the horns were of the rough, thick, old Highland type, but the body was heavy, and he was clearly a back-going beast. After a wait of some twenty minutes he got up and gave me a chance at about two hundred yards, and I dropped him dead with a shot in the neck, which was the only part of him clear.

It was for me the first stag of the season, and it is always a pleasant moment when the tension relaxes and you light your pipe and look around you. As soon as the gralloch was over I proposed lunch, and we found for the purpose a little nook by a spring. We were within a few hundred yards of the Haripol march, which there does not run along the watershed but crosses the corrie about half a mile below the col. In the old days of sheep there had been a fence, the decaying posts of which could be observed a little way off on a knoll. Between the fence and the col lay some very rough ground, where the Alt-na-Sidhe had its source, ground so broken that it was impossible, without going a good way up the hill, to see from it the watershed ridge.

I finished Mary's stuffed scones and ginger biscuits, and had a drink of whisky and spring water, while Angus and Kennedy ate their lunch a few yards off in the heather. I was just lighting my pipe, when a sound made me pause with the match in my hand. A rifle bullet sang over my head. It was not very near—fifty feet or so above me, and a little to the left.

"The tamned towrists!" I heard Angus exclaim.

I knew it was Medina as certainly as if I had seen him. He was somewhere in the rough ground between the Haripol march and the col—probably close to the col, for the sound of the report seemed to come from a good way off. He could not have been aiming at me, for I was perfectly covered, but he must have seen me when I stalked the stag. He had decided that his chance was not yet come, and the shot was camouflage—to keep up the reputation of Haripol for wild shooting.

"It would be the staggie that went over the march," grunted Angus. "The towrists—to be shooting at such a wee beast!"

I had suddenly made up my mind. I would give Medina the opportunity he sought. I would go and look for him.

I got up and stretched my legs. "I'm going to try a stalk on my own," I told Angus. "I'll go over to Corrie Easain. You had better pull this beast down to the burnside, and then fetch the pony. You might send Hughie and the other pony up Glenaicill to the Mad Burn. If I get a stag I'll gralloch him and get him down somehow to the burn, so tell Hughie to look out for my signal. I'll wave a white handerchief. The wind is backing round to the north, Angus. It should be all right for Corrie Easain, if I take it from south."

"It would be better for Sgurr Dearg," said Angus, "but that's ower far. Have you the cartridges, sir?"

"Plenty," I said, patting a side pocket. "Give me that spare rope, Kennedy. I'll want it for hauling down my stag, if I get one."

I put my little .240 into its cover, nodded to the men, and turned down the gully to the main burn. I wasn't going to appear on the bare hill-side so long as it was possible for Medina to have a shot at me. But soon a ridge shut off the view from the Haripol ground, and I then took a slant up the face of Bheinn Fhada.

Mary had spent most of the morning at the big telescope in the library window. She saw us reach the rim of the corrie and lost us when we moved up the side of Clonlet. We came into view again far up the corrie, and she saw the stalk and the death of the stag. Then she went to luncheon, but hastened back in the middle of it in time to see me scrambling alone among the screes of Bheinn Fhada. At first she was reassured because she thought I was coming home. But when she realised that I was mounting higher and was making for Corrie Easain her heart sank, and, when I had gone out of view, she could do nothing but range miserably about the garden.

II: 2.15 P.M. TO ABOUT 5 P.M.

It was very hot on Bheinn Fhada, for I was out of the wind, but when I reached the ridge and looked down on Corrie Easain I found a fair breeze, which had certainly more north than east in it. There was not a cloud in the sky, and every top for miles round stood out clear, except the Haripol peaks which were shut off by the highest part of the ridge I stood on. Corrie Easain lay far below—not a broad cup like Corrie-na-Sidhe, but a deep gash in the hills, inclined at such an angle that the stream in it was nothing but white water. We called it the Mad Burn—its Gaelic name, I think, was the Alt-a-mhuillin— and halfway up and just opposite me a tributary, the Red Burn, came down from the cliffs of Sgurr Dearg. I could see the northern peak of that mountain, a beautiful cone of rock, rising like the Matterhorn from its glacis of scree.

I argued that Medina would have seen me going up Bheinn Fhada and would assume that I was bound for Corrie Easain. He would recross the col and make for the Haripol side of the *beallach* which led from that corrie to the Reascuill. Now I wanted to keep to the higher ground, where I could follow his movements, so it was my aim to get to the watershed ridge looking down on Haripol before he did. The wind was a nuisance, for it was blowing from me and would move any deer towards him, thereby giving him a clue to my whereabouts. So I thought that if I could once locate him, I must try to get to the lee side of him. At that time I think I had a vague notion of driving him towards Machray.

I moved at my best pace along the east face of Bheinn Fhada towards the *beallach*—which was a deep rift in the grey rock-curtain through which deer could pass. My only feeling was excitement, such as I had never known before in any stalk. I slipped and sprawled among the slabs, slithered over the screes, had one or two awkward traverses round the butt-end of cliffs, but in about twenty minutes I was at the point where the *massif* of Bheinn Fhada joined the watershed ridge. The easy way was now to get on to the ridge, but I dared not appear on the sky-line, so I made a troublesome journey along the near side of the ridge-wall, sometimes out on the face of sheer precipices, but more often involved in a chaos of loose boulders which were the débris of the upper rocks. I was forced pretty far down, and eventually struck the *beallach* path about five hundred feet below the summit.

At the crest I found I had no view of the Reascuill valley—only a narrow corrie blocked by a shoulder of hill and the bald top of Stob Coire Easain beyond. A prospect I must have, so I turned east along the watershed ridge in the direction of Sgurr Dearg. I was by this time very warm, for I had come at a brisk pace; I had a rifle to carry, and had Angus's rope round my shoulders like a Swiss guide; I was wearing an old grey suit, which, with bluish stockings, made me pretty well invisible on that hill-side. Presently as I mounted the ridge, keeping of course under the sky-line, I came to a place where a lift of rock enabled me to clear the spurs and command a mile or so of the Reascuill.

The place was on the sky-line, bare and exposed, and I crawled to the edge where I could get a view. Below me, after a few hundred yards of rocks and scree, I saw a long tract of bracken and deep heather sweeping down to the stream. Medina, I made sure, was somewhere thereabouts, watching the ridge. I calculated that with his recrossing of the col at the head of Corrie-na-Sidhe and his working round the south end of Bheinn Fhada, he could not have had time to get to the *beallach*, or near the *beallach*, before me, and must still be on the lower ground. Indeed I hoped to catch sight of him, for, while I was assured he was pursuing me, he could not know that I was after him and might be off his guard.

But there was no sign of life in that sunny stretch of green and purple, broken by the grey of boulders. I searched it with my glass and could see no movement except pipits, and a curlew by a patch of bog. Then it occurred to me to show myself. He must be made to know that I had accepted his challenge.

I stood up straight on the edge of the steep, and decided to remain standing till I had counted fifty. It was an insane thing to do, I daresay, but I was determined to force the pace. . . . I had got to forty-one without anything happening. Then a sudden instinct made me crouch and step aside. That movement was my salvation. There was a sound like a twanged fiddle-string, and a bullet passed over my left shoulder. I felt the wind of it on my cheek.

The next second I was on my back wriggling below the sky-line.

Once there I got to my feet and ran—up the ridge on my left to get a view from higher ground. The shot, so far as I could judge, had come from well below and a little to the east of where I had been standing. I found another knuckle of rock, and crept to the edge of it, so that I looked from between two boulders into the glen.

The place was still utterly quiet. My enemy was hidden there, probably not half a mile off, but there was nothing to reveal his presence. The light wind stirred the bog cotton, a merlin sailed across to Stob Coire Easain, a raven croaked in the crags, but these were the only sounds. There was not even a sign of deer.

My glass showed that halfway down an old ewe was feeding—one of those melancholy beasts which stray into a forest from adjacent sheep-ground, and lead a precarious life among the rocks, lean and matted and wild, till some gillie cuts their throats. They are far sharper-eyed and quicker of hearing than a stag, and an unmitigated curse to the stalker. The brute was feeding on a patch of turf near a big stretch of bracken, and suddenly I saw her raise her head and stare. It was the first time I had ever felt well disposed towards a sheep.

She was curious about something in a shallow gully which flanked the brackens, and so was I. I kept my glass glued on her, and saw her toss her disreputable head, stamp her foot, and then heard her whistle through her nose. This was a snag Medina could not have reckoned with. He was clearly in that gully, working his way upward in its cover, unwitting that the ewe was giving him away. I argued that he must want to reach the high ground as soon as possible. He had seen me on the ridge, and must naturally conclude that I had beaten a retreat. My first business, therefore, was to reassure him.

I got my rifle out of its cover, which I stuffed into my pocket. There was a little patch of gravel just on the lip of the gully, and I calculated that he would emerge beside it, under the shade of a blaeberry-covered stone. I guessed right . . . I saw first an arm, and then a shoulder part the rushes, and presently a face which peered up-hill. My glass showed me that the face was Medina's, very red, and dirty from contact with the peaty soil. He slowly reached for his glass, and began to scan the heights.

I don't know what my purpose was at this time, if indeed I had any purpose. I didn't exactly mean to kill him, I think, though I felt it might come to that. Vaguely I wanted to put him out of action, to put the fear of God into him, and make him come to terms. Of further consequences I never thought. But now I had one clear intention—to make him understand that I accepted his challenge.

I put a bullet neatly into the centre of the patch of gravel, and then got my glass on it. He knew the game all right. In a second like a weasel he was back in the gully.

I reckoned that now I had my chance. Along the ridge I went, mounting fast, and keeping always below the sky-line. I wanted to get to the lee side of him and so be able to stalk him up wind, and I thought that I had an opportunity now to turn the head of the Reascuill by one of the steep corries which descend from Sgurr Dearg. Looking back, it all seems very confused and amateurish, for what could I hope to do, even if I had the lee-side, beyond killing or wounding him? and I had a chance of that as long as I had the upper ground. But in the excitement of the chase the mind does not take long views, and I was enthralled by the crazy sport of the thing. I did not feel any fear, because I was not worrying about consequences.

Soon I came to the higher part of the ridge and saw frowning above me the great rock face of Sgurr Dearg. I saw, too, a thing I had forgotten. There was no way up that mountain direct from the ridge, for the tower rose as perpendicular as a house-wall. To surmount it a man must traverse on one side or the other—on the Machray side by a scree slope, or on the Haripol side by a deep gully which formed the top of the corrie into which I was now looking. Across that corrie was the first of the great buttresses which Sgurr Dearg sends down to the Reascuill. It was the famous Pinnacle Ridge (as mountaineers called it); I had climbed it three weeks before and found it pretty stiff; but then I had kept the ridge all the way from the valley bottom, and I did not see any practicable road up the corrie face of it, which seemed nothing but slabs and rotten rocks, while the few chimneys had ugly overhangs.

I lay flat and reconnoitred. What was Medina likely to do? After my shot he could not follow up the ridge—the cover was too poor on the upper slopes. I reasoned that he would keep on in the broken ground up the glen till he reached this corrie, and try to find a road to the high ground either by the corrie itself or by one of the spurs. In that case it was my business to wait for him. But first I thought I had better put a fresh clip in my magazine, for the shot I had fired had been the last cartridge in the old clip.

It was now that I made an appalling discovery. I had felt my pockets and told Angus that I had plenty of cartridges. So I had, but they didn't fit. . . . I remembered that two days before I had lent Archie my .240 and had been shooting with a Mannlicher. What I had in my pocket were Mannlicher clips left over from that day. . . . I might chuck my rifle away, for it was no more use than a poker.

At first I was stunned by the fatality. Here was I, engaged in a duel on a wild mountain with one of the best shots in the world, and I had lost my gun! The sensible course would have been to go home. There was plenty of time for that, and long before Medina reached the ridge I could be in cover in the gorge of the Mad Burn. But that way out of it never occurred to me. I had chosen to set the course, and the game must be played out here and now. But I confess I was pretty well in despair and could see no plan. I think I had a faint hope of protracting the thing till dark and then trusting to my hill-craft to get even with him, but I had an unpleasant feeling that he was not likely to oblige me with so long a delay.

I forced myself to think, and decided that Medina would either come up the corrie or take the steep spur which formed the right-hand side of it and ran down to the Reascuill. The second route would give him cover, but also render him liable to a surprise at close quarters if I divined his intention, for I might suddenly confront him four yards off at the top of one of the pitches. He would there-fore prefer the corrie, which was magnificently broken up with rocks, and seamed with ravines, and at the same time gave a clear view of all the higher ground.

With my face in a clump of louse-wort I raked the place with my glass; and to my delight saw deer feeding about halfway down in the right-hand corner. Medina could not ascend the corrie without dis-turbing these deer—a batch of some thirty hinds, with five small and two fairish stags among them. Therefore I was protected from that side, and had only the ridge to watch.

But as I lay there I thought of another plan. Medina, I was pretty certain, would try the corrie first, and would not see the deer till he was well inside it, for they were on a kind of platform which hid them from below. Opposite me across the narrow corrie rose the great black wall of the Pinnacle Ridge, with the wind blowing from me towards it. I remembered a trick which Angus had taught me— how a stalker might have his wind carried against the face of an opposite mountain and then, so to speak, reflected from it and brought back to his own side, so that deer below him would get it and move away from it up *towards him*. If I let my scent be carried to the Pinnacle Ridge and diverted back, it would move the deer on the platform up the corrie towards me. It would be a faint wind, so they would move slowly away from it—no doubt towards a gap under the tower of Sgurr Dearg which led to the little corrie at the head of the Red Burn. We never stalked that corrie because it was impossible to get a stag out of it without cutting him up, so the place was a kind of sanctuary to which disturbed deer would naturally resort.

I stood on the sky-line, being confident that Medina could not yet be within sight, and let the wind, which was now stronger and nearly due north, ruffle my hair. I did this for about five minutes, and then lay down to watch the result, with my glass on the deer. Presently I saw them become restless, first the hinds and then the small stags lifting their heads and looking towards the Pinnacle Ridge. Soon a little fellow trotted a few yards up-hill; then a couple of hinds moved after him; and then by a sudden and simultaneous impulse the whole party began to drift up the corrie. It was a quiet steady advance; they were not scared, only a little doubtful. I saw with satisfaction that their objective seemed to be the gap which led over to the Red Burn.

Medina must see this and would assume that wherever I was I was not ahead of the deer. He might look for me on the other side, but more likely would follow the beasts so as to get the high ground. Once there he could see my movements, whether I was on the slopes of the Pinnacle Ridge, or down on the Machray side. He would consider no doubt that his marksmanship was so infinitely better than mine that he had only to pick me out from the landscape to make an end of the business.

What I exactly intended I do not know. I had a fleeting notion of lying hidden and surprising him, but the chances against that were about a million to one, and even if I got him at close quarters he was armed and I was not. I moved a little to the right so as to keep my wind from the deer, and waited with a chill beginning to creep over my spirit. . . . My watch told me it was five o'clock. Mary and Peter John would be having tea among the Prince Charlie roses, and Greenslade and Archie coming up from the river. It would be heavenly at Machray now among greenery and the cool airs of evening. Up here there was loveliness enough, from the stars of butterwort and grass of Parnassus by the well-heads to the solemn tops of Sgurr Dearg, the colour of stormy waves against a faint turquoise sky. But I knew now that the beauty of earth depends on the eye of the beholder, for suddenly the clean airy world around me had grown leaden and stifling.

III: 5 P.M. TO ABOUT 7.30 P.M.

It was a good hour before he came. I had guessed rightly, and he had made the deduction I hoped for. He was following the deer towards the gap, assuming that I was on the Machray side. I was in a rushy hollow at a junction of the main ridge and the spur I have mentioned, and I could see him clearly, as, with immense circumspection and the use of every scrap of cover, he made his way up the corrie. Once he was over the watershed, I would command him from the higher ground and have the wind to my vantage. I had some hope now, for I ought to be able to keep him on the hill till the light failed, when my superior local knowledge would come to my aid. He must be growing tired, I reflected, for he had had far more ground to cover. For myself I felt that I could go on forever.

That might have been the course of events but for a second sheep. Sgurr Dearg had always been noted for possessing a few sheep even on its high rocks—infernal tattered outlaws, strays originally from some decent flock, but now to all intents a new species, unclassified by science. How they lived and bred I knew not, but there was a legend of many a good stalk ruined by their diabolical cunning. I heard something between a snort and a whistle behind me, and, screwing my head round, saw one of these confounded animals poised on a rock and looking in my direction. It could see me perfectly, too, for on that side I had no cover.

I lay like a mouse watching Medina. He was about half a mile off, almost on the top of the corrie, and he had halted for a rest and a spy. I prayed fervently that he would not see the sheep.

He heard it. The brute started its whistling and coughing, and a novice could have seen that it suspected something and knew where that something was. I observed him get his glass on my lair, though from the place where he was he could see nothing but rushes. Then he seemed to make up his mind and suddenly disappeared from view.

I knew what he was after. He had dropped into a scaur, which would take him to the sky-line and enable him to come down on me from above, while he himself would be safe from my observation.

There was nothing to do but to clear out. The spur dropping to the Reascuill seemed to give me the best chance, so I started off, crouching and crawling, to get round the nose of it and on to the steep glen-ward face. It was a miserable job till I had turned the corner, for I expected every moment a bullet in my back. Nothing happened, however, and soon I was slithering down awesome slabs on to insecure ledges of heather. I am a fairly experienced mountaineer, and a lover of rock, but I dislike vegetation mixed up with a climb, and I had too much of it now. There was perhaps a thousand feet of that spur, and I think I must hold the speed record for its descent. Scratched, bruised, and breathless, I came to anchor on a bed of screes, with the infant Reascuill tumbling below me, and beyond it, a quarter of a mile off, the black cliffs of the Pinnacle Ridge.

But what was my next step to be? The position was reversed. Medina was above me with a rifle, and my own weapon was useless. He must find out the road I had taken and would be after me like a flame. . . . It was no good going down the glen; in the open ground he would get the chance of twenty shots. It was no good sticking to the spur or the adjacent ridge, for the cover was bad. I could not hide for long in the corrie. . . . Then I looked towards the Pinnacle Ridge and considered that, once I got into those dark couloirs, I might be safe. The Psalmist had turned to the hills for his help—I had better look to the rocks.

I had a quarter of a mile of open to cross, and a good deal more if I was to reach the ridge at a point easy of ascent. There were chimneys in front of me, deep black gashes, but my recollection of them was that they had looked horribly difficult, and had been plentifully supplied with overhangs. Supposing I got into one of them and stuck. Medina would have me safe enough. . . . But I couldn't wait to think. With an ugly cold feeling in my insides I got into the ravine of the burn, and had a long drink from a pool. Then I started downstream, keeping close to the right-hand bank, which mercifully was high and dotted with rowan saplings. And as I went I was always turning my head to see behind and above me what I feared.

I think Medina, who of course did not know about my rifle, may have suspected a trap, for he came on slowly, and when I caught sight of him it was not on the spur I had descended but farther up the corrie. Two things I now realised. One was that I could not make the easy end of the Pinnacle Ridge without exposing myself on some particularly bare ground. The other was that to my left in the Ridge was a deep gully which looked climbable. Moreover the foot of that gully was not a hundred yards from the burn, and the mouth was so deep that a man would find shelter as soon as he entered it.

For the moment I could not see Medina, and I don't think he had yet caught sight of me. There was a trickle of water coming down from the gully to the burn, and that gave me an apology for cover. I ground my nose into the flowe-moss and let the water trickle down my neck, as I squirmed my way up, praying hard that my enemy's eyes might be sealed.

I think I had got about halfway, when a turn gave me a view of the corrie, and there was Medina halted and looking towards me. By the mercy of Providence my boots were out of sight, and my head a little lower than my shoulders, so that I suppose among the sand and gravel and rushes I must have been hard to detect. Had he used his telescope I think he must have spotted me, though I am not certain. I saw him staring. I saw him half raise his rifle to his shoulder, while I heard my heart thump. Then he lowered his weapon, and moved out of sight.

Two minutes later I was inside the gully.

The place ran in like a cave with a sandy floor, and then came a steep pitch of rock, while the sides narrowed into a chimney. This was not very difficult. I swung myself up into the second storey, and found that the cleft was so deep that the back wall was about three yards from the opening, so that I climbed in almost complete darkness and in perfect safety from view. This went on for about fifty feet, and then, after a rather awkward chockstone, I came to a fork. The branch on the left looked hopeless, while that on the right seemed to offer some chances. But I stopped to consider, for I remembered something.

I remembered that this was the chimney which I had prospected three weeks before when I climbed the Pinnacle Ridge. I had prospected it from above, and had come to the conclusion that, while the left fork *might* be climbed, the right was impossible or nearly so, for modestly as it began, it ran out into a fearsome crack on the face of the cliff, and did not become a chimney again till after a hundred feet of unclimbable rotten granite.

So I tried the left fork, which looked horribly unpromising. The first trouble was a chockstone, which I managed to climb round, and then the confounded thing widened and became perpendicular. I remembered that I had believed a way could be found by taking to the right-hand face, and in the excitement of the climb I forgot all precautions. It simply did not occur to me that this face route might bring me in sight of eyes which at all costs I must avoid.

It was not an easy business, for there was an extreme poverty of decent holds. But I have done worse pitches in my time, and had I not had a rifle to carry (I had no sling), might have thought less of it. Very soon I was past the worst, and saw my way to returning to the chimney, which had once more become reasonable. I stopped for a second to prospect the route, with my foot on a sound ledge, my right elbow crooked round a jag of rock, and my left hand, which held the rifle, stretched out so that my fingers could test the soundness of a certain handhold.

Suddenly I felt the power go out of those fingers. The stone seemed to crumble and splinters flew into my eye. There was a crashing of echoes, which drowned the noise of my rifle as it clattered down the precipice. I remember looking at my hand spread-eagled against the rock, and wondering why it looked so strange.

The light was just beginning to fail, so it must have been about half-past seven.

IV: 7.30 P.M. AND ONWARDS

Had anything of the sort happened to me during an ordinary climb I should beyond doubt have lost my footing with the shock and fallen. But, being pursued, I suppose my nerves were keyed to a perpetual expectancy, and I did not slip. The fear of a second bullet saved my life. In a trice I was back in the chimney, and the second bullet spent itself harmlessly on the granite.

Mercifully it was now easier going—honest knee-and-back work, which I could manage in spite of my shattered fingers. I climbed feverishly with a cold sweat on my brow, but every muscle was in order, and I knew I would make no mistake. The chimney was deep, and a ledge of rock hid me from my enemy below. . . . Presently I squeezed through a gap, swung myself up with my right hand and my knees to a shelf, and saw that the difficulties were over. A shallow gully, filled with screes, led up to the crest of the ridge. It was the place I had looked down on three weeks before.

I examined my left hand, which was in a horrid mess. The top of my thumb was blown off, and the two top joints of my middle and third fingers were smashed to pulp. I felt no pain in them, though they were dripping blood, but I had a queer numbness in my left shoulder. I managed to bind the hand up in a handkerchief, where it made a gory bundle. Then I tried to collect my wits.

Medina was coming up the chimney after me. He knew I had no rifle. He was, as I had heard, an expert cragsman, and he was the younger man by at least ten years. My first thought was to make for the upper part of the Pinnacle Ridge, and try to hide or to elude him somehow till the darkness. But he could follow me in the transparent Northern night, and I must soon weaken from loss of blood. I could not hope to put sufficient distance between us for safety, and he had his deadly rifle. Somewhere in the night or in the dawning he would get me. No, I must stay and fight it out.

Could I hold the chimney? I had no weapon but stones, but I

might be able to prevent a man ascending by those intricate rocks. In the chimney at any rate there was cover, and he could not use his rifle. But would he try the chimney? Why should he not go round by the lower slopes of the Pinnacle Ridge and come on me from above?

It was the dread of his bullets that decided me. My one passionate longing was for cover. I might get him in a place where his rifle was useless and I had a chance to use my greater muscular strength. I did not care what happened to me provided I got my hands on him. Behind all my fear and confusion and pain there was now a cold fury of rage.

So I slipped back into the chimney and descended it to where it turned slightly to the left past a nose of rock. Here I had cover, and could peer down into the darkening deeps of the great couloir.

A purple haze filled the corrie, and the Machray tops were like dull amethysts. The sky was a cloudy blue sprinkled with stars, and mingled with the last flush of sunset was the first tide of the afterglow. . . . At first all was quiet in the gully. I heard the faint trickle of stones which are always falling in such a place, and once the croak of a hungry raven. . . . Was my enemy there? Did he know of the easier route up the Pinnacle Ridge? Would he not assume that if I could climb the cleft he could follow, and would he feel any dread of a man with no gun and a shattered hand?

Then from far below came a sound I recognised—iron hobnails on rock. I began to collect loose stones and made a little pile of such ammunition beside me . . . I realised that Medina had begun the ascent of the lower pitches. Every breach in the stillness was perfectly clear—the steady scraping in the chimney, the fall of a fragment of rock as he surmounted the lower chockstone, the scraping again as he was forced out on to the containing wall. The light must have been poor, but the road was plain. Of course I saw nothing of him, for a bulge prevented me, but my ears told me the story. Then there was silence. I realised that he had come to the place where the chimney forked.

I had my stones ready, for I hoped to get him when he was driven out on the face at the overhang, the spot where I had been when he fired.

The sounds began again, and I waited in a desperate choking calm. In a minute or two would come the crisis. I remember that the after-glow was on the Machray tops and made a pale light in the corrie below. In the cleft there was still a kind of dim twilight. Any moment I expected to see a dark thing in movement fifty feet below, which would be Medina's head.

But it did not come. The noise of scraped rock still continued, but it seemed to draw no nearer. Then I realised that I had misjudged the situation. Medina had taken the right-hand fork. He was bound to, unless he had made, like me, an earlier reconnaissance. My route in the half-light must have looked starkly impossible.

The odds were now on my side. No man in the fast-gathering darkness could hope to climb the cliff face and rejoin that chimney after its interruption. He would go on till he stuck—and then it would not be too easy to get back. I reascended my own cleft, for I had a notion that I might traverse across the space between the two forks, and find a vantage point for a view.

Very slowly and painfully, for my left arm was beginning to burn like fire and my left shoulder and neck to feel strangely paralysed, I wriggled across the steep face till I found a sort of *gendarme* of rock, beyond which the cliff fell smoothly to the lip of the other fork. The great gully below was now a pit of darkness, but the after-glow still lingered on this upper section and I saw clearly where Medina's chimney lay, where it narrowed and where it ran out. I fixed myself so as to prevent myself falling, for I feared I was becoming light-headed. Then I remembered Angus's rope, got it unrolled, took a coil round my waist, and made a hitch over the *gendarme*.

There was a smothered cry from below, and suddenly came the ring of metal on stone, and then a clatter of something falling. I knew what it meant. Medina's rifle had gone the way of mine and lay now among the boulders at the chimney foot. At last we stood on equal terms, and, befogged as my mind was, I saw that nothing now could stand between us and a settlement.

It seemed to me that I saw something moving in the half-light. If it was Medina, he had left the chimney and was trying the face. That way I knew there was no hope. He would be forced back, and surely would soon realise the folly of it and descend. Now that his rifle had gone my hatred had ebbed. I seemed only to be watching a fellow-mountaineer in a quandary.

He could not have been forty feet from me, for I heard his quick breathing. He was striving hard for holds, and the rock must have been rotten, for there was a continuous dropping of fragments, and once a considerable boulder hurtled down the couloir.

"Go back, man," I cried instinctively. "Back to the chimney. You can't get further that way."

I suppose he heard me, for he made a more violent effort, and I thought I could see him sprawl at a foothold which he missed, and then swing out on his hands. He was evidently weakening, for I heard a sob of weariness. If he could not regain the chimney, there was three hundred feet of a fall to the boulders at the foot.

"Medina," I yelled, "I've a rope. I'm going to send it down to you. Get your arm in the loop."

I made a noose at the end with my teeth and my right hand, working with a maniac's fury.

"I'll fling it straight out," I cried. "Catch it when it falls to you."

My cast was good enough, but he let it pass, and the rope dangled down into the abyss.

"Oh, damn it, man," I roared, "you can trust me. We'll have it out when I get you safe. You'll break your neck if you hang there."

Again I threw, and suddenly the rope tightened. He believed my word, and I think that was the greatest compliment ever paid me in all my days.

"Now you're held," I cried. "I've got a belay here. Try and climb back into the chimney."

He understood and began to move. But his arms and legs must have been numb with fatigue, for suddenly that happened which I feared. There was a wild slipping and plunging, and then he swung out limply missing the chimney, right on to the smooth wall of the cliff.

There was nothing for it but to haul him back. I knew Angus's ropes too well to have any confidence in them, and I had only the one good hand. The rope ran through a groove of stone which I had covered with my coat, and I hoped to work it even with a single arm by moving slowly upwards.

"I'll pull you up," I yelled, "but for God's sake give me some help. Don't hang on the rope more than you need."

My loop was a large one and I think he had got both arms through it. He was a monstrous weight, limp and dead as a sack, for though I could feel him scraping and kicking at the cliff face, the rock was too smooth for fissures. I held the rope with my feet planted against boulders, and wrought till my muscles cracked. Inch by inch I was drawing him in, till I realised the danger.

The rope was grating on the sharp brink beyond the chimney and might at any moment be cut by a knife-edge.

"Medina"—my voice must have been like a wild animal's scream —"this is too dangerous. I'm going to let you down a bit so that you can traverse. There's a sort of ledge down there. For heaven's sake go canny with this rope."

I slipped the belay from the *gendarme*, and hideously difficult it was. Then I moved farther down to a little platform nearer the chimney. This gave me about six extra yards.

"Now," I cried, when I had let him slip down, "a little to your left. Do you feel the ledge?"

He had found some sort of foothold, and for a moment there was a relaxation of the strain. The rope swayed to my right towards the chimney. I began to see a glimmer of hope.

"Cheer up," I cried. "Once in the chimney you're safe. Sing out when you reach it."

The answer out of the darkness was a sob. I think giddiness must have overtaken him, or that atrophy of muscle which is the peril of rock-climbing. Suddenly the rope scorched my fingers and a shock came on my middle which dragged me to the very edge of the abyss.

I still believe that I could have saved him if I had the use of both my hands, for I could have guided the rope away from that fatal knife-edge. I knew it was hopeless, but I put every ounce of strength and will into the effort to swing it with its burden into the chimney. He gave me no help, for I think—I hope—that he was unconscious.

Next second the strands had parted, and I fell back with a sound in my ears which I pray God I may never hear again—the sound of a body rebounding fully from crag to crag, and then a long soft rumbling of screes like a snowslip.

I managed to crawl the few yards to the anchorage of the *gendarme* before my senses left me. There in the morning Mary and Angus found me.

ALFRED DENIS GODLEY

1856–1925

A. D. Godley was, in the phrase of a memorialist, "one of the blessed company of purely natural scholars." For most of his life he was associated with Oxford, as an undergraduate and from 1883 to 1912 as a fellow and tutor of Magdalen College. In 1910 he was appointed Public Orator. After his retirement he became an honorary fellow and in 1919 consented to receive an honorary doctorate. Even his war service was Oxonian. He commanded the regiment of Oxfordshire Volunteers, engaged largely in home defense and guard duty. He achieved a colonelcy and was awarded the Order of the British Empire, Fourth Class.

His works of serious scholarship include an edition of Tacitus, translations of Horace and Herodotus, *Socrates and Athenian Society*, and *Oxford in the Eighteenth Century*. More famous is his light verse, which appeared in a variety of journals of belles lettres, particularly the *Oxford Magazine*. Partisans have contended that his four volumes of humorous poetry—*Verses to Order, Lyra Frivola, Second Strings*, and *The Casual Ward*—entitle him to a rank equal with that of Charles Stuart Calverley among the bards of mirth.

Godley first visited Switzerland in 1875 and returned to climb many times thereafter. He exerted himself in the Lake District, and at Oxford he was known as a mighty walker. He became a member of the Alpine Club in 1870 and a Vice-President in 1923. His Alpine papers, though few, are direct expressions of a quiet and engaging personality—witty, conservative, and slightly melancholy. The editor of two volumes of *Reliquiae* believes them "almost the best of his prose writings."

The following selection, first published in *The Alpine Journal*, XXXVII (May, 1925), 107–17, is reprinted from *Reliquiae A. D. Godley*, two volumes, edited by C. R. L. Fletcher, Oxford, University Press, 1926, by permission of the Alpine Club.

Mountains and the Public

THE SUBJECT . . . of this paper being mountaineering and the popular attitude towards it, it is convenient for me that the Dean of St. Paul's should have lately written an article on the same theme: a paper which might, indeed, have provided mine with a reason for existence. . . .

The Dean has published some strictures on the mental attitude of those who go, like ourselves, to mountains for recreation. Dr. Inge, who is satisfied with so few things in this present world, is sadly dissatisfied with our manner of life in our holidays among mountains; he says so in an article which he calls "The Return to Barbarism." [1] Now we need not quarrel with the title, which, indeed, shows the author in a mood of comparative optimism; for if we return to barbarism, we must at some time have temporarily emerged from it, and I think you will acknowledge that that is a striking admission, for the Dean. . . . But in the article itself the writer relapses into his usual severity. We do not adopt a proper mental attitude in face of mountain scenery. We take our Wordsworth to the hills (so Dr. Inge says, and I am sincerely glad to hear it), but this laudable practice does us very little good. For a man may have Wordsworth in his pocket, yet not be a Wordsworthian; he does not meditate as he ought, he spends far too little of his time in pure contemplation; so the vision of Wordsworth is not for him. "Most of us," says the Dean, "have to confess, with great disappointment, that we cannot feel what the poet did." The Dean is disappointed about a great many things; but I hardly think that most of us have a right to feel surprised and discouraged because we cannot reproduce Wordsworth's feelings in our own minds. Indeed, it seems that the poet himself had serious difficulties in this matter. . . . Can we hope to succeed where the poet himself sometimes failed? Assuredly the vision of Wordsworth is not for most of us; nor was it always even for him: "the things that I have seen I now can see no more."

[1] Unfortunately for the inquiring reader, Mr. Godley does not mention the name of the periodical in which the article appeared, and a search of contemporary files fails to disclose it.

Trying to recapture one's own emotions is a difficult business; trying to recapture someone else's rather recalls the stock definition of metaphysics—a blind man in a coal-cellar at midnight looking for a black hat which isn't there.

However this be, we might at least (says the Dean, and it is here that he does not quite see eye to eye with this Club) try to follow a better rule of life in the mountains. We ought to meditate more. "Most people," we are told, "hardly know what meditation means. They would be astonished if a philosopher told them that contemplation is the highest form of activity. Their idea of activity is the activity of a squirrel in a cage. So they approach the mountains in a wrong spirit. A mountain for them is a sort of glorified greased pole to be swarmed up. Perhaps some of them know what is best for them; but the vision of Wordsworth is not for them."

In this matter of meditation I cannot help thinking that the Dean demands too much of human nature—which is, after all, in its blind groping fashion, pursuing the Ultimate Good, but even in the mountains finds itself hampered by mortal weaknesses. . . . Meditation is indeed the highest form of activity: fortunate are they who can practice it! But how few of us, alas, have that command of their mental machinery which should enable them to meditate at will! It is, I fear, a matter of common experience; direct a man's attention to the grandiose and inspiring surroundings which meet his eyes, and command him to exercise his mind in such speculations as ought to be prompted by scenes of surpassing beauty or interest: will he attune his thinking faculties to his environment? The spirit is willing, the flesh is weak. With the best intentions in the world, he will in all probability at once become incapable of any kind of consecutive thinking. He will be smitten by a mental paralysis. If he retains any power of thought at all, he will find himself reflecting not on the great problems of Man, of Nature, and of human life, but rather on such topics as the relative advisability of walking down from the Riffel and going down by train, or the arguments for and against having afternoon tea again when he gets to the village; and it is not, I conceive, such topics as these which are commended to us by Dr. Inge. It is, in short, no good to tell people to meditate. They would if they could; but they can't. Anyhow, it is useless to suggest that they will meditate any better by avoiding the practice of going up mountains. I agree that the practice is impossible, or at least very difficult, at the moment of ascending the Grepon, or Doe Crag. He who in the act of scaling those altitudes should set himself to meditate coherently and consecutively on the Absolute would probably not have the opportunity of doing it again. But it does not follow that he will be the most inclined to meditation by looking at the mountains from below; for either he will go to sleep, or be a merely passive recipient of images of sensuous beauty; and neither state is consistent with truly philosophic contemplation.

Dr. Inge, it will be observed, includes under the same condemnation all who visit the mountains. Yet these are too vast and miscellaneous a multitude to be dealt with in this undiscriminating way. Now, after six years of restored peace and of post-war travel, with all its attendant embarrassments, we are perhaps in a position to consider the habits of those who once more go to the mountains for recreation. We can make some attempt to grapple with the psychology of new Europe, as we do with its geography. Even the Alps have not remained unchanged: it is there, in fact, that some of the characteristic impulses of modern times can be studied in a concentrated form. While the glacier, encouraged, no doubt, by its survey of the territorial readjustments which remodel Europe, descends with increasing boldness and increasing disregard of the convenience of its neighbors into the contiguous valley, the valley is also menaced by the irruptions of human hordes from below; and it is much to the credit of the original inhabitants that they make the best of such space as is still left to them, and derive an increasing advantage from both the glacier and the tourist. It is not my intention to speak at length of the glacier. As for the tourist, his multiplication is in part due to the war—the war, and the herd-like habit of congregation which is one of the inheritances which we derive from it. Partly from the self-protective herd-instinct, and partly from the difficulty of finding any other places of residence, we congregate in hotels, and we live and move by preference in crowds; and where shall you find more hotels and more crowds than in the Alps? And there have been particular national forces also at work. It was from no discourtesy but rather from a compelling sense of truth that must be uttered, that a Swiss traveller once enlarged to me on the welcome opportunity which the war had given to his countrymen of regaining possession of their own mountains during the temporary absence of the usual occupants. They had their opportunity; they took it. The Swiss have recovered their mountain resorts, and they keep them. . . . Meantime the beneficent activities of tourist agencies, among which it would be dangerous to select any for special commendation, continue to make trains a very fair imitation of the Black Hole of Calcutta—to inundate the shores of Lovely Lucerne—to devour like locusts all the available provisions of Glorious Grindelwald—and, no doubt, to gladden the hearts of shareholders in the Jungfrau Railway. But amid these miscellaneous multitudes, comparable to the migrant races of antiquity, there is but a small proportion of mountaineers. More and more climbers become, in most regions, a class separate and distinct. Where there are roads as well as mountains—in the Dolomites, for instance—the general public finds what danger it wants in motoring, and has nothing to do with the lesser perils of the Langkofel pinnacles or the Cimone della Pala. Ask your hotels of the mountaineer; they know him not, nor he them. There are refuges among the hills, where the necessaries of life can be obtained; among them the local climber lives and moves, only descending to the valleys—so we are told—when he wants a bath. . . .

There is, then, among the crowds who go to the mountains a gulf fixed between those who are mountaineers and those who are not. This is a general truth; and it is of the essence of a general truth that it remains valid in spite of observed facts which may appear to disprove it. There *are* such contradictory phenomena. Thus, it may be said (not without truth) that the world is not so sharply divided. There are people who visit the mountains in a proper spirit, although also in a *char-à-banc*. They are spiritually mountaineers; yet not in the highest and truest sense of the word, for which you will probably agree with me that a modicum of physical ascent is essential. Nevertheless, it is possible to allege that there may be mountaineers outside clubs. Then again, how are we to classify those persons who go up one mountain and no more? We must first know why they do it; and that is very difficult to ascertain. The commonly received account is, I believe, that they wish to say they have done it. This is very improbable; for by adopting an easy and obvious alternative they might save themselves some physical exertion, besides the tariff for a guide and porter. In the absence of any certain motive, it may be doubted by the judicious whether these occasional conformists should be assigned to the sheep or the goats. Personally, I am inclined to suspect the *animus* (though, it is true, a subsequent career may do something to rehabilitate them) of people who begin their career by ascending a peak which enjoys a great reputation: I cannot help fearing that their guiding motive may be the same as that which leads so many of you to the Amusements department at Wembley.

Observed facts, therefore, point to the conclusion that climbers are a class apart, aloof from the general public, which is out of sympathy with their aims and ideals. At least, this is my hypothesis; and it is supported by the criticisms of the Dean of St. Paul's. For there we have a writer and preacher of high intelligence and wide knowledge of the world, not only setting up impossible standards for mountaineers and even for tourists, but permitting himself to use intemperate language about greased poles and squirrels in cages; standing, in fact, as a type of that opinion which is based on a total misunderstanding of the spirit which animates this Club. For the Dean is not alone. He is giving eloquent expression to the sentiments entertained, I fear, by the majority of his countrymen; who, if they do not express themselves as picturesquely as the Dean, do for the most part regard the Alpine Club and its occupations with regrettable indifference—with a neutrality which is rather less than benevolent. This, of course, cannot be seriously excused; but it is susceptible of explanation. You will not, I trust, suspect me of any tendency to backsliding if I endeavour to set out the case against us as, no doubt, it presents itself to the public mind.

I will deal, therefore, with the influence exerted by the three great motives of Authority, Environment, and Inclination.

Authority, I fear, is not on the side of Alpinism. Take antiquity first: were I to weary you with a complete list of all the classical writers who have said very little about mountains, and nothing at all about their ascent, the record would include every author from the Trojan war to the fall of the Byzantine empire. You will tell me, no doubt, that Homer compares a warrior to a snowy mountain. He does so; but obviously it is because he wishes to illustrate the inconvenience and danger caused by the hero to those in his immediate proximity. The Romans, again, called mountains horrid. Some of you may argue that the proper meaning of *horridus* is not horrid in our sense, but simply bristling or spiky. I fear I have no time to discuss these points of scholarship, which do not invalidate the general truth that businesslike nations like the Greeks and Romans had no particular use for mountain scenery, and certainly none for mountain-climbing. To come to more recent periods: it is commonly held that Rousseau was the chief of those who taught our modern admiration of nature and scenery; but Rousseau's natural world was the world of the valleys and sub-Alpine hills. Our own great nature-poets of the Romantic period were, no doubt, attracted and inspired by mountain scenery; they saw the grandeur of the heights, but they did not see them as points to be attained; they did not countenance actual climbing. Even so lately as some eighty years ago Tennyson did not say "Come up, O maid, to yonder mountain height"; on the contrary, the lady, who is presumably climbing Alpine peaks, is definitely advised not to walk with Death and Morning on the silver horns, but to come down into the valley, where life offers a variety of far greater attractions.[2] Among poems of the nineteenth century, while many have celebrated the majesty of mountains, there is only one which is apparently in praise of climbing; and even there the fate of the climber is left problematical. I allude to *Excelsior*.

The case is not much better when we turn to eminent writers of prose; for Ruskin, who wrote beautifully about the form of mountains, condemned with no uncertain voice those who presumed to make a sport of climbing them.[3] It may be said that to set against

---

[2] See *The Princess*, VII, ll. 177–207.
[3] "You have despised Nature. . . . The Alps themselves which your own poets used to love so reverently, you look upon as soaped poles in a bear-garden, which you set yourselves to climb and slide down again." ("Of Kings' Treasuries," in *Sesame and Lilies* [Lecture 1, 1864], in *The Works of John Ruskin*, ed. by E. T. Cook and Alexander Wedderburn, London, George Allen, New York, Longmans, Green & Co., 1905, XVIII, 89–90.) Although Ruskin was not a mountaineer in the usual sense, he did some modest climbing in the Alps and was a member of the Alpine Club from 1869 to 1882. He "wrote beautifully about the form of mountains" principally in Volume IV of *Modern Painters*.

this we have the great Alpine literature of the nineteenth century. Alas! men do not, I fear, read their Leslie Stephen, their Tyndall, their Forbes, their Moore, their Coolidge, till they are on the right road already; the reading of these authors is more often the concomitant than the cause of conversion. And if literature speaks with no authoritative voice, much less does the example of our rude forefathers 150 years ago, or later. It was they who regarded the Apennines as bad enough, but less disgusting (to a man of taste and sensibility) than the Alps. It was they who, when conducted to the summit of Skiddaw, requested that the physical effects of that dangerous altitude might be corrected by blood-letting and they themselves conveyed to some place of comparative safety in the adjacent valley. Where, then, are we to look for sanction from authority? The Church itself denies us its consolations. It is true that this Club has been blessed by his Holiness the Pope: [4] but the successor of St. Peter is far away in the Vatican, while no distance mitigates for us the denunciations of the Dean of St. Paul's.

Turn now from the influence exerted on the potential Alpinist by authority, to the insensible promptings of his environment. What does he see around him? What encouragement is he likely to receive from the classes which still possess prestige and the masses which have recently acquired power? Practically none. He observes with dismay that among dukes, captains of industry, and other millionaires, the percentage of mountaineers is practically negligible; and should he enquire of the ranks of trade unionism, the response will be even less encouraging. Title and wealth have other diversions; and the trade unionist's cherished principle of limited hours of work is not really compatible with the practice of this Club—except, perhaps, that of its youngest and swiftest members. Thus he is confronted with the hostility or indifference of the two classes which most

[4] Pope Pius XI was an active friend of mountaineering. Before his elevation he climbed extensively in the Alps, particularly in the Monte Rosa chain. His adventures are described in a book translated under the title *Climbs on Alpine Peaks* (1923). In 1923 Pope Pius XI named as patron of all mountaineers Saint Bernard of Menthon. As Vicar General to the Bishop of Aosta Saint Bernard habitually visited remote Alpine valleys. Being much concerned for the safety and comfort of travelers he established the hospices on the two St. Bernard passes. He died in 1008. (*The Book of Saints* . . . , compiled by the Benedictine Monks of St. Augustine's Abbey . . . , New York, Macmillan, 1942, p. 45.)

affect public opinion. He is driven to the conclusion that mountaineering is confined to the bourgeoisie; and that is a class to which no young man in these days can wish to belong. I pass to another important part of environment. Magazine fiction (that great educator) habitually presents Alpine adventure in a singularly unattractive aspect: the incidents described are seldom such as the man in the train would wish to see reproduced in his own daily life; neither heroes nor villains appear to him to offer models for his imitation. You know the kind of thing. The hero and the villain—both, I regret to say, described as members of this Club—go out to pluck for the lady who ensnares their rival affections the prize of Alpine adventure—the *edelweiss*, which, as is well known, blooms only on the least accessible of the snow-clad summits.[5] In pursuit of this coveted vegetable, the hero inevitably slips into a *bergschrund;* his companion sees the opportunity for disposing of a hated rival, and cuts the rope. But kindly Nature defeats the machinations of villainy; for the glacier, sweeping swiftly and steadily downward, takes charge of the fallen mountaineer, and duly delivers him safe and sound in the valley, just in time to prevent the villain from leading the heroine to the hymeneal altar. Such narratives are seldom founded on actual experience and knowledge; but the public does not know that. When golf or cricket or Mah Jong is the subject of fiction, the reader is accustomed to a high standard of accuracy. He sees these pastimes presented by experts in a correct form; naturally, therefore, he infers that the same is the case with mountaineering. Or, if he does recognise that the writer is moving about in worlds not realised, his natural conclusion is that a game cannot be worth playing which is not worth describing accurately, like the other pastimes which I have mentioned. . . .

It appears then that we have dangerous enemies in both authority and environment, both of which prove mountaineering to be unreasonable. Yet it is one of the Englishman's sources of pride that he is not, like some Latin nations, a slave to reason; and mere logic might well fail, if counteracted by inborn instinct and natural in-

---

[5] "It [edelweiss] is a favorite . . . Alpine subject for rock gardens though sometimes grown in pots." (*The New Garden Encyclopedia*, ed. by E. L. D. Seymour, New York, Wm. H. Wise and Co., 1941, p. 415.)

clination. Unfortunately, in the present case, the natural feelings of the majority of our fellow-countrymen are on the side of tradition, and allied with the promptings of environment. Does Nature, for instance, suggest to them that mountains are beautiful? We in this Club, and perhaps some others, are apt to assume that they are. . . . But I ask you, gentlemen, to clear your minds of cant—to examine your conclusions and your premisses . . . and then to show for the public's satisfaction to what canons of beauty so many yards of snow or ice or rock placed on an inclined plane do really conform; and why these singular formations should be admired by humanity. If we accept the Ruskinian canon which makes utility a necessary ingredient of beauty, what are we to say of mountains, which are really of no substantial use to anyone except hotel-keepers and guides? According to this rule, a mountain which has no hotel near it (fortunately, there are very few such) cannot be said to be beautiful; it becomes beautiful when you build a hotel at the base, and still more so if you build one at the top; and it will always be more beautiful to the hotel-keeper than to anyone else. A friend of mine, not an hotel-keeper, but a man of keen sensibilities and correct judgment, could find little to please him in Alpine scenery. He did not like the mountains, which, he said, obstructed the view, and should be got rid of. Evidently we are on no safe ground here. Further, in order to go up most mountains, you must walk; now the British public has a natural disinclination to walk. The feeling is overcome sometimes, but it is there. The late Hugh Sidgwick says somewhere in his delightful *Walking Essays* that Elizabeth Bennet in *Pride and Prejudice* was the first real English walker. Perhaps the habit is not of quite so recent origin as that; but it is certain that the general public in this country does not yet care to walk for the sake of exercise or amusement, and regards those who do as slightly abnormal. They are in a mild way, suspect; it is better, on the whole, to do business with a man who uses a motor, as nature meant that he should. And if walking in general is hardly yet popular, still less so is walking uphill. That, for most of us, is abhorrent to our most deeply ingrained instinct. There was a man (I heard him, for I happened to be passing by) who sat by the side of the path leading up to the Riffel Alp, and when his companions urged him to press on a little farther—perhaps, as far as the first restaurant—replied to them in words which I do not think were meant for poetry, though they had the poignant sincerity of a great poetic fragment—"No matter where it leads me, the downward path for me." That might be sung in churches; and if it were, I am sure that most of the congregation at any mountaineering centre would join in with exceptional heartiness. In short, the great majority of average persons have no use at all for going up hills. Listen to them talking to each other, and you will hear them proclaim it, glorying in their shame. When they are in better company (our company) they will sometimes condescend to the tribute of hypocrisy which vice is said to pay to virtue: they will make excuses; they will protest a bad heart, or more frequently a bad head, which is unequal to the terrific exigencies of mountain-climbing. Nor are they always insincere; for steep hills are replete with imagined perils of the most desperate kind. It is not surprising; the draughtsmen who illustrate such fiction as I have alluded to above invariably portray a mountain-side as perpendicular at best, and frequently overhanging; nor does the Press tend to encouragement. Every now and then its emissaries penetrate into fastnesses of Snowdonia or the Lakes; and when that happens, the public sups its full of horrors. I have known the day when climbing parties, whose chief desire and ruling passion was for personal safety, have shuddered to see themselves pilloried before the alarmed eyes of their distant and anxious friends under the taking title of "The Brotherhood of Peril." Is it then surprising if householders and rate-payers and breadwinners hesitate before they engage in enterprises so unfashionable, so unauthorised, so repugnant to the primal self-protective instincts of humanity?

No; it is not surprising at all. It is more unaccountable that there are so many devotees; that their number does in some strange and fortunate way increase. The fact is, I suppose, that mountaineering is (as was once shown in a paper read here) a religion; and it is an inevitable attribute of all real religions that it is much easier to assail them from outside than to demonstrate their appeal. Only the faithful comprehend, and to comprehend is not always the same thing as to make your comprehension intelligible to others. It is a religion; it has its sermons (this is one), it has even its hymns;

and from time to time there is a collection. It has also its books of devotion, a great many of them. But these devotional works are mostly (as we see to be the case with most religions) for the elect, who are predestined to a state of grace, predestined to the vision which can recognise mountain-climbing as one of the few really stable good things amid the shifting values of modern moral and intellectual currency. Inevitably, that vision is not for all, or most. Nor indeed, can it be wished that the case were otherwise. Excessive popularity might have its dangers. Let the public *en masse* take to climbing, and we may well imagine that there might be a cry for Brighter Mountaineering; we can conceive an appeal to make the Matterhorn Safe for Democracy. Things are better as they are.

ALBERT FREDERICK MUMMERY

THE FOLLOWING SELECTION is reprinted from A. F. Mummery, *My Climbs in the Alps and the Caucasus*. See also pp. 152–153.

The Pleasures and Penalties of Mountaineering

WELL-KNOWN CLIMBERS, whose opinions necessarily carry the greatest weight, have recently declared their belief that the dangers of mountaineering no longer exist. Skill, knowledge, and text-books have hurled them to the limbo of exploded bogies. I would fain agree with this optimistic conclusion, but I cannot forget that the first guide to whom I was ever roped, and one who possessed—may I say it?—more knowledge of mountains than is to be found even in the Badminton library,[1] was none the less killed on the Brouillard Mont Blanc, and his son, more recently, on Koshtantau. The memory of two rollicking parties, comprising seven men, who one day in 1879 were climbing on the west face of the Matterhorn, passes with ghost-like admonition before my mind and bids me remember that of these seven, Mr. Penhall was killed on the Wetterhorn, Ferdinand Imseng on the Macugnaga Monte Rosa, and Johann Petrus on the Fresnay Mont Blanc. To say that any single one of these men was less careful and competent, or had less knowledge of all that pertains to the climber's craft, than we who yet survive, is obviously and patently absurd. Our best efforts must sometimes be seconded by

[1] See p. 163 n.

the great goddess of Luck; to her should the Alpine Club offer its vows and thanksgivings.

Indeed, if we consider for a moment the essence of the sport of mountaineering, it is obvious that it consists, and consists exclusively, in pitting the climber's skill against the difficulties opposed by the mountain. Any increase in skill involves, *pari passu*, an increase in the difficulties grappled with. From the Breuil ridge of the Matterhorn we pass on to the Dru, and from the Dru to the Aiguille de Grépon: or to take a yet wider range, from the Chamonix Mont Blanc to the same mountain by way of the Brenva glacier and the Aiguille Blanche de Peuteret. It can scarcely be argued that Bennen and Walters were less fit to grapple with the cliff above the "Linceul" than we moderns to climb the Grépon "crack"; or that Jacques Balmat was less able to lead up the "Ancien passage" than Emile Rey to storm the ghastly precipices of the Brenva Peuteret. But if it be admitted that the skill of the climber has not increased relatively to the difficulties grappled with, it would appear to necessarily follow that climbing is neither more nor less dangerous than formerly.

It is true that extraordinary progress has been made in the art of rock climbing, and that consequently, any given rock climb is much easier now than thirty years since, but the essence of the sport lies, not in ascending a peak, but in struggling with and overcoming difficulties. The happy climber, like the aged Ulysses, is one who has "Drunk delight of battle with his peers," and this delight is only attainable by assaulting cliffs which tax to their utmost limits the powers of the mountaineers engaged. This struggle involves the same risk, whether early climbers attacked what we now call easy rock, or whether we moderns attack formidable rock, or whether the ideal climber of the future assaults cliffs which we now regard as hopelessly inaccessible. Doubtless my difference with the great authorities referred to above is, in the main, due to a totally different view of the *raison d'être* of mountaineering. Regarded as a sport, some danger is, and always must be, inherent in it; regarded as a means of exercise amongst noble scenery, for quasi-scientific pursuits, as the raw material for interesting papers, or for the purposes of brag and bounce, it has become as safe as the ascent of the Rigi or Pilatus was to the climbers of thirty years since. But these pursuits are not mountaineering in the sense in which the founders of the Alpine Club used the term, and they are not mountaineering in the sense in which the elect—a small, perchance even a dwindling body—use it now. To set one's utmost faculties, physical and mental, to fight some grim precipice, or force some gaunt, ice-clad gully, is work worthy of men; to toil up long slopes of screes behind a guide who can "lie in bed and picture every step of the way up, with all the places for hand and foot," is work worthy of the fibreless contents of fashionable clothes, dumped with all their scents and ointments, starched linen and shiny boots, at Zermatt by the railway.

The true mountaineer is a wanderer, and by a wanderer I do not mean a man who expends his whole time in travelling to and fro in the mountains on the exact tracks of his predecessors—much as a bicyclist rushes along the turnpike roads of England—but I mean a man who loves to be where no human being has been before, who delights in gripping rocks that have previously never felt the touch of human fingers, or in hewing his way up ice-filled gullies whose grim shadows have been sacred to the mists and avalanches since "Earth rose out of chaos." In other words, the true mountaineer is the man who attempts new ascents. Equally, whether he succeeds or fails, he delights in the fun and jollity of the struggle. The gaunt, bare slabs, the square, precipitous steps in the ridge, and the black, bulging ice of the gully, are the very breath of life to his being. I do not pretend to be able to analyse this feeling, still less to be able to make it clear to unbelievers. It must be felt to be understood, but it is potent to happiness and sends the blood tingling through the veins, destroying every trace of cynicism and striking at the very roots of pessimistic philosophy.

Our critics, curiously enough, repeat in substance Mr. Ruskin's original taunt, that we regard the mountains as greased poles.[2] I must confess that a natural and incurable denseness of understanding does not enable me to feel the sting of this taunt. Putting aside the question of grease, which is offensive and too horrible for contemplation in its effects on knickerbockers—worse even than the structure-destroying edges and splinters of the Grépon ridge—I

[2] See note 3, p. 381.

do not perceive the enormity or sin of climbing poles. At one time, I will confess, I took great delight in the art, and, so far as my experience extends, the taste is still widespread amongst English youth. It is possible, nay even probable, that much of the pleasure of mountaineering is derived from the actual physical effort and from the perfect state of health to which this effort brings its votaries, and, to this extent, may plausibly be alleged to be the mere sequence and development of the pole and tree climbing of our youth. The sting of the taunt is presumably meant to lurk in the implication that the climber is incapable of enjoying noble scenery; that, in the jargon of certain modern writers, he is a *"mere* gymnast." But why should a man be assumed incapable of enjoying aesthetic pleasures because he is also capable of the physical and non-aesthetic pleasures of rock climbing?

A well-known mountaineer asserts that the fathers of the craft did not regard "the overcoming of physical obstacles by means of muscular exertion and skill" as "the chief pleasure of mountaineering." But is this so? Can any one read the great classic of mountaineering literature, "The Playground of Europe," without feeling that the overcoming of these obstacles was a main factor of its author's joy? Can any one read "Peaks, Passes, and Glaciers" and the earlier numbers of *The Alpine Journal* without feeling that the various writers gloried in the technique of their craft? Of course the skilful interpolation of "chief" gives an opening for much effective dialectic, but after all, what does it mean? How can a pleasure which is seated in health and jollity and the "spin of the blood" be measured and compared with a purely aesthetic feeling? It would appear difficult to argue that as a man cultivates and acquires muscular skill and knowledge of the mountains, he correspondingly dwarfs and impairs the aesthetic side of his nature. If so, we magnify the weak-kneed and the impotent, the lame, the halt and the blind, and brand as false the Greek ideal of the perfect man. Doubtless a tendency in this direction may be detected in some modern thought, but, like much else similarly enshrined, it has no ring of true metal. Those who are so completely masters of their environment that they can laugh and rollick on the ridges, free from all constraint of ropes or fear of danger, are far more able to appreciate the glories of the "eternal hills" than those who can only move in constant terror of their lives, amidst the endless chatter and rank tobacco smoke of unwashed guides.

The fact that a man enjoys scrambling up a steep rock in no way makes him insensible of all that is beautiful in nature. The two sets of feelings are indeed wholly unconnected. A man may love climbing and care naught for mountain scenery; he may love the scenery and hate climbing; or he may be equally devoted to both. The presumption obviously is that those who are most attracted by the mountains and most constantly return to their fastnesses, are those who to the fullest extent possess both these sources of enjoyment— those who can combine the fun and frolic of a splendid sport with that indefinable delight which is induced by the lovely form, tone, and colouring of the great ranges.

I am free to confess that I myself should still climb, even though there were no scenery to look at, even if the only climbing attainable were the dark and gruesome potholes of the Yorkshire dales. On the other hand, I should still wander among the upper snows, lured by the silent mists and the red blaze of the setting sun, even though physical or other infirmity, even though in after aeons the sprouting of wings and other angelic appendages, may have sunk all thought of climbing and cragsmanship in the whelming past.

It is frequently assumed, even by those who ought to know better, that if mountaineering involves danger of any sort, it should never be indulged in—at all events by such precious individuals as the members of the English Alpine Club. Before considering this most pernicious doctrine, it is well to remember, that though the perils of mountaineering may not have been wholly dissipated into space by the lightning-like flashes of the Badminton and All England series,[3] yet, nevertheless, these perils are not very great. With a single exception, the foregoing pages [4] contain an account of every difficulty I have experienced which has seemed to render disaster a possible contingency. As my devotion to the sport began in 1871, and has continued with unabated vigour ever since, it will be evident

[3] See note, p. 163.
[4] The chapter reprinted here is the last in *My Climbs in the Alps and the Caucasus* (1895).

that the climber's perils—in so far as a modest individual may regard himself as typical of the class—are extremely few and very rarely encountered. Such, however, as they have been, I would on no account have missed them. There is an educative and purifying power in danger that is to be found in no other school, and it is worth much for a man to know that he is not "clean gone to flesh pots and effeminacy." It may be admitted that the mountains occasionally push things a trifle too far, and bring before their votaries a vision of the imminence of dissolution that the hangman himself with all his paraphernalia of scaffold, gallows, and drop, could hardly hope to excel. But grim and hopeless as the cliffs may sometimes look when ebbing twilight is chased by shrieking wind and snow and the furies are in mad hunt along the ridges, there is ever the feeling that brave companions and a constant spirit will cut the gathering web of peril, "forsan et haec olim meminisse juvabit."

The sense of independence and self-confidence induced by the great precipices and vast silent fields of snow is something wholly delightful. Every step is health, fun, and frolic. The troubles and cares of life, together with the essential vulgarity of a plutocratic society, are left far below—foul miasmas that cling to the lowest bottoms of reeking valleys. Above, in the clear air and searching sunlight, we are afoot with the quiet gods, and men can know each other and themselves for what they are. No feeling can be more glorious than advancing to attack some gaunt precipitous wall with "comrades staunch as the founders of our race." Nothing is more exhilarating than to know that the fingers of one hand can still be trusted with the lives of a party, and that the lower limbs are free from all trace of "knee-dissolving fear," even though the friction of one hobnail on an outward shelving ledge alone checks the hurtling of the body through thin air, and of the soul (let us hope) to the realms above.

I am of course aware that it is an age which cares little for the more manly virtues, and which looks askance at any form of sport that can, by any stretch of extremest imagination, be regarded as dangerous: yet since we cannot all, for most obvious reasons, take our delight "wallowing in slimy spawn of lucre," something may surely be urged in favour of a sport that teaches, as no other teaches, endurance and mutual trust, and forces men occasionally to look death in its grimmest aspect frankly and squarely in the face. For though mountaineering is not, perhaps, more dangerous than other sports, it undoubtedly brings home to the mind a more stimulating sense of peril; a sense, indeed, that is out of all proportion to the actual risk. It is, for instance, quite impossible to look down the tremendous precipices of the Little Dru without feeling in each individual nerve the utter disintegration of everything human which a fall must involve; and the contingency of such a fall is frequently brought before the mind—indeed, throughout the ascent, constant and strenuous efforts are needed to avoid it. The love of wager, our religious teachers notwithstanding, is still inherent in the race, and one cannot find a higher stake—at all events in these materialistic days, when Old Nick will no longer lay sterling coin against the gamester's soul—than the continuity of the cervical vertebrae; and this is the stake that the mountaineer habitually and constantly wagers. It is true the odds are all on his side, but the off-chance excites to honesty of thought and tests how far decay has penetrated the inner fibre. That mountaineering has a high educational value, few, who have the requisite knowledge to form a fair judgment, would deny. That it has its evil side I frankly admit. None can look down its gloomy death-roll without feeling that our sport demands a fearful price.

Mountaineering being a sport not wholly free from danger, it behoves us to consider the directions from which this danger may come, and the methods by which it may usually be met and conquered. Amongst the mountains, as elsewhere, "the unexpected always happens." It is the momentary carelessness in easy places, the lapsed attention, or the wandering look that is the usual parent of disaster. It may appear that to this extent dangers are avoidable, and the high authorities referred to above justified in their optimism. But which of us can boast that his attention to the slope and his companions never flags, that his eyes are always on the watch for falling stones, for loose rocks, for undercut ice, and all the traps and pitfalls that Madame Nature scatters with such profusion among the "lonely hills"? The chief source of danger is this need for incessant care, the unvarying readiness of ice, snow, and rock to punish relentlessly an instant's forgetfulness, or the most trifling neglect. The first lesson the novice has to learn is to be ever on his guard, and it is one that the oldest climber rarely fully masters. Unfortunately it is one which the beginner must find out for himself, it is a habit that must be acquired, and to which no road other than constant practice, will ever lead him. It wants long experience to impress upon the mind that the chief danger of extremely difficult climbing is to be found on the easy places by which it is followed; that it lies less in the stress of desperate wrestling with the crags than in the relaxed attention which such work is apt to induce on the return to comparatively easy ground. Nothing is more usual than to hear a man say after some very formidable ascent—it may even be read in *The Alpine Journal*—that on the way up, certain preliminary rocks appeared distinctly difficult, but on the way down, after the terrible grapple with the cliffs above, these same rocks appeared "ridiculously easy." It is the delusive appearance of safety presented by these "ridiculously easy rocks" that swells the list of Alpine victims. . . .

There is, again, the impossibility of learning, except by actual experience, the length of time during which the nervous system may be relied on. The protracted strain of a long ice slope tells on men in wholly different ways. To some it means merely the sharpening of their faculties, and with every hour they get steadier and safer in their steps; with others it means utter exhaustion and collapse. It is distinctly unpleasant when a companion, who you think is enjoying himself, suddenly informs you that he is doubtful of his power to stand in the steps, that his knees are wobbling, and that he may be expected to slip at any moment. . . . It may be said that such a man should not go climbing; but how is he to know that he is affected in this way till he has so gone? A man can never know his capabilities till he has tried them, and this testing process involves risk. Going over ground where a slip would not be serious is of no use; so long as this is the case he may be as good or better than his companions. It is the knowledge that he holds the lives of the party in his hand that masters and conquers him, not the mere technical difficulties of the slope, which, to a man who has good steps cut for him, may be practically nil.

It will be evident that all these dangers press on the novice far more than on the old and seasoned mountaineer. Those who have learnt the craft, and spent fifteen or twenty summers amongst the mountains, are scarcely likely to be unaware of their own failings and weaknesses, and may be trusted to be generally on the alert. The dangers to which such "old hands" are subject come in the main from other directions, and are chiefly connected with "new expeditions." In the Alps, such ascents can only be found on previously unclimbed sides of peaks, and the mountaineer usually has the knowledge that if he reaches the top he can descend by an easy and well-known route. The temptation to persevere in an ascent, especially if anything very formidable has already been passed, is extremely great, and a party may even be urged forward by the fear of retreat. This fear should, however, never be yielded to; it may easily result in forcing the party into difficulties from which they have neither the time nor the ability to extricate themselves. If a place cannot be descended it should never be climbed.

A somewhat similar and still more deceitful peril is involved by the ascent in the early morning of gullies, which, though fairly safe at that hour, are known to be the channel of avalanches and falling stones in the afternoon. Should any unforeseen cause stop the party high up on the mountain, no safe line of retreat is open. . . . Unless, therefore, the climber is absolutely certain that the ascent can be completed, it is in the highest degree perilous to enter such gullies, and those who do so should clearly recognise that they are running very serious risks. If, however, the risk has been run and the party is checked high up on the mountain, it is usually the better course to spend the night on the rocks, and wait till frost has sealed up the loose stones, snow and ice. This expedient has been adopted more than once by my old guide, Alexander Burgener. On the memorable descent of the Col du Lion, it undoubtedly saved both Dr. [Paul] Güssfeldt's life and his own. I am aware that this procedure involves some slight risk from adverse changes in the weather, and extreme discomfort from cold, and possibly hunger, but these latter are mere trifles to strong men, properly clad; and as for the former, such places as the great couloir of the western Matterhorn are far safer in a snowstorm than when the setting sun is blazing on the great slopes above. Indeed, when snow falls at a low temperature it instantly dries up the trickles of water, stops the melting of the great pendent icicles, and generally checks the fall of missiles, thus rendering slopes and couloirs, which one dare not climb in fine weather, fairly safe. On the other hand, a summer snow squall followed by a wind above freezing point (a not infrequent phenomenon), will convert rock slopes, usually innocent, into cascades of water, armed and rendered terrible by stones and dislodged crags. It will thus be seen that most knowledge for this judgment is hardly to be obtained till the climber has learnt, by dangerous experience, to grasp the exact nature of the storm, and the effect it is likely to have on the slope he is dealing with.

Climbers sometimes write as though it were possible to avoid all slopes down which stones or ice can ever fall. In actual fact, though such slopes may, to some extent, be avoided on the days and at the hours when such falls may be most expected, it is impossible to keep wholly clear of them.

Mountaineers of the widest experience and most approved prudence, even presidents and ex-presidents of the Alpine Club, have been known to descend, for hours on end, shelterless slopes of rock and ice, liable at any moment to be raked from top to bottom by falling stones and ice. The orthodox critic may protest, but none the less those who seek to effect new passes will occasionally find themselves in positions which leave them no endurable alternative. The pseudo mountaineer can, it is true, almost wholly avoid these dangers. Accompanied by guides who know every step of the way, he is led by a fairly sheltered route, or, if none such exists, he is told this fact before he starts, and can alter his plans accordingly. But the repetition of an accurately timed and adjusted performance, under the rigid rule of a guide as stage manager, does not commend itself to the real mountaineer. His delight and pleasure in the sport are chiefly derived from the very uncertainty and difficulties which it is the main function of such a guide to eliminate. Even if the pass is not exactly new, he likes to encounter it without the exact knowledge of the route which reduces it to a mere tramp of so many hours duration, and as a consequence he cannot invariably avoid all risk.

As a matter of fact, very few of the usual and customary ascents are quite free from ice and rock falls. . . . There is . . . no absolute immunity from this danger, and it is desirable, therefore, that the young mountaineer should learn the various methods by which it may most suitably be grappled. To acquire the art of watching a falling stone, and, at the critical moment, to remove oneself from the line of fire, is essential to the cragsman. To attain the knowledge requisite to judge where and when ice and snow avalanches may be expected to fall, is equally necessary for the safe guidance of a party. It requires, however, the best teaching that the oldest and steadiest guides can give, combined with a long experience of the upper snows. . . . Beginners are apt to forget that at no time is falling ice more greatly to be feared than when protracted sunshine has wrought havoc amongst the leering monsters poised above their track. To adapt the expedition to the weather is frequently of critical importance, and may make not merely the difference between success and failure, but even between health and jollity, and irremediable disaster.

In this connection it is desirable to notice that an unroped party is safer than a roped one, and that its chances of escape from the missiles at the mountain's disposal vary, at the very least, inversely with its size. With three on the rope the middle man is more or less of a fixture, and has very little chance of saving himself from falling stones unless cover is close at hand. If no cover is available, the fact that the party is spread over a considerable extent of rock renders it highly probable that the true line of escape for its first and last members will lie in opposite directions. Should this be the case no movement is immediately possible, and the middle man occupies a most unenviable position. Personally I much prefer discarding the rope in all such places, and if this is not desirable, consider two quite the maximum permissible. I may add that this opinion is shared by such men as Alex. Burgener and Emile Rey. I have known each of them object to add a third to the party, on the ground that it would prevent rapidity of movement in places where such rapidity might be desirable. There is also the very serious risk of stones upset by the leader, and which may acquire very dangerous velocity before they pass the lowest man when several climbers are on the slope. During the first ascent of the Rothhorn from Zermatt, disaster was narrowly escaped from this very cause.

There are many gullies in which it is absolutely impossible to avoid dislodging stones, and as a consequence large parties are forced to "close up." Whilst this, to some extent, obviates the risk from falling stones, it negatives any advantage from the rope, and frequently compels all but the first man to be simultaneously on bad ground. Even then I have, more than once, seen a man badly hurt by such stones, and it is difficult to avoid the conclusion that some unexplained accidents may have resulted from a dislodged stone knocking a companion out of his steps, and his fall dragging the members of a "closed up" party, one after another, from their hold. On very steep ice, again, the leader is sometimes seriously hampered by the existence of a large party below him, and the consequent necessity of only cutting small pieces of ice with each stroke of the axe, and absolutely to avoid, on reaching rocks, any endeavour to clear the ice from them; the chance of detaching a fragment sufficiently large to knock a companion seventy or eighty feet below from his steps, being greater than the advantage of getting reliable footing.

These considerations of roping and numbers apply with even greater force to any danger arising from ice avalanches. Every additional man on the rope means a serious decrease of the extreme speed at which the party can move, and it is in speed, and in speed alone, that a party so surprised can hope for safety. . . .

Of course if an incompetent man is included, the rope must be worn constantly, and at least two sound and reliable mountaineers must be watching over his idiosyncrasies; but parties so hampered should avoid such gullies as that ascended on the way up the Schreckhorn, or the pitiless slopes of the Italian side of the Col des Hirondelles.

There is one other condition in which the rope seriously increases the risks of competent mountaineers. In the event of an avalanche being started, a roped party is almost helpless. It may be frequently possible for any one of the party to escape from the seething snow, but he is, if roped, of necessity dragged back by his companions. In such a case escape from the avalanche is only possible if all can

jump from the sliding snow on the same side and at the same moment, and even then only if they can free the rope from the wet
masses of snow in which it is certain to have become somewhat
involved. It is obvious, that under circumstances which may afford
each single member of the party a dozen chances of escape, it will
be highly improbable that all of them will get a simultaneous
chance, and the rope in such a case is a veritable death-trap. In larger
avalanches, where the utmost the climber can do is to keep his head
above the crest of the wave, the roped climber is hampered, as a
swimmer in a furious surf would be hampered, by the entanglement
of his companions. One has only to read the account of the death of
Bennen to realise how disastrous a rope may be.[5]

I have no wish to advocate the disuse of the rope, but merely to
point out certain well-known facts that have been lost sight of
in recent contributions to the literature of mountaineering. As a
general rule it is of the utmost value, and where climbers are of unequal skill and experience, its constant use is demanded by the
primary feelings of comradeship and good faith. There is, however,
some danger of its being regarded as a sort of Providence, always
ready to save the reckless and incompetent, no matter how slight
their experience, no matter how little they may be fitted for the
expeditions they undertake. Though I have dwelt at some length
on the occasional disadvantages the rope entails, and said but little
about the safety it so constantly assures, this is merely because there
seems no danger of the latter being overlooked, and much that the
former will be wholly forgotten. It is, moreover, to be remembered
that the conduct of guideless parties has been chiefly in view. Since
each member of such a party should be absolutely certain never to
slip, the monotony of this precaution may in many places be relaxed
with safety, and sometimes even with advantage.

I am, of course, aware that high authorities assert that a party
should always be roped, and that it should never consist of less than
three—does not the All England series tell that "whatever number
may be right, two is wrong"? I must, however, confess that I fail
to apprehend the reasons which have led to this unqualified dictum.
It would rather appear that the best number depends on a variety

[5] See John Tyndall, *Hours of Exercise in the Alps*, pp. 204–205.

of conditions, which vary with the expedition in view. For instance, on the Col du Lion, two is undoubtedly the best and safest number. Not merely is it desirable to reduce to the smallest dimensions the target offered to the mountain musketry and big guns, but it is also essential to move with the utmost speed attainable. Wherever this is the case each additional man is a source of danger.

Much recent writing on this question assumes that on steep slopes or cliffs three men are safer than two. It would, however, appear obvious that this is an error. If the leader slips, it almost of necessity involves the destruction of the party. In any case the whole impact of his fall must come on the man next him in the line, and if this man is dragged from his hold it is absurd to suppose that the third will be able to support the shock of the two men falling. Exactly the same may be said of a traverse; if the leader slips he must be held, if he is held at all, by the man next him in the line. No matter how many may be behind, they will, of necessity, be dragged, one after another, from their hold. It is obvious that if the leader is held by the man next him in the line, two are sufficient for safety; if he is not so held, then three, or any greater number, are equally doomed to destruction. Writers on this subject seem to assume that a party of three or more have no ends to the rope—that each member of the party is between two others—in which case, doubtless, fairly efficient help could be given. It is needless to point out, however, that this is impossible. In every party there are two men, the slip of either of whom, on a steep traverse, is extremely dangerous, if not fatal. The insertion reduces or diminishes this danger, though, in circumstances which can readily be imagined, it may gravely add to it.

The truth would appear to be, that if from a party of three you remove the worst climber, the two remaining men will, on steep slopes, be distinctly safer than the whole party. If, on the other hand, from the party of three you remove either of the more competent men, then the remaining two will be very much less safe. It must be remembered that I am not arguing in favour of a party consisting of one mountaineer and a duffer, but of two men, equally competent and skilled in all that pertains to the climber's craft.

A careful consideration of the various possibilities that can assail the mountaineer on the steeper slopes would appear to lead to the conclusion that a party of three or four is as often too many, as a party of two is too few. The loss of time and the danger of upset stones, and even of ice and snow hewn out in the process of step cutting, appear to fairly balance the advantages of a greater number.

These advantages are chiefly, that in places where the second man is giving the leader a shoulder, a third man may be able to anchor the party with a hitched rope; or where the upper lip of a schrund is almost out of reach, a third man can materially aid in the work of lifting and holding the leader on the shoulders of his companion whilst the necessary steps are being cut. It is also desirable, in all expeditions where much backing up is required, that the second man should be free from the encumbrance of the knapsack, spare rope, etc., and this, necessarily, involves a third to act as porter. It would appear then, that so far as the steeper slopes are concerned, the number of the party should be adapted to the nature of the expedition, and no attempt should be made to lay down any hard and fast rule.

The main strength of the objection to two men climbing alone is, perhaps, to be found in the common belief that if one man falls into a crevasse, his companion will be unable to pull him out. With regard to this extremely unpleasant supposition, it may be pointed out that there is no particular reason for him to fall in. . . . It is, of course, a quite unnecessary incident, and one which is not, perhaps, nearly so frequently indulged in as some people imagine. Once only have I been near falling into a crevasse, but on that occasion, being unroped, I felt it desirable to abandon such pleasure as this proceeding may afford.

A crevasse, except immediately after fresh snow, is always visible to any one who takes the trouble to look for it; and even if the leader is careless and does break through, the rope, if used with any readiness and skill, ought to check his going in beyond his waist.

It is a curious fact, that, from the very earliest days of mountaineering, two guides, dismissed after crossing a pass, have been in the habit of returning home by themselves. So far as I have been able to learn, no single crevasse accident has ever happened to them.

When it is remembered that such extensive and fissured fields of névé, as those traversed by the routes over the Col du Géant, the Mönch Joch, the Weiss Thor, the Col d'Hérens and the Brèche de la Meije, are amongst those which have been habitually crossed by two guides alone, it would appear that the danger to such parties is almost or quite non-existent. It is, indeed obvious that if such parties *were* exposed to the danger alleged, it would be little short of criminal to take two men across an ice pass and dismiss them under conditions which practically involve their climbing two on a rope. To permit guides to run risks, which their employer is warned on no account to face, would be, to say the least of it, contrary to the traditions of Englishmen at large and the Alpine Club in particular.

The difficulty of reconciling practice and teaching on this point leads me to suppose that, possibly, these denunciations are levelled, not against parties of two mountaineers, but against parties of one mountaineer and one duffer. Politeness, that arch-corrupter of truth, has, perchance, led our teachers to say "a party should never consist of less than three, of whom two should be guides," in preference to saying that "a party should always consist of two mountaineers, with or without one or more pieces of animate luggage." It would, indeed, be passing strange, if my old friends Alex. Burgener and Emile Rey, being seized with a desire to cross the Col du Géant, were compelled to obtain the help of some weakly school girl, or decrepit tourist, before being able to face the perils of the pass! Yet this is the conclusion to which the doctrines of our prophets necessarily lead! Truly those who aspire to walk with the "quiet gods" on more than Olympian heights should shun the formal politeness which conceals truth and say their whole meaning, regardless of the feelings of the incompetent and the duffer. . . . If from a party of three you abstract the weakest member, the party is very materially strengthened and improved, and . . . two competent climbers constitute a far safer and better party than the two guides and a traveller, so dear to the orthodox authorities on mountaineering. . . .

The habit of climbing alone is open to far other and more serious objections. It is true that under very exceptional circumstances, when, for instance, settled fine weather has rendered every crevasse visible, snow fields may be crossed in the early morning without much risk. At such times I have strolled over the Trift Joch, the Weiss Thor, the Col du Géant and other passes without experiencing any symptom of danger; but the sense of loneliness, a sense which, when fog and mists curl round the ridges, becomes almost painful, is apt to affect a man's steadiness and resource. It is certainly undesirable to push such solitary wanderings beyond very narrow limits.

On the other hand, nothing develops a man's faculties so rapidly and completely. No one detects a crevasse so readily as the man who is accustomed to traverse snow fields by himself. No one takes such careful note of the line of ascent as the cragsman who has got to find his way back alone. The concentration of all responsibility and all the work on a single individual forces him to acquire an all-round skill which is hardly to be gained in any other way. Climbing in parties is apt to develop one-sidedness. One man cuts the steps, another climbs the rocks, and a third always knows the way. Division of labour is doubtless excellent, and perchance deserves all that Adam Smith has said in its favour, but it does not develop the ideal mountaineer. In this department of human duty Mr. William Morris gives sounder advice. Of course this is merely another way of saying that the chamois hunter—*i.e.*, the solitary mountaineer— is the best raw material for a guide. The fact that a man has been in the habit of climbing alone, means that the law of the survival of the fittest has had full and ample opportunity of eliminating him should he be, in any way, a careless or incapable mountaineer.

From the individual's point of view this elimination may not, perhaps, appear wholly desirable. Yet, judging from his habits, the faithful climber, carried away by altruistic feelings and thinking merely of the welfare of future companions, prefers that the law of the survival of the fittest should have full scope and should pass him through its searching fires. . . . The man so proved is quite independent of the rope, and moves as freely, or more freely, without it than with. He suggests at every step that he adds to the pool of safety that may be regarded as embodied in it. Those on the other hand, who are imbued with the textbooks, and fear to move hand or foot when free from the trammels of loops and knots, insensibly suggest that they subtract from this same pool of safety.

It must not be supposed that I am an advocate of solitary climbing. It requires but a trifling knowledge of the average amateur to feel assured that at least nine out of every ten will break their necks if they seriously attempt it. All that it is desirable to do, is to point out to those who wish to go without guides, the direction in which they may seek for reliable companions. The more orthodox method of ascending peaks, between two good guides, has much to recommend it, but its votaries had best be avoided by those who aspire to face the great ridges, trusting exclusively in their own right arms and slowly won experience.

The rope should, indeed, be regarded by each member of the party, exclusively as an aid and protection to his companions. Those who feel its constant use essential to their own comfort, should regard this as indisputable evidence that they are engaging in expeditions too difficult for them; a practice which will never make good and self-reliant climbers. To be able to move safely and freely on a mountain slope should be the one object which the young mountaineer sets before himself. At occasional "mauvais pas" he may legitimately ask his companions to look after him and either give actual help, or rescue him from disaster should he slip, but this help should be quite exceptional. If he finds on any expedition that this protection is constantly required, he should frankly recognise that he is attempting work for which he is unfit. . . .

Whilst the true mountaineer is undoubtedly

". . . the noblest work of God,"

a thing that is pushed and hustled up peaks by Swiss peasants, and which is so wholly unable to take care of itself that it cannot be trusted to sit on a crag unroped, is as contemptible an object as may easily be imagined. A man should never knowingly and deliberately thrust himself into places where he is hopelessly mastered and dominated by his environment. He who does this is regarded by his guides as a sort of "vache au lait," a convenient source of tariffs and Trinkgeld; a butt for small jokes and witticisms; an object to smear with grease, to decorate with masks and veils, and to button up in strange, chain-clad gaiters; a thing to be wound up with wine and brandy, and which must never be lost sight of till safely handed over to the landlord of an inn. It is difficult to apprehend how men, who in other departments of life are not wanting in a sufficient sense of their own personal dignity, should consent to be treated in this way. It is not, even, as if it were the only form of mountain expedition open to them. Work within the powers of the least competent is abundant in every Alpine valley, much of it surrounded by the noblest scenery both of ice and snow. The art of mountaineering consists in being able to climb easily and securely, in being able to relate one's skill to the difficulties of the slopes above and around, and it may, to some extent, be practised and enjoyed, consistently with reasonable safety and self-respect, by every man, no matter how slight his natural aptitude and training may be. It is merely necessary that he should recognise the limits so imposed.

High proficiency in the sport is only attainable when a natural aptitude is combined with long years of practice, and not without some, perhaps much, danger to life and limb. Happily, the faithful climber usually acquires this skill at an age when the responsibilities of life have not yet laid firm hold upon him, and when he may fairly claim some latitude in matters of this sort. On the other hand he gains a knowledge of himself, a love of all that is most beautiful in nature, and an outlet such as no other sport affords for the stirring energies of youth; gains for which no price is, perhaps, too high. It is true the great ridges sometimes demand their sacrifices, but the mountaineer would hardly forego his worship though he knew himself to be the destined victim. But happily to most of us the great brown slabs bending over into immeasurable space, the lines and curves of the wind-moulded cornice, the delicate undulations of the fissured snow, are old and trusted friends, ever luring us to health and fun and laughter, and enabling us to bid a sturdy defiance to all the ills that time and life oppose.

SIR LESLIE STEPHEN

THE FOLLOWING SELECTION is reprinted from Sir Leslie Stephen, *The Playground of Europe*, edited by H. E. G. Tyndale, Oxford, Basil Blackwell, Ltd., 1936, by permission of Longmans, Green & Co., Ltd. See also pp. 3–4.

The Regrets of a Mountaineer

I HAVE OFTEN FELT a sympathy, which almost rises to the pathetic, when looking on at a cricket-match or boat-race. Something of the emotion with which Gray regarded the "distant spires and antique towers" [1] rises within me. It is not, indeed, that I feel very deeply for the fine ingenuous lads, who, as somebody says, are about to be degraded into tricky, selfish Members of Parliament. I have seen too much of them. They are very fine animals; but they are rather too exclusively animal. The soul is apt to be in too embryonic a state within these cases of well-strung bone and muscle. It is impossible for a mere athletic machine, however finely constructed, to appeal very deeply to one's finer sentiments. I can scarcely look forward with even an affectation of sorrow for the time when, if more sophisticated, it will at least have made a nearer approach to the dignity of an intellectual being. It is not the boys who make me feel a touch of sadness; their approaching elevation to the dignity of manhood will raise them on the whole in the scale of humanity; it is the older spectators whose aspect has in it something affecting. The shaky old gentleman, who played in the days when it was decidedly less dangerous to stand up to bowling than to a cannon-ball, and who now hobbles about on rheumatic joints, by the help

[1] "Ode on a Distant Prospect of Eton College," l. 1. Slightly altered.

of a stick; the corpulent elder, who rowed when boats had gangways down their middle, and did not require as delicate a balance as an acrobat's at the top of a living pyramid—these are the persons whom I cannot see without an occasional sigh. They are really conscious that they have lost something which they can never regain; or, if they momentarily forget it, it is even more forcibly impressed upon the spectators. To see a respectable old gentleman of sixty, weighing some fifteen stone, suddenly attempt to forget a third of his weight and two-thirds of his years, and attempt to caper like a boy, is indeed a startling phenomenon. To the thoughtless, it may be simply comic; but without being a Jaques, one may contrive also to suck some melancholy out of it.

Now, as I have never caught a cricket-ball, and, on the contrary, have caught numerous crabs in my life, the sympathy which I feel for these declining athletes is not due to any great personal interest in the matter. But I have long anticipated that a similar day would come for me, when I should no longer be able to pursue my favorite sport of mountaineering. Some day I should find that the ascent of a zigzag was as bad as a performance on the treadmill; that I could not look over a precipice without a swimming in the head; and that I could no more jump a crevasse than the Thames at Westminster.

None of these things have come to pass. So far as I know, my physical powers are still equal to the ascent of Mont Blanc or the Jungfrau. But I am no less effectually debarred—it matters not how—from mountaineering. I wander at the foot of the gigantic Alps, and look up longingly to the summits, which are apparently so near, and yet know that they are divided from me by an impassable gulf. In some missionary work I have read that certain South Sea Islanders believed in a future paradise where the good should go on eating for ever with insatiable appetites at an inexhaustible banquet. They were to continue their eternal dinner in a house with open wickerwork sides; and it was to be the punishment of the damned to crawl outside in perpetual hunger and look in through the chinks as little boys look in through the windows of a London cookshop. With similar feelings I lately watched through a telescope the small black dots, which were really men, creeping up the high flanks of Mont Blanc or Monte Rosa. The eternal snows represented for me the Elysian fields, into which entrance was sternly forbidden, and I lingered about the spot with a mixture of pleasure and pain, in the envious contemplation of my more fortunate companions.

I know there are those who will receive these assertions with civil incredulity. Some persons assume that every pleasure with which they cannot sympathise is necessarily affectation, and hold, as a particular case of that doctrine, that Alpine travellers risk their lives merely from fashion or desire for notoriety. Others are kind enough to admit that there is something genuine in the passion, but put it on a level with the passion for climbing greased poles. They think it derogatory to the due dignity of Mont Blanc that he should be used as a greased pole, and assure us that the true pleasures of the Alps are those which are within reach of the old and the invalids, who can only creep about villages and along highroads. I cannot well argue with such detractors from what I consider a noble sport.

As for the first class, it is reduced almost to a question of veracity. I say that I enjoy being on the top of a mountain, or, indeed, half-way up a mountain; that climbing is a pleasure to me, and would be so if no one else climbed and no one ever heard of my climbing. They reply that they don't believe it. No more argument is possible than if I were to say that I liked eating olives, and some one asserted that I really eat them only out of affectation. My reply would be simply to go on eating olives; and I hope the reply of mountaineers will be to go on climbing Alps. The other assault is more intelligible. Our critics admit that we have a pleasure; but assert that it is a puerile pleasure—that it leads to an irreverent view of mountain beauty, and to oversight of that which should really most impress a refined and noble mind. To this I shall only make such an indirect reply as may result from a frank confession of my own regrets at giving up the climbing business—perhaps for ever.

I am sinking, so to speak, from the butterfly to the caterpillar stage, and, if the creeping thing is really the highest of the two, it will appear that there is something in the substance of my lamentations unworthy of an intellectual being. Let me try. By way of preface, however, I admit that mountaineering, in my sense of the word, is a sport. It is a sport which, like fishing or shooting, brings one into contact with the sublimest aspects of nature; and, without setting their enjoyment before one as an ultimate end or aim, helps one indirectly to absorb and be penetrated by their influence. Still it is strictly a sport—as strictly as cricket, or rowing, or knurr and spell—and I have no wish to place it on a different footing. The game is won when a mountain top is reached in spite of difficulties; it is lost when one is forced to retreat; and, whether won or lost, it calls into play a great variety of physical and intellectual energies, and gives the pleasure which always accompanies an energetic use of our faculties. Still it suffers in some degree from this undeniable characteristic, and especially from the tinge which has consequently been communicated to narratives of mountain adventures.

There are two ways which have been appropriated to the description of all sporting exploits. One is to indulge in fine writing about them, to burst out in sentences which swell to paragraphs, and in paragraphs which spread over pages; to plunge into ecstasies about infinite abysses and overpowering splendours, to compare mountains to archangels lying down in eternal winding-sheets of snow, and to convert them into allegories about man's highest destinies and aspirations. This is good when it is well done. Mr. Ruskin has covered the Matterhorn, for example, with a whole web of poetical associations, in language which, to a severe taste, is perhaps a trifle too fine, though he has done it with an eloquence which his bitterest antagonists must freely acknowledge. Yet most humble writers will feel that if they try to imitate Mr. Ruskin's eloquence they will pay the penalty of becoming ridiculous. It is not everyone who can with impunity compare Alps to archangels.[2]

Tall talk is luckily an object of suspicion to Englishmen, and, consequently most writers, and especially those who frankly adopt the sporting view of the mountains, adopt the opposite scheme: they affect something like cynicism; they mix descriptions of scenery with allusions to fleas or to bitter beer; they shrink with the prevailing dread of Englishmen from the danger of overstepping the limits of the sublime into its proverbial opposite; and they humbly try to amuse us because they can't strike us with awe. This, too, if I may venture to say so, is good in its way and place; and it seems

2 See note 3, p. 381.

rather hard to these luckless writers when people assume that, because they make jokes on a mountain, they are necessarily insensible to its awful sublimities. A sense of humour is not incompatible with imaginative sensibility; and even Wordsworth might have been an equally powerful prophet of nature if he could sometimes have descended from his stilts. In short, a man may worship mountains, and yet have a quiet joke with them when he is wandering all day in their tremendous solitudes.

Joking, however, is, it must be admitted, a dangerous habit. I freely avow that, in my humble contributions to Alpine literature, I have myself made some very poor and very unseasonable witticisms. I confess my error, and only wish that I had no worse errors to confess. Still I think that the poor little jokes in which we mountaineers sometimes indulge have been made liable to rather harsh constructions. We are accused, in downright earnest, not merely of being flippant, but of an arrogant contempt for all persons whose legs are not as strong as our own. We are supposed seriously to wrap ourselves in our own conceit, and to brag intolerably of our exploits. Now I will not say that no mountaineer ever swaggers; the quality called by the vulgar "bounce" is unluckily confined to no profession. Certainly I have seen a man intolerably vain because he could raise a hundredweight with his little finger; and I daresay that the "champion bill-poster," whose name is advertised on the walls of this metropolis, thinks excellence in bill-posting the highest virtue of a citizen. So some men may be silly enough to brag in all seriousness about mountain exploits. However, most lads of twenty learn that it is silly to give themselves airs about mere muscular eminence; and especially is this true of Alpine exploits—first, because they require less physical prowess than almost any other sport, and secondly, because a good amateur still feels himself the hopeless inferior of half the Alpine peasants whom he sees. You cannot be very conceited about a game in which the first clodhopper you meet can give you ten minutes' start in an hour. Still a man writing in a humourous vein naturally adopts a certain bumptious tone, just as our friend *Punch* ostentatiously declares himself to be omniscient and infallible. Nobody takes him at his word, or supposes that the editor of *Punch* is really the most conceited man in all England.

But we poor mountaineers are occasionally fixed with our own careless talk by some outsider who is not in the secret. We know ourselves to be a small sect, and to be often laughed at; we reply by assuming that we are the salt of the earth, and that our amusement is the first and noblest of all amusements. Our only retort to the good-humoured ridicule with which we are occasionally treated is to adopt an affected strut, and to carry it off as if we were the finest fellows in the world. We make a boast of our shame, and say, if you laugh we must crow. But we don't really mean anything: if we did, the only word which the English language would afford wherewith to describe us would be the very unpleasant antithesis to wise men, and certainly I hold that we have the average amount of common sense. When, therefore, I see us taken to task for swaggering, I think it a trifle hard that this merely playful affectation of superiority should be made a serious fault. For the future I would promise to be careful, if it were worth avoiding misunderstanding of men who won't take a joke. Meanwhile, I can only state that when Alpine travellers indulge in a little swagger about their own performances and other people's incapacity, they don't mean more than an infinitesimal fraction of what they say, and that they know perfectly well that when history comes to pronounce a final judgment upon the men of the time, it won't put mountain-climbing on a level with patriotism, or even with excellence in the fine arts.

The reproach of real bona fide arrogance is, so far as I know, very little true of Alpine travellers. With the exception of the necessary fringe hanging on to every set of human beings—consisting of persons whose heads are weaker than their legs—the mountaineer, so far as my experience has gone, is generally modest enough. Perhaps he sometimes flaunts his ice-axes and ropes a little too much before the public eye at Chamonix, as a yachtsman occasionally flourishes his nautical costume at Cowes; but the fault may be pardoned by those not inexorable to human weaknesses. This opinion, I know, cuts at the root of the most popular theory as to our ruling passion. If we do not climb the Alps to gain notoriety, for what purpose can we possibly climb them? That same unlucky trick of joking is taken to indicate that we don't care much about the scenery; for who, with a really susceptible soul, could be facetious under the cliffs of the Jungfrau or the ghastly precipices of the Matterhorn? Hence people who kindly excuse us from the blame of notoriety-hunting generally accept the "greased-pole" theory. We are, it seems, overgrown schoolboys, who, like other schoolboys, enjoy being in dirt, and danger, and mischief, and have as much sensibility for natural beauty as the mountain mules. And against this, as a more serious complaint, I wish to make my feeble protest, in order that my lamentations on quitting the profession may not seem unworthy of a thinking being.

Let me try to recall some of the impressions which mountaineering has left with me, and see whether they throw any light upon the subject. As I gaze at the huge cliffs where I may no longer wander, I find innumerable recollections arise—some of them dim, as though belonging to a past existence; and some so brilliant that I can scarcely realise my exclusion from the scenes to which they belong. I am standing at the foot of what, to my mind, is the most glorious of all Alpine wonders—the huge Oberland precipice, on the slopes of the Faulhorn or the Wengern Alp. Innumerable tourists have done all that tourists can do to cocknify (if that is the right derivative from cockney) the scenery; but, like the Pyramids or a Gothic cathedral, it throws off the taint of vulgarity by its imperishable majesty. Even on turf strewn with sandwich-papers and empty bottles, even in the presence of hideous peasant-women singing "*Stand er auf*" for five centimes, we cannot but feel the influence of Alpine beauty. When the sunlight is dying off the snows, or the full moon lighting them up with ethereal tints, even sandwich-papers and singing women may be forgotten. How does the memory of scrambles along snow arêtes, of plunges—luckily not too deep—into crevasses, of toil through long snowfields, towards a refuge that seemed to recede as we advanced—where, to quote Tennyson with due alteration, to the traveller toiling in immeasurable snow—

> Sown in a wrinkle of the monstrous hill
> The chalet sparkles like a grain of salt;— [3]

how do such memories as these harmonise with the sense of superlative sublimity?

[3] "Will," ll. 19–20. For "chalet" read "city."

One element of mountain beauty is, we shall all admit, their vast size and steepness. That a mountain is very big, and is faced by perpendicular walls of rock, is the first thing which strikes everybody, and is the whole essence and outcome of a vast quantity of poetical description. Hence the first condition towards a due appreciation of mountain scenery is that these qualities should be impressed upon the imagination. The mere dry statement that a mountain is so many feet in vertical height above the sea, and contains so many tons of granite, is nothing. Mont Blanc is about three miles high. What of that? Three miles is an hour's walk for a lady—an eighteen-penny cab-fare—the distance from Hyde Park Corner to the Bank—an express train could do it in three minutes, or a racehorse in five. It is a measure which we have learnt to despise, looking at it from a horizontal point of view; and accordingly most persons, on seeing the Alps for the first time, guess them to be higher, as measured in feet, than they really are.

What, indeed, is the use of giving measures in feet to any but the scientific mind? Who cares whether the moon is 250,000 or 2,500,-000 miles distant? Mathematicians try to impress upon us that the distance of the fixed stars is only expressible by a row of figures which stretches across a page; suppose it stretched across two or across a dozen pages, should we be any the wiser, or have, in the least degree, a clearer notion of the superlative distances? We civilly say, "Dear me!" when the astronomer looks to us for the appropriate stare, but we only say it with the mouth; internally our remark is "You might as well have multiplied by a few more millions whilst you were about it." Even astronomers, though not a specially imaginative race, feel the impotence of figures, and try to give us some measure which the mind can grasp a little more conveniently. They tell us about the cannon-ball which might have been flying ever since the time of Adam, and not yet have reached the heavenly body, or about the stars which may not yet have become visible, though the light has been flying to us at a rate inconceivable by the mind for an inconceivable number of years; and they succeed in producing a bewildering and giddy sensation, although the numbers are too vast to admit of any accurate apprehension.

We feel a similar need in the case of mountains. Besides the bare statement of figures, it is necessary to have some means for grasping the meaning of the figures. The bare tens and thousands must be clothed with some concrete images. The statement that a mountain is 15,000 feet high is, by itself, little more impressive than that it is 3,000; we want something more before we can mentally compare Mont Blanc and Snowdon. Indeed, the same people who guess of a mountain's height at a number of feet much exceeding the reality, show, when they are cross-examined, that they fail to appreciate in any tolerable degree the real meaning of the figures. An old lady one day, about 11 A.M., proposed to walk from the Eggishorn to the Jungfraujoch, and to return for luncheon—the distance being a good twelve hours' journey for trained mountaineers. Every detail of which the huge mass is composed is certain to be underestimated. A gentleman the other day pointed out to me a grand ice-cliff at the end of a hanging glacier, which must have been at least 100 feet high, and asked me whether that snow was three feet deep.

Nothing is more common than for tourists to mistake some huge pinnacle of rock, as big as a church tower, for a traveller. The rocks of the Grands Mulets, in one corner of which the chalet is hidden, are often identified with a party ascending Mont Blanc; and I have seen boulders as big as a house pointed out confidently as chamois. People who make these blunders must evidently see the mountains as mere toys, however many feet they may give them at a random guess. Huge overhanging cliffs are to them steps within the reach of human legs; yawning crevasses are ditches to be jumped; and foaming waterfalls are like streams from penny squirts. Everyone knows the avalanches on the Jungfrau, and the curiously dispropor-tionate appearance of the little puffs of white smoke, which are said to be the cause of the thunder; but the disproportion ceases to an eye that has learnt really to measure distance, and to know that these smoke-puffs represent a cataract of crashing blocks of ice.

Now the first merit of mountaineering is that it enables one to have what theologians would call an experimental faith in the size of mountains—to substitute a real living belief for a dead intellectual assent. It enables one, first, to assign something like its true magnitude to a rock or a snow-slope; and, secondly, to measure that magnitude in units. Suppose that we are standing upon the Wengern Alp; between the Mönch and the Eiger there stretches a round white bank with a curved outline, which we may roughly compare to the back of one of Sir E. Landseer's lions. The ordinary tourists—the old man, the woman, or the cripple, who are supposed to appreciate the real beauties of Alpine scenery—may look at it comfortably from their hotel. They may see its graceful curve, the long straight lines that are ruled in delicate shading down its sides, and the contrast of the blinding white snow with the dark blue sky above; but they will probably guess it to be a mere bank—a snowdrift, perhaps, which has been piled by the last storm. If you pointed out to them one of the great rocky teeth that projected from its summit, and said that it was a guide, they would probably remark that he looked very small, and would fancy that he could jump over the bank with an effort.

Now a mountaineer knows, to begin with, that it is a massive rocky rib, covered with snow, lying at a sharp angle, and varying perhaps from 500 to 1,000 feet in height. So far he might be accompanied by men of less soaring ambition; by an engineer who had been mapping the country, or an artist who had been carefully observing the mountains from their bases. They might learn in time to interpret correctly the real meaning of shapes at which the uninitiated guess at random. But the mountaineer can go a step further, and it is the next step which gives the real significance to those delicate curves and lines. He can translate the 500 or 1,000 feet of snow-slope into a more tangible unit of measurement. To him, perhaps, they recall the memory of a toilsome ascent, the sun beating on his head for five or six hours, the snow returning the glare with still more parching effect; a stalwart guide toiling all the weary time, cutting steps in hard blue ice, the fragments hissing and spinning down the long straight grooves in the frozen snow till they lost themselves in the yawning chasm below; and step after step taken along the slippery staircase, till at length he triumphantly sprang upon the summit of the tremendous wall that no human foot had scaled before. The little black knobs that rise above the edge represent for him huge impassable rocks, sinking on one side in scarped slippery surfaces towards the snowfield, and on the other stooping in one tremendous cliff to a distorted glacier thousands of feet below.

The faint blue line across the upper névé, scarcely distinguishable to the eye, represents to one observer nothing but a trifling undulation; a second, perhaps, knows that it means a crevasse; the mountaineer remembers that it is the top of a huge chasm, thirty feet across, and perhaps ten times as deep, with perpendicular sides of glimmering blue ice, and fringed by thick rows of enormous pendent icicles. The marks that are scored in delicate lines, such as might be ruled by a diamond on glass, have been cut by innumerable streams trickling in hot weather from the everlasting snow, or ploughed by succeeding avalanches that have slipped from the huge upper snowfields above. In short, there is no insignificant line or mark that has not its memory or its indication of the strange phenomena of the upper world. True, the same picture is painted upon the retina of all classes of observers; and so Porson and a schoolboy and a peasant might receive the same physical impression from a set of black and white marks on the page of a Greek play; but to one they would be an incoherent conglomeration of unmeaning and capricious lines, to another they would represent certain sounds more or less corresponding to some English words; whilst to the scholar they would reveal some of the noblest poetry in the world, and all the associations of successful intellectual labour.

I do not say that the difference is quite so great in the case of the mountains; still I am certain that no one can decipher the natural writing on the face of a snow-slope or a precipice who has not wandered amongst their recesses, and learnt by slow experience what is indicated by marks which an ignorant observer would scarcely notice. True, even one who sees a mountain for the first time may know that, as a matter of fact, a scar on the face of a cliff means, for example, a recent fall of a rock; but between the bare knowledge and the acquaintance with all which that knowledge implies—the thunder of the fall, the crash of the smaller fragments, the bounding energy of the descending mass—there is almost as much difference as between hearing that a battle has been fought and being present at it yourself. We have all read descriptions of Waterloo till we are sick of the subject; but I imagine that our emotions on seeing the shattered wall of Hougoumont are very inferior to those of one of the Guard who should revisit the place where he held out for a long day against the assaults of the French Army.

Now to an old mountaineer the Oberland cliffs are full of memories; and, more than this, he has learnt the language spoken by every crag and every wave of glacier. It is strange if they do not affect him rather more powerfully than the casual visitor who has never been initiated by practical experience into their difficulties. To him, the huge buttress which runs down from the Mönch is something more than an irregular pyramid, purple with white patches at the bottom and pure white at the top. He fills up the bare outline supplied by the senses with a thousand lively images. He sees tier above tier of rock, rising in a gradually ascending scale of difficulty, covered at first by long lines of the débris that have been splintered by frost from the higher wall, and afterwards rising bare and black and threatening. He knows instinctively which of the ledges has a dangerous look—where such a bold mountaineer as John Lauener might slip on the polished surface, or be in danger of an avalanche from above. He sees the little shell-like swelling at the foot of the glacier crawling down the steep slope above, and knows that it means an almost inaccessible wall of ice; and the steep snow-fields that rise towards the summit are suggestive of something very different from the picture which might have existed in the mind of a German student, who once asked me whether it was possible to make the ascent on a mule.

Hence, if mountains owe their influence upon the imagination in a great degree to their size and steepness, and apparent inaccessibility—as no one can doubt that they do, whatever may be the explanation of the fact that people like to look at big, steep, inaccessible objects—the advantages of the mountaineer are obvious. He can measure those qualities on a different scale from the ordinary traveller. He measures the size, not by the vague abstract term of so many thousand feet, but by the hours of labour, divided into minutes—each separately felt—of strenuous muscular exertion. The steepness is not expressed in degrees, but by the memory of the sensation produced when a snow-slope seems to be rising up and smiting you in the face; when, far away from all human help, you are clinging like a fly to the slippery side of a mighty pinnacle in mid-air. And as for the inaccessibility, no one can measure the difficulty of climbing a hill who has not wearied his muscles and brain in struggling against the opposing obstacles. Alpine travellers, it is said, have removed the romance from the mountains by climbing them. What they have really done is to prove that there exists a narrow line by which a way may be found to the top of any given mountain; but the clue leads through innumerable inaccessibilities; true, you can follow one path, but to right and left are cliffs which no human foot will ever tread, and whose terrors can only be realised when you are in their immediate neighbourhood. The cliffs of the Matterhorn do not bar the way to the top effectually, but it is only by forcing a passage through them that you can really appreciate their terrible significance.

Hence I say that the qualities which strike every sensitive observer are impressed upon the mountaineer with tenfold force and intensity. If he is as accessible to poetical influences as his neighbours—and I don't know why he should be less so—he has opened new avenues of access between the scenery and his mind. He has learnt a language which is but partially revealed to ordinary men. An artist is superior to an unlearned picture-seer, not merely because he has greater natural sensibility, but because he has improved it by methodical experience; because his senses have been sharpened by constant practice, till he can catch finer shades of colouring, and more delicate inflexions of line; because, also, the lines and colours have acquired new significance, and been associated with a thousand thoughts with which the mass of mankind has never cared to connect them. The mountaineer is improved by a similar process. But I know some sceptical critics will ask, does not the way which he is accustomed to regard mountains rather deaden their poetical influence? Doesn't he come to look at them as mere instruments of sport, and overlook their more spiritual teaching? Does not all the excitement of personal adventure and the noisy apparatus of guides, and ropes, and axes, and tobacco, and the fun of climbing, rather dull his perceptions and incapacitate him from perceiving

> The silence that is in the starry sky,
> The sleep that is among the lonely hills? [4]

Well, I have known some stupid and unpoetical mountaineers; and, since I have been dismounted from my favourite hobby, I think I have met some similar specimens among the humbler class of tourists. There are persons, I fancy, who "do" the Alps; who look upon the Lake of Lucerne as one more task ticked off from their memorandum book, and count up the list of summits visible from the Gornergrat without being penetrated with any keen sense of sublimity. And there are mountaineers who are capable of making a pun on the top of Mont Blanc—and capable of nothing more. Still I venture to deny that even punning is incompatible with poetry, or that those who make the pun can have no deeper feeling in their bosoms which they are perhaps too shamefaced to utter.

The fact is that that which gives its inexpressible charm to mountaineering is the incessant series of exquisite natural scenes, which are for the most part enjoyed by the mountaineer alone. This is, I am aware, a round assertion; but I will try to support it by a few of the visions which are recalled to me by these Oberland cliffs, and which I have seen profoundly enjoyed by men who perhaps never mentioned them again, and probably in describing their adventures scrupulously avoided the danger of being sentimental.

Thus every traveller has occasionally done a sunrise, and a more lamentable proceeding than the ordinary view of a sunrise can hardly be imagined. You are cold, miserable, breakfastless; have risen shivering from a warm bed, and in your heart long only to creep into bed again. To the mountaineer all this is changed. He is beginning a day full of the anticipation of a pleasant excitement. He has, perhaps, been waiting anxiously for fine weather, to try conclusions with some huge giant not yet scaled. He moves out with something of the feeling with which a soldier goes to the assault of a fortress, but without the same probability of coming home in fragments; the danger is trifling enough to be merely exhilatory, and to give a pleasant tension to the nerves; his muscles feel firm and springy, and his stomach—no small advantage to the enjoyment of scenery—is in excellent order. He looks at the sparkling stars with

[4] Wordsworth, "Song at the Feast of Brougham Castle," ll. 163–64.

keen satisfaction, prepared to enjoy a fine sunrise with all his faculties at their best, and with the added pleasure of a good omen for his day's work. Then a huge dark mass begins to mould itself slowly out of the darkness, the sky begins to form a background of deep purple, against which the outline becomes gradually more definite; one by one, the peaks catch the exquisite Alpine glow, lighting up in rapid succession, like a vast illumination; and when at last the steady sunlight settles upon them, and shows every rock and glacier, without even a delicate film of mist to obscure them, he feels his heart bound, and steps out gaily to the assault—just as the people on the Rigi are giving thanks that the show is over and that they may go to bed.

Still grander is the sight when the mountaineer has already reached some lofty ridge, and, as the sun rises, stands between the day and the night—the valley still in deep sleep, with the mists lying between the folds of the hills, and the snow-peaks standing out clear and pale white just before the sun reaches them, whilst a broad band of orange light runs all round the vast horizon. The glory of sunsets is equally increased in the thin upper air. The grandest of all such sights that live in my memory is that of a sunset from the Aiguille du Goûter. The snow at our feet was glowing with rich light, and the shadows in our footsteps a vivid green by the contrast. Beneath us was a vast horizontal floor of thin level mists suspended in mid-air, spread like a canopy over the whole boundless landscape, and tinged with every hue of sunset. Through its rents and gaps we could see the lower mountains, the distant plains, and a fragment of the Lake of Geneva lying in a more sober purple. Above us rose the solemn mass of Mont Blanc in the richest glow of an Alpine sunset. The sense of lonely sublimity was almost oppressive, and although half our party was suffering from sickness, I believe even the guides were moved to a sense of solemn beauty.

These grand scenic effects are occasionally seen by ordinary travellers, though the ordinary traveller is for the most part out of temper at 3 A.M. The mountaineer can enjoy them, both because his frame of mind is properly trained to receive the natural beauty, and because he alone sees them with their best accessories, amidst the silence of the eternal snow, and the vast panoramas visible from the

loftier summits. And he has a similar advantage in most of the great
natural phenomena of the cloud and the sunshine. No sight in the
Alps is more impressive than the huge rocks of a black precipice
suddenly frowning out through the chasms of a storm-cloud. But
grand as such a sight may be from the safe verandahs of the inn at
Grindelwald, it is far grander in the silence of the Central Alps
amongst the savage wilderness of rock and snow.

Another characteristic effect of the High Alps often presents
itself when one has been climbing for two or three hours, with
nothing in sight but the varying wreaths of mist that chased each
other monotonously along the rocky ribs up whose snow-covered
backbone we were laboriously fighting our way. Suddenly there is
a puff of wind, and looking round we find that we have in an
instant pierced the clouds, and emerged, as it were, on the surface
of the ocean of vapour. Beneath us stretches for hundreds of miles
the level fleecy floor, and above us shines out clear in the eternal
sunshine every mountain, from Mont Blanc to Monte Rosa and the
Jungfrau. What, again, in the lower regions, can equal the mysterious charm of gazing from the edge of a torn rocky parapet into
an apparently fathomless abyss, where nothing but what an Alpine
traveller calls a "strange formless wreathing of vapour" indicates the
storm-wind that is raging below us?

I might go on indefinitely recalling the strangely impressive
scenes that frequently startle the traveller in the waste upper world;
but language is feeble indeed to convey even a glimmering of what
is to be seen to those who have not seen it for themselves, whilst to
them it can be little more than a peg upon which to hang their own
recollections. These glories, in which the mountain spirit reveals
himself to his true worshippers, are only to be gained by the appropriate service of climbing—at some risk, though a very trifling
risk, if he is approached with due form and ceremony—into the
furthest recesses of his shrines. And without seeing them, I maintain that no man has really seen the Alps.

The difference between the exoteric and the esoteric school of
mountaineers may be indicated by their different view of glaciers.
At Grindelwald, for example, it is the fashion to go and "see the glaciers"—heaven save the mark! Ladies in costumes, heavy German

professors, Americans doing the Alps at a gallop, Cook's tourists, and other varieties of a well-known genus, go off in shoals and see —what? A gigantic mass of ice, strangely torn with a few of the exquisite blue crevasses, but defiled and prostrate in dirt and ruins. A stream foul with mud oozes out from the base; the whole mass seems to be melting fast away; the summer sun has evidently got the best of it in these lower regions, and nothing can resist him but the great mounds of decaying rock that strew the surface in confused lumps. It is as much like the glacier of the upper regions as the melting fragments of snow in a London street are like the surface of the fresh snow that has just fallen in a country field. And by way of improving its attractions a perpetual picnic is going on, and the ingenious natives have hewed a tunnel into the ice, for admission to which they charge certain centimes.

The unlucky glacier reminds me at his latter end of a wretched whale stranded on a beach, dissolving into masses of blubber, and hacked by remorseless fishermen, instead of plunging at his ease in the deep blue water. Far above, where the glacier begins his course, he is seen only by the true mountaineer. There are vast amphitheatres of pure snow, of which the glacier known to tourists is merely the insignificant drainage, but whose very existence they do not generally suspect. They are utterly ignorant that from the top of the icefall which they visit you may walk for hours on the eternal ice. After a long climb you come to the region where the glacier is truly at its noblest; where the surface is a spotless white; where the crevasses are enormous rents sinking to profound depths, with walls of the purest blue; where the glacier is torn and shattered by the energetic forces which mould it, but has an expression of superabundant power, like a full stream fretting against its banks and plunging through the vast gorges that it has hewn for itself in the course of centuries. The bases of the mountains are immersed in a deluge of cockneyism—fortunately a shallow deluge—whilst their summits rise high into the bracing air, where everything is pure and poetical.

The difference which I have thus endeavoured to indicate is more or less traceable in a wider sense. The mountains are exquisitely beautiful, indeed, from whatever points of view we contemplate them; and the mountaineer would lose much if he never saw the beauties of the lower valleys, of pasturages deep in flowers, and dark pine-forests with the summits shining from far off between the stems. Only, as it seems to me, he has the exclusive prerogative of thoroughly enjoying one—and that the most characteristic, though by no means only, element of the scenery. There may be a very good dinner spread before twenty people; but if nineteen of them were teetotallers, and the twentieth drank his wine like a man, he would be the only one to do it full justice; the others might praise the meat or the fruits, but he would alone enjoy the champagne; and in the great feast which Nature spreads before us (a stock metaphor, which emboldens me to make the comparison), the high mountain scenery acts the part of the champagne. Unluckily, too, the teetotallers are very apt, in this case also, to sit in judgment upon their more adventurous neighbours. Especially are they pleased to carp at the views from high summits. I have been constantly asked, with a covert sneer, "Did it repay you?"—a question which involves the assumption that one wants to be repaid, as though the labour were not itself part of the pleasure, and which implies a doubt that the view is really enjoyable.

People are always demonstrating that the lower views are the most beautiful; and at the same time complaining that mountaineers frequently turn back without looking at the view from the top, as though that would necessarily imply that they cared nothing for scenery. In opposition to which I must first remark, that, as a rule, every step of an ascent has a beauty of its own, which one is quietly absorbing even when one is not directly making it a subject of contemplation, and that the view from the top is generally the crowning glory of the whole.

It will be enough if I conclude with an attempt to illustrate this last assertion; and I will do it by still referring to the Oberland. Every visitor with a soul for the beautiful admires the noble form of the Wetterhorn —the lofty snow-crowned pyramid rising in such light and yet massive lines from its huge basement of perpendicular cliffs. The Wetterhorn has, however, a further merit. To my mind—and I believe most connoisseurs of mountain tops agree with me—it is one of the most impressive summits in the Alps. It is not a sharp pinnacle like the Weisshorn, or a cupola like Mont Blanc, or a grand rocky tooth like Monte Rosa, but a long and nearly horizontal knife-edge, which, as seen from either end, has of course the appearance of a sharp-pointed cone. It is when balanced upon this ridge—sitting astride of the knife-edge on which one can hardly stand without giddiness—that one fully appreciates an Alpine precipice. Mr. Justice Wills has admirably described the first ascent, and the impression it made upon him, in a paper which has become classical for succeeding adventurers.[5] Behind you the snow-slope sinks with perilous steepness towards the wilderness of glacier and rock through which the ascent has lain. But in front the ice sinks with even greater steepness for a few feet or yards. Then it curves over and disappears, and the next thing that the eye catches is the meadowland of Grindelwald, some 9,000 feet below.

I have looked down many precipices, where the eye can trace the course of every pebble that bounds down the awful slopes, and where I have shuddered as some dislodged fragment of rock showed the course which, in case of accident, fragments of my own body would follow. A precipice is always, for obvious reasons, far more terrible from above than from below. The creeping, tingling sensation which passes through one's limbs—even when one knows oneself to be in perfect safety—testifies to the thrilling influence of the sight. But I have never so realised the terrors of a terrific cliff as when I could not see it. The awful gulf which intervened between me and the green meadows struck the imagination by its invisibility. It was like the view which may be seen from the ridge of a cathedral roof, where the eaves have for their immediate background the pavement of the streets below; only this cathedral was 9,000 feet high. Now, anyone standing at the foot of the Wetterhorn may admire their stupendous massiveness and steepness; but, to feel their influence enter into the very marrow of one's bones, it is necessary to stand at the summit, and to fancy the one little slide down the short ice-slope, to be followed apparently by a bound into clear air and a fall down to the houses, from heights where only the eagle ventures to soar.

This is one of the Alpine beauties, which, of course, is beyond

[5] Alfred Wills's *Wanderings in the High Alps* (1856) was influential in Stephen's early sporting career.

the power of art to imitate, and which people are therefore apt to
ignore. But it is not the only one to be seen on the high summits.
It is often said that these views are not "beautiful"—apparently because they won't go into a picture, or, to put it more fairly, because
no picture can in the faintest degree imitate them. But without
quarrelling about words, I think that, even if "beautiful" be not
the most correct epithet, they have a marvellously stimulating effect
upon the imagination. Let us look round from this wonderful pinnacle in mid-air, and note one or two of the most striking elements
of the scenery.

You are, in the first place, perched on a cliff, whose presence
is the more felt because it is unseen. Then you are in a region over
which eternal silence is brooding. Not a sound ever comes from
there, except the occasional fall of a splintered fragment of rock,
or a layer of snow; no stream is heard trickling, and the sounds of
animal life are left thousands of feet below. The most that you can
hear is some mysterious noise made by the wind eddying round
the gigantic rocks; sometimes a strange flapping sound, as if an unearthly flag was shaking its invisible folds in the air. The enormous
tract of country over which your view extends—most of it dim
and almost dissolved into air by distance—intensifies the strange
influence of the silence. You feel the force of the line I have quoted
from Wordsworth—

> The sleep that is among the lonely hills.

None of the travellers whom you can see crawling at your feet has
the least conception of what is meant by the silent solitudes of the
High Alps. To you, it is like a return to the stir of active life, when,
after hours of lonely wandering, you return to hear the tinkling
of the cowbells below; to them the same sound is the ultimate limit
of the habitable world.

Whilst your mind is properly toned by these influences, you
become conscious of another fact, to which the common variety
of tourists is necessarily insensible. You begin to find out for the
first time what the mountains really are. On one side, you look back
upon the huge reservoirs from which the Oberland glaciers descend.
You see the vast stores from which the great rivers of Europe are re-

plenished, the monstrous crawling masses that are carving the mountains into shape, and the gigantic bulwarks that separate two great quarters of the world. From below these wild regions are half invisible; they are masked by the outer line of mountains; and it is not till you are able to command them from some lofty point that you can appreciate the grandeur of the huge barriers, and the snow that is piled within their folds.

There is another half of the view equally striking. Looking towards the north, the whole of Switzerland is couched at your feet; the Jura and the Black Forest lie on the far horizon. And then you know what is the nature of a really mountainous country. From below everything is seen in a kind of distorted perspective. The people of the valley naturally think that the valley is everything— that the country resembles old-fashioned maps, where a few sporadic lumps are distributed amongst towns and plains. The true proportions reveal themselves as you ascend. The valleys, you can now see, are nothing but narrow trenches scooped out amidst a tossing waste of mountain, just to carry off the drainage. The great ridges run hither and thither, having it all their own way, wild and untamable regions of rock or open grass or forest, at whose feet the valleys exist on sufferance. Creeping about amongst the roots of the hills, you half miss the hills themselves; you quite fail to understand the massiveness of the mountain chains, and, therefore, the wonderful energy of the forces that have heaved the surface of the world into these distorted shapes. And it is to a half-conscious sense of the powers that must have been at work that a great part of the influence of mountain scenery is due.

Geologists tell us that a theory of catastrophes is unphilosophical; but, whatever may be the scientific truth, our minds are impressed as though we were witnessing the results of some incredible convulsion. At Stonehenge we ask what human beings could have erected these strange grey monuments, and in the mountains we instinctively ask what force can have carved out the Matterhorn, and placed the Wetterhorn on its gigantic pedestal. Now, it is not till we reach some commanding point that we realise the amazing extent of country over which the solid ground has been shaking and heaving itself in irresistible tumult.

Something, it is true, of this last effect may be seen from such mountains as the Rigi or the Faulhorn. There, too, one seems to be at the centre of a vast sphere, the earth bending up in a cup-like form to meet the sky, and the blue vault above stretching in an arch majestical by its enormous extent. There you seem to see a sensible fraction of the world at your feet. But the effect is far less striking when other mountains obviously look down upon you; when, as it were, you are looking at the waves of the great ocean of hills merely from the crest of one of the waves themselves, and not from some lighthouse that rises far over their heads; for the Wetterhorn, like the Eiger, Mönch, and Jungfrau, owes one great beauty to the fact that it is on the edge of the lower country, and stands between the real giants and the crowd of inferior, though still enormous, masses in attendance upon them. And, in the next place, your mind is far better adapted to receive impressions of sublimity when you are alone, in a silent region, with a black sky above and giant cliffs all round; with a sense still in your mind, if not of actual danger, still of danger that would become real with the slightest relaxation of caution, and with the world divided from you by hours of snow and rock.

I will go no further, not because I have no more to say, but because descriptions of scenery soon become wearisome, and because I have, I hope, said enough to show that the mountaineer may boast of some intellectual pleasures; that he is not a mere scrambler, but that he looks for poetical impressions, as well as for such small glory as his achievements may gain in a very small circle.

Something of what he gains fortunately sticks by him: he does not quite forget the mountain language; his eye still recognises the space and the height and the glory of the lofty mountains. And yet there is some pain in wandering ghostlike among the scenes of his earlier pleasures. For my part, I try in vain to hug myself in a sense of comfort. I turn over in bed when I hear the stamping of heavily nailed shoes along the passage of an inn about 2 A.M. I feel the skin of my nose complacently when I see others returning with a glistening tight aspect about that unluckily prominent feature, and know that in a day or two it will be raw and blistered and burning. I think, in a comfortable inn at night, of the miseries of those who are trying to sleep in damp hay, or on hard boards of chalets, at once cold and stuffy and haunted by innumerable fleas. I congratulate myself on having a whole skin and unfractured bones, and on the small danger of ever breaking them over an Alpine precipice. But yet I secretly know that these consolations are feeble. It is little use to avoid early rising and discomfort, and even fleas, if one also loses the pleasures to which they were the sauce—rather too *piquante* a sauce occasionally, it must be admitted.

The philosophy is all very well which recommends moderate enjoyment, regular exercise, and a careful avoidance of risk and overexcitement. That is, it is all very well so long as risk and excitement and immoderate enjoyment are out of your power; but it does not stand the test of looking on and seeing them just beyond your reach. In time, no doubt, a man may grow calm; he may learn to enjoy the pleasures and the exquisite beauties of the lower regions—though they, too, are most fully enjoyed when they have a contrast with beauties of a different, and pleasures of a keener excitement. When first debarred, at any rate, one feels like a balloon full of gas, and fixed by immovable ropes to the prosaic ground. It is pleasant to lie on one's back in a bed of rhododendrons, and look up to a mountain top peering at one from above a bank of cloud; but it is pleasantest when one has qualified oneself for repose by climbing the peak the day before and becoming familiar with its terrors and its beauties.

In time, doubtless, one may get reconciled to anything; one may settle down to be a caterpillar, even after one has known the pleasures of being a butterfly; one may become philosophical, and have one's clothes let out; and even in time, perhaps—though it is almost too terrible to contemplate—be content with a mule or a carriage, or that lowest depth to which human beings can sink, and for which the English language happily affords no name, a *chaise à porteurs:* and even in such degradation the memory of better times may be pleasant; for I doubt much whether it is truth the poet sings—

That a sorrow's crown of sorrow is remembering happier things.[6]

Certainly, to a philosophical mind, the sentiment is doubtful. For my part, the fate which has cut me off, if I may use the expression,

[6] Tennyson, "Locksley Hall," l. 76.

in the flower of my youth, and doomed me to be a non-climbing animal in the future, is one which ought to exclude grumbling. I cannot indicate it more plainly, for I might so make even the grumbling in which I have already indulged look like a sin. I can only say that there are some very delightful things in which it is possible to discover an infinitesimal drop of bitterness, and that the mountaineer who undertakes to cut himself off from his favourite pastime, even for reasons which he will admit in his wildest moods to be more than amply sufficient, must expect at times to feel certain pangs of regret, however quickly they may be smothered.

BRIEF GLOSSARY

Aiguille: a needle-shaped peak.

Alp: a single peak or (in plural) a range, especially in Switzerland, France, Germany, and Italy. Originally an upland meadow or mountain pasture.

Arête: any acute ridge or knife-edge. The analogy is with a spine.

Bergschrund: a crevasse occurring near the head of a glacier, where ice and rock join.

Brae: (1) a slope or hill; (2) a glacier (Norway).

Col: a high pass between two peaks.

Corrie: any hollow or circular declivity in the side of a mountain; a cirque.

Couloir: a deep gorge in a mountainside.

Cwm: same as corrie.

Gabbro: any of several kinds of igneous rock.

Glissade: the act of sliding down a snow slope in a sitting or standing position.

Joch: a mountain pass.

Massif: a major mountain mass or extensive upland.

Névé: the semi-compacted snow on the surface toward the head of a glacier; more generally, any field of granular snow.

Roches moutonnées: slabs of rock on which the passage of a glacier has left a series of ridges in more or less parallel lines.

Scree: rocky débris at the foot of a steep slope.

Sérac: a pinnacle of ice on a glacier; also a block of ice broken off a glacier and standing upright.

Stob: a peak which appears blunted (Scotland).

Talus: same as scree.

Tind: a mountain or peak (Norway).

Traverse: (1) a route cut or forced across the face of a cliff, also the cliff thus crossed; (2) a climb up one side of a mountain and down the other.

SUGGESTIONS FOR FURTHER READING

ALMOST ALL of the sources from which selections have been taken for this anthology will yield further reading. Much more is available. The lists which follow include some of the best of the writings in English which have not been represented.

BELLES-LETTRES

Auden, W. H., and Christopher Isherwood. The Ascent of F6; a Tragedy in Two Acts. 1937.

Belloc, Hilaire. The Path to Rome. 1902. An account of a pilgrimage, physical and spiritual, from Toul, through Switzerland, to the Eternal City.

Buchan, John. Comments and Characters. 1940. See the essays entitled "The Alps" and "The Dolomites."

[Clemens, Samuel L.]. A Tramp Abroad. . . . Copyright 1879; several times reprinted. Contains satirical sketches of many aspects of Alpine *tourisme*.

Mason, A. E. W. Running Water. 1907; new ed., 1928. A novel.

Montague, C. E. The Right Place: a Book of Pleasures. 1924. A collection of essays.

—— Right off the Map. 1927. A political romance.

Pilkington, Lawrence. An Alpine Valley and Other Poems. 1924.

—— The Hills of Peace. 1930. Poems.

Roberts, Michael. Poems. 1936. See particularly "Elegy for the Fallen Climbers."

Ruskin, John. Modern Painters. 5 vols. 1851–1860. Volume IV is entitled *Of Mountain Beauty*.

Smythe, Frank S. Secret Mission: a Mountain Thriller. 1942.

Todd, Ruthven. Over the Mountain. 1939. A political allegory, somewhat reminiscent of *The Ascent of F6*.

Trollope, Anthony. The West Indies and the Spanish Main. 1860. Contains an amusing account of Trollope's ascent of Mount Irazu in Costa Rica.

Young, Geoffrey Winthrop. April and Rain. 1923. Poems.

—— Freedom. 1914. Poems.

—— Wind and Hill. 1909. Poems.

JOURNALS

Alpine Journal, The. Published since 1863 by the Alpine Club, London. Described on the title page as "a record of mountain adventure and scientific observation," this is the oldest and best known of the periodicals. Its ancestors were two volumes entitled *Peaks, Passes, and Glaciers,* which appeared in 1859 and 1862.

American Alpine Journal, The. Published since 1929 by the American Alpine Club, New York.

Appalachia. Published since 1876 by the Appalachian Mountain Club, Boston.

Cambridge Mountaineering. Published irregularly by the Cambridge University Mountaineering Club. The latest volume appeared in 1946.

Canadian Alpine Journal. Published since 1907 by the Alpine Club of Canada, Banff, Alberta.

Climbers' Club Journal, The. Published since 1898 by the Climbers' Club of London.

Harvard Mountaineering. Published irregularly since 1927 by the Harvard Mountaineering Club, Cambridge, Massachusetts.

Himalayan Journal, The. Published from 1929 to 1948 by the Himalayan Club, Calcutta.

Iowa Climber, The. Published since 1945 by the Iowa Mountaineers, Inc., State University of Iowa, Iowa City, Iowa.

Journal of the Fell and Rock Climbing Club of the English Lake District, The. Published since 1907.

Journal of the Mountain Club of South Africa, The. Published since 1897 by the Cape Town Section.

Mazama. Published since 1896 by the Mazamas of Portland, Oregon.

Mountaineer, The. Published since 1907 by the Mountaineers, Inc., Seattle, Washington.

New Zealand Alpine Journal, The. Published since 1892 by the New Zealand Alpine Club, Christchurch, New Zealand.

Rucksack Club Journal, The. Published since 1907 by the Rucksack Club, Manchester.

Scottish Mountaineering Club Journal, The. Published since 1890 by the Scottish Mountaineering Club, Edinburgh.

Sierra Club Bulletin. Published since 1893 by the Sierra Club, Berkeley, California.

TRAVEL, DESCRIPTION, AND PERSONAL REMINISCENCE

Baker, Ernest A. Moors, Crags, and Caves of the High Peak. . . . n.d. Explorations in the Pennine Chain between Sheffield and Manchester.
—— On Foot in the Highlands. 1932.
Bates, Robert H., et al. Five Miles High. . . . 1939. A full report of the American Alpine Club expedition to K2 (Mount Godwin-Austen) in the Karakoram Himalaya in 1938.
Belloc, Hilaire. The Pyrenees. 1909.
Brewer, William H. Up and Down California in 1860–1864. . . . 1930.
Browne, Belmore. The Conquest of Mount McKinley. . . . 1913. An ascent of the highest peak (20,300 feet) in North America.
Bruce, C. G., et al. The Assault on Mount Everest, 1922. 1923.
Collie, J. Norman. Climbing on the Himalaya and Other Mountain Ranges. 1902.
Conway, William Martin Conway, Baron. The Bolivian Andes. . . . 1901.
—— Mountain Memories; a Pilgrimage of Romance. 1920.
Dent, Clinton. Above the Snow Line. . . . 1885. Chiefly Alpine sketches.
FitzGerald, E. A. Climbs in the New Zealand Alps. . . . 1896.
Freshfield, Douglas W. The Exploration of the Caucasus. 1896.
—— Italian Alps (1875); new ed., 1937.
—— Round Kangchenjunga. 1903. An account of one of the earliest complete reconnaissances.
Harrison, Frederic. My Alpine Jubilee, 1851–1907. 1908.
Hinchliff, Thomas W. Summer Months among the Alps. . . . 1857.
Jones, Owen Glynne. Rock-Climbing in the English Lake District. 1897.
Kain, Conrad. Where the Clouds Can Go. Ed. J. Monroe Thorington. 1935. The autobiography of a guide, with several chapters by other hands.
Kingdon-Ward, F. Burma's Icy Mountains. 1949.
Knowlton, Elizabeth. The Naked Mountain. 1933. The history of the German-American attempt on Nanga Parbat in 1932.
Lunn, Arnold. The Mountains of Youth. 2d ed. 1949.
Moore, A. W. The Alps in 1864 (1902); new ed., 1939.
Norton, E. F., et al. The Fight for Everest, 1924. 1925.
Noyce, Wilfrid. Mountains and Men. 1947.
Palmer, Howard. Mountaineering and Exploration in the Selkirks . . . , 1908–1912. 1912.

Pascoe, John. Unclimbed New Zealand. . . . 1939.

Russell, Scott. Mountain Prospect. 1946.

Smith, Janet Adam. Mountain Holidays. 1946.

Smythe, Frank S. Kamet Conquered. 1932.

—— The Kangchenjunga Adventure. 1931. An attempt undertaken in 1930 by an international party.

—— Over Tyrolese Hills. 1935.

—— The Valley of Flowers. 1949. Botanizing and climbing in the Himalaya.

Tilman, H. W. The Ascent of Nanda Devi. 1937. The narrative of the campaign on the highest mountain yet climbed.

—— Mount Everest, 1938. 1948. The account of the latest major expedition.

—— Snow on the Equator. 1937. The mountains of Africa.

—— When Men and Mountains Meet. 1946.

Tyndale, H. E. G. Mountain Paths. 1949.

Tyndall, John. Hours of Exercise in the Alps. 1871. Several later eds.

Ullman, James Ramsey, ed. The Kingdom of Adventure: Everest. 1947. A composite narrative, mainly from primary sources, of attempts on Mount Everest.

Whymper, Edward. Scrambles amongst the Alps in the Years 1860–'69. 1871; often reprinted.

—— Travels among the Great Andes of the Equator. 1892.

Wilcox, Walter D. The Rockies of Canada. 1900.

Wills, Alfred. Wanderings in the High Alps. 1856; new ed., 1937.

GUIDE-BOOKS AND MANUALS

Barford, J. E. Q., ed. Climbing in Britain. 1947.

Beckey, Fred. Climber's Guide to the Cascade and Olympic Mountains. 1949.

Coulter, Henry and Merrill F. McLane. Mountain Climbing Guide. 1947.

Fisher, Joel E. Bibliography of American Mountain Ascents. 1946. An exhaustive list, published by the American Alpine Club.

Henderson, Kenneth. The American Alpine Club's Handbook of American Mountaineering. 1942.

Mountaineers, Inc. Mountaineer's Handbook: the Techniques of Mountain Climbing. 1948.

Palmer, Howard and J. Monroe Thorington. A Climber's Guide to the Rocky Mountains of Canada. 3d ed. 1940–43.

Peattie, Roderick. Mountain Geography; a Critique and Field Study. 1936.

—— ed. The Berkshires: the Purple Hills. 1948. This and the three following items are volumes in the American Mountains Series.

—— The Friendly Mountains, Green, White, and Adirondacks. 1942.

—— The Great Smokies and the Blue Ridge; the Story of the Southern Appalachians. 1943.

—— The Sierra Nevada: the Range of Light. 1947.

Thorington, J. Monroe. A Climber's Guide to the Interior Ranges of British Columbia. 2d ed. 1947.

—— The Purcell Range of British Columbia. 1946.

Young, Geoffrey Winthrop. Mountain Craft. 7th ed. 1949.

HISTORY AND MISCELLANEOUS

Clark, Donald. The Early Alpine Guides. 1949.

Coolidge, W. A. B. The Alps in Nature and History. 1908.

Irving, R. L. G. The Romance of Mountaineering. 1935. An historical survey.

—— ed. The Mountain Way, an Anthology in Prose and Verse. 1938.

Lunn, Arnold, ed. The Englishman in the Alps. . . . 2d ed. 1927. An anthology.

Thorington, J. Monroe. Mont Blanc Sideshow: the Life and Times of Albert Smith. 1934. Biography of a very popular mid-nineteenth century lecturer, whose favorite subject was Mont Blanc.

Ullman, James Ramsey. High Conquest: the Story of Mountaineering. 1941.

INDEX

the stones which the mountain had fired at us (fortunately with rather a bad aim) for the first half-hour on the rock. We breakfasted then followed a difficult and dangerous climb. It was difficult because the rocks were exceedingly steep, every now and then we had to creep up and out of the common hard chimney—one in particular about mid-day, I remember, because we subsequently had the very deuce of a time coming down it, or round the face of a tower or cut our way across an ice couloir between two gendarmes and it was dangerous because the whole rock was so treacherous. I found this out very early in the morning by putting my hand into the crack of a rock which looked as if it went into the very foundations of things. About 2 feet square of rock tumbled out upon me and knocked me a little way down the hill till I managed to part company with it on a tiny ledge. I got back on to my feet without being pulled up by the rope, which was as well for a little later I happened to pass the rope through my hands and found that it had been cut half through about a yard from my waist when the rock had fallen on it. This was rather a nuisance as it shortened a rope we often wanted long to allow of our going up difficult chimneys in turn. So on and on we went up the arête and the towers multiplied like rabbits above and grew steeper and steeper and about 2 o'clock I looked round and saw great black clouds rolling up from the west. But by this time looking up we also saw the topmost tower of the arête far above us still, and the summit of the mountain further still and though we could not yet see what the top of the arête was like we were cheered and pushed on steadily for another hour while the weather signs got worse and worse. At 3 just as the first snow flakes began to fall, we got into full view of the last two gendarmes—and the first one was quite impossible. The ridge had been growing narrow, its sides steeper as we mounted, so that we had been obliged for some time to stick quite to the backbone of it; then it threw itself up into a great tower leaning over to the right and made of slabs set like slates on the top with a steep drop of some 20 feet below them on to the col. We were then 1000 feet below the summit I should guess, perhaps rather less, anyway we could see our way up, not easy but possible, above this tower and once on the top we could get down the other side in any weather. It had to be tried: we sat down to eat a few mouthfuls the snow falling fast, driven by a strong wind, and a thick mist marching up the valley below, over the Finsteraar joch, then we crept along the knife edge of a col, fastened a rope firmly round a rock and let Ulrich [Führer] down on to a ledge below the overhang of the tower. He tried it for a few moments and then gave it up. The ledge was very narrow, sloped outwards and was quite rotten. Anything was better than that. So we tried the left side of the tower: there was a very steep iced couloir running up at the foot of the rock on that side for about 50 feet, after which all would be well. Again we let ourselves down on the extra rope to the foot of the tower, again to find that this way also was impossible. A month later in the year I believe this couloir would go; after a warm August there would be no ice in it, and though it is very steep the rocks so far as one could see under the ice, looked climbable. But even with the alternative before us of the descent down the terrible arête, we decided to turn back; already the snow was blowing down the couloir in a small avalanche, small but blinding, and the wind rushed down upon us carrying the mists with it. If it had been fine weather we should have tried down the arête a little and then a traverse so as to get at the upper rocks by another road. I am not sure that it could be done but we should have tried anything—but by the time we had been going down for half-an-hour we could see nothing of the mountain side to the right or to the left except an occasional glimpse as one cloud rolled off and another rolled over. The snow fell fast and covered the rocks with incredible speed. Difficult as they had been to go up, you may imagine what they were like going down when we could no longer so much as see them. There was one corner in particular where we had to get around the face of a tower.

We came round the corner, down a very steep chimney, got on to a sloping out rock ledge with an inch of new snow on it; there was a crack in which you could stand and with one hand hold in the rock face, from whence you had to drop down about 8 feet on to steep snow. We fixed the extra rope and tumbled down one after the other on to the snow; it was really more or less safe because one had the fixed rope to hold on to, but it felt awful: I shall remember every inch of that rock face for the rest of my life. It was now near 6. Our one idea was to get down to the chimney—the mid-day chim-